READINGS ON
WRITING

Ohio University Composition Committee

Readings on Writing

Ohio University Composition Committee

Printed in Ohio

Printed in the United States of America

10 9 8 7 6 5 4 3 2 1

ISBN: 978-1-61740-071-1

Van-Griner Publishing
Cincinnati, Ohio
www.van-griner.com

Rouzie 071-1 F12

Copyright © 2013

Contents

Vocabulary of Comics
SCOTT McCLOUD

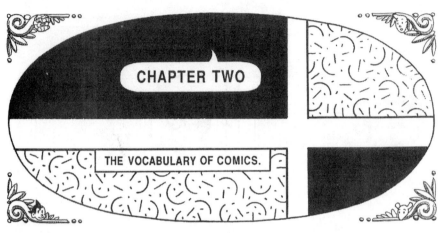

THIS IS NOT A MAN.

THESE ARE NOT IDEAS.

THIS IS NOT A COUNTRY.

THIS IS NOT A LEAF

THESE ARE NOT PEOPLE

THIS IS NOT MUSIC.

THIS IS NOT A COW.

WELCOME TO THE *STRANGE* AND *WONDERFUL* *WORLD* OF THE *ICON!*

THIS IS NOT MY VOICE.

THIS IS NOT SOUND.

THESE ARE NOT FLOWERS.

THIS IS NOT ME.

THIS IS NOT LAW.

THIS IS NOT A PLANET.

THIS IS NOT FOOD.

THIS IS NOT A CAR.

THIS IS NOT A COMPANY.

THIS IS NOT A FACE.

THESE ARE NOT SEPARATE MOMENTS.

NOW, THE WORD *ICON* MEANS MANY THINGS.

THIS IS PAPER

THIS IS *INK* ON PAPER

FOR THE PURPOSES OF THIS CHAPTER, I'M USING THE WORD *"ICON"* TO MEAN ANY IMAGE USED TO REPRESENT A A PERSON, PLACE, THING OR *IDEA*.

ICON

THAT'S A BIT BROADER THAN THE DEFINITION IN MY DICTIONARY, BUT IT'S THE CLOSEST THING TO WHAT I NEED HERE.

"SYMBOL" IS A BIT TOO *LOADED* FOR ME.

THE SORTS OF IMAGES WE USUALLY *CALL* SYMBOLS ARE ONE *CATEGORY* OF ICON, HOWEVER.

THESE ARE THE IMAGES WE USE TO REPRESENT *CONCEPTS, IDEAS* AND *PHILOSOPHIES*.

THEN THERE ARE THE ICONS OF *LANGUAGE, SCIENCE* AND *COMMUNICATION*.

A	B	C	D
1	2	3	4
?	:	!	*
田	森	雨	石
+	=	×	÷
$	%	©	¢

ICONS OF THE *PRACTICAL* REALM.

AND FINALLY, THE ICONS WE CALL *PICTURES*: IMAGES DESIGNED TO ACTUALLY *RESEMBLE* THEIR SUBJECTS.

BUT AS RESEMBLANCE VARIES, SO DOES THE LEVEL OF ICONIC CONTENT.

OR TO PUT IT SOMEWHAT *CLUMSILY,* SOME PICTURES ARE JUST MORE ICONIC THAN OTHERS.

IN THE *NON-PICTORIAL* ICONS, MEANING IS *FIXED* AND *ABSOLUTE.* THEIR APPEARANCE DOESN'T AFFECT THEIR MEANING BECAUSE THEY REPRESENT *INVISIBLE IDEAS.*

IN *PICTURES,* HOWEVER, MEANING IS *FLUID* AND *VARIABLE* ACCORDING TO APPEARANCE. THEY DIFFER FROM *"REAL-LIFE"* APPEARANCE TO VARYING *DEGREES.*

WORDS ARE TOTALLY *ABSTRACT* ICONS. THAT IS, THEY BEAR NO RESEMBLANCE AT ALL TO THE *REAL McCOY.*

EYE

BUT IN PICTURES THE *LEVEL* OF ABSTRACTION *VARIES.* SOME, LIKE THE FACE IN THE *PREVIOUS* PANEL, SO CLOSELY RESEMBLE THEIR *REAL-LIFE COUNTERPARTS* AS TO ALMOST *TRICK THE EYE!*

OTHERS, LIKE YOURS TRULY, ARE QUITE A BIT *MORE* ABSTRACT AND, IN FACT, ARE VERY MUCH *UNLIKE* ANY HUMAN FACE YOU'VE EVER SEEN!

LET'S SEE IF WE CAN PUT THESE *PICTORIAL ICONS* IN SOME SORT OF ORDER.

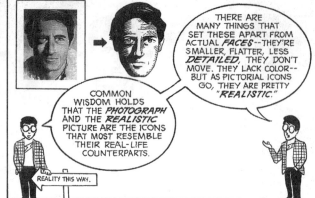

THERE ARE MANY THINGS THAT SET THESE APART FROM ACTUAL *FACES*--THEY'RE SMALLER, FLATTER, LESS *DETAILED,* THEY DON'T MOVE. THEY LACK COLOR-- BUT AS PICTORIAL ICONS GO, THEY ARE PRETTY *"REALISTIC."*

COMMON WISDOM HOLDS THAT THE *PHOTOGRAPH* AND THE *REALISTIC* PICTURE ARE THE ICONS THAT MOST RESEMBLE THEIR REAL-LIFE COUNTERPARTS.

REALITY THIS WAY.

Scott McCloud

WHY-- --ARE-- --WE-- --SO-- --INVOLVED?

WHY WOULD *ANYONE,* YOUNG OR OLD, RESPOND TO A CARTOON AS MUCH OR MORE THAN A *REALISTIC IMAGE?*

WHY IS OUR CULTURE *SO IN THRALL* TO THE *SIMPLIFIED REALITY* OF THE *CARTOON?*

DEFINING THE CARTOON WOULD TAKE UP AS MUCH SPACE AS DEFINING *COMICS,* BUT FOR *NOW,* I'M GOING TO EXAMINE CARTOONING AS A FORM OF *AMPLIFICATION THROUGH SIMPLIFICATION.*

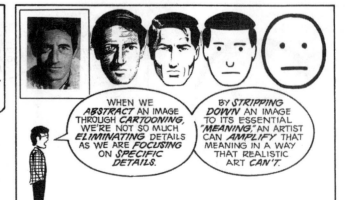

WHEN WE *ABSTRACT* AN IMAGE THROUGH *CARTOONING,* WE'RE NOT SO MUCH *ELIMINATING* DETAILS AS WE ARE *FOCUSING* ON *SPECIFIC DETAILS.*

BY *STRIPPING DOWN* AN IMAGE TO ITS ESSENTIAL *"MEANING,"* AN ARTIST CAN *AMPLIFY* THAT MEANING IN A WAY THAT REALISTIC ART *CAN'T.*

8

FILM CRITICS WILL SOMETIMES DESCRIBE A *LIVE-ACTION* FILM AS A "CARTOON" TO ACKNOWLEDGE THE STRIPPED-DOWN *INTENSITY* OF A SIMPLE STORY OR VISUAL STYLE.

THOUGH THE TERM IS OFTEN USED *DISPARAGINGLY,* IT CAN BE EQUALLY WELL APPLIED TO MANY *TIME-TESTED CLASSICS.* SIMPLIFYING CHARACTERS AND IMAGES TOWARD A *PURPOSE* CAN BE AN EFFECTIVE TOOL FOR STORYTELLING IN *ANY* MEDIUM.

CARTOONING ISN'T JUST A WAY OF *DRAWING,* IT'S A WAY OF *SEEING!*

FOLLOW! FOLLOW!

THE ABILITY OF CARTOONS TO *FOCUS* OUR ATTENTION ON AN IDEA IS, I THINK, AN IMPORTANT PART OF THEIR SPECIAL POWER, BOTH IN COMICS AND IN DRAWING GENERALLY.

ONE

A FEW

THOUSANDS

MILLIONS

(NEARLY) ALL

ANOTHER IS THE *UNIVERSALITY* OF CARTOON IMAGERY. THE MORE CARTOONY A FACE IS, FOR INSTANCE, THE MORE PEOPLE IT COULD BE SAID TO *DESCRIBE.*

BUT I BELIEVE THERE'S SOMETHING *MORE* AT WORK IN OUR MINDS WHEN WE VIEW A CARTOON--ESPECIALLY OF A HUMAN FACE-- WHICH WARRANTS FURTHER INVESTIGATION.

WHAT   ARE YOU

REALLY   SEEING?

THE FACT THAT YOUR MIND IS *CAPABLE* OF TAKING A *CIRCLE, TWO DOTS* AND A *LINE* AND TURNING THEM INTO A *FACE* IS NOTHING SHORT OF *INCREDIBLE!*

BUT STILL *MORE* INCREDIBLE IS THE FACT THAT YOU CANNOT *AVOID* SEEING A FACE HERE. YOUR MIND WON'T *LET* YOU!

ASK A FRIEND TO DRAW YOU SOME SHAPES ON A PIECE OF PAPER. THEY SHOULD BE *CLOSED CURVES*, BUT *OTHER- WISE* CAN BE AS *WEIRD* AND *IRREGULAR* AS HE OR SHE *WANTS*.

LET'S SAY THE RESULTS LOOK SOMETHING LIKE *THIS*.

NOW-- YOU'LL FIND THAT NO MATTER WHAT THEY *LOOK* LIKE, EVERY SINGLE *ONE* OF THOSE SHAPES *CAN* BE MADE INTO A FACE WITH ONE SIMPLE ADDITION.

YOUR MIND HAS NO TROUBLE AT ALL CONVERTING SUCH SHAPES INTO FACES, YET WOULD IT EVER MISTAKE *THIS*--

--FOR *THIS?*

WE HUMANS ARE A SELF-CENTERED RACE.

ALL SET?

GOOD.

NOW, *SMILE*.

C'MON, NOBODY'S LOOKING.

GOOD. NOW, WHAT *CHANGED* WHEN YOU SMILED? WHAT DID YOU SEE?

NOTHING, RIGHT.

YET, YOU *KNOW* YOU SMILED! NOT JUST BECAUSE YOU FELT YOUR CHEEKS COMPRESS OR THE CRINKLING AROUND YOUR EYES!

YOU *KNOW* YOU SMILED BECAUSE YOU TRUSTED THIS MASK CALLED YOUR FACE TO *RESPOND!*

BUT THE FACE YOU SEE IN YOUR *MIND* IS NOT THE SAME AS *OTHERS* SEE!

WHEN TWO PEOPLE INTERRACT, THEY USUALLY LOOK DIRECTLY *AT* ONE ANOTHER, SEEING THEIR PARTNER'S FEATURES IN *VIVID DETAIL*.

EACH ONE *ALSO* SUSTAINS A CONSTANT AWARENESS OF HIS OR HER *OWN* FACE, BUT *THIS* MIND-PICTURE IS NOT NEARLY SO VIVID; JUST A SKETCHY ARRANGEMENT... A SENSE OF SHAPE... A SENSE OF *GENERAL PLACEMENT.*

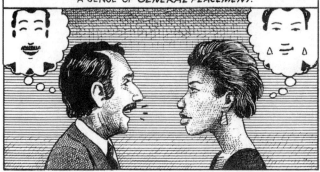

SOMETHING AS *SIMPLE* AND AS *BASIC--*

--AS A CARTOON.

THUS, WHEN YOU LOOK AT A PHOTO OR REALISTIC DRAWING OF A FACE--

--YOU SEE IT AS THE FACE OF ANOTHER.

BUT WHEN YOU ENTER THE WORLD OF THE *CARTOON--*

-- YOU SEE YOURSELF.

I BELIEVE THIS IS THE *PRIMARY CAUSE* OF OUR CHILDHOOD FASCINATION WITH *CARTOONS,* THOUGH OTHER FACTORS SUCH AS *UNIVERSAL IDENTIFICATION, SIMPLICITY* AND THE *CHILDLIKE FEATURES* OF MANY CARTOON CHARACTERS ALSO PLAY A PART.

THE CARTOON IS A *VACUUM* INTO WHICH OUR *IDENTITY* AND *AWARENESS* ARE *PULLED...*

...AN *EMPTY SHELL* THAT WE INHABIT WHICH *ENABLES* US TO TRAVEL IN *ANOTHER REALM.*

WE DON'T JUST *OBSERVE* THE CARTOON, WE *BECOME* IT!

THAT'S WHY I DECIDED TO *DRAW* MYSELF IN SUCH A SIMPLE *STYLE.*

WOULD YOU HAVE *LISTENED* TO ME IF I LOOKED LIKE *THIS??*

Credit

McCloud, Scott. "Vocabulary of Comics," pages 24-37 from *Understanding Comics: The Invisible Art* by Scott McCloud. Copyright © 1993, 1994 by Scott McCloud. Reprinted by permission of HarperCollins Publishers.

David Bartholomae

Must We Mean What We Say?

DAVID BARTHOLOMAE

1   I recognize words as mine when I see that I have to forgo them to use them. Pawn them and redeem them to own them.

—Stanley Cavell, *Philosophical Passages* (103)

2   Meaning what one says becomes a matter of making one's sense present to oneself. This is the way I understand Wittgenstein's having described his later philosophy as an effort to "bring words back" to their everyday use, as though the words we use in philosophy, in any reflection about our concerns, are away.

—Stanley Cavell, *Must We Mean What We Say?* (xxxiii)

3 It is Fall, 2010, and I'm headed toward the final weeks of a first year writing course, a course I've taught every Fall since 1972. I have received a paper I've read many times before, and I am preparing to teach it in class. I will distribute a copy, read it out loud, ask an opening question, and organize the discussion. If you have taught this course, you've received this paper. It is a standard theme. It is student writing—the writing produced from a certain well-defined (and over-determined) cultural and institutional space.

4   In this version, the student was asked to think about himself as a representative case and to write about the forces that shaped a young person's life here and now—in the US at this moment in time. I'll speak more about context later, but the prompt was framed by a reading of Anthony Appiah's essay, "Race, Culture, Identity." To think about audience, I asked my Pittsburgh students to consider my students in Bilbao, Spain, where I have taught off and on since 1982, and where my Bilbao students have written essays for a Pittsburgh audience considering the shaping forces, the "scripts" to use Anthony Appiah's terms, that circulate widely and powerfully in the Basque country in the North of Spain.

5   The writer of this paper had come to college in Fall 2010 after serving in the Third Ranger Battalion as part of the Army Special Operations Command. Although everyone in the class knew that he had been in the armed services, no one knew the details. This was the first and only personal essay I had assigned; his essay was eagerly anticipated and eagerly read. When it came time for class discussion, however, there was only one paragraph that seemed to command attention:

6   We were on a mission in Afghanistan, and while we were setting into position we began taking fire. This was not uncommon for Afghanistan, because the people there are much more aggressive than in Iraq. Usually the gun fights last only a few minutes, but this one lasted eight hours, during which we took three casualties. One casualty had a gunshot wound to the shoulder, and one had a gunshot wound to the foot. These two only spent a few days in the hospital. The third casualty, Benjamin Stephen Kopp, had a gunshot wound to the leg which severed his femoral artery. This wound would ultimately lead to his death eight days later. This was by far the most difficult time of my life, but I think I have become a better man because of it. After learning to deal with pain that extreme, I can easily say that there is not a situation that I can't handle. Problems that seemed so difficult before are now easily solved. It is a horrible way to learn a lesson, but it is important to learn from every situation in life no matter how good or bad it is.

7 When I asked the class, "What is it that makes this passage notable, remarkable?", the students wanted to talk about the quality of the sentences. The prose [they said] was calm, confident, understated; you felt the authority of the writer; there was, they said, the ring of truth. Someone mentioned Hemingway. The best sentence, by acclaim, was the one with the name: "The third casualty, Benjamin Stephen Kopp, had a gunshot wound to the leg which severed his femoral artery."

8 I asked what other sentences they could find that had a similar charge, that could only have been written by someone who was there, part of this story, with this expertise, immersed here, speaking from this experience, present on the page. And they pointed to the first sentence and the phrase, "setting into position," a phrase that is not a common one. And they pointed to the sentence about the differences between firefights in Iraq and Afghanistan:

9 We were on a mission in Afghanistan, and while we were setting into position we began taking fire. This was not uncommon for Afghanistan, because the people there are much more aggressive than in Iraq. Usually the gun fights last only a few minutes, but this one lasted eight hours, during which we took three casualties. One casualty had a gunshot wound to the shoulder, and one had a gunshot wound to the foot. These two only spent a few days in the hospital. The third casualty, Benjamin Stephen Kopp, had a gunshot wound to the leg which severed his femoral artery. This wound would ultimately lead to his death eight days later.

10 No one wanted to talk about the sentences that followed, and these are the sentences I want to talk about today:

11 This was by far the most difficult time of my life, but I think I have become a better man because of it. After learning to deal with pain that extreme, I can easily say that there is not a situation that I can't handle. Problems that seemed so difficult before are now easily solved. It is a horrible way to learn a lesson, but it is important to learn from every situation in life no matter how good or bad it is.

12 This simplest thing to say is that these sentences mark a break from the previous sentences—there is a shift in tone and intent, they don't say the same thing and they don't have the same presence—although they clearly announce the essay's theme and they are clearly there and they clearly fit. But they could also be the concluding sentences to any number of essays telling any number of stories: My Parent's Divorce, My Automobile Accident, My Summer Job, My Sports Injury, Not Making the Cut for the Student Musical, the End of a Romance.

13 As a class, we were too committed to the opening of the paragraph (and too necessarily respectful of the writer's service) to spend much time on its closing. And as much as I wanted to make the point that what we have here is a writing problem (or, to point to the Cavell passages at the head of this essay, a "philosophical" problem, a problem of words and what they do and what they say), I had too little confidence in my ability to manage the discussion to ask the class to linger on the second half of the paragraph.

14 It would not have taken much to make these sentences sound flat or thoughtless or even shocking for how distant and disconnected they seem from the event: "I think I have become a better man because of it." "Problems that seemed so difficult before are now easily solved." These are true, I'm sure, as statements, but as voiced, they seem far too eager to turn away from the experience of a fire fight and the death of Benjamin Stephen Kopp--to stop thinking, to end recall, to keep the words away, to make the event trivial, to return to the comfort of the commonplace.

15 As a point of contrast, here are passages from a paper written to the same assignment; this one telling the story of a college freshman attending a Jewish service on a campus far from home. I believe this was an easier paper to write (although not necessarily an easier paper to revise). I am not, however, trying to rank student essays or student writers. I want to use the comparison to think about problems and possibilities common to student writing. I'll start two paragraphs into the essay:

16 [The] Shima ended and the people sat and I came in. I could see some of the kids I sat with for shabbot services up in the front, but there were no empty seats. So, I sat almost in the back. I found my page; the service continued. They had brought an actual rabbi in for the High Holy Days. Every so often, he stopped and talked about the joy that was supposed to be behind the Amidah or some similar New Age crap. Not to say I hated it—honestly it was nice to have an adult speaking for once. I am far too comforted by the presence of adults.

17 That is a great line, "I am far too comforted by the presence of adults." This is a feature of the style of this essay—it speaks from different positions, inside and outside the commonplace, with and in spite of What One is Supposed To Say. Here is more. (The essay is charming and so I can't help but provide a healthy chunk):

18 Services are an audial experience—the whisper of pages turning, the moment besides the monotone drone of well-known passages when the voices join together into one beautiful, rising tone. I could hear one of my friends above everyone else. She had an amazing voice, pure and clean and deep, a flash of water evident all the course of the fall. I loved sitting next to her on Friday nights because I could picture myself listening to a CD of prayers done folk-style, her on the case wearing a long denim skirt and holding a guitar. Other than that I found her a little irritating at times: she had an ego approximately as large as mine and I in my stubbornness kept trying to determine how exactly I could exceed her in my right to be self-righteous. I could see her over there and she looked like she was having fun. I pushed the lonely jealousy back and concentrated on praying.

...

19 The rabbi asked a question about how in the days of the Temple the Bar'chu used to serve as a call to prayer like in Islam, about where you felt the sacred. I raised my hand for that one and I think I said something about outside or around old buildings, the way the infinite shoots up over your head and the wind blows through the grass. I sat down, satisfied. The room had excellent acoustics.

20 Shacharit ended and some people left....I took the opportunity to come up to the front, near my friends, and there was a brief exchange of smiles and pleasantries before Mussaf began. And it did. I realized that although my dress went past my knees and I had a sweater covering my shoulders, it didn't have a top button but rather had a deep V that ended a little over the waist. The dress was deeply cut and I realized now that it was rather inappropriate. I didn't have a pin, so I held it closed with my hand, trying to make it appear a natural thing to do while holding a book.

21 There were Torah readings. They'd brought an actual Torah down (but not a second, so they read the second selection from a sheet of paper) and you could feel its presence rippling through the room. The rabbi had a method of giving Aliyahs to special people. He started with the Cohens, then the Levis, of course, but then he asked for everyone who was experiencing their first Rosh Hashanah away from home. Which was me, but I didn't raise my hand. I shrunk down into my seat with half of the other cowardly freshmen in that room, and left it to the happy few that had led services before and another of my friends, who with her socks and sandals went up and struggled through the blessing, for she wasn't very good at Hebrew or used to it, and beamed the entire time with that energy that kept her skimming through the prayer book after everyone else was filing off to get dinner. Hagar was stumbling through the desert after being cast from Abraham's camp along with her son. I was holding my sweater shut and my hand was cramping. The rabbi called for anyone who had taken a great journey or made a life change. That could have applied to me. I was far away from home and all by myself. I sat and listened as they read through, sat as they finished.

22 There are great lines in this essay: "I am far too comforted by the presence of adults," "the room had great acoustics," "Hagar was stumbling through the desert." These, though, could certainly be said to be as equally rehearsed as "I have become a better man because of it." What is different between these two uses of everyday language?

23   I'd point to two things. The speaker at shabbot service stays within the language of the story she is recounting; she remains in character as a character. At no point, and this is part of the strength of the essay, does she stop and explain the ritual of the service, define a word, like Aliyah, or explain the point about the two Torahs. And this speaker, the narrator, is such a rich character, full of mixed motives, double voiced; she speaks within and without the range of the expected; she is aware of the script as "scripted," she is both spiritually serious about her Judaism and a sassy, independent young woman. And the writing celebrates this doubleness. Words matter. ("Pawn them and redeem them to own them." That's how Cavell puts it.)

24   This essay has not yet announced its theme, but it is easy to imagine that it is not unlike the theme of the first. Both undertake a difficult intellectual project—thinking (along with Anthony Appiah, I would add) about the very real dilemma of identification. In this essay: what does a young woman gain and lose by identifying with the institution of religion, its practices, its politics and its history. How can one be both sassy and pious? In this previous essay: what does a young man gain and lose by identifying with the institutions of warfare, the history of US military action, including the military action in Afghanistan?

25   For years I have been opening my composition class with a book of poems. This year it was Tony Hoagland's 2003 book, *What Narcissism Means to Me*. I asked students to read it—as I asked them to read the book of prose I assigned, *Color Conscious: The Political Morality of Race*, by K. Anthony Appiah and Amy Gutmann—as though it were a writing textbook. It enacts a set of lessons. It is about writing. What lessons does it hold for you?

26   For this class, as I started reading their Hoagland papers, the lesson was clearly about voice and persona—about an aggressive voice that moved into different registers and spoke from different points of view.

27   Here is a poem from early in the book. It is titled "The Change."

28
> The season turned like the page of a glossy fashion magazine.
> In the park the daffodils came up
> And in the parking lot, the new car models were on parade.
> Sometimes I think that nothing really changes—
> The young girls show the latest crop of tummies,
> and the new president proves that he's a dummy.
> But remember the tennis match we watched that year?
> Right before our eyes
> some tough little European blonde
> pitted against that big black girl from Alabama,
> cornrowed hair and Zulu bangles on her arms,
> some outrageous name like Vondella Aphrodite—
> We were just walking past the lounge
> and got sucked in by the screen above the bar,
> and pretty soon
> we started to care about who won,
> putting ourselves into each whacked return
> as the volleys went back and forth and back
> like some contest between the old world and the new,
> and you loved her complicated hair
> and her to-hell-with-everybody stare,
> and I,
> I couldn't help wanting
> the white girl to come out on top,
> because she was one of my kind, my tribe,
> with her pale eyes and thin lips
> and because the black girl was so big

and so black,
so unintimidated,
hitting the ball like she was driving the Emancipation Proclamation
down Abraham Lincoln's throat,
like she wasn't asking anyone's permission.

29 And then the poem, like a Harvard Essay, makes a turn toward a Conclusion. The speaker steps back to reflect on the meaning of it all--and to tidy things up a bit, a gesture not completely unlike the one in the Afghanistan paper.

30
There are moments when history
Passes you so close
you can smell its breath,
you can reach your hand out
and touch it on its flank,
and I don't watch all that much Masterpiece Theatre,
but I could feel the end of an era there
in front of those bleachers full of people in their Sunday tennis-watching clothes
as that black girl wore down her opponent
then kicked her ass good
then thumped her once more for good measure
and stood up on the red clay court
holding her racket over her head like a guitar.
And the little pink judge
had to climb up on a box
to put the ribbon on her neck,
still managing to smile into the camera flash,
even though everything was changing
and in fact, everything had already changed—
Poof, remember? It was the twentieth century almost gone,
we were there,
and when we went to put it back where it belonged,
it was past us
and we were changed.

31 Carl Dennis, in his book, *Poetry as Persuasion*, categorizes Hoagland as a political poet; he says Hoagland's poems are all about America as she shapes and determines who we are, what can be said, thought and done. This poem clearly engages (and continues to engage) US racial politics. At the February 2011 annual conference of the AWP (the Association of Writers and Writing Programs), Claudia Rankine had the poem read aloud and then responded, describing her discomfort at reading/hearing the poem.

32 She began, "I don't like using the word racist because if you use it it means you are an angry black person." And she talked about the difficulty she had placing herself and the poet, the Tony Hoagland who was her colleague, in relation to the language and the speaker in this poem. She refers to an exchange of words between the two of them in a classroom at the University of Houston, when she spoke of her discomfort in reading and teaching this poem, an encounter in which, by her account, Hoagland did not choose his words carefully and was quick to temper. As was she. This was a heated moment. In describing it (and the change in their relationship) Rankine says she recalls thinking, "Who let America in the room?"[1]

33 Hoagland, in a written response to Rankine, says that Rankine is (and was at the time of the exchange) "naïve when it comes to the subject of American racism." He argues that the poem, "The Change," is not "racist" but "racially complex." Just as she finds the posture of the "angry black person" simplistic, he finds the posture of the "'apologetic liberal white person' not just boring, but useless." He says in his response: "The poet plays with the devil; that is, she or he traffics in repressed energies. The poet's job is elasticity, mobility of perspective, trouble-making, clowning and truth telling."[2]

34   One of the poems in *What Narcissism Means to Me* is titled "America." It is a great teaching poem, since it addresses the figure of the student. (I like to read it as a rewriting of Frost's "Mending Wall.") It begins:

35
> Then one of the students with blue hair and a tongue stud
> Says that America is for him a maximum-security prison
> Whose walls are made of Radio Shacks and Burger Kings, and
> MTV episodes
> Where you can't tell the show from the commercials,
>
> And as I consider how to express how full of shit I think he is,
> He says that even when he's driving to the mall in his Isuzu
>
> Trooper with a gang of his friends, letting rap music pour over them
> Like a boiling Jacuzzi full of ballpeen hammers, even then he feels
>
> Buried alive, captured and suffocated in the folds
> Of the thick satin quilt of America
>
> And I wonder if this is a legitimate category of pain,
> or whether he is just spin doctoring a better grade,
>
> And then I remember that when I stabbed my father in the dream
> last night,
> It was not blood but money
>
> That gushed out of him, bright green hundred-dollar bills
> Spilling from his wounds, and—this is the weird part—,
>
> He gasped, "Thank god—those Ben Franklins were
> Clogging up my heart—
>
> And so I perish happily,
> Freed from that which kept me from my liberty"—
>
> Which is when I knew it was a dream, since my dad
> Would never speak in rhymed couplets,
>
> And I look at the student with his acne and cell phone and phony
> ghetto clothes
> And I think, "I am asleep in America too,"
>
> And I don't know how to wake myself up either,"
> And I remember what Marx said near the end of his life:
>
> "I was listening to the cries of the past,
> When I should have been listening to the cries of the future."
>
> But how could he have imagined 100 channels of 24-hour cable
> Or what kind of nightmare it might be
>
> When each day you watch rivers of bright merchandise run past you
> And you are floating in your pleasure boat upon this river
>
> Even while others are drowning underneath you
> And you see their faces twisting in the surface of the waters
>
> And yet it seems to be your own hand
> Which turns the volume higher?

36 The first writing assignment of the course was a description of a Hoagland poem and what it was doing—not what it says but what it does. Here is an introductory paragraph:

37
> In *What Narcissism Means to Me*, Tony Hoagland struggles to find meaning in the everyday, from its ordinariness to its complexity. His search for truth reminds us of the mission and importance of poetry and poets.

38 I passed out a list of opening paragraphs, and when we talked these through in class, the obvious question was, "How are these sentences in conversation with a figure like Tony

Hoagland, as you've seen him in his book? What is he doing?—that was the original question. What are you doing in return?"

39 The revised essays had beginnings like this one:

40 When I picked us this book, *What Narcissism Means to Me*, I thought: Great, another narcissistic asshole to add to my asshole-saturated life. And then I started reading: Rap music; bullying; a sunset in August; high-school band rehearsals; an automobile accident; a girl singing on the radio. These all appear ordinary enough; what's interesting, though, is watching the poet, Hoagland, trying to make them meaningful, to give them what some might call "deeper" meaning. As I followed his travels, I changed my mind about his motives. [This may sound like the writer of the Rosh Hashana paper, but it is not.]

41 I am not promoting "ass-hole" as a critical term, but I think this student (and the class) had quickly made an important turn. There is more to work with in the revised opening: a writer with a performative sense of herself and her relationship to her audience; a way of reading that thinks about persona, the reader, and about the experience of a book across time; and there is a positioning against the usual ways of thinking about poetry and "deep meaning," the latter phrase now necessarily in scare quotes. But this was copying, one student said, a routine, a caricature of Hoagland. It is rude.

42 And, of course, it is a routine; it is not original; it is a caricature, and it is, in more than one sense, rude. But this opening belonged to this writer on this occasion; it was hers, as much as any of us ever owns our writing, and it was smart (a gesture toward the kind of thinking we think of as smart), it was stylish and voiced.

43 And it works. As I said to the class, it was the first paragraph I had read that sounded like writing rather than the dreadful standard issue of the English class: "the struggle to find meaning in the everyday." That language, too, is prepared, learned, available; but it is not the language of adults speaking about things that matter to them, and so it is not a language I want to encourage.

44 In a later paper, a revision of the earlier one, I had students working with a published review of *What Narcissism Means to Me*. I was teaching my students how to work with sources, how to have an idea in response to someone else's ideas, how to get a word in edgewise.

45 Here is what the poet and critic Craig Arnold had to say in the *Yale Review* about Hoagland and his book.[3] This passage attracted much attention in class discussion, and it is a passage almost all of the students used in their essays:

46 It is important to distinguish between persona and the writing-workshop orthodoxy of "finding one's voice," which stems, I think, from a wish to trademark or brand one's own unique style. Personae are meant, rather, for the public domain, as types or rhetorical commonplaces; they extend, as it were, the range of our affections. (172)

47 Rhetorical commonplaces. Topoi. And (and now Arnold is talking about two poets, Hoagland and Olena Kalytiak Davis):

48 It is against this vanity, I think, that Hoagland and Davis are writing. Their personae require them to simplify and reduce themselves to caricatures, but we are not so very complicated organisms—at least, not as much as our vanity would have us think. They recognize themselves as the flawed, contingent beings that they are; but although they are both self-aware and self-critical, they are never so self-conscious as to bite their tongues….their personae become common property, on hand for anyone who needs them. We learn to put on their masks, and adopt their attitudes, new ways of speaking, of gesturing, new turns of phrase and tones of voice, and perhaps we will muscle through the business of living with a bit more grace or confidence or humility. (186)

49 The courage to offer caricature. Personae as common property. New turns of phrase and tones of voice; new ways of speaking and gesturing; muscling "through the business of living with a bit more grace or confidence or humility." The leverage one gains by being rude. I am willing to say that my students learned something like this from reading Hoagland.[4]

50   But I began with the Afghanistan essay. There is an earlier passage in this student's paper that suggests he is prepared to think about a more performative, complicated sense of identity and identification (or to think about the difference between character and caricature):

51   In a place like my unit, you worked very closely with the same people on a daily basis. I wanted to make friends with these people, so I tried acting like the guy who I thought was the coolest guy in high school. I actually talked like him and used his same mannerisms, but I found it got exhausting trying to be someone else. A funny thing happens when you go somewhere that nobody knows who you are. You can be absolutely whoever you want to be. If you want to act just like the coolest kid from your high school, you can do just that. But after trying out different identities, that is when you really figure what kind of person you want to become—your identity, so to speak. I don't see "identity" as an ending point, but more as a path. Little things like tastes and feelings can all change on a daily basis, so I see identity as more of a path made up of certain beliefs that lead in a specific direction. Even though the traveler might change a little, he will still end up going the same way.

52   This is, among other things, a quiet allusion to a section in the essay by Anthony Appiah ("Race, Culture, Identity: Misunderstood Connections") that students had read in class, a passage we read over and over again for purposes of discussion, a passage the students wanted to take time with. As used above, it is inflected, of course, by a young person's desire for certainty—for the moment "when you really figure out who you are and become comfortable with it"—but I'd use the presence of this passage in the essay to say that the problem with the firefight paragraph is a writing problem, of imagining a space on the page that allows for multiple voices, many coming from a single source, for a philosophical consideration of the problems of language and identity as they reside in a moment (and an act) when a writer struggles to find words that work in a narrative description.

53   Here is Appiah:

54   We make up selves from a tool kit of options made available by our culture and society.... We do make choices, but we don't determine the options among which we choose. (96).

55   Later he refers to "scripts," "narratives that people can use in shaping their life plans and in telling their life stories." Some of these are restrictive; some, he says, can be "glorious." But we need to be wary of the tendency of collective identities to "go imperial." And thus, he concludes

56   it is crucial to remember always that we are not simply black or white or yellow or brown, gay or straight or bisexual, Jewish, Christian, Moslem, Buddhist, or Confucian but that we are also brothers and sisters; parents and children; liberals, conservatives and leftists; teachers and lawyers and auto-makers and gardeners; fans of the Padres and the Bruins; amateurs of grunge rock and lovers of Wagner; movie buffs; MTV-holics, mystery-readers; surfers and singers; poets and pet-lovers; students and teachers; friends and lovers. (103-104)

57   And he advises: "live with fractured identities; engage in identity play; find solidarity, yes, but recognize contingency; and, above all, practice irony"(104).[5]

58   Here is Tony Hoagland, again from his written response to Claudia Rankine in the back and forth over "The Change."

59   I am not trying to side-step—of course I am racist; and sexist, a homophobe, a classicist, a liberal, a middle class american, a college graduate, a drop out, an egotist, Diet Pepsi

drinker, a Unitarian, a fool, a Triple A member, a citizen of Texas, a lover of women, a teacher, a terrible driver, and a single mother. Purity is not my claim, my game, nor a thing remotely within my grasp. I'm an American; this tarnished software will not be rectified by good intentions, or even good behavior.

60 You would have thought Hoagland had just finished reading Appiah. (Perhaps he did; after all, they were both in my class.)

61   And here is the revised conclusion to the paragraph above on the death of Benjamin Stephen Kopp:

62   The third casualty, Benjamin Stephen Kopp, had a gunshot wound to the leg which severed his femoral artery. This wound would ultimately lead to his death eight days later. We held an informal ceremony for him in Afghanistan; only the people who escorted his corpse home got to go to the funeral. The picture of the soldier kneeling in front of the boots and helmet of another soldier is a cool decoration until it's you on a knee in front of your friend's boots. [In the margin, I wrote: "What if this paragraph ended here?" What would be lost? What would be gained? Richard Ohmann, as I note below, would most likely say that everything would be lost. I'm not so sure. I think the turn against the image of the soldier kneeling in front of the boots and helmet of another soldier is sufficient, creating a space by rejecting the advertising image, the soldiers the army is wearing this year.] As I stood up from in front of his memorial, I tried with all my might to hide that I was crying until I saw the entire formation of guys that I worked with in tears. Only two of the guys really stood out to me, my boss Taylor and my best friend Ray. Taylor was perfect at his job and exactly what I wanted to be there, and the only word I can think of to describe Ray is badass. Some guys promise their wives that they won't talk to girls when they go out; Ray had to promise he wouldn't fight, and I have yet to see him lose. You couldn't defeat them at anything, and yet there they stand in tears. I have been mad at people and held grudges, but until this day, I can say with complete confidence that I have never known hate or misery. Today I find it difficult to get truly angry at someone, and I don't think I've had any grudges since about three months after his death.

63 In a classic essay, "Use Definite, Specific, Concrete Language," Richard Ohmann said:

64   In an epoch when so much of the language students hear or read comes from distant sources, via the media, and when so much of it is shaped by advertisers and other corporate experts to channel their thoughts and feelings and needs, I think it a special pity if English teachers are turning students away from critical scrutiny of the words in their heads, especially from those that are most heavily laden with ideology. When in the cause of clarity of liveliness we urge them toward detail, surfaces, the sensory, as mere expansion of ideas or as a substitute for abstraction, we encourage them to accept the empirical fragmentation of consciousness that passes for common sense in our society, and hence to accept the society itself as just what it most superficially seems to be. (397)

65 "A critical scrutiny of the words in their heads." Ohmann has always been a hero for me. I have admired the urgency and the critical sophistication he brought to freshman English as a topic in the late 60s and early 70s, an urgency informed by the legacy of war, in this case the Vietnam war. And I take to heart what he says about an attention to detail—linguistic or literary—as a substitute for critical reflection, as the mere expansion of set ideas.

66   And, let me assure you, I know how to doubt every word of this student paper, how to say "Wait a minute. That is not his story; that is standard issue, a story told over and over again and to the same ends." The master narrative of critique as applied to the master narrative of war. I was part of a generation that went to graduate school to learn how to call such language into question; I was also part of a generation of men who went to graduate school to avoid the Vietnam war.

67   In my account of the class, I said I (we) had to respect his service. I think we need to

respect the starting point of any piece of student writing; here, though, there is (for me, at least) an urgency. Still, there are many reasons why I won't just say No to this piece of student writing, not the least of which is that this narrative still circulates. It works. I can't make it disappear with a wave of the hand, even if I wanted to. It is current; it is legible. The students knew to name it after Hemingway. It is what student writers (all US writers) have to work with; it is where this writing class began. I am preparing a new generation to work on their writing and, in doing so, to work on narratives like this one. In my account of this class, I am reporting on what students had to say, what they could and couldn't do in revision, and what I said and did along the way.

68 And I don't think abstract statement (as an enactment or articulation of ideological critique) is the only or necessary result of a critical scrutiny of the words in our heads. What we can teach writers is revision (as a form of practical criticism); we can ask them to write what they have written over again, differently, and to think about the consequences of the differences. And, here, in the Afghanistan paper, as the project begins in narrative, the revision requires work with narrative. I don't think any other work is worthwhile—not if we want a critical scrutiny of the words in their heads, if we want to bring words back to their everyday use. "Meaning what one says becomes a matter of making one's sense present to oneself." I'd say the revision above is evidence of this (including its final confusion and incompleteness, where the writer struggles to find his way in these sentences). "I recognize words as mine when I see that I have to forgo them to use them." I would say that the student was able to rewrite this essay as he did (and, to my mind, as a step forward) because he had read Hoagland and Appiah, trying out his life, at least for the moment, in their terms. (Just as I have found it useful to consider their work through the writing of Stanley Cavell.)

69 Or, to put it another way, I think the writer is wisely following the example of Anthony Appiah, who insists that a critical consideration of culture and identity be available to ordinary language and to the practice and the representation of our everyday lives. This is why I teach first year writing courses, to give students a rich sense of the words they use and are used by.

...

70 Where does student writing come from? As a teacher, I don't find it useful to think about hearts and minds. The work is on the page. Nor do I find it useful, as a writing teacher, to place the student text in the context of a national political culture—even a national literary culture—to say, for example, that the problem with the Afghanistan paper is the problem of American foreign policy: it promotes blindness; it requires evasion or deception. The connection is too remote to be useful in a writing class.

71 I do, however, think that we can reference a more immediate textual context—a collection of books, movies, songs, essays and utterances, a material presence that is a writer's source and inspiration. This is what Appiah has in mind when he speaks of a "tool kit."

72 I prefer to think about a library or reading list or syllabus, a collection of books, including fragments of books, and passages. The web of citation (an unspecified set of references that emerge in students' writing, often in surprising ways, almost always unacknowledged), this collection is something we can enrich, which is why I always develop a composition course around a set of readings. We can expand the range of reference; we can make old texts newly readable. We can do what we do: assign readings, prepare assignments, suggest ways of working with written language.

73 In an odd and surprising essay, "Self Writing," Foucault locates this idealized space of reading and writing in the hupomn mata, an individual notebook used widely during the first two centuries of the Greco-Roman empire: "They constituted a material record of things read, heard, or thought, thus offering them up as a kind of accumulated treasure for subsequent rereading and meditation" (209). And, in talking about their use, he says (in a passage that, citing Seneca, cites, for me, Appiah and Hoagland):

74 Through the interplay of selected readings and assimilative writing, one should be able to form an identity through which a whole spiritual genealogy can be read. In a chorus there are tenor, bass, and baritone voices, men's and women's tones: "The voices of the individual singers are hidden; what we hear is the voices of all together....I would have my mind of such a quality as this; it should be equipped with many arts, many precepts, and patterns of conduct taken from many epochs of history; but all should blend harmoniously into one."[6] (214)

75 Here is what I say to my students in week one, in my course description:

76 The subject of this course is writing. Writing, as I think of it, is an action, an event, a performance, a way of asserting one's presence. It is a way of asserting one's presence but, paradoxically, in a language that makes the writer disappear. (No matter what you write, the writing is not yours; it is part of a larger text, one with many authors, begun long ago.) And its end is outside your control. In spite of what you think you are saying, your text will become what others make of it, what they say you said.

77 One of my goals in this course is to arrange your work to highlight your relationship (as a writer) to the past and to the words of others (to history, literature, and culture). This is the reason for the assigned readings, and this is the primary role reading will play in this writing course. You will be asked to read a series of assigned texts and to write in response to what you have read. I want to foreground the ways in which your writing takes place in relation to the writing of others. My goal, as your teacher, will be to make that relationship interesting, surprising, and productive. These meetings between the past and the present, writing and a writer, those places in your essays where you work with someone else's words and ideas represent, to my mind, the basic scene of instruction; they are the workplaces, the laboratories, the arenas of what is often called a "liberal" education.

78 Did some combination of Appiah and Hoagland write these papers? No. Are students citing Appiah and Hoagland in these papers? Not directly. Did students write about being black, white, brown or yellow; Jewish, Christian or Buddhist; parents or children, friends or lovers, liberals or conservatives, fans of the Pirates or Steelers, etc. Yes. Over and over again. Did they practice irony? Often.

79 Where did these papers come from? I'd say they came from my class, a kind of odd and arbitrary reading room. They wrote and read. I organized and managed a set of readings, helped students to learn to read their own papers, to read them as rich with other voices, rich with reference, spaces within which they could have something to say.

80 The essays they wrote were allusively connected to what they read, informed by what they read, just as, to be sure, were their readings of Appiah and Hoagland informed by the work they had done as writers, writing about Afghanistan and Rosh Hashanah. Mutually informing. And this is why I think a writing class and a reading class are the same thing, best imagined as part of the same project, set in a single space.

Notes

[1] The various conversations on the internet (and I haven't begun to review them all) seem to conclude that the poem and the poet are racist. As I read the text of Rankine's talk, she is careful not to say this. (You can see Rankine's talk and Hoagland's response at Claudia Rankine's website http://claudiarankine.com/).

[2] Hoagland made a similar point in "Negative Capability: How to Talk Mean and Influence People" in Real Sofistikashun: Essays on Poetry and Craft. Graywolf Press, 2006. 193-201.

[3] This example provides an insight into the kind of research that might accompany a composition course. I was in search of a review of What Narcissism Means to Me that would both serve as a model (as an exemplary piece of academic writing) and that could be usefully read by (or that

would cast useful echoes for) a reader of Anthony Appiah's essay in Color Conscious. When I found the Craig Arnold review, I found a piece worth teaching as a piece of writing, I found a productive way to characterize (and externalize) a reading of Hoagland's book (with Arnold as the character), and I found an essay that gave additional language to use in talking about What Narcissism Means to Me as a textbook for a composition course.

[4] This is how I now understand Bill Coles' prescript that learning is a "stylistic response to style" (1). For most readers, The Plural I is a confrontation between a teacher (and his style) and his students (and theirs). It is easy to see why the book might be read this way, but to read it this way robs the book of the real force of its argument. In The Plural I, as in the examples I provide above, students measure their linguistic performance against figures in texts. The classroom does not have to be a battle ground. Which is not to say that this teaching is easy or without violence.

[5] Appiah refers to this as a "banal postmodernism." I'd prefer to refer to it as an ordinary or everyday.

Credit _____

Bartholomae, David. "Must We Mean What We Say?" From *Writing on the Edge* 22.1 (2011): 17–33. Reprinted with the author's permission.

The Inspired Writer vs. The Real Writer

SARAH ALLEN

1   Several years ago, in a first year writing course, a student nervously approached me after class, asking if we could talk about her latest draft of a formal paper.* She was worried about the content of the draft, about the fact that in writing about her writing process (the assignment for the paper), she found her tone to be at best frustrated, at worst grumbling and whiney. "I don't really like writing. Is that okay?" she asked.

2   This is the first time that I remember a student confessing aloud (to me) that she did not like writing, and I remember struggling for an appropriate response—not because I couldn't fathom how she had the gall to admit this to me, a writing teacher, but because I couldn't understand why admitting to not liking writing worried her. In the next class, I asked my students if they liked writing. I heard a mixed response. I asked them if they assumed that someone like me, a writing teacher/scholar, always liked writing. The answer was a resounding "yes." I rephrased, "So you believe that every day I skip gleefully to my computer?" Again, though giggling a bit, my students answered "yes." And, at last, one student piped up to say, "Well, you're good at it, right? I mean, that's what makes you good at it."

3   My student, quoted above, seems to suggest that I am good at writing because I like doing it. But I'd have to disagree on at least two points: First, I wouldn't describe my feelings toward writing as being a "like" kind of thing. It's more of an agonistic kind of thing. Second, I am not "good" at writing, if being good at it means that the words, the paragraphs, the pages come easily.

4   On the contrary, I believe that I write because I am driven to do so—driven by a will to write. By "will," I mean a kind of purposefulness, propensity, diligence, and determination (which, I should mention, does not lead to perfection or ease . . . unfortunately). But, I should qualify this: the will to write is not innate for me, nor is it always readily available. In fact, the common assumption that a will to write must be both innate and stem from an ever-replenishing source never ceases to surprise (and annoy) me. I've worked with a lot of enviably brilliant and wonderful writers—teachers, students, scholars, and freelancers. I've yet to meet one who believes that she/he is innately and/or always a brilliant writer, nor have I met one who says she/he always wants to write.

5   And yet, I confess that I find myself to be genuinely surprised when some well-respected scholar in my field admits to struggling with his writing. For example, David Bartholomae (a very successful scholar in the field of Rhetoric and Composition) confesses that he didn't learn to write until after he completed his undergraduate studies, and that he learned it through what must have been at least one particularly traumatic experience: his dissertation was rejected for being "poorly written" (22–23).

6   If at first glance the rejection of a dissertation means little to you, let me explain: imagine spending years (literally, years) on a piece of writing (a very long piece of writing), for which you've sacrificed more than you ever thought you'd sacrifice for anything (your time, your freedom, sleep, relationships, and even, at times, your sanity), only to have it rejected. And worse, it's rejected for being "poorly written," which is like being booted off of a pro-league baseball team for not being able to tie your shoes properly. We're talking basics here, or so we (writers) like to think. And yet, if writing were nothing more than "practicing the basics," why's it so hard—hard even for one of the best of the best in my field?

7   It's alarming how many great scholars have admitted to struggling with writing. Bartholomae is not the only one. In a rather famous admission, one of the "fathers" of the field of Rhetoric and Composition, Peter Elbow—the guy who put freewriting on the map, wrote one of the first book-length studies of the writing process, and has been the virtual MLK, Jr. for voice-in-writing (yeah, that guy)—dropped out of graduate school because he suffered so badly from writer's block.[1]

8   My own story of my frustrated struggle with writing is not nearly so heroic as Elbow's or Bartholomae's. I did not fight the dragon beasts of poor writing skills or writer's block, return to the (writing) field as the victorious knight, and then settle in for a long, successful reign as one of the rulers of the land of Rhetoric and Composition. Rather, mine was (and, sometimes, still is) more Hamlet-like, more like a battle with a ghost—the ghost being the "Inspired Writer."

9   The Inspired Writer, as I understand her/him, is a figure for whom writing comes easily—the sort of Romantic hero who writes purely out of an awe-full state, generating perfect prose without the frustrated process of revision (or failure). This Inspired Writer is everywhere, in all the great stories of great writers who were so full of "writerliness" that they were tormented by their need to write; they were relentlessly pursued by their muses . . . as was evidenced by their inked hands, tangled hair, ringed eyes, and profoundly watchful stares. They did not have to go crawling about in the muck of what-everybody's-already-written, across the desert of what-could-I-possibly-say, and over the mountain of an-audience-who-probably-knows-a-lot-more-than-I-do.

10   Of course, the great irony of this figure's story is that the Inspired Writer is really the transcendent distortion of real-life writers. It's much more likely that most of those great, real-life writers got their inked hands from gripping too hard their quills or pens in frustration, as they hovered over pages with more slashes, margin-notes, and edits than clean, untouched sentences set in perfect lines. They probably got their tangled hair from wrenching it; their ringed eyes from spending too many hours staring at black squiggles over white pages; and their profoundly watchful stares from their consequent, bad eyesight.

11   The fact is that they, too, had to answer to the great works that had been written before them; they, too, had to struggle with their own fears about sounding stupid; and they, too, had to answer to an often discerning and demanding audience. Yet, despite reality, the awesome figure of the Inspired Writer still holds sway, hovering over us like bad lighting, blinding us to our own work.

12   The pervasiveness of this myth of the Inspired Writer and the continued celebration of her/him works against us, as writers, for we often assume that if writing does not come easily, then our writing is not good—and in turn, that we cannot be good writers. Consequently, we believe that the writing that comes easily is the only good writing, so we will turn in papers that have been drafted quickly and without revision, hoping for the best (grade).

13   Now, in the days when I was clawing my way through classes as an English major, literature teachers didn't spend much time on revision. I don't ever remember being told anything about strategies for revision. I remember doing peer reviews, where we read each other's drafts and marked punctuation problems, having no idea how to examine—much less comment on—structure and analysis. Other than the five-paragraph formula I'd learned in high school, I had no idea what a paper should or could look like. In other words, when I was learning to write college papers some fifteen years ago, I was totally on my own. The most useful strategy in my bag of tricks? Trial and error. And believe me, good grades or no, having had the opportunity recently (thanks to my mother moving and insisting, "take your STUFF!") to look at the papers I wrote back then, I see an awful lot of the latter.

14   You see, the awful, honest truth is that I'm no rabbit, no natural digger, no lover of thick, tangled messes, and I had no idea how to find my way through the knotted ideas at work in any first drafts, much less how to dig my way into more root (e.g. to go further with my claims, to push the analysis, to discover the "so what" of my work). I didn't find

this place (the page) to be a comfy, hide-out-worthy home. In fact, I confess that I still don't. I have always loved to read, but writing has been much more work than I ever anticipated. And even after so many years of graduate school, and even more years of teaching writing and of writing scholarship, when one might think I should have fully embraced and embodied the status of "veteran" digger, I still, very often feel like I'm trudging through some thick of hard branches and harder roots to find my way down a page.

15   After years of reflecting on this trudging and of talking with students about how they, too, often feel as though they are trudging down a page—through ideas, among the cacophony of words (our own and others')—I've come to this (admittedly, unimpressive) realization: this is, for many of us, an alien discourse. I'm not like my two closest friends from graduate school, whose parents were academics. We didn't talk at breakfast about "the problematic representations of race in the media." Instead, my father told racist jokes that my sisters and I didn't recognize—until later—were racist. We didn't talk at dinner about "the mass oppression of 'other(ed)' cultures by corporate/national tyrants." My sisters and I talked about how the cheerleaders were way cooler than we were because they had better clothes, cars, hair, bodies, and boyfriends, and that we would, consequently, be losers for the rest of our lives.

16   Again, this is an alien discourse, even now. Well, not this. This is more like a personal essay, but the papers I was supposed to write for my literature classes, those were strange. I didn't normally think in the order that a paper would suggest—first broadly, then moving to specifics, which are treated as isolated entities, brought together in transitions and at the end of the paper. I didn't understand, much less use, words like "Marxism," "feminism," or even "close reading." I didn't know that Shakespeare may not have been Shakespeare. I didn't know that Hemingway was a drunk. I didn't know that really smart people spent their entire careers duking it out about who Shakespeare really was and whether Hemingway's alcoholism influenced his work.

17   I didn't know the vocabulary; I didn't know the issues; I didn't think in the right order; I didn't quote properly; and I was far too interested in the sinking, spinning feeling that writing—and reading— sometimes gave me, instead of being interested in the rigorousness of scholarly work, in modeling that work, and in becoming a member of this strange discourse community. Consequently, when a teacher finally sat me down to explain that this was, in fact, a community—one that occurred on pages, at conferences, in coffee shops, and over listservs—and that if I wanted to stay on the court, I'd have to learn the rules of the game, I was both intrigued and terrified. And no surprise, writing then became not just a way to induce the sinking, spinning thing of which I spoke earlier, but a way to think, a way to act—e.g. a way to figure out little things, like who "Mr. W.H." is in Shakespeare's dedication to his Sonnets, as well as big things, like how we can better fight the "isms" of this world.

18   No doubt, the sinking, spinning feeling that I experience when I write or read comes and goes now, but it always did. I feel it alternately, as it shares time with the "trudging" feeling I described earlier. But, please don't think that this trudging comes from having to learn and practice the writing conventions of an alien community. Rather, the feeling of "trudging" is a consequence, again, of that haunting specter, the Inspired Writer. The feeling comes from the expectation that writing should come from "the gods" or natural talent, and it is a consequence, too, of the expectation that this inspiration or talent should be always available to us—always there, though sometimes hidden, in some reservoir of our beings.

19   Thus, even now, when I hit a blank spot and the sentence stumbles off into white space, I feel . . . inadequate . . . or worse, like a fraud, like I'm playing a game that I've got no business playing. The reader is gonna red-card me. And what makes it worse: I

have to write. Writing teacher and scholar or not, I have to write memos and emails and resumes and reports and thank you notes and on and on.

20 But the upshot of all of this is that you'd be amazed what talking about this frustration (and all of the attendant fears) will do for a writer, once she/he opens up and shares this frustration with other writers, other students, teachers . . . with anyone who has to write. For example, once my students see that everyone sitting in this classroom has a gnawing fear about their work failing, about how they don't have "it," about how they don't feel justified calling themselves "writers," because most of them are "regular folks" required to take a writing class, well . . . then we can have ourselves a getting-down-to-it, honest and productive writing classroom. Then, we can talk about writer's block—what it is, what causes it, and what overcomes it. We can talk about how to develop "thick skins"—about how to listen to readers' commentaries and critiques without simultaneously wanting to rip our writings into tiny pieces, stomp them into a trashcan, and then set fire to them. And most importantly, then, we can talk about writing as a practice, not a reflection of some innate quality of the writer.

21 My work, for example, is more a reflection of the scholarship I spend the most time with than it is a reflection of me, per se. One strategy I learned in graduate school (and I swear, I picked it up by watching my first year composition students) is to imitate other, successful pieces of writing. By "imitate," of course I don't mean plagiarize. I mean that I imitate the form of those texts, e.g. the organization, and the ways that they engage with, explore, and extend ideas.

22 For example, a Rhetoric and Composition scholar named Patricia Bizzell has written scholarship that I use a lot in my own work. In fact, even when I don't use her work directly, I can see her influence on my thinking. A couple of years ago, after reading one of her books for about the hundredth time (seriously), I noticed that her articles and chapters are organized in predictable kinds of ways (not predictable as in boring, but predictable as in she's-a-pro). She seems to have a formula down, and it works. Her work is consistently solid—i.e. convincing, important—and using that formula, she's able to tackle really dense material and make it accessible to readers.

23 To be more specific, she tends to start with an introduction that demonstrates, right away, why the coming work is so important. For example, in "Foundationalism and Anti-Foundationalism in Composition Studies," she starts off the article by reminding us, basically (I'm paraphrasing here), that everybody's down with "the social," that we are all invested in examining how language—and writing—occurs in a context and how that context dictates meaning. So, for example, the word "we" in the previous sentence is a reference to Rhetoric and Composition teachers and scholars; however, in this sentence, it's not a reference to a group of people, but to the word "we," as it occurs in the previous sentence. See? Meaning changes according to context.

24 So, Bizzell starts with this premise: that everybody's down with the social, that we're invested in examining contexts, that we know that meaning happens in those contexts. Then, she introduces the problem: that we still want something pre-contextual (e.g. I know what "we" means because I can step outside of any contexts—including this one—and examine it objectively). Then, she gives two in-depth examples of where she sees the problem at work in the field. She then examines how we've tried to address that problem, then how we've failed at addressing it, and then she poses another/new perspective on the problem and, consequently, another/new way of addressing it.

25 This is her formula, and I imitate it, frequently, in my own work. It's rigorous, thorough, and like I said earlier, accessible. It works. But, sometimes I'm working on something totally different, something new (to me), and that formula starts to box me in too much; the formula becomes a tomb instead of a foundation. That's when I turn to outside readers.

26 Now, this one, actually, is a tougher strategy to use . . . because it requires that you

share a piece of work that looks like a train wreck to you with another human being—ideally, another smart, patient, open-minded human being. I have four people I send my work out to consistently. One is my boss; one my mentor; one a (very successful) peer; and the other, a senior colleague I come dangerously close to worshipping. In other words, I don't send my stuff to my mom. I don't give it to my best friend, my boyfriend, my dance teacher, or my sisters. I only send my stuff to people who seem to be a lot better at writing scholarship than I feel like I am.

27   Again, it's hard to do, but I can't tell you how many students I'll see in my office over the course of a semester who will say, "But my mom read my paper, and she says it looks great"—while gripping a paper marked with a D or F. Mom may have been the final authority when you were negotiating curfews and driving and dating, but unless Mom's a (college-level) writing teacher, she'll be no more of an expert in college-level writing than your dentist will. Send it to her if you want an outside reader, but don't expect her final word to be similar to your teacher's final word. And while I'm on my soapbox . . . don't let anyone edit your papers . . . including your mom. It's called "collusion"—a kind of plagiarism—and it's really easy to spot, especially if you were the Comma Splice King in the first paper and use commas flawlessly in the second.

28   More importantly, keep in mind that if you only use your mom, or your coach, or some other person who's not in the same class, then you may be making the revision process (and the reading for that person) more difficult than necessary, since that reader will have no idea what you've read in class, what you've talked about in class, or what the assignment guidelines and grading criteria are. Writing occurs—and is assessed—in a context, remember?

29   The best strategy for finding and using readers is to start with the teacher (no, it's not cheating). Ask him/her to read a draft before you submit the final. Then, share the paper with a classmate, as well as someone who's not in the class. That way, you'll get an "insider's" perspective as well as an "outsider's."[2] I've heard students say that using anyone but the teacher for feedback seems to be a waste of time. However, I find that when a student brings me a draft, I (and most writing professors) read it in terms of how it should be revised, not how I'd grade it. So, after you revise based on the teacher's feedback, get other readers to take a look, again, at the newly revised version and have them read it as a finished product. This will help you get a better sense of how it's working as a text that will be graded.

30   The best piece of advice I can give you, though, is to tell the Inspired Writer to shut up and let you write. If you have to, find out about a few of your favorite writers. I guarantee that they struggle, too. If not them, try talking to your classmates and/or your teacher. Again, if they have written anything in their lives worth writing, then it took some effort to do so. And, once the insecurities are out there, so to speak, and not trapped in Pandora's little box to drive us mad with their "what if" whispers, you may discover that there's more to the writing process than just getting lost in branches and stumbling over roots.

31   There's nothing quite like finding that the black squiggles you typed onto that white page actually invoke a feeling in or change the mind of your reader(s). Of course, too, there's the emotion, revelation, clench of teeth, slackening of shoulders, or any other response, that a text elicits from even its own writer. The latter is, for my part, the biggest reason why I write—even now, and even and especially as I write scholarship. For me, the text is like a fire in the room. And I am often awed by the way it moves, sleeps, devours, and sustains, while I am simultaneously trying to master it (knowing full well that if I let it go, it will run riot, but knowing, too, that I can't push too hard or it will disappear altogether).

32   For what I've found in my own relationship to writing, and in talking to my students

about theirs, is that it's about the connection, really—even if the connection is an antagonistic one. We like to think that thinking isn't for nothing; that communicating with another (even and especially with ourselves) is never entirely in vain; that what we have to say is perhaps/probably not brilliant but is, still, worth the attempt of saying, of writing, and of considering/being considered. No doubt, a whole lot of practice can give us the means to write in such a way that not only we, the writers, but others will want to listen, will want to read. And in that listening-talking, reading-writing relation, a collision, the inevitable momentary connection, happens.

33   Maybe we smack the dirt and roots; maybe we smack white space. Maybe a reader's jaw drops at the "gets it" insight of some obscure line in your paper that you don't even remember writing because you spent forty-five minutes working on the line right after it. Maybe you make someone stop and think for just a moment about something they've never considered before. Maybe you make friends with a bunch of classmates because of that story you wrote about the road trip you took last summer to a music festival. Maybe you inspired a heated class debate because of that paper you wrote about your personal project for saving the world.

34   But for all the misunderstandings, all the fears and so-called failings that happen among writer and paper and reader, there's always another white page, and there's always more to say. This is why we must write, why we must continue to practice: to keep talking, keep thinking, keep revising. Nobody's ever got the final word, not even on the page. We've all got the will to write: it's called "communication." Maybe you do so in music or in paint or in graphics or, even, in gossip. But here, in these black squiggles on this white page, you've listened to something I've had to say. Maybe you've not listened closely; maybe you're yawning or rolling your eyes. But if this is a decent piece of writing, you're giving some response right now—a smile? An exasperated sigh? A tensed shoulder? A clenched fist? Whatever the case, here, response is happening. And that's at least a (good) start.

Credit

Allen, Sarah. "The Inspired Writer vs. The Real Writer." From *Writing Spaces: Readings on Writing Vol. 1.* Charles Lowe and Pavel Zemliansky, Eds. West Lafayette: Parlor Press, 2010: 34–44. Reprinted with the author's permission.

Seeing the Text

STEPHEN A. BERNHARDT

1 The physical fact of the text, with its spatial appearance on the page, requires visual apprehension: a text can be seen, must be seen, in a process which is essentially different from the perception of speech. The written mode necessitates the arrangement of script or typeface, a process which gives visual cues to the verbal organization of the text. We might think of texts arranged along a continuum, from texts at one end which convey relatively little information visually, to texts at the opposite end which reveal substantial information through such visible cues as white space, illustrations, variation in typeface, and use of nonalphabetic symbols, such as numbers, asterisks, and punctuation. In terms of this continuum, an essay would fall well toward the non-visually informative end. Certainly, paragraph indentation, margins, capitalization, and sentence punctuation provide some information to the reader, but such information is extremely limited, with most of the cues as to organization and logical relations buried within the text. At the other extreme of the continuum would be texts which display their structure, providing the reader/ viewer with a schematic representation of the divisions and hierarchies which organize the text.

2 If we were to encourage students to experiment with visible features of written texts, we would increase their ability to understand and use hierarchical and classificatory arrangements. Because of the opportunities it offers for visual inspection, writing heightens awareness of categories and divisions, changing the ways people conceive classificatory relations. Goody has suggested that the earliest uses of writing in a society-making lists, keeping accounts, recording events-sharpen awareness of categories and classes through the very fact of placing items physically on a page where they can be inspected and arranged. The graphic quality of writing, in contrast to the flow of speech, underscores the discontinuity, the boundaries, and the order which is possible in visual organization.[1] Ong derives similar conclusions concerning the introduction of typography, suggesting that printing "gave urgency to the very metaphor that ideas were items which could be 'spread,'" in two senses: the printing press spread books throughout the culture, but also opened new possibilities for spreading type on the page, possibilities which were not open to scribes.[2] Writing, especially when visually informative, encourages the writer to be exact about grouping related ideas, delineating beginnings and endings, and using cues to signal to the reader a graphic representation of cognitive organization. By studying and writing texts which display their structures through white space, graphic patterning, enumerative sequences, and so on, student writers can gain a heightened sense of categories, divisions, and orderly progression.[3]

3 Though classroom teaching often assumes essay organization as the norm, outside the classroom visually informative prose is pervasive, and not just in scientific or technical fields. As a starting point, we might consider the ubiquitous, insistent presence of advertising, with its continual striving for attractive and convincing visual/verbal stategies. The graphic arts generally attend to the intersection of print and graphic media.[4] Texts designed for public audiences typically adopt visually informative strategies. Thousands of informational pamphlets, brochures, and forms flow from government agencies, special interest groups, businesses, and community groups, attempting to gather information, to sell ideas, to explain programs, to describe rights and responsibilities to an affected public, or to seek support for one program or another.

4 Legal writing also displays a "tendency to make more and more use of layout and other graphetic and graphological devices as a means of revealing structure, content, and logical progression."[5] Business writing exhibits similar visual patterning in everything from formal reports, to procedures, to correspondence, to memos-all make liberal use of conventional partitioning, white space, headings, schematics, lists, and other visible cues. The same can be claimed for writing in scientific and technical fields, much of which follows familiar formats with text layout determined by conventional practices.

5   At all levels of structure, texts which are highly informative visually share features not characteristic of texts which do not exploit the graphic potential of written language. We can assume that visually informative texts achieve rhetorical organization, just as do texts which are relatively non-informative visually. Both types must provide direction to the reader as to how the text is to be read: what transaction is intended, what the major divisions are, what is considered important, and what relations exist amongst the various subpoints. But the manner in which visually informative texts achieve rhetorical control differs in important ways from that in the non-visually informative text, at all levels of organization: in the whole discourse, in the paragraph, and in the sentence.

6   In a non-visually informative expository text, rhetorical control is typically exercised through the familiar strategies of essay composition. Introduction/ body/conclusion partitioning is frequently in evidence, with each section per-forming predictable functions. Topics are introduced and broken down in the initial section; the sequence for the following paragraphs is anticipated by statements that preview the full text or announce a plan of organization. Paragraph-to-paragraph movement is often facilitated by transitional links to show logical connection. From time to time, readers are reminded of their place in the progression of the text, reminded anaphorically of what has come before and prepared cataphorically for what is to follow. Topic or core sentences enter into coordinate relations with other topic or core sentences in other paragraphs, and into relations of generalization and support with sentences within the paragraph. Sentence to sentence relations are controlled semantically through cohesive ties: one must actually read what is written to get any sense of how one point is related to the next. The net effect, or at least that which is intended, is one of smooth progression from beginning to end, a careful leading of the reader through the text to the final acceptance of and satisfaction with the conclusion. Linear progression characterizes both the execution and the intended reader's approach to the text.

7   In sentences, the non-visually informative text evidences a consistency of structure. The vast majority of sentences are major syntactic forms as opposed to minor; they exhibit typical patterns of subject/verb/object, cast in a preponderance of declarative mood constructions. Minor forms or use of fragments is generally rare, as are uses of interrogative or imperative mood. The typical classroom essay is composed of sentences which resemble each other in their full, declarative structures, arranged in paragraphs with low visual identity (except for boundaries, signalled by indentation). The essay appears on the page as essentially unbroken, undifferentiated print, an effect which is heightened by printing processes which justify margins and further homogenize the texture of the page.

8   Admittedly, this characterization of expository text is based on one sort of writing, that enshrined in the handbooks of our trade. But this characterization does seem sufficiently influential within our discipline to be considered the norm, the product we encourage in our practice within the "current-traditional paradigm."[6] The control of rhetorical relations is strictly internal to the text, integrated within the paragraph and sentence structures. And the closer our models come to literary norms, to the norms of the polite, personal, anthologized essay typical of the Eastern literary "establishment," the greater are the demands on the student to produce essays which are subtle in their organizational schemes, leading rather than showing and telling, with no authorial recourse to meta-discoursal commentary on the structure or logic of the exposition.

9   To gain a sense of just how divergent these rhetorical values are from those evidenced in other, more visually informative prose patterns, it is necessary to look at and think

about the achievement of rhetorical control in a visible text. The sample text reproduced below as Figure 1, a fact sheet on wetlands, is part of a larger project, *The Great*

Wetlands

Every year in the Great Lakes region an estimated 20,000 acres of valuable wetlands are filled, drained, or developed for residential, commercial and other uses. No one is certain how many acres of wetlands remain in the Great Lakes region, because the last complete national inventory was done in 1955, but losses have been significant. The most common types of wetlands found in the Great Lakes are coastal wetlands, marshes, wet meadows, shrub and wooded swamps, ponds, and bogs - all remnants of the shallow lakes left by the glaciers. These areas are wet all or part of the year.

Wetlands are valuable to the Great Lakes because they provide many free and natural environmental services. These services range from helping preserve water quality in the lakes to shoreline protection to providing a habitat for valuable wildlife such as waterfowl, fur bearing animals, and spawning fish - all important to the regional economy.

But despite their potential value, incremental losses of wetlands continue. Why? One reason is that the public has historically been ignorant about the value of wetlands, seeing them as useless property - swamps filled with mosquitoes. Secondly, many wetlands are found along the coastline of the Great Lakes or in the region's rich agricultural areas. Therefore, they are economically desirable land for development and agriculture. Thirdly, few studies exist which quantify the economic and environmental value of wetlands. And lastly, there is no comprehensive and coordinated state or federal policy for the management of wetlands.

The importance of wetlands to the Great Lakes

Free and natural water treatment	Wetlands purify surface and ground-water by filtering and absorbing sediments, nutrients, and chemicals from runoff.
Flood control	Wetlands can absorb and hold large quantities of water from flooding rivers and streams, effectively reg-ulating extreme water levels which often occur in the Great Lakes.
Shoreline erosion prevention	The thickly rooted aquatic vegeta-tion in wetlands can buffer the shore against waves in sheltered lakes and bays.
Tourist and recreation areas	Wetlands are rich natural areas which are good for birdwatching, fishing, and hunting.
Produce food crops	Wetlands are excellent growing and gathering areas for wild rice, cran-berries, and blueberries.
Produce wildlife	Wetlands provide a habitat for wa-terfowl, fish, like northern pike, large-mouthed bass, and muskies, and other wildlife such as valuable fur bearing muskrats, racoons, and minks
Replenish groundwater supplies	Wetlands act like natural reservoirs trapping rain and melting snow which later flows into underground water systems.

Figure 1. Reduced photocopy of wetlands fact sheet from *The Great Lakes Notebook*.

How can wetlands be protected? _____

- By legislation which prevents the drainage, filling, or development of wetland areas without state review and permit.
- By state or federal acquisition of private wetlands in order to protect important wetlands.
- By tax reductions and other incentives to private owners to protect and preserve their wetlands.
- By identification of wetlands which have special environmental importance.
- By educating people about the many values of wetlands.

Status of Federal Wetlands Protecitons

There are no comprehensive federal laws to protect wetlands, however limited protection is found under: 1) section 404 of the Clean Water Act which requires permits to dredge and fill in wetlands and prohibits construction of wastewater treatment plants in wetlands; 2) the National Flood Insurance Program which limits development in wetlands near floodplains; 3) the U.S. Fish and Wildlife Coordination Act which requires consultation on all water projects to protect rare habitats; and 4) Executive Order 11990 of May 1977 which instructs federal agencies to implement programs to protect wetlands.

Great Lakes Region – status of wetlands protection

ILLINOIS: Few wetlands in Great Lakes portion of state. Limited protection through floodplain management and dredging legislation.

INDIANA: One third of the state's wetlands are in the Great Lakes basin. Limited wetlands protection under the state's Natural Scenic and Recreational Rivers Act and Nature Preserve Program.

MICHIGAN: One half of all Great Lakes wetlands are in Michigan. The wetlands Protection Act enacted in 1979 regulates the filling, dredging, development or drainage of wetlands primarily 5 acres or more and smaller significant wetlands.

MINNESOTA: The state owns or controls many of the state's numerous and important wetlands. The Public Waters Act and several other acts indirectly protect many wetland areas.

NEW YORK: Has one of the most comprehensive state wetlands protection laws, the Freshwater Wetlands Act of 1975. The act protects wetlands larger than 12.4 acres and those with special significance.

OHIO: One-half of the state's wetlands are in the Great Lakes basin. The Nature Preserve Program which acquires land for endangered species habitat and the Critical Areas Program are used to protect wetlands.

PENNSYLVANIA: Special wetlands area along Lake Erie. Floodplain management legislation and the state's administrative code which allows state acquisition of valuable wetlands afford protection.

WISCONSIN: The state has many wetland areas in the basin. The Shoreland Zoning Act limits development in shoreland wetlands, and the Floodplain Management Act and other legislation offer protection of other wetlands.

ONTARIO: Two thirds of the province's wetlands are located in the Great Lakes basin. These are protected under the provincial Beach Protection Act which requires permits for, and review of, any work in wetlands.

Prepared by the Great Lakes Basin Commission, Box 999, Ann Arbor, MI 48106l/8l.

Figure 1 Continued.

Lakes Notebook, undertaken by the Great Lakes Basin Commission.[7] *The Great Lakes Notebook* was conceived and composed by Sandra Gregerman, information officer for the Commission and a graduate of the University of Michigan's School of Natural Resources Master's degree program in Environmental Communications. Those in the environmental sciences know that to be successful they must communicate with diverse audiences, and this text attempts to increase public awareness of the importance of wetlands protection in the Great Lakes area. The importance of this sheet was heightened by the fact that at the time of its release, conservation groups and interested legislators in Michigan were working to pass a wetlands protection act. The primary audiences for the text were legislators, educators and their students, and the general public. Gregerman's purpose was larger than public relations: she hoped to convey important, substantial information in an intelligent manner in order to influence the ecological administration of the region.

10   These multiple considerations of audience and purpose functionally constrain the text, influencing its shape and structure. The intention was to produce a document which would satisfy a number of functional considerations of cost and distribution, while being attractive enough to draw reader attention and substantial enough to encourage the reader to keep the sheet, compile it with others in the series, and use it. Especially in legislative and bureaucratic spheres, where the flow of print information is heavy, documents compete for attention, and to be effective readers must be drawn into the text.[8] The wetlands fact sheet insured attention through the use of high quality, heavy weight paper and crisp, well-defined print, qualities chosen to encourage the reader to notice and keep the sheet. Though each sheet of the Notebook was a different color (the wetlands sheet a light brown), all attained a high visual identity through headings across the top and sides and identifying symbols in the upper right hand corners.[9] The sheets were distributed one at a time in an effort to shorten initial production time and to allow for subsequent revisions, so it was important that they be recognized as part of a series. Their compilation was encouraged by the use of punched paper, and headings spaced vertically along the right margin increased the identity of the sheets and usefully served as a thumb index once the sheets were compiled.

11   Also important in the design of the fact sheet was the distribution of printed information on the page. To attend to the layout of the text requires considering the text as a visual gestalt, focusing attention on the total visual impact of the text on a prospective reader. Cataldo suggests that the principles codified by experiments in perception can be usefully applied to the visual/verbal design of graphic texts.[10] Perhaps the most relevant law is that of equilibrium, or *pragnanz*, which suggests that items in a visual field strive for balance or equilibrium with other items in the field. The wetlands text works well, in part, because the distribution of print on the first page achieves equilibrium simultaneously along several axes: horizontally, vertically, and diagonally. A horizontal axis balances the material above and below the widely spaced heading: *The importance of wetlands to the Great Lakes.* A vertical axis divides the lower half of the page, balancing the widely spaced headings along the left side against the explanatory material on the right. Finally, diagonal axes work toward symmetry; the lined margins on the top and right balance each other, the continuous text in the upper-left balances the shorter, detached statements in the lower right, and the logo in the upper-right balances the spaced headings of the lower-left.

12   A second law of gestalt, that of *good continuation,* or good figure, suggests that visual perception works to pull figures out of the background, to give them definition against the undistinguished field in which they are located. In the sample text on wetlands, good continuation is achieved through the clear black print on a light-brown background, through the headings, and through the groupings of related information which are set

off by blank space. The typeface variation further reinforces the high definition of figure against ground. With a poorly reproduced text with low contrast of figure to ground, the reader has to strain to make out the text, in the process invoking a third law of gestalt, that of *closure*. When good continuation or good figure is not provided by the visual stimulus, the perceiver has a tendency to fill in the missing gaps, to provide the missing definition, as evidenced by the ability of readers to process even highly degraded copy, in which much of the information provided by the shape of letters is missing. In the sample text reproduced here, the quality of the printing and the arrangement of type on the page make for good figure and the reader need not strive for closure.

13 The law of good continuation or good figure also underlies the effect of emphasis in a visible text. Figures which are more strongly defined against their field will tend to appear more important than other figures which share the same ground. On the first page, an emphasis on wetland values is achieved by isolating the list under a major heading in the middle of the page and then calling attention visually to the list of functions and values with bold-faced headings along the left margin. The emphasis on this section may be further increased by its location in the lower-left area of the visual field, an area which, it has been suggested, is favored by visual stress.[11]

14 A fourth law of gestalt, the law of *similarity*, suggests that units which resemble each other in shape, size, color, or direction will be seen together as a homogenous grouping. The groupings of the wetlands sheet are highly distinct, reinforced by spacing between sections and headings in various type sizes which clearly delineate boundaries, allowing the text to display its structure. Good use of the law of similarity, as obvious a principle as it may seem, is an accomplishment, not a given, as has been amply demonstrated by Anderson's discussion of the visual organization of written texts.[12] Anderson shows how texts which fail to convey to the reader the intended groupings of information under the law of similarity can be profitably rewritten.

15 The sample text on wetlands makes good use of "visual syntax," to use Dondis' phrase, in the creation of a harmonious, balanced, attractive text which conveys information to the reader about textual organization through visible means. The visual impact of the front side is certainly greater than that of the reverse, but that is as it should be, for if the reader is sufficiently engaged with the text to flip the sheet over and look at the reverse, then the visual appeal has already proven effective. Through these laws of gestalt, visual features take over the load of structuring and organizing the reader's processing, thus reducing the role of those semantic features which organize a form like the essay. Instead of a smooth, progressive realization of the text through initial previewing and a chain of logic which ties each paragraph or section to the preceding or following one, the visible text relies on localization, on a heightening of the boundaries, edges, and divisions of the text. In an integrated, non-visually informative text, the desideratum is a seamless text. In the visible text, the goal is to call the reader's attention visually to semantically grouped information, focusing the reader's attention on discrete sections. Fowler captures the distinction well in his contrast between progressive and localized text structures:

16 A text is progressive if its structure leads the reader onwards, projects him forward from one segment of text to a succeeding one. Textual surface structure may be said to be localizing when it operates to hold up the reader's attention at a specific place in the total syntagm.[13]

17 Each section of the wetlands text is its own locale; it has its own function, which is likely to differ from previous and subsequent sections. Instead of a cumulative movement, the text has a localized focus in each section, with separateness rather than integration characterizing the text both semantically and visually.

18 In the sample text on wetlands, each section is self-contained and available to the reader without reference to other sections. Unconstrained by linear presentation, the reader can move about, settle on certain sections, read some sections lightly, some intently, some not at all, and still have a good idea of what the text is about. The legal audience, for example, may be less interested in or already familiar with the values of wetlands, but very interested in existing state and federal legislation. Students in a biology class may be highly motivated to look at the information on the first page, but uninterested in that on the second. The localization of the text makes possible the selective use of the text by varied audiences for varied purposes.

19   With a visible text, it may not be fruitful to talk about paragraphs in terms of topic sentences and support, or opening and closing sentences, or sentences of transition. In fact, it may not be useful to speak of paragraphs at all, but of sections or chunks. In the visible text, the headings take over the task of generalizing or identifying the topic. Levels of subordination are indicated by variation in typeface, type size, or placement of headings, rather than through subordinators or cohesive ties which indicate semantically dependent relations. For example, the initial section, written in integrated paragraphs, makes heavy use of deictics (*the, these*), pronominals (*their, they*), conjuncts (*but, one, secondly, thirdly, therefore, and lastly*), and ellipsis (*Why?, One reason is .. .*), to link each sentence to the next through some expressed logical relation or through the carrying over of the topic. But in sections two, three, and five, with the exception of lexical ties, there are no cohesive ties indicating logical relations, nor any transitional ties between sections. With subordinate relations indicated visually, the contents of each section tends to be a series or list of coordinate points, each item having equal status.

20   The move toward serial, coordinate development of sections exerts a shaping influence over the syntax of the listed items. Parallel grammatical structures tend to predominate, as in the second section of the wetlands text, wherein each statement of the values or functions of wetlands, with one exception, begins with the word *wetlands*, which serves simultaneously as the topic for the following comment, the subject of the sentence, and the agent of the actions or qualities described. The visual isolation of the information interrupts the flow of discourse, exerting a localizing effect which is reflected in parallel syntax. The sentence beginning *The thickly rooted aquatic vegetation* calls attention to itself because it does not fit the abstract context, that is, a visible parallel list. A better fit would be provided by beginning the sentence like the others, with initial phrasing such as *Wetlands buffer*, with *vegetation* planted within an instrumental clause later in the sentence. Traditional advice to vary sentence structure or sentence openings to avoid boring the reader or to keep sentences from sounding choppy would be misdirected here, where structural isomorphism must be maintained.

21   In addition to heightening the demands for parallel form, localization tends to reduce syntax from full sentences to phrases. In the third section of the sample text, for instance, the question *How can wetlands be protected?* is followed by a list of prepositional phrases beginning with *by*, each of which answers the question. Each carries over elliptical information from the lead question, which would take the form "*Wetlands can be protected ...*" were it written out in full form. In this instance, the individual items do not complete a syntactic structure begun in a lead sentence, even though the items are punctuated like sentences. The fourth section of the text offers a contrast, in that the syntax of a single sentence is carried over from item to item in the list, resulting in one long sentence which is at once a single sentence and a list of sentences. It is worth noting that no term for this sort of construction exists, to my knowledge, in the lexicon of composition, rhetoric, or linguistics, and yet the pattern is extremely widespread in writing from many fields. Such *expanded sentences* require careful control, demanding a series of elements which are syntactically parallel, each completing a sentence by adding a phrase which complements the initiating phrase.

22   The sentences of the final section of the sample text evidence still another kind of

41

syntactic patterning. This section demonstrates an easy movement from full sentences to fragments in an unpredictable sequence. The effect is a casual tone, almost as though we were reading someone's notes rather than a finished written product.

23   The wetlands fact sheet thus offers quite a contrast to texts composed within traditional essay format, employing as it does a variety of strategies on both large (full text and sectioning) and small (sentence and section development) scales. It avoids linear, progressive organization, allowing a reader to break in at any point in the text with full comprehension. It combines graphic techniques of layout and typeface variation with verbal passages which achieve cohesion in a variety of ways through integrated paragraphs, expanded sentences, isolated sentences, and organized fragments of various sorts. The text reflects decisions by the author to adopt a variety of strategies in response to varying ideational content and in the interest of assembling the information attractively for various audiences. Any of the sections might have been written in integrated paragraphs, but the choices made capitalize on the visual potential of written language.

24   The table below summarizes those features which distinguish visually informative from non-visually informative texts. Not all features will necessarily be present in any given text, but texts at one end of the continuum or the other are likely to share some combination of these features.

25   There are no hard and fast rules for designing effective visually informative texts, though empirical research has begun to offer some tentative findings. For example, in studies at the Document Design Center, complicated FCC regulations were rewritten and simplified through a visually informative format of questions and answers. The new rules enabled readers to find information more quickly and more accurately.[14] Not all research findings are so clear, however. A report by Frase and Schwartz made a strong claim which bears directly on visual design:

26   Our results show that lines may be short or they may be long, a page may have neat margins or ragged margins. No matter. What is critical is whether the lines represent meaningful groups of information. It is this matching of visual design to the constraints of cognitive processing that makes for efficiency.[15]

27   The conclusion seems logical and is not qualified by the authors. And yet an attempt to replicate the study under similar conditions did not find significant gains in comprehension which could be attributed to visual, semantically-based groupings.[16] Great difficulties beset the researcher who attempts to demonstrate changed reader behavior as a function of text design, since texts which fall toward the visually informative end of the continuum encourage selective reading and extracting of information. The design strategies make the texts accessible at various depths to suit the purposes of various readers. This aspect of interaction between text and reader is difficult to evaluate or build into experimental design.[17]

28   Instead of attempting to base teaching practice on scant and tentative results, we may find it more expedient to view the rhetoric of visual design as an evolving art. As is true of other arts, more profit can be gained in the early stages of research from looking at what practitioners do than from attempting to induce and measure changes in experimental variables. If teachers would begin to look at naturally-occurring discourse forms which have evolved outside the classroom, they would begin to develop a descriptive base for visual design. A preoccupation with conventional essay format allows little attention to visual features. Instead of helping students learn to analyze a situation and determine an appropriate form, given a certain audience and purpose, many writing assignments merely exercise the same sort of writing week after week, introducing only topical variation. Texts with visually organized, localized development, and features such as headings, expanded sentences, meaningful white space, or question-and-answer strategies are typically neglected.

Visual Organization of Written Texts

Visually Informative		Non-visually Informative
	Rhetorical Control	
varied surface offers aesthetic possibilities; can attract or repel reader through the shape of the text; laws of equilibrium, good continuation, good figure, closure, similarity.	Visual Gestalt	homogenous surface offers little possibility of conveying information; dense, indistinguished block of print; every text presents the same face; formidable appearance assumes willing reader.
localized: each section is its own locale with its own pattern of development; arrests reader's attention.	Development	progressive: each section leads smoothly to the next; projects reader forward through discourse-level previewing and backwards through reviewing.
iconic: spacing, headings reveal explicit, highly visible divisions; reader can jump around, process the text in a non-linear fashion, access information easily, read selectively.	Partitioning	integrated: indentations give some indication of boundaries, but sections frequently contain several paragraphs and some-times divisions occur within paragraphs; reader must read or scan linearly to find divisions.
emphasis controlled by visual stress of layout, type size, spacing, headings.	Emphasis	emphasis controlled semantically through intensifiers, conjunctive ties; some emphasis achieved by placement of information in initial or final slots in sentences and paragraphs.
subordinate relations signaled through type size, headings, indenting.	Subordinate Relations	controlled semantically within linear sequence of paragraphs and sentences.
signalled through listing structures, expanded sentences, parallel structures, enumerated or iconically signalled by spacing, bullets, or other graphic devices.	Coordinate Relations	controlled semantically through juxtaposition, parallel structures, and cohesive ties, especially additive ties.
linkage controlled visually; little or no use of semantic ties between sentences and sections; reliance on enumerative sequences or topicalization of a series.	Linking/ Transitional/ Intersentential Relations	liberal use of cohesive ties, especially conjunctives and deictics; frequent interparagraph ties or transitional phrases.
variety in mood and syntactic patterning; much use of Q/A sequences, imperatives; fragments and minor forms; phrases used in isolation.	Sentence Patterns	complete sentences with little variation in mood; sentences typically declarative with full syntax.

29 Classroom practice which ignores the increasingly visual, localized qualities of information exchange can only become increasingly irrelevant. Influenced especially by the growth of electronic media, strategies of rhetorical organization will move increasingly toward visual patterns presented on screens and interpreted through visual as well as verbal syntax. Written texts will gain flexibility in organization through branching and recursion, characteristics more closely associated with speech than writing. Further use of isolated, localized passages also seems likely, with information called up in short snatches in interactional patterns, rather than in extended, rhetorically integrated, progressive texts.

30 By studying actual texts as they function in particular contexts, we can gain an improved understanding of what constitute appropriate, effective strategies of rhetorical organization. At the same time, we can learn from such studies how successful texts are composed and what part schools can play in encouraging students to become able, creative composers.

Notes

[1] Jack Goody, The Domestication of the Savage Mind (Cambridge, England: Cambridge University Press, 1977), p. 81.

[2] Walter J. Ong, S. J., Rhetoric, Romance, and Technology (Ithaca: Cornell University Press, 1971), p. 167.

[3] See Anne Ruggles Gere, "A Cultural Perspective on Talking and Writing," in Exploring Speaking-Writing Relationships: Connections and Contrasts, ed. Barry M. Kroll and Roberta J. Vann (Urbana, IL: National Council of Teachers of English, 1981), pp. 111-123.

[4] See especially John W. Cataldo, Graphic Design and Visual Communication (Scranton: International Textbook Company, 1966); Arthur T. Turnbull and Russell N. Baird, The Graphics of Communication (New York: Holt, Rinehart & Winston, 1975).

[5] David Crystal and Derek Davy, Investigating English Style (Bloomington: Indiana University Press, 1969), p. 198. See also David Mellinkoff, The Language of the Law (Boston: Little, Brown and Company, 1963).

[6] Richard Young, "Paradigms and Problems: Needed Research in Rhetorical Invention," in Research on Composing: Points of Departure, ed. Charles R. Cooper and Lee Odell (Urbana, IL: National Council of Teachers of English, 1978), pp. 29-47.

[7] A commission which has, unfortunately but like so many other environmental advocacy groups, been eliminated by Federal budget cuts.

[8] Roland Harweg draws a nice distinction between texts which must seek out an audience vs. those which have an assured audience, outlining characteristic ways of beginning for each: "Beginning a Text," in Discourse Processes, 3 (October–December, 1980), 313-326.

[9] It is unfortunate that the attractive qualities of the sheet cannot be appreciated in the reduced, black and white version printed here. Standard print journalism, with its homogenization of the text's surface and reduction of the physicality of the text, levels qualities active in more graphic media. For examples of how print journalism can extend the possibilities of the printed page, see any issue of Visible Language: The Research Journal Concerned with All That Is Involved in Our Being Literate.

[10] Cataldo, Chapters 2, 3, 4, and 5.

[11] Donis Dondis, A Primer of Visual Literacy (Cambridge: MIT Press, 1973), pp. 28-29.

[12] Paul V. Anderson," Organizing Is Not Enough,"in Courses, Components,and Exercises in Technical

Communication (Urbana, IL: National Council of Teachers of English, 1981), pp. 163-184.

[13] Roger Fowler, "Cohesive, Progressive, and Localizing Aspects of Text Structure," in Grammars and Descriptions, ed. Teun A. Van Dijk and Jinos Petöfi (Berlin: de Gruyter, 1977), pp. 64-84.

[14] Reported by Robin Battison and Joanne Landesmanin "The Cost Effectiveness of Designing Simpler Documents," SimplyStated,16 (April, 1981), pp. 1, 3.

[15] L. T. Frase and B. J. Schwartz," Typographical Cues that Facilitate Comprehension," Journal of Educational Psychology, 71 (April, 1979), p. 205.

[16] James Hartley, "Spatial Cues in Text," Visible Language, 14 (1980), 62-79.

[17] Experimental studies on text design are reported in P. A. Kolers, M. E. Wrolstad, and H. Bouman, ed., Processing of Visible Language,1, 2 (New York: Plenum, 1979, 1980); D. Wright reviews the research and concludes "there is no ubiquitously good way of presenting technical information" in "Presenting Technical Information: A Survey of Research Findings," Instructional Science, 6 (April, 1977), 93-134. For an overview of writings on visual literacy, see Dennis W. Pett, "Visual Literacy," in Classroom Relevant Research in the Language Arts, ed. Harold G. Shane and James Walden (Washington, DC: Association for Curriculum Development, 1978), pp. 8-17.

Credit _____

Voice in Writing Again: Embracing Contraries
PETER ELBOW

The Voice Story

1 *Voice* used to be a hot critical term in the pages of the journals, but our current scholarly conversation has gone rather quiet. I think there's something to be gained if we reawaken the discussion.

2 Starting around the 1960s, there was a surge of enthusiasm for getting voice into writing. Those of us who were in that surge were not all saying the same thing, but we were all promoting voice in one sense or another: *Voice is an important dimension of texts and we should pay lots of attention to it. Everyone has a real voice and can write with power. Writing with a strong voice is good writing. Sincere writing is good writing. My voice is my true self and my rhetorical power. The goal of teaching writing is to develop the self.*

3 But then came skeptics. They weren't all saying the same thing either, but they were all being critical in one sense or another: *Let's not pay so much attention to the voice in texts. Voice is a misleading metaphor. We don't write with a "voice" that is ours. We do not write, we are written by our culture. We are socially constructed, and what we mistake for a self is a subject position that changes as we are differentially interpellated from one social context of our life to another. Sincerity is not a useful goal for writing.*

4 Interestingly, the enthusiasts *and* the critics tended to share the same anti-elitist political desire for a fairer and less oppressive society—a desire to give more power to students in the classroom and citizens at large. So, when the skeptical line of thought seemed to go so far as to deprive individual persons of any agency to make a difference in the world (*we cannot write, we can only reproduce larger more powerful forces around us*), there were various and continuing attempts to rescue agency. Paul Smith and Randall Freisinger gave some early and sophisticated versions. *We may be constructed by culture, but if we learn to analyze carefully enough how this happens, then we can actually work toward a fairer world.*

5 This conflict about voice in our field echoes a much older conflict about the self in language. The Greek sophists offered, in effect, to help craft any voice for any speech to help win any argument or law case—no matter what kind of self. Plato, in reaction, argued that the power of language derived, to some real extent, from the nature of the rhetor's self: only a good rhetor can create really good words. To learn to speak or write better, we need also to work on being better persons.

6 Aristotle refused this either/or conflict. He wrote that "We believe good men more fully and more readily than others" (*Rhetoric* 1356a), but then he went on to acknowledge that speakers can fool listeners and persuade them with a consciously constructed voice. He talks about the ability to "make ourselves *thought* to be sensible and morally good. [. . .]" (1378a, my emphasis)— noting that this is a matter of skill, not character:

7 We can now see that a writer must disguise his art and give the impression of speaking naturally and not artificially. Naturalness is persuasive, artificiality is the contrary; for our hearers are prejudiced and think we have some design against them. (1404b)

8 I hear Aristotle giving a kind of pragmatic, common sense affirmation of both positions: *It helps to be trustworthy; but, if you're skilled, you can fake it.* These are crux passages and certainly not unambiguous. Some readers hear him saying that craft and disguise are the only things that matter. Nan Johnson's scholarship and stature convince me to see Aristotle affirming both sides: not *just* that we can fool readers, but also that good men *do* have an advantage and that genuine naturalness *is* persuasive (more about this later) .

9   I'm intrigued by a more recent avoidance of either/or thinking about voice in writing. It started as a local culture, spread, and then had a nontrivial influence on composition studies at large. It was spawned by a noteworthy first-year English course at Amherst College that was inaugurated and directed by Theodore Baird from 1938 to 1966 (see Robin Varnum on this course). Walker Gibson, Roger Sale, and William Coles were deeply influenced by teaching in it; David Bartholomae was strongly influenced through Coles, and Joseph Harris through Bartholomae and Coles. Harris wrote admiringly about Coles in these pages (see his "Plural Text"). A list of others who also taught or were influenced is striking: Reuben Brower, Neil Hertz, Richard Poirier, Gordon Pradl, and William Pritchard. Lurking significantly in the background at Amherst College was Robert Frost, with his own strong preoccupation with a voice in written language.

10   Baird and the others developed a rich and sophisticated attitude toward voice. On the one hand, participants spent a great deal of time scorning sincerity and skewering students and colleagues who were naive or foolhardy enough to defend it. They insisted that a text gives no window at all on the actual self of the writer. Yet, on the other hand, they were deeply preoccupied with the voice in a text and tended (more than most New Critics) to see voice as perhaps the central and operative dimension of a text. They developed some of the best ears around for the nuances of voice. They engaged in what Pritchard called "ear training" in his perceptive essay of that title. They *were* interested in the self in a text but insisted that this self was continually made and remade by langua ge—not a reflection of the historical self or author. In their fascination with voice, they sometimes seemed to want a voice that was true or right *in itself*, fitting the writer or speaker—not just a voice that is appropriate to the audience or genre.[1]

The Current Situation

11   So there's been lots of interesting thinking about voice over the centuries and the topic is far from settled, but now we don't see much scholarly critical writing about it. (For a notable exception, see the 2001 special issue of the Journal of Second Language Writing, guest edited by Belcher and Hirvela.) The concept of voice in writing seems to have been successfully discredited in our journals and books: who can find a writer arguing for voice (much less "true self" or "real self") in any enthusiastic, nonironic or noncritical sense in the pages of *College Composition and Communication* or *College English* for the last ten or fifteen years? Yet the concept of voice (without quotation marks) keeps not going away. Darsie Bowden herself makes this very case:

12   A longtime critic of voice, I rail against its use in my courses. Despite this, the term
        invariably emerges, often sheepishly from one of my students and, more frequently
        than I'd like to admit, from me as I stumble over my own inability to describe what
        I mean. ("Voice" 285)

13   So voice is alive in our classrooms. Students at all levels instinctively talk and think about voice, or their voice in their writing, and tend to believe they have a real or true self—despite the best efforts of some of their teachers. [Jane Danielewicz quotes a comment by one of her students: "I turned down your suggestion for revising just because I thought it took away some of my personal voice in some places" (personal conversation)]. If Bowden herself falls into using the term, think of how many other teachers use it in some of their responses to student papers. It seems intuitive in our culture to speak, for example, about a "hesitant, uncertain voice" at this point in a paper, or an "intolerant voice," or a "confusing change in voice in the second section." And when teachers work with a student for fourteen weeks, it's often hard not to slip into a comment that links the voice in the paper to the student's character or personality. ("You're usually so forthright when you make points in class. Why do you use such a hesitant voice in this

written argument?")

14   Voice is also alive in politics. George Bush was probably elected because his voice was more persuasive and believable to more voters. We're left with a widespread perplexity about whether that down-home "nucular" voice is *him* or a clever ruse. It would be nice if our next election were decided entirely on the basis of substantive issues, but—unless we have more culturewide discussions about the complexities of voice, the relations between voice and the actual character—voter feelings about self-in-voice will surely carry the day again. Political advertising tends to be based on research about perceptions of self-in-voice.

15   Voice is alive on the Internet and via email. It used to be that most writing occurred in school or at work (although we shouldn't underestimate how many people wrote mostly privately in other settings; see D. Barton and R. Ivanic). Much or most writing used to be addressed to a judging authority who knew more about writing or the topic than the writer did. What a huge change the Internet has brought to the experience of writing: so many more writers; so much more writing in the world; so much writing for *strangers!* Instead of writers only wondering about what teachers will find right and wrong in their words, more and more writers wonder less defensively what kind of person readers will think they are. (As the *New Yorker* cartoon dog says to his friend: "Online, they don't know you're a dog.") On blogs and websites such as MySpace, lots of people eagerly use written words to reveal "who they really are," while just as many use the same websites to "construct" a self. Among the latter group, some want to disguise what they feel are their "real selves," some want to give voices to what they experience as multiple selves, and some don't feel they have actual selves at all until they create them with language.

16   So, as I look at our journals, our classrooms, and the larger world, I see a kind of stalemate about voice in writing. The concept is alive and well, yet no one comes forward any more in our field to argue for it or even to explore very seriously why it's so alive. Critics get tired of criticizing something that no one defends, tired of not reaching people who don't listen to them. Thus, critical commentary goes on to other topics, such as digital media, public writing, service learning. (The growing discussion of World Englishes and nonmainstream versions of English cries out for more attention to voice.) We're left with an unresolved contrary that strikes me as unhealthy and unproductive: many critiques seem valid, yet voice stays alive, even in the most "naive" forms that have been most powerfully critiqued. My goal here is to wake up this slumbering contradiction.

Either/Or Battle

17   How do people respond when they are party to a contradiction? The most common response is to try to win—to engage in an either/or, zero-sum attempt to discredit the other view. I want to illustrate the dangers of this impulse by looking at how Joseph Harris makes his argument about voice. His chapter on it in *A Teaching Subject* is a classic compare/contrast essay between an approach he approves of and one he criticizes. "Picture two writing classrooms" (23), he starts off, and, when he gets to the heart of his argument, he writes: "These contrasting views of what ought to go on in a writing classroom stem from deep and conflicting intuitions about how language and the self are related" (42). As his chapter unfolds, his either/or analysis of two approaches to voice becomes a larger analysis of two approaches to the teaching of writing. He launches his analysis by quoting me as follows:

18   "The underlying metaphor," writes Peter Elbow, ". . . is that we all have a chest cavity unique in size and shape so that each of us naturally resonates to one pitch alone" (Harris *Subject* 24; *Power* 281-82).

19   He uses my metaphor not just as an example, but as an icon to stand for the kind of writing classroom he disapproves of. Thus, toward the end of his argument, he sums up the good approach as one that avoids this idea of voice issuing from "'a chest cavity unique in size and shape'" (34). And he keeps referring back to this metaphor to characterize my position.

20   What's striking to me, however, is that he quotes only half of my metaphorical treatment of voice (and ignores my nonmetaphorical analysis). He fails to note that I go on immediately to argue that such a simple notion is wrong. Here's what he doesn't quote from me:

21   In this metaphorical world, then, even if we figure out the system, we are stuck. If we want to be heard we are limited to our single note. If we want to sing other notes, we will not be heard.

22   And yet, if we are brave and persistent enough to sing our note at length— to develop our capacity for resonance—gradually we will be able to "sing ourselves in": to get resonance first into one or two more frequencies and then more. Finally, we will be able to sing whatever note we want to sing, even to sing whatever note others want to hear, and to make every note resound with rich power. But we only manage this flowering if we are willing to start off singing our own single tiresome pitch for a long time and in that way gradually teach the stiff cells of our bodies to vibrate and be flexible. (*Power* 282)

23   Working in an adversarial zero-sum model where one side must be wrong for the other to be right, Harris couldn't seem even to *register* this second idea. It *had* to be that, if I said we only had one note, I couldn't possibly be going on to say the contrary. So he also couldn't notice the previous paragraph, where I'd set up my both/and metaphor with an explicit analogy of a "clunky violin" that needs to be "played in" before it can resonate to a wider range of pitches.

24   This either/or mental framework dominates again when Harris says that I equate voice in writing with "a certain type of prose" (34). Yet I repeatedly argue in the chapter he was analyzing that voice correlates with no kind of writing:

25   There are no outward linguistic characteristics to point to in writing with real voice. [...] Real voice is not necessarily personal or sincere. Writing about your personal concerns is only one way and not necessarily the best. Such writing can lead to gushy or analytical words about how angry you are today: useful to write, an expression of strong feelings, a possible source of future powerful writing, but not resonant or powerful for readers as it stands. (*Power* 312–13)[2]

26   Because I have been so often cited as representing a whole "school" in composition studies, I think that this kind of misreading somehow got ingrained and that it has affected how many people understand the landscape of composition studies— tending to see it as a site for either/or, zero-sum conflict between positions. The representation of my work has often been based on an inability to imagine myself carving out a both/and analysis and making arguments that embrace contraries. For example, when I argue strongly for unplanned, uncensored freewriting, people often ignore my stated commitments to careful, planned, skeptical revising. When I argue for the believing game, I'm not heard insisting on the need for the skeptical, logical, critical thinking of the doubting game. When I argue for private personal individual writing, people have trouble seeing me affirm the social dimension of language and writing.[3]

Compromise

27   Compromise is surely a healthier way to deal with conflict or contradiction. *If we're going to avoid war, you can't have your position and I can't have mine. They are mutually incompatible. We both have to give in a bit—back down some—and work out a middle* *position of some sort.*

28 I don't know whether the Amherst College group thought of themselves as compromising between previous extreme positions about voice (Baird was explicitly influenced by Korzybski and his theory of general semantics). But their position on voice invites itself to be seen as a compromise. On the one hand, they affirm a main principle of the *enthusiasts* for voice: that we should look at texts in terms of the voices there— and that this kind of textual voice is interesting, central, and powerful. On the other hand, they loudly affirm a main principle of the critics of voice: a textual voice gives no window at all onto the real character of the author. Also, Thomas Newkirk's book *The Performance of Self in Student Writing* takes what strikes me as a more or less compromise position. But his book was strikingly criticized in the pages of *College Composition and Communication* and *College English*, perhaps because partisan ideological lines had already been drawn.

29 Even though compromise is a precious skill that life continually asks us to learn, I want to point to the *limitations* of compromise as a way of dealing with contradiction. Normal compromise doesn't free us from the conflict-based framework of either/or, black/white thinking. It's a method for letting each side lose as little as possible. For a true win/ win outcome, we need a way to *break out* of this either/or frame of reference.

30 Aristotle's position on voice (as I understand it) illustrates what's involved in going beyond compromise and breaking out of the either/or thinking. He's not saying that rhetors should find a halfway position where they are *a little bit* good and natural and *a little bit* clever at disguising. Being only somewhat good and somewhat clever is a formula for mediocrity. My both/and reading of the crux passage is consistent with the kind of thinking that Aristotle uses in various places in his work. He often deals with tricky issues by saying, "in one sense, X; but, in another sense, Y." That is, he often implies that we can understand a complex topic well only if we can look at it first through one lens and then through a contrary lens. So I read him to be saying, "Analyzed through one frame of reference, good ethos requires good character; but, analyzed through another frame of reference, good ethos is available to skill alone."

31 In *Writing Without Teachers*, I emphasized the limitations of compromise in the writing process (and summarized the point as follows in my essay on "binary thinking"): The path to really good writing, then, is seldom the path of compromise or the golden mean. If we are only sort of generative and sort of critical, we write mediocre stuff: we don't have enough to choose from, and we don't reject ideas and words we ought to reject. We need extremity in both directions. Instead of finding one point on the continuum between two extremes, we need as it were to occupy two points near both ends. (54)

Handling the Stalemate by Embracing Contraries

32 If a stalemate is strong and ingrained, the competing positions themselves are probably valuable and necessary. In such a situation, we need the benefit of the competing positions in all of their strength—and, for that, we need both/and thinking or embracing contraries. So, with the voice stalemate, we need to stop trying to find out which of the competing positions is right—or trying to work out some watered down middle position.

33 In this essay, I show that we can affirm the validity of both conflicting positions— even in their contradiction—and benefit from them. I start with a theoretical overview. (By the way, although I used a *kind* of both/and thinking in the chapter that Harris quotes, I wasn't using it to embrace contraries; I was using it to argue for voice.)

34 We have a choice about how to think about written language: through the lens of text or that of *voice*. There is no problem with either. The only a problem is when people try to outlaw one as wrong. They see a debate between right and wrong when it's really a choice between two lenses or "terministic screens" (to use Burke's term). We need both because each shows us something about language that the other obscures.

35   In their root literal senses, "text" stands for words on a page and "voice" for the spoken medium of language. Thus, the text lens highlights the visual and spatial features of language as print (etymologically, "text" comes from weaving—note "textile"); the voice lens highlights language as sounded, heard, and existing in time. The text lens foregrounds language as an abstract system (Saussure's *langue*) in which words have the same meaning whoever utters them in whatever context—words as interchangeable and not attached to persons; the voice lens highlights how language issues from individual persons and physical bodies and how the same words differ, depending on who says them and how. Two people's use of the word "cat" is the same as text, but the words sound very different as spoken or voiced. (Handwriting is more personal and body-connected than typing, so handwritten words are often experienced as more "voiced" than typed or printed words. With the resources of word processing, people sometimes try to create or bring out a voice by using certain fonts.)

36   Insofar as we consider language purely through the text lens, it is disembodied language; no one is speaking to anyone. The paradigm cases are mathematics and logic. Mathematics is a language, in certain ways the best one that we have. The symbols do nothing but proclaim a relationship: that something is the case or means something or equals something. If we look at written or spoken language through this narrow text lens—stripping away the people, the historical drama, the body, and the actual person trying to do something to someone else—we can analyze better the bare root meaning, logic, and patterns that voice and rhetorical drama can obscure, thus highlighting the value of putting an argument into symbolic logic.

37   In contrast, insofar as we consider discourse as voiced utterance, it is *rhetorical*: this lens brings back into focus the historical and material and social context. This rhetorical lens has been usefully celebrated in our era, and it has helped us fight free of any temptation to see language only as grammar books and handbooks see it—as pure text or naked meaning ("The cat is on the mat").

38   But no one is tempted any more to take this narrow, nonhistorical or nonrhetorical view as the only lens for language. (It's become a cliché to accuse the New Critics of taking a completely ahistorical stance toward literary texts, but Clara Claiborne Park has written an important and fascinating essay showing that it's not so simple. And before falling into clichéd condescension, let's remember that we have a legacy from the New Critics of close reading of words and the intricate relations among them in a text—a kind of careful reading that was comparatively rare in scholarship until they came along.)

39   Currently, however, there is some temptation to see the rhetorical lens as the only right one for language: *All discourse is always already rhetorical*. But the telltale "always already" shows that the claim is a lens claim. As such, it cannot refute another lens claim. That is, a rhetorical lens shows us a rhetorical dimension in *all* discourse. But, by the same token, a pure text lens shows us a naked meaning dimension that is "always already" in all discourse.

40   Even a piece of mathematical discourse that consists mostly of equations can helpfully be viewed through both lenses. It may look as though it's just sitting there as a piece of text or semiosis laying out a semantic relationship; but the equations can also be seen as someone's response to someone else's equations.[4]

41   In short, we benefit from both metaphors or lenses and we lose out if either is outlawed. In what follows, I lay out concrete opposing reasons why, in our teaching and our own discourse, we need to engage in two contrary activities: paying lots of attention to voice and pushing away considerations of voice. My premise is that, if we acknowledge the realm of time—seeing how it can trump logic—we don't have to choose only one approach or create a watery compromise, but rather can easily follow contradictory advice.

Reasons for Attending to Voice in Texts

42 *When readers hear a voice in a piece of writing, they are often more drawn to read it—and that audible voice often makes the words easier to understand. Robert Frost put this in oracular terms:*

43   A dramatic necessity goes deep into the nature of the sentence. . . . All that can save [written language] is the speaking tone of voice somehow entangled in the words and fastened to the page for the ear of the imagination.

44 This is helpful knowledge for writers. With practice, people can learn to write prose that "has a voice" or "sounds like a person," and, interestingly, when they do, their words are more effective at *carrying meaning*. For when we hear naturally spoken language—or when we hear a difficult text read aloud well—we don't have to work so hard to understand the meaning. Intonation or prosody enacts some of the meanings so that we can "hear" them. (Here are some of the audible elements in spoken language that carry meaning: variations in pitch, accent, volume, speed, timbre, rhythm. I like to illustrate this in a miniworkshop where each person tries to say a single word, such as *hello*, in such a way as to carry a different meaning.) Of course written words are literally silent, but it is possible to learn to write language that readers actually *hear in their minds* (or, if you prefer, that readers have the illusion of hearing). Readers usually experience "audible" voiced writing as clearer than writing they don't hear.

45   But what makes writing audible? This is a theoretical mystery (that I've enjoyed pursuing), yet there's a simple technique that helps students produce it. When students have the repeated experience of reading their writing aloud, they are more likely to *listen* to their words and write sentences that are inviting and comfortable to speak, which, in turn, makes the sentences better for readers reading in silence. For centuries, writers and rhetoricians have advised reading aloud (more on this in my "Three Mysteries").

46   *Attention to voice helps rhetorical effectiveness.* Merely *getting* a voice into one's writing is not enough. If the voice is wrong, it backfires. Throughout the centuries of rhetorical tradition, teachers have urged speakers and writers to think about the audience and find the most appropriate voice (or *ethos* or implied author or persona). By analyzing the voice in lots of texts and by reading drafts aloud—and trying out different readings to manipulate the voice in various ways—we can learn to hear better the voice that readers are most likely to hear. It's particularly important to learn to hear the voice or voices that readers *won't consciously* hear but that may well affect their reaction. (Is there a subliminal arrogance or timidity that turns off readers who aren't already sympathetic to the argument?) This kind of "ear training" was one of the main goals of the Amherst College group. (Walker Gibson has what are probably the most elegant and useful books that help with ear training: *Tough, Sweet,* and *Stuffy,* and *Persona*).

47   Aristotle famously observed that *ethos* often trumps *logos* or *pathos* in persuading an audience. Most writing, especially student writing, is a mixture of weaknesses and strengths. When we find ourselves noticing weaknesses more, it's often because of a problematic voice. A winning, believable, and attractive voice probably makes us notice virtues more. It's surely appropriate that voice is a prominent rubric in many statewide writing exams.

48   The *metaphor of "voice" helps students improve their writing.* Many of the textual features that people describe in terms of voice can also be described as matters of *style*. And there's a huge and sophisticated scholarly literature about style in writing. But the voice metaphor often works better for students and others who are not sophisticated about language. Compare these two phrasings:

49   You have too many passives and nominative constructions here.

50   You sound kind of distant, uninvolved, or bureaucratic to me here.

51 Of course, the style formulation is more accurate and trustworthy. Passives and nominative constructions are "true facts." The voice formulation is a personal subjective projection—and it implies a subjective guess about how others will react and even about the mind and feelings of the writer. Nevertheless, the voice formulation has advantages. Few students are sophisticated about the grammatical and other technical linguistic features needed for style analysis—whatever the merits. Yet, ever since they were toddlers, they have been getting more sophisticated about the effects of different voices on listeners. ("Don't you use that tone with me, young man!") And they've had to work at psyching out various voice games—for example, in the realm of dating.

52 Even the subjectivity of voice judgments has an advantage. Style-based comments may be more authoritative, but they often imply a misleadingly technical or impersonal stance toward language. "Too many passive verbs" invokes an impersonal universal standard, when the real truth is unavoidably subjective: how many passive verbs are right for these particular readers in this rhetorical context? When style comments imply objective verdicts from an impersonal judge (or a high-stakes testing agency), they sometimes lead students to forget that writing is a transaction between humans (language as "dramatism" in Burke's term).

53 In addition, voice-based responses are sometimes better for helping students make large-scale and pervasive revisions. When writers change their felt relationship to their readers ("Maybe I could let readers hear how much I care about my ideas"; "Maybe I shouldn't imply that only an idiot could disagree with me"), they usually instinctively come up with better wording—and even more effective thinking.

54 *Thinking in terms of voice can help people enjoy writing more*. When people are helped to treat writing as a process of "just using your own regular voice," they usually become less intimidated by writing—often finding words and ideas more easily and even coming to enjoy writing. Admittedly, in many cases one's own comfortable voice is inappropriate. It's often too casual for lots of school and business tasks. (But let's not forget that some of the most ineffective and even tangled student writing comes from trying too hard to avoid a "regular voice.") And the voice that comes easily and "feels like how I want to say this" may carry some problematic features—for example, some anger, resentment, or fear about the topic. Small or large adjustments in voice may be necessary in revising. But this very process—noticing what voice turns up naturally, thinking about how readers might react to it, and learning to make necessary revisions— is exactly the kind of rhetorical training that makes better writers.

55 *Attention to voice can help with reading*. Many students have trouble understanding and enjoying the kinds of texts we teach and, especially, feeling a connection to them. Teachers commonly enlist voices when they play a good recording of a complex poem or show a video of a Shakespearean play. But this leaves students in a passive role. I prefer to enlist the students' own voices. In teaching a hard text, I used to say, "Your homework is to read this very carefully until you understand it very well." Now I say, "Your homework is to prepare yourself to read this text aloud so that listeners without a text will really understand it." This "simple task" actually forces students to work out the meanings in remarkable detail and actually *feel* those meanings in their bodies. (This also works well for nonfiction or even scholarly essays. If the text is long, I specify a crux passage for reading aloud.)

56 When we hear and discuss the readings in class (everyone in pairs and then some volunteers reading for all of us), I like to press for conflicting readings, even ones that go against the grain. Every out loud reading is an interpretation, and, by comparing and discussing them, we bring out different interpretations and also highlight various critical concepts such as implied author, unreliable narrator, irony, and tone.

57 *It's a question of voice and self.* I've argued in this essay for creating an audible voice that helps reach readers and carry meaning and for crafting a voice that fits the audience. But can I argue that writers should try to make their writing reflect their actual selves? I do, in a sense, but given the electricity around this issue, I will tiptoe carefully as I try to describe two kinds of voice linked to the self of the writer.

58 (1) *Sincerity.* Sincerity isn't the same as good writing; it can be awful and tinny. But sincerity is one style or voice, and it is useful for *some* occasions, if it's believable. The need for sincerity (or the illusion of it) is most obvious in letters of apology or proposal. The fact is that *some* effective writing seems to get its power from convincing readers that the writer is not calculating the right stance or voice but is allowing his or her sincere self to show. Sometimes this voice is odd or "wrong" or dangerous in some way, but it wins readers over nevertheless by seeming so genuine. For many readers, one of the pleasures in reading is a sense of making contact with the writer.[5]

59 (2) *Resonance.* When I am reading a text of some length, I sometimes sense bits of what I want to call "resonance": I experience them as pieces of added weight, richness, or presence— even if they are bits of irony, play, metaphor, or even silliness. Sometimes, these are little changes of tone, eruptions, asides, or digressions, even lapses of a sort. Resonance is not at all the same as sincerity nor does it give an accurate picture of what the writer is like. My hypothesis here is completely speculative, but I sense that these are places where the writer has gotten a bit more of his or her self *in* or *behind* or *underneath* the words—often a bit of the unconscious self. Some important dimension of perception or thinking or feeling formerly kept out of the writing is now allowed in. (Good musicians often get a bit more of themselves *into* or *under* the notes— notes which do not show a picture of the player.)

60 I'm not calling these places "good writing." They may even be places where the writing breaks down. Resonant passages are often holes or cracks in the structure or voice that the writer was trying to use. Often, the piece is going to have to get worse before it can realize the potential resonance that is trying to get in. But I think I've noticed myself and other writers benefiting from having these passages pointed out. Often the writer can say, "Yes, I have a proprioceptive sense that something different was going on for me as I was writing those passages." I suspect it helps if someone is good at noticing such passages and then says, "Try for more of that." Although the advice often doesn't help in revising the piece (especially if the deadline is near), I sense that it helps one's long-term growth as a writer.[6]

Reasons for Not Attending to Voice in Texts

61 Thus, I'm arguing that we should put lots of attention on voice in all of the ways I've just described. But now I'll argue that we should *not* pay attention to voice—in all the following ways.

62 *Ignoring voice is necessary for good reading.* Students improve their ability to see and analyze the semantic, intellectual content of what they read if we help them learn not just to ignore voice, but to push aside forcibly any effects of the "voice" (or illusion of voice) that is "saying" these things. Since speaking and listening were people's first experiences with words—and continue as primary language experiences—most readers tend to hear a voice in written words if the language halfway allows it. (When the language is tangled, clogged, and unsayable—or when people are speed-reading at a furious clip—it's harder to hear a text.) New readers often mouth written words, and it's not uncommon even for experienced readers to move their lips. The auditory nerves of most readers probably show electrical activity, perhaps even the throat nerves.

63 Not only do most readers hear voices in texts as they read, they tend to hear people in the texts. Written words may be silent semiotic signs, but, when humans read (and write), they usually infer a person behind the words and build themselves a relationship of some sort with that person. I needn't make this argument at length since it's made so well by Deborah Brandt in *Literacy as Involvement.*

64   It's this powerful default tendency in so many human readers that shows the importance of learning to *push away* the effects of voice. If students are going to learn how to read critically, they need to understand that voice will often mislead them. A textual voice often functions like a persuasive courtroom lawyer; it can distract readers from the details of the cognitive, logical, semantic meaning itself. Small children (and animals) often decide whether to trust a spoken message on the basis of who the speaker is and what tone of voice is used. One could describe the goal of schooling and literacy as learning *not* to listen and read that way.

65   Because scholars are not immune to the effects of prestige, the APA citation system suppresses gender and first names. Critical reading and critical thinking involve (among other things) using the doubting game to cut through the "rhetoric" so as to see flaws in thinking. Aristotle's *Rhetoric* is a book for rhetors; he's saying, in effect, "If you want to persuade, you can override *logos* with *ethos* and *pathos*." If he'd written book for listeners and readers, he'd have said, "Beware of *ethos* and *pathos*— zero in on *logos*." In various books, Roy Harris has developed a powerful argument why writing is essentially different from speech and why we get a distorted and misleading understanding of writing if we think of it as a record of spoken language.

66   In recent years, people in our field have enjoyed emphasizing the lens of rhetoric and criticizing Plato and Ramus for valuing dialectic more than rhetoric. But there is a dialectic dimension to *all* discourse—purely logical, semantic, analytic, cognitive—no matter how small that dimension is: all discourse can be helpfully viewed through the lens of dialectic. So, we need to train students to use this lens—to push away the rhetorical lens and test out the pure reasoning. When they do that, they'll find many flaws they didn't see before. This helps explain why logicians make use of artificial symbolic languages. Students won't get good at disciplined thinking if we emphasize *only* voice and rhetoric.

67   *Ignoring voice is necessary for teaching writing.* As with reading, we need to teach students how to reduce their drafts to unvoiced outlines and diagrams—pure message and logic—even in the case of personally persuasive or "merely ceremonial" writing tasks. Of course, they write better if they call on the considerable voice skills they have learned from the rhetoric of conversational argument, but, if that's their only resource, they'll fall into all kinds of weak reasoning. Those who cannot both read and write while tuning out voice, tone, and feelings—who cannot concentrate on strict meaning and logic alone—are literally "nonliterate": their perception of *visual letters* is clouded by *sounded voice.*

68   So I. Hashimoto was right in his complaint: if writing teachers emphasize only voice or emphasize it too much, they tend to mislead students into thinking that good writing requires only voice (especially "your own" voice). "The problem, of course, is that writing is an intellectual endeavor" (76) and requires learned skills and conscious techniques. (In making this valid argument, Hashimoto unfortunately uses exaggerated strawman pictures of figures he charges, including me. Like Harris, he portrays me as saying that writing with voice is the same as good writing—an assertion I explicitly deny [Power 313, quoted earlier].)

69   *If we can empty a text of voice, we enlarge possibilities for meaning and interpretation; whereas, when we hear written language as voiced (or when we hear actual speech), meaning and interpretation are restricted.* One of the main goals of schooling and literacy is to help students work out multiple meanings. We succeed best by pushing away interpretative pressure that comes from a strong voice. The restrictive effect of voice is clearest in the case of actual performance. For example, a Shakespearean play (unless it's incoherently performed) necessarily settles on one interpretation and tends to block others in the minds of the audience. The effect is insidious. Even when we read a text after hearing a strong performance of it (or read a book after seeing the movie), the words on the page often seem permanently infected by that interpretation. This effect is particularly strong when we are not aware that we are being influenced by voice. The problem is worst with unskilled readers. In contrast, Shakespeare's silent texts invite many interpretations, and, over the years, they have successfully *permitted* wider interpretations that seemed contrary to the spirit of the text.

70   But to get this benefit, we have to train students not to rely on voice or projected voice when they read. We need to teach them to separate language and thinking from the author (especially if it's a famous or respected author) and to see multiple and even contrary interpretations of a text, even when a strong-voiced text tries to seduce them into a particular reading. As often as not, "reading against the grain" means reading against the voice. Just as we train children not to read by moving their lips, we should train adolescents not to read by using their ears too much.

71   *Avoidance of voice is a powerful tool for a writer.* In various writing situations, writers understandably don't want readers to feel their presence; they want readers to encounter only the message—the data or ideas or thinking. A felt voice in a text often distorts how readers perceive a message. Scientists, for example, often write their research and scholarly arguments in a way that seeks to be impersonal. Of course, good scientists know that pure impersonality (like pure objectivity) is not attainable. Nevertheless, the impersonal conventions of scientific publications (e.g., blind reviews and APA citations that omit first names) testify to the recognition that unobtainable goals such as objectivity and impersonality are sometimes worth aiming *toward*. That is, for scholarly work, we don't want reviewers and readers judging validity on the basis of the reputation or even the gender of the writer—nor on the basis of the blandishments of "human" rhetoric. It's understandable that impersonality conventions such as those in APA are widely used in the natural sciences, the social sciences, and even education.[7]

72   Through the ages, writers, especially members of underestimated or stigmatized groups, have used anonymous or pseudonymous publication to keep readers from being distracted by knowing whose words these are. Women have traditionally used anonymous publication to prevent their words from being read as "female." Even when anonymous or pseudonymous writing has a strong voice, the technique still avoids that single most vexed dimension of voice— the link between the words on the page and the person of the actual author.

73   *"Voice" is too vague a metaphor to be useful.* It means so many things to so many people that it leads to confusion and undermines clear thinking about texts. In any given usage, it's seldom clear what the term is actually pointing to. For example, "voice" is commonly used to point to a feature that's only found in some writing—yet it's also commonly used to point to a feature found in all writing. (The voice can be blah, impersonal, bureaucratic, or even computer-speak, but there's always a voice.) I tried to deal with ambiguities in "voice" by carefully distinguishing five distinct senses (audible voice, dramatic voice, recognizable or distinctive voice, voice with authority, and resonant voice; see "Introduction"). I believe my analysis was helpful, yet I clearly failed to get people to use those distinctions. We already have a number of helpful terms that are less metaphorical, ambiguous, and fraught: *style, ethos, implied author,* and *persona.* The last two are particularly helpful when voice is problematic: distinguishing between character in the text and character in the author. Bowden suggests metaphors from a different realm: "Web" and "network" (Mythology 194).

74 *The notion of "voice in writing" does harm in our culture.* Even though the term has no stable meaning—or means wildly different things to different people—it turns out to have implications that are resonantly potent for many people in our culture. Indeed, its peculiar resonance comes from the way it reinforces some pervasively harmful mythic assumptions.

75 That is, the concept of voice tricks many students and would-be writers into believing that, if they can achieve "their own unique voice," they will, by definition, be good writers. (Shakespeare is a prime counterexample: he was radically deficient with respect to "his own voice."") And the "voice" concept harms the way many people think about the nature of identity and self. It reinforces a powerful cultural assumption that we have single, unique, unchanging selves; that we are not "written" or need not be written by the culture around us; that our goal in life is to learn to be the unique individuals that we inherently are. The mystique about finding and uncovering or recovering our "own unique voice" tends to foreground personal power in a way that reinforces the pervasive cultural assumption that everyone's goal is to learn to grab the microphone and stand out as a star in the world—a world that's modeled as a zero-sum competitive arena. Organizations of awesome wealth and power do their amazing best to persuade people that, if they buy the right clothes or perfume or car, they can express and be their true selves. We also suffer from the notion that sincerity overcomes all shortcomings. This argument against cultural and ideological implications is the one most frequently made against voice. (Bowden argues at length that the term crystallizes the widespread but misleading idea that writing issues from one person and obscures the importance of culture and intertextuality in the production of all writing.)

76 Do all these arguments against voice contradict the earlier arguments for it? Yes. Do they cancel or diminish them? I insist not. The conflicting positions are incompatible in logic—even the informal logic of common experience: we cannot both pay attention and not pay attention to something. But there is no strain on logic or experience once we introduce the dimension of time. It's easy to pay attention and also not pay attention—at two different points in time. We don't have to read or write the same way all of the time.

Conclusion: Meta-Issues

77 I have two goals for this essay. First, I'm trying to help us learn to adopt contrary stances toward voice—reading texts through the lens of voice and also reading them through the lens of "text" or not-voice. We need the different and complementary insights we get from each kind of reading. In a recent book, Richard Lanham argues for a practice he calls *oscillatio*: he says we read best when we attend alternately to substance and to style and when we are conscious of the alternation. Lyn Brown and Carol Gilligan, in listening to tapes of girls and women, found that they could understand and learn best if they listened more than once to the same tapes of interviews with young women—each time listening in the language for a different dimension of development and psychology. Denis Donoghue praises Ricoeur for this idea about voice and reading:

78 Paul Ricoeur [. . .] proposes, in effect, that we read the text twice; once for print, once for the voice. He would let the ideology of writing have its day first and then give the reader the freedom of another destiny by recourse to voice:

79 We can, as readers, remain in the suspense of the text, treating it as a worldless and authorless object; in this case, we explain the text in terms of its internal relations, its structure. On the other hand, we can lift the suspense and fulfill the text in speech, restoring it to living communication; in this case, we interpret the text. These two possibilities both belong to reading, and reading is the dialectic of these two attitudes. (Donoghue 120)

80 But I have another wider meta-goal for this essay. I'm asking us to learn to be wiser in our scholarly thinking and writing. Especially if an issue is vexed and disputed, we can learn to step outside of either/or thinking (usually adversarial) and work out a both/and approach that embraces contraries. Such thinking can often release us from dead-end critical arguments that are framed by the unexamined assumption that, if two positions seem incompatible, only one can be valid. (Dewey was tireless in warning of the traps that come from inappropriate either/or thinking).

81 Finally, I need to add a meta-meta note. I'm not arguing *against* either/or thinking; I'm arguing only for *the addition* of both/and thinking to our methodology. That is, I'm taking a both/and stance toward both/and thinking. I've always acknowledged the necessity of either/or thinking for one of our intellectual modes: critical thinking or the doubting game. This mode rests on a foundation of logic, which, in turn, depends on either/or thinking. Logic and either/or thinking are our best tools for uncovering hidden flaws in thinking that *sounds* right or in ideas that we are drawn to believe because "our crowd" believes them.

82 But, by the same token, we need to learn *in addition* to set aside critical thinking and either/or thinking and use the contrasting intellectual mode of the believing game, which can involve embracing contraries that are logically contradictory. We need this mode because it can show us good ideas or virtues in discredited ideas that we remain blind to if we use only critical thinking or the doubting game. Just as we can see more about texts if we learn to look at them through two lenses in succession—the lens of voice and the not voice—so, too, in our thinking we need to learn use both intellectual modes: the doubting and believing games.[8]

Notes

[1] We see this particularly clearly in Coles's treatment of Holden Caulfield. Coles is entertainingly furious at Salinger for *Catcher in the Rye*, but most livid of all at generations of readers (especially young readers) who *like* the voice there. A cool rhetorical analysis would grant that Salinger brilliantly crafted *exactly* the voice required for his audience, genre, and exigence. Coles has no beef there. "The amateurish sounding voice of the passage, for example, is actually a very slick professional achievement; there is no question of Salinger's skill to manipulate dead language to produce the illusion of a sensitive and knowing creature." But Coles nevertheless calls that created voice a "fraud" and a "lie" because it doesn't match any real character behind it. Indeed, Coles charges that no human person could fit that voice. It's the voice of the "myth of the Natural Sophisticate"—the myth "that the capacity for appreciation and the ability to discriminate *can* exist in total independence of the understanding, that in fact one *may* live on a level other than the languages he knows" (164–5). There is an empirical question here: I would disagree with Coles, because I think that humans commonly do know and express more than they can understand with conscious language, but that's not the point. What's at stake for this exploration of voice in writing is Coles's complaint that a written voice is bad if it doesn't match a real human character. (For more about the centuries-long historical conversation about voice and self, see my *Landmark Essays on Voice and Writing* and my long introduction to it.)

[2] Harris supports his claim that I link voice to a certain type of prose by quoting from an entirely different essay of mine where I am talking not about voice, but about personal writing—which naturally I do define as a type of discourse ("Foreword"). Harris likes to call attention to the importance of careful quoting. In evaluating student writing, we must "look at how this writing responds to other texts . . . . The power and meaning of a text is seen to stem largely from the stance it takes toward other texts." The student's job "is one of finding her way into a written world, of gaining control over a set of textual conventions . . . ." (*Subject* 24)

[3] In particular, because I celebrate private writing and the benefits of ignoring the audience while exploring and drafting, I am often read as uninterested in the social dimension of writing. In fact, my *Writing Without Teachers* in 1973 was probably the main influence that brought peer feedback to the profession. In my theoretical appendix essay, I ground peer response in a social

theory of language itself: not just that the effectiveness of a text is determined by a community of readers (rather than a single teacher!), but indeed that the very *meaning* of any word or discourse is determined by the tug of war between various communities of readers. (See especially 151ff.) For my emphasis on embracing contraries in general, see my 1986 book of that title, my 1975 *Oppositions in Chaucer*, and my 1993 essay "The Uses of Binary Thinking."

[4] Sharp-eyed readers will have noticed that I've snuck in the word "rhetorical" and linked it to the voice lens. Obviously, I'm using the words "voice" and "text" in a more schematic and dichotomous way than they are often used in general. "Text" in particular has expanded its range of meaning—especially as "voice" has fallen out of favor—until it's sometimes used for all language. Given the way linguists use "text" for any stretch of language, written or spoken, and given the "linguistic turn" that has occurred in the humanities and social sciences in the twentieth century, I sense that scholars have come to feel the word "text" as a more scholarly and impressive word for language. And also—in reaction to the heyday of New Criticism—we've also had a "rhetorical turn" in our field—emphasizing language always taking place in time with speakers and writers trying to have an effect on others in a particular context. And so, as scholars have fallen into using the word "text" for all language, they have used it even in arguing for this rhetorical, human-interaction dimension of language.

But I'm insisting here—in a theoretical vein—on noting how the concept of "voice," tied as it is to the material body existing in time, is the appropriate lens or metaphor for language as material and historical—language as the stuff with which humans try to reach and affect other humans. Of course, this violates much current word-usage, but I would point to Bakhtin who gave so much emphasis to the word "voice" for highlighting the social, rhetorical, and interactional dimension of language: language as issuing from historically situated persons. Yet as a linguist, he acknowledges that discourse can *also* be analyzed as disembodied language. Here's a useful passage:

Where linguistic analysis sees only words and the interrelations of their abstract factors (phonetic, morphological, syntactic, and so on), there, for living artistic perception and for concrete sociological analysis, relations among people stand revealed, relations merely reflected and fixed in verbal material. Verbal discourse is the skeleton that takes on living flesh only in the process of creative perception— consequently, only in the process of living social communication. ("Discourse" 109)

Finally, I'd insist that both words, "text" and "voice," have come, in fact, to be metaphors. "Text" *sounds* more literal—especially when applied to writing—but it morphs into metaphor once it's been widely applied to spoken language too. It's very much a "metaphor we live by" (in Lakoff and Johnson's terms): a way of seeing even written language that foregrounds certain dimensions and obscures others. (For some of this section of the essay, I've drawn on my Introduction to *Landmark* Essays, especially xii–xiv.)

[5] Coles thought Holden Caulfield's voice was fraudulently sincere, but it convinced many readers. While *Catcher in the Rye* didn't pretend to be autobiography, *The Education of Little Tree* presented itself as the authentic product of an authentic Native American—and convinced many good readers. But it turned out to be written by a white member of the Ku Klux Klan. Sincerity mattered in a nontrivial way during the Vietnam War. Young people who wanted conscientious objector status had to convince their draft boards in writing that their objection was based on a "sincere" religious belief. The content of the belief didn't matter; only the sincerity. I failed this writing test and would have had to go to Canada or jail—or into the army!—if I hadn't gotten too old before they called me up. It must be admitted that written sincerity helps with not a few teachers of writing.

[6] I think Auden is describing resonance in his poem, "The Truest Poetry Is the Most Feigning." It tells of a poet who writes a love poem about his decidedly not-beautiful beloved—but describes her as the most beautiful creature that ever lived; then a dictator takes power in a coup and the poet resexes the pronouns to create a hymn of praise to *Il Duce*; so the poet dies in bed rather than in prison—wealthy and successful. In later years, readers of the ode to the dictator say, "Ah, how fair she must have been." I hear Auden saying that there is a precious kind of resonance or presence or authenticity that good writers can create and good readers can appreciate—but that it comes not at all from telling the truth. In fact, he's using the title from Shakespeare to imply that trying for truth can get in the way

Resonance seems to me what gives Bill Clinton much of his rhetorical success. One can never trust that he is telling the truth, and yet, in or underneath or behind much of his discourse, there's a notable power over listeners or readers—a power that seems to come from something deeper than mere clever voice-crafting. I think this hypothesis about resonance also explains the success of the *Little Tree* hoax. Resonance seems a useful and paradoxical model for textual voice linked to the writer's actual self. *Resonance* seems a more helpful word than *authenticity* and *presence* because they are so controversial. (But see George Steiner's Real Presences for a remarkably sophisticated and learned argument for presence in texts.)

[7] Admittedly, the conventions of scientific impersonal writing and the APA guidelines are sometimes used to justify bad writing, but writing can be impersonal and still clear and strong. Note, by the way, that the APA Handbook has long *recommended* use of the first person for certain appropriate situations. First person voice (in the grammatical sense) does not necessarily produce a strong or personal voice. So, in trying to teach students to write well, we can teach them the ability—for certain writing situations—to write clear, strong prose that nevertheless prevents readers from feeling their presence, mood, or attitude.

[8] I've written a succession of essays about the believing game, starting with the 1973 appendix to *Writing Without Teachers*. I cite the two most recent essays in the works cited here—essays where I make most pointedly the argument that I cannot develop here: that, even though the goal of critical thinking or the doubting game is to uncover hidden flaws, it often fails significantly in helping people find flaws in *their own* thinking or point of view. For that task, the believing game works better.

I've been working on the present essay for a long time. (The germ was a talk I gave at Stony Brook in the fall of 2002.) I've gotten significant help from more people than I can remember or thank here. But I'm particularly grateful to Don Jones, Irene Papoulis, John Schilb, and the *College English* reviewers.

Credit _____

Elbow, Peter. "Voice in Writing Again: Embracing Contraries." *College English* 70.2. Copyright © 2007 by the National Council of Teachers of English. Reprinted by permission.

Good English and Bad
BILL BRYSON

1 Consider the parts of speech. In Latin, the verb has up to 120 inflections. In English it never has more than five (e.g., *see, sees, saw, seeing, seen*) and often it gets by with just three (*hit, hits, hitting*). Instead of using loads of different verb forms, we use just a few forms but employ them in loads of ways. We need just five inflections to deal with the act of propelling a car – *drive, drives, drove, driving,* and *driven* – yet with these we can express quite complex and subtle variations of tense: "I drive to work every day," "I have been driving since I was sixteen," "I will have driven 20,000 miles by the end of this year." This system, for all its ease of use, makes labeling difficult. According to any textbook, the present tense of the verb *drive* is *drive*. Every junior high school pupil knows that. Yet if we say, "I used to drive to work but now I don't," we are clearly using the present tense *drive* in a past tense sense. Equally if we say, "I will drive you to work tomorrow," we are using it in a future sense. And if we say, "I would drive if I could afford to," we are using it in a conditional sense. In fact, almost the only form of sentence in which we cannot use the present tense form of *drive* is, yes, the present tense. When we need to indicate an action going on right now, we must use the participial form *driving*. We don't say, "I drive the car now," but rather "I'm driving the car now." Not to put too fine a point on it, the labels are largely meaningless.

2 We seldom stop to think about it, but some of the most basic concepts in English are naggingly difficult to define. What, for instance, is a sentence? Most dictionaries define it broadly as a group of words constituting a full thought and containing, at a minimum, a subject (basically a noun) and predicate (basically a verb). Yet if I inform you that I have just crashed your car and you reply, "What!" or "Where?" or "How!" you have clearly expressed a complete thought, uttered a sentence. But where are the subject and predicate? Where are the noun and verb, not to mention the prepositions, conjunctions, articles, and other components that we normally expect to find in a sentence? To get around this problem, grammarians pretend that such sentences contain words that aren't there. "What!" they would say, really means "What are you telling me – you crashed my car?" while "Where?" is shorthand rendering of "Where did you crash it?" and "How?" translates as "How on earth did you manage to do that, you old devil you?" or words to that effect. The process is called *ellipsis* and is certainly very nifty. Would that I could do the same with my bank account. Yet the inescapable fact is that it is possible to make such sentences conform to grammatical precepts only by bending the rules. When I was growing up we called that cheating.

3 In English, in short, we possess a language in which the parts of speech are almost entirely notional. A noun is a noun and a verb is a verb largely because the grammarians say they are. In the sentence "I am suffering terribly" *suffering* is a verb, but in "My suffering is terrible," it is a noun. Yet both sentences use precisely the same word to express precisely the same idea. *Quickly* and *sleepily* are *adverbs* but *sickly* and *deadly* are adjectives. *Breaking* is a present tense participle, but as often as not it is used in a past tense sense ("He was breaking the window when I saw him"). *Broken*, on the other hand, is a past tense participle but as often as not it is employed in a present tense sense ("I think I've just broken my toe") or even future tense sense ("If he wins the next race, he'll have broken the school record"). To deal with all the anomalies, the parts of speech must be so broadly defined as to be almost meaningless. A noun, for example, is generally said to be a word that denotes a person, place, thing, action, or quality. That would seem to cover almost everything, yet clearly most actions are verbs and many words that denote qualities – *brave, foolish, good* – are adjectives.

4 The complexities of English are such that the authorities themselves often stumble.

Each of the following, penned by an expert, contains a usage that at least some of his colleagues would consider quite wrong.

5 "Prestige is one of the few words that has had an experience opposite to that described in 'Worsened Words.'" (H.W. Fowler, *A Dictionary of Modern English Usage*, second edition) It should be "one of the few words that have had."

6 "Each of the variants indicated in boldface type count as an entry." (*The Harper Dictionary of Contemporary Usage*) It should be "each...counts."

7 "It is of interest to speculate about the amount of dislocation to the spelling system that would occur if English dictionaries were either proscribed or (as when Malory or Sir Philip Sidney were writing) did not exist." (Robert Burchfield, *The English Language*) Make it "*was* writing."

8 "A range of sentences forming statements, commands, questions and exclamations cause us to draw on a more sophisticated battery of orderings and arrangements." (Robert Burchfield, *The English Language*) It should be "causes."

9 "The prevalence of incorrect instances of the use of the apostrophe...together with the abandonment of it by many business firms... suggest that the time is close at hand when his moderately useful device should be abandoned." (Robert Burchfield, *The English Language*) The verb should be *suggests*.

10 "If a lot of the available dialect data is obsolete or almost so, a lot more of it is far too sparse to support any sort of reliable conclusion." (Robert Claiborne, *Our Marvelous Native Tongue*) *Data* is a plural.

11 "His system of citing examples of the best authorities, of indicating etymology, and pronunciation, are still followed by lexicographers." (Philip Howard, *The State of the Language*) His system are?

12 "When his fellowship expired he was offered a rectorship at Boxworth... on condition that he married the deceased rector's daughter." (Robert McCrum, et al., *The Story of English*) A misuse of the subjunctive: It should be "on condition that he marry."

13 English grammar is so complex and confusing for the one very simple reason that its rules and terminology are based on Latin – a language with which it has precious little in common. In Latin, to take one example, it is not possible to split an infinitive. So in English, the early authorities decided, it should not be possible to split an infinitive either. But there is no reason why we shouldn't, any more than we should forsake instant coffee and air travel because they weren't available to the Romans. Making English grammar conform to Latin rules is like asking people to play baseball using the rules of football. It is a patent absurdity. But once this insane notion became established grammarians found themselves having to draw up ever more complicated and circular arguments to accommodate the inconsistencies. As Burchfield notes in *The English Language*, one authority, F. Th. Visser, found it necessary to devote 200 pages to discussing just one aspect of the present participle. That is as crazy as it is amazing.

14 The early authorities not only used Latin grammar as their model, but actually went to the almost farcical length of writing English grammars in that language, as with Sir Thomas Smith's *De Recta et Emendata Linquae Anglicae Scriptione Dialogus* (1568), Alexander Gil's *Logonomia Anglica* (1619), and John Wallis's *Grammatica Linguae Anglicanae* of 1653 (though even he accepted that the grammar of Latin was ill-suited to English). For the long-est time it was taken entirely for granted that the classical languages *must* serve as models. Dryden spoke for an age when he boasted that he often translated his sentences into Latin to help him decide how best express them in English.

15 In 1660, Dryden complained that English had "not so much as a tolerable dictionary or a grammar; so our language is in a manner barbarous." He believed there should be an academy to regulate English usage, and for the next two centuries many others

would echo his view. In 1664, the Royal Society for the Advancement of Experimental Philosophy formed a committee "to improve the English tongue," though nothing lasting seems to have come of it. Thirty-three years later in his *Essay Upon Projects*, Daniel Defoe was calling for an academy to oversee the language. In 1712, Jonathan Swift joined the chorus with a *Proposal for Correcting, Improving and Ascertaining the English Tongue*. Some indication of the strength of feeling attached to these matters is given by the fact that in 1780, in the midst of the American Revolution, John Adams wrote to the president of Congress appealing to him to se up an academy for the purpose of "refining, correcting, improving and ascertaining the English language" (a title that closely echoes, not to say plagiarizes, Swift's pamphlet of sixty-eight years before). In 1806, the American Congress considered a bill to institute a national academy and in 1820 an American Academy of Language and Belles Lettres, presided over by John Quincy Adams, was formed, though again without any resounding perpetual benefits to users of the language. And there were many other such proposals and assemblies.

16 The model for all these was the Académie Francaise, founded by Cardinal Richelieu in 1635. In its youth, the academy was an ambitious motivator of change. In 1762, after many years of work, it published a dictionary that regularized the spellings of some 5,000 words – almost a quarter of the words then in common use. It took the *s* out of words like *estre* and *fenestre*, making them *être* and *fenêtre*, and it turned *roy* and *loy* into *roi* and *loi*. In recent decades, however, the academy has been associated with an almost ayatollah-like conservatism. When in December 1988 over 90 percent of French schoolteachers voted in favor of a proposal to introduce the sort of spelling reforms the academy itself had introduced 200 years earlier, the forty venerable members of the academy were, to quote the London Sunday *Times*, "up in apoplectic arms" at the thought of tampering with something as sacred as French spelling. Such is the way of the world. Among the changes the teachers wanted and the academicians did not were the removal of the circumflex on *être*, *fenêtre*, and other such words, and taking the *–x* off plurals such as *bureaux, chevaux*, and *chaveaux* and replacing it with an *–s*.

17 Such actions underline the one almost inevitable shortcoming of national academies. However progressive and far-seeing they may be to begin with, they almost always exert over time a depressive effect on change. So it is probably fortunate that the English-speaking world never saddled itself with such a body, largely because as many influential users of English were opposed to academies as favored them. Samuel Johnson doubted the prospects of arresting change and Thomas Jefferson thought it in any case undesirable. In declining an offer to be the first honorary president of the Academy of Language and Belles Letters, he noted that had such a body been formed in the days of the Anglo-Saxons English would now be unable to describe the modern world. Joseph Priestley, the English scientist, grammarian, and theologian, spoke perhaps most eloquently against the formation of an academy when he said in 1761 that it was "unsuitable to the genius of a free nation… We need make no doubt but that the best forms of speech will, in time, establish themselves by their own superior excellence; and in all controversies, it is better to wait the decisions of time, which are slow and sure, than to take those of synods, which are often hasty and injudicious." [Quoted by Baugh and Cable, page 269]

18 English is often commended by outsiders for its lack of a stultifying authority. Otto Jespersen as long ago as 1905 was praising English for its lack of rigidity, its happy air of casualness. Likening French to the severe and formal gardens of Louis XIV, he contrasted it with English, which he said was "laid out seemingly without any definite plan, and in which you are allowed to walk everywhere according to your own fancy without having to fear a stern keeper enforcing rigorous regulations." [*Growth and Structure of the English Language*, page 16]

19   Without an official academy to guide us, the English-speaking world has long relied on self-appointed authorities such as the brothers H.W. and F.G. Fowler and Sir Ernest Gowers in Britain and Theodore Bernstein and William Safire in America, and of course countless others. These figures write books, give lectures, and otherwise do what they can (i.e., next to nothing) to try to stanch (not staunch) the perceived decline of the language. They point out that there is a useful distinction to be observed between *uninterested* and *disinterested*, between *imply* and *infer*, *flaunt* and *flout*, *fortunate* and *fortuitous*, *forgo* and *forego*, and *discomfort* and *discomfit* (not forgetting *stanch* and *staunch*). They point out that *fulsome*, properly used, is a term of abuse, not praise, that *peruse* actually means to read thoroughly, not glance through, that *data* and *media* are plurals. And from the highest offices in the land are ignored.

20   In the late 1970s, President Jimmy Carter betrayed a flaw in his linguistic armory when he said: "The government of Iran must realize that it cannot flaunt, with impunity, the expressed will and law of the world community." *Flaunt* means to show off; he meant *flout*. The day after he was elected president in 1988, George Bush told a television reporter he couldn't believe the enormity of what had happened. Had President-elect Bush known that the primary meaning of *enormity* is wickedness or evilness, he would doubtless have selected a more apt term.

21   When this process of change can be seen happening in our lifetimes, it is almost always greeted with cries of despair and alarm. Yet such change is both continuous and inevitable. Few acts are more salutary than looking at the writings of language authorities from recent decades and seeing the usage that heightened their hackles. In 1931, H.W. Fowler was tutting over *racial*, which he called "an ugly word, the strangeness of which is due to our instinctive feeling that the termination-al has no business at the end of a word that is not obviously Latin." (For similar reasons he disliked *television* and *speedometer*.) Other authorities have variously – and sometimes hotly – attacked *enthuse*, *commentate*, *emote*, *prestigious*, *contact* as a verb, *chair* as a verb, and scores of others. But of course these are nothing more than opinions, and, as is the way with other people's opinions, they are generally ignored. So if there are no officially appointed guardians for the English language, who sets down all those rules that we all know about from childhood – the idea that we must never end a sentence with a preposition or begin one with a conjunction, that we must use *each other* for two things and *one another* for more than two, and that we must never use *hopefully* in an absolute sense, such as "Hopefully it will not rain tomorrow"? The answer, surprisingly often, is that no one does, that when you look into the background of these "rules" there is often little basis for them.

22   Consider the curiously persistent notion that sentences should not end with a preposition. The source of this stricture, and several other equally dubious ones, was one Robert Lowth, an eighteenth-century clergyman and amateur grammarian whose *A Short Introduction to English Grammar*, published in 1762, enjoyed a long and distressingly influential life both in his native England and abroad. It is to Lowth we can trace many a pedant's most treasured notions: the belief that you must say *different from* rather than *different to* or *different than*, the idea that two negatives make a positive, the rule that you must not say "the heaviest of the two objects," but rather "the heavier," the distinction between *shall* and *will*, and the clearly nonsensical belief that *between* can apply only to two things and *among* to more than two. (By this reasoning, it would not be possible to say that St. Louis is between New York, Los Angeles, and Chicago, but rather that it is among them, which would impart a quite different sense.) Perhaps the most remarkable and curiously enduring of Lowth's many beliefs was the conviction that sentences ought not to end with a preposition. But even he was not didactic about it. He recognized that ending a sentence with a preposition was idiomatic and common in both speech and informal writing. He suggested only that he thought it generally better and more graceful, not crucial, to place the preposition before its relative "in solemn and elevated" writing. Within a hundred years this had been converted from a piece of questionable advice into an immutable rule. In a remarkable outburst of literal-mindedness, nineteenth-century academics took it as read that the very name *preposition* meant it must come before something – anything.

23 But then this was a period of the most resplendent silliness, when grammarians and scholars seemed to be climbing over one another (or each other; it doesn't really matter) in a mad scramble to come up with fresh absurdities. This was the age when, it was gravely insisted, Shakespeare's *laughable* ought to be changed to *laugh-at-able* and *reliable* should be made into *relionable*. Dozens of seemingly unexceptionable words – *lengthy, standpoint, international, colonial, brash* – were attacked with venom because of some supposed etymological deficiency or other. Thomas de Quincy, in between bouts of opium taking, found time to attack the expression *what on earth*. Some people wrote *mooned* for *lunatic* and *foresayer* for *prophet* on the grounds that the new words were Anglo-Saxon and thus somehow more pure. They roundly castigated those ignoramuses who impurely combined Greek and Latin roots into new words like *petroleum* (Latin *petro* + Greek *oleum*). In doing so, they failed to note that the very word with which they described themselves, *grammarians*, is itself a hybrid made of Greek and Latin roots, as are many other words that have lived unexceptionably in English for centuries. They even attacked *handbook* as an ugly Germanic compound when it dared to show its face in the nineteenth century, failing to notice that it was a good Old English word that had simply fallen out of use. It is one of the felicities of English that we can take pieces of words from all over and fuse them into new constructions – like *trusteeship*, which consists of a Nordic stem (*trust*), combined with a French affix (*ee*), married to an Old English root (*ship*). Other languages cannot do this. We should be proud of ourselves for our ingenuity and yet even now authorities commonly attack almost any new construction as ugly or barbaric.

24 Today in England you can still find authorities attacking the construction *different than* as a regrettable Americanism, insisting that a sentence such as "How different things appear in Washington than in London" is ungrammatical and should be changed to "How different things appear in Washington from how they appear in London." Yet *different than* has been common in England for centuries and used by such exalted writers as Defoe, Addison, Steele, Dickens, Coleridge, and Thackeray, among others. Other authorities, in both Britain and America, continue to deride the absolute use of *hopefully*. *The New York Times Manuel of Style and Usage* flatly forbids it. Its writers must not say, "Hopefully the sun will come out soon," but rather are instructed to resort to a clumsily passive and periphrastic construction such as "It is to be hoped that the sun will come out soon." The reason? The authorities maintain that *hopefully* in the first sentence is a misplaced modal auxiliary—that it doesn't belong to any other part of the sentence. Yet they raise no objection to dozens of other words being used in precisely the same unattached way—*admittedly, mercifully, happily, curiously*, and so on. No doubt the reason hopefully is not allowed is that somebody at *The New York Times* once had a boss who wouldn't allow it because his professor had forbidden it, because *his* father thought it was ugly and inelegant, because *he* had been told so by his uncle who was a man of great learning…and so on.

25 Considerations of what makes for good English or bad English are to an uncomfortably large extent matters of prejudice and conditioning. Until the eighteenth century it was correct to say "you was" if you were referring to one person. It sounds odd today, but the logic is impeccable. *Was* is a singular verb and *were* a plural one. Why should *you* take a plural verb when the sense is clearly singular? The answer—surprise, surprise—is

that Robert Lowth didn't like it. "I'm hurrying, are I not?" is hopelessly ungrammatical, but "I'm hurrying, aren't I?"—merely a contradiction of the same words—is perfect English. *Many* is almost always a plural (as in "Many a man was there"), but not when it is followed by *a*, as in "Many a man was there." There's no inherent reason why these things should be so. They are not defensible in terms of grammar. They are because they are.

26   Nothing illustrates the scope for prejudice in English better than the issue of the split infinitive. Some people feel ridiculously strongly about it. When the British Conservative politician Jock Brue-Gardyne was economic secretary to the Treasury in the early 1980s, he returned unread any departmental correspondence containing a split infinitive. (It should perhaps be pointed out that a split infinitive is one in which an adverb comes between to and a verb, as in to *quickly look*.) I can think of two very good reasons for not splitting an infinitive.

27   **1.** Because you feel that the rules of English ought to conform to the grammatical precepts of a language that died a thousand years ago.

28   **2.** Because you wish to cling to a pointless affectation of usage that is without the support of any recognized authority of the last 200 years, even at the cost of composing sentences that are ambiguous, inelegant, and patently contorted.

29   It is exceedingly difficult to find any authority who condemns the split infinitive— Theodore Bernstein, H.W. Fowler, Ernest Gowers, Eric Partridge, Rudolph Flesch, Wilson Follett, Roy H. Copperud, and others too tedious to enumerate here all agree that there is no logical reason not to split an infinitive. Otto Jespersen even suggests that, strictly speaking, it isn't actually possible to split an infinitive. As he puts it: " 'To'… is no more an essential part of an infinitive than the definite article is an essential part of a nominative, and no one would think of calling 'the good man' a split nominative." [*Growth and Structure of the English Language*, page 222]

30   Lacking an academy as we do, we might expect dictionaries to take up the banner of defenders of the language, but in recent years they have increasingly shied away from the role. A perennial argument with dictionary makers is whether they should be *prescriptive* (that is, whether they should prescribe how language should be used or *descriptive* (that is, merely describe how it is used without taking a position). The most notorious example of the descriptive school was the 1961 *Webster's Third New International Dictionary* (popularly called *Webster's Unabridged*), whose editor, Philip Gove, believed that distinctions of usage were elitist and artificial. As a result, usages such as *imply* as a synonym for *infer* and *flout* being used in the sense of *flaunt* were included without comment. The dictionary provoked further antagonism, particularly among members of the U.S. Trademark Association, by refusing to capitalize trademarked words. But what really excited outrage was its remarkable contention that ain't was "used orally in most parts of the U.S. by many cultivated speakers."

31   So disgusted was *The New York Times* with the new dictionary that it announced it would not use it but would continue with the 1934 edition, prompting the language authority Bergen Evans to write: "Anyone who solemnly announces in the year 1962 that he will be guided in matters of English usage by dictionary published in 1934 is talking ignorant and pretentious nonsense," and he pointed out that the issue of the *Times* announcing the decision contained nineteen words condemned by the *Second International*.

32   Since then, other dictionaries have been divided on the matter, *The American Heritage Dictionary*, first published in 1969, instituted a usage panel of distinguished commentators to rule on contentious points of usage, which are discussed, often at some length, in the text. But others have been more equivocal (or prudent or spineless depending on how you view it). The revised *Random House Dictionary of the English Language*, published in 1987, accepts the looser meaning for most words, though often noting that the newer usage is frowned on "by many"—a curiously timid approach that at once acknowledges the existence of expert opinion and yet constantly places it at a distance. Among the looser meanings it accepts are *disinterested* to mean uninterested and infer to mean imply. It even accepts the existence of *kudo* as a singular—prompting a reviewer from *Time* magazine to ask if one instance of pathos should now be a patho.

33   It's a fine issue. One of the undoubted virtues of English is that it is a fluid and democratic language in which meanings shift and change in response to the pressures of common usage rather than the dictates of committees. It is a natural process that has been going on for centuries. To interfere with that process is arguably both arrogant and futile, since clearly the weight of usage will push new meanings into currency no matter how many authorities hurl themselves into the path of change.

34   But at the same time, it seems to me, there is a case for resisting change—at least slapdash change. Even the most liberal descriptivist would accept that there must be *some* conventions of usage. We must agree to spell *cat* c-a-t and no e-l-e-p-h-a-n-t, and we must agree that by that word we mean a small furry quadruped that goes *meow* and it sits comfortably on one's lap and not a large lumbering beast that grows tusks and is exceedingly difficult to housebreak. In precisely the same way, clarity is generally better served if we agree to observe a distinction between *imply* and *infer*, *forego* and *forgo*, *fortuitous* and *fortunate*, *uninterested* and *disinterested*, and many others. As John Ciardi observed, resistance may in the end prove futile, but at least it tests the changes and makes them prove their worth.

35   Perhaps for our last words on the subject of usage we should turn to the last words of the venerable French grammarian. Dominique Bonhours, who proved on his deathbed that a grammarian's work is never done when he turned to those gathered loyally around him and whispered: "I am about to—or I am going to –die; either expression is used."

Credit

Bryson, Bill. "Good English and Bad" from *The Mother Tongue: English and How It Got That Way* by Bill Bryson. Copyright © 1990 by Bill Bryson. Reprinted by permission of HarperCollins Publishers.

Writing a Life: The Composing of Grace

MYRNA HARRIENGER

1 This chapter presents an ethnographic case study of Grace, an eighty-year old woman institutionalized after suffering right frontal lobe damage caused by two slight strokes. Grace's oral and written discourse spanned a sixty-two year period, from her eighteenth year until she died in 1988. I am currently studying this work in relation to medical views of old, sick women. Here, I offer a portrait of Grace as a writer, because she used language to control and to name her life in every detail –and to narrate is as well. The sketch illustrates what our composition research has not yet studied, composing as its everyday experience becomes a life-defining practice: it describes the role played by composing through the stages in one woman's adult life, including illness in old age. Janice Lauer correctly notes that "our field knows very little about writing in old age and nothing about writing in illness." Yet in light of our aging, medicalized society where the majority of the old are women, we have a great need to understand what people like Grace can tell us (see Kahana and Kahana; Riley).

2 Because Grace's writing extends over the sixty-two years of her adult-hood, it illustrates what often eludes shorter- term studies, namely, the enormous potential of rhetoric, especially in its written form, to construct, empower, and validate the ordinary life. Written discourse was central to Grace's mode of life, her self-concept, and her sense of worth and defined her relationship with the persons and events of her lived experience.

3 Having cared for my mother before she died and later for a friend whose rare disease required constant patient care, I came to Grace's illness keenly aware of what Adrienne Rich notes: "The powerful decide for the powerless . . . the well for the ill" (39). What I now know about medicine, illness, and caregiving began then, with reading, listening to patients, interviewing doctors, and observing caregivers. I was struck by the tendency to treat the chronically ill and the old as if they would become well and by the extent to which health care workers, family, and others attended to the voice of medical authority while being relatively deaf to discourse of the ill (see Stoeckle; Kleinman). I remain incredulous that the central and often insurmountable difficulty of being old or sick—the sense of loss—goes virtually unnoticed (see Cassel; Zaner).

4 I first met Grace in April 1987 when her niece Mary, a colleague at a midwestern university, moved her aunt from Florida to a nursing home in the city where Mary lives. After her arrival, Grace and I visited at the nursing home three or four times each week. I found Grace alert, intelligent, articulate, and talented. We shared a no- nonsense approach toward life, perhaps because, as oldest daughters, we had each had to assume early family responsibility. We both enjoyed reading, sewing, and needlework.

5 "Some things you do because you love to; I guess I have always loved words." Grace's own literacy accounts, frequent and intense, suggested what her writing assured, that composing was a centripetal force in her adult life. Her writing evidences an enormously literate, broadly educated person, even though Grace lacked a college education and had not held the type of job whose work-related writing compositionists currently study. A brief overview of her adulthood writing gives a sense of how language and Grace composed each other.

6 Three interrelated aspirations –literacy, independence, and relationships—characterize Grace and explain her self- defining involvement with language and the fundamental role of discourse in her personal and professional life. These values are the reasons she wrote. Grace often wrote to share literacy events. She did not write to learn. For persons of her age cohort educated in current-traditional curricula, writing is evidence of, not a means to, literacy. Learning experiences provide purpose and content for much of her completed discourse. Writing allowed her to share these experiences and information while also maintaining relationships with her friends and relatives. Finally, she wrote to maintain that control we associate with independence. For Grace, order and organization were critical elements of this control. Until her illness, Grace's writing included travel booklets and scripts for slide presentations, letters, organization-related writing including club minutes, a dictionary of unfamiliar words, newspaper articles, a eulogy for a friend, and postcards, as well as several kinds of what Shirley Brice Heath calls jottings, including labels, lists, and files.

7 Until recently, Grace's discourse would have fallen outside the scope of composition studies. However, Louise Wetherbee Phelps, in her influential work *Composition as a Human Science*, argues convincingly for a broader notion of composition. Defining writing as the practice of composing meaning, a function of reflection as complement to experience, Phelps identifies composition as the potential for such meaning and assigns to composition studies the responsibility for attending to that t reflection (65,67). Using Heath's term, "literate behavior," Phelps includes within the domain of composition the broad panoply of such practices as "writing, reading, speaking, listening, inner speech" (67). This chapter affords us an on-line/off-line reading of one persons composing of meaning and meaning of composing. It illustrates Phelp's view of dynamic interplay between composition and life "outside the text." Grace exemplifies the intertextual character of a life imbricated in discourse.

8 Whereas today camcorders and thirty-five millimeter cameras record and store our memories, memories of the 1930s come to us in neatly labeled albums of black-and-white photos and in scrapbooks. Even in the thirties, though, Grace's travel books were unusual. She produces a travel book for each of twelve auto trips taken with friends during the thirties and early forties to such places as New England, various national parks, Mexico, and world's fairs. For each, she transcribed and typed shorthand notes taken throughout the trip. She then bound each text into a fifty-page booklet nine inches square, which she machine –stitched at the spine and glued to a stiff, blue cover. On the front of each, thin cork letters identify the trip. Besides text, these books include photos, pertinent information form magazines or brochures, and an appendix with a distance and mileage charts, addresses, and a list of tour guide books. Grace's copies also contain an itemized list of her expenses and, occasionally, one or two personal comments. This is where I learned, for example, that she had been more impressed by Mount Rushmore (where only the head of Washington was completed at the time) than by Yellowstone and that, at the Grand Canyon, "having stolen out into predawn hush before the world had wakened, [she] stood wide-eyed before the rising sun."

9 Like most of her personal writing, these booklets address a specific, known audience, those who shared the group experiences the piece records. The collective nature of the pieces, then, may account for the lack of self- reference. Almost as an observer, Grace built her narratives around what the group did, where they went, and how much it cost. Rarely did she provide a personal view, thought, impression, or reaction. Even telling about the Mexico trip when her luggage never arrived, Grace's writing is subdued: "I was this side of panic. Here I was with only the clothes on my back with a three week Mexican tour just starting . . . . Make the best of a bad situation and hope . . . . Spent a warm and worried night." This tendency to avoid self –revelation, of course, is more evident in these booklets than in her letters, though her writing generally exhibits the reserve and dry humor interviewees identified with Grace. In such audience-directed prose, the rare, inadvertent self- reference catches one unaware. The sudden shift in tense of the remembrance jettisons the reader into an event fifty years past: "Here I am using Arlie's hair appointment, sitting under a dryer writing my impressions." Through the inadvertent inclusion of shorthand marginalia, the reader is momentarily privy to

Grace talking to herself: "Remember when you get home to write a Christina a note" or "Have Mom order one of these."

10 These books also include significant amounts of geographic, historical, or demographic information, duly credited to sources Grace either used to prepare the trip or acquired en route. Like most of her writing, factual information overshadows both particulars about the trips and personal reflections. On one trip, Grace and a companion both wrote travel accounts. They both told similar version of evenings with the cowboys during a stay at a dude ranch near Yellowstone, but how the stories are told contrasts sharply. Louise's account is witty, informal, and written in a familiar style that employs slang, while Grace's references are less direct and less personal, even though she is the anonymous traveler involved in several described incidents. She uses first-person plural pronouns but refers to herself as "Grace" when using the singular. While Grace admits playing the piano most of the evening, we learn from Louise that she played until after midnight to avoid one of the cowboys. Grace also provides more factual information: numbers, names, and times. Louise, though, provides a view of Grace as a writer: "There's Gracie writing in the car, at the picnic table, and propped up in bed. She'll turn squiggles into stories, memories of fun in the sun, wait 'n see."

11 At about the same time Grace was writing about these vacations, her composition also turned an artistic project into a public presentation. A course in puppetry led Grace and her two sisters to make several marionettes for which they developed skits to entertain their nieces. Using these skills as a basis, the sisters organized an act divided into scenes, and Grace wrote the scripts for the marionettes: a clown whose trained seal dances while juggling a ball on its nose; a pair of Spanish dancers; a tall, frail, white-haired pianist who shares his piano with a torch singer; a ballerina; and three marionettes whose faces and clothes match those of Grace and her sisters. The three performed this act locally for several years.

12 During her marriage of the next fifteen years, Grace photographed but did not write about trips, since, as she explained, "Jack and I could talk about them." Their move from city to farm brought a halt to entries in the notebook listing both movies and plays Grace had attended and over a thousand books she had read during the previous twenty years. "I have new records to keep," Grace wrote then. "My writing has always been tied to what I'm doing, you know," she continued. Too busy for extensive writing, "I stitched curtains instead of pages." 'Except for letters, mostly to Ellen after she moved [west], my writing dealt with the farm and the house. Maybe you and Mary wouldn't call it real writing, though." Many of the jottings mentioned below date from this time on the farm. My favorite example, reflecting the frugality of people from Depression years, is a three-by-five –inch notebook whose current label covers another label that reads, "Eggs Sold: 1951-52."

13 In later years, as a widow living and working again in the city, Grace replaced travel booklets with written scripts to accompany slide presentations she arranged for friends. Those trips to places in Europe, Canada, Mexico, and Japan were also literacy events for Grace. "What I enjoyed most about these trips," she writes to a friend, "is learning all I could about the place and people." Following the trip's chronology but no longer intended as a record for the travel group, these scripts are filled with information about places and events. Meticulous about details, Grace carefully credits her sources, whether tour guide, residents of countries visited, or printed material.

14 Because Grave was socialized at a time when Americans used long-distance telephone only for emergencies and depended upon written correspondence to maintain family ties and friendships, letters make up the largest category of her writing. In early adulthood, Grace corresponded with her mother's family in Pennsylvania. (The earliest sample of her writing, though, a kind of journal entry, tells about being graduated from business school, a two-year program Grace completed in six months, and finding a job the next week.) Besides family, friends prompted Grace to write. Interestingly, notes as follow-ups to chance meetings initiated several long-term friendships. To Grace, such follow-ups were part of being literate, which she took to include being cultured: "It's important to be thoughtful, and people appreciate it when you take time to write." "It takes a great deal of time to maintain friendships, and much of that goes into correspondence."

15   Written first in shorthand and the typed single spaced, Grace's letters average two pages, becoming shorter after she retired. By then, her correspondence list had grown and she was very busy. As well, she had always valued exactness and succinctness. Length was not a value in itself, as Grace note in a letter to her sister: "When you have something to say, say it. I don't think going on and on is a virtue. No one has time for that and few the interest." Always personal and thoughtful, Grace's letters ask about family members, remember special days, comment upon previous correspondence, and respond to problems. Often she encloses some remembrance—a photo, slide, article, or gift. "One reason I've done so much tatting in Florida," she told me, "is because it fits so well in an envelope." "Remembering is so important to people; I try never to forget a birthday, anniversary, or what have you." Her small, thirty-year-old datebook is filled with dates significant to friends, co-workers, club members, and their families.

16   Whereas most letter depict Grace as a friend, letters to Ellen, her youngest sister and seven years her junior, portray her as an oldest sister. In these, the caring interest and warm concern common to all her letters are more explicit, probably because in them Grace is somewhat less reserved. They express a clear, preferential love for her "baby" sister. "I'm so proud of you; you looked beautiful," Grace wrote. "Just the thought that you made it! Thank you." "Finally, others recognize your artistic ability." "How far your candle throws its light." In these letters, too, can sometimes be heard the impatient, even abrupt, sound of authority that punctuates my own interaction with my youngest sister. Orders: "Get your rest. . . .Don't waste your time. . . [or] want to accomplish too much in one day" ;opinions: " you must decide . . .[it] isn't very reasonable"; and impatience: "Of course, I know what calligraphy is" are offered out of sisterly concern: "Sorry I sound harsh, but it's out of love I write to you this way."

17   Except for a few years during her marriage, Grace worked all her adult life as an executive secretary, retiring at age seventy. In 1925, secretarial work was considered a suitable job for women—as were library and clerical work, nursing, and nonuniversity teaching. Basically scribal work, they required language ability of a functional, noncreative sort. Women in these jobs copied, documented, recorded, and filed the language and discourse produced by others, nearly always men. But Grace did more than move around the words of male-dominated language and tidy up a corner of the masculine work world. If rhetoric deals with the functionality of language in context, Grace's job was as discursively constructed as her personal life. "I guess I've worked with words all my life," she told me. "I loved my job for that reason." Grace voiced satisfaction: "My secretarial friends at other companies made more money, but, you know, I never felt I was only working with someone else's words; they were. It may be a man's world, but not all of it. My old boss used to tell me that the King's English is sometimes owned by queens."

18   Co-workers concurred. "Grace had such a command of English, she certainly made Mr. Hires look great on paper. Foreign-born and self made, Jack Hires knew his trade better than his English." "You know, if 1930 had been 1990," another colleague laughed, "Grace would've been company president." "She did not just type and take shorthand," Betty assured me. "Whether Jack just outlined its contents, which he usually did, or actually dictated it, Grace really composed nearly every document. She loved words, you know, and never let an unfamiliar word go unnoticed. She knew all the technical language of the production end."

19 "I still wrote, typed and filed, but at home," Grace said of her retirement. She continued to type ninety-two words a minute and to use shorthand "for everything— phone messages, composing letters, taking notes, at a meeting or on a trip." In Florida, she wrote a weekly social column for a local paper, was secretary for the local chapter of the Federal Mobile Home Owners' Association, and wrote a piece for *Needlework* (November 1987), the journal of Embroiderers' Guild of America. Her move to Florida also occasioned continuous correspondence. In fact, a record of her correspondence for the two years before her strokes indicates that Grace wrote an average of three letters a day.

20 Jottings, lists, labels, and files were extremely important to Grace, for the satisfied her desire and ability to maintain order and organization in every facet of her life. Her upbringing by German parents, her training and employment, and her own artistic talent all contributed to her equating order with control. A brief tour of her house convinced me that Grace had kept a list of, a label on, or a file about everything important to her.

21 A jar of rice, for example, was labeled and the recipe taped to the top. Tine labels atop spice containers facilitated identification. A typed list of foodstuffs to be found in the cupboard sat on one self. On another kitchen cupboard, one envelope read "large plastic bags," another "small plastic bags." On the inside edge of each curtain was printed "left" or "right." Labels also identified boxes, utensil, and appliances. Attached to several utensils, small cards explained cleaning procedures; taped to the back of the television set, a label noted its make and serial number and the date, place and circumstance of its purchase. Music boxes, unusual dishes, and handmade item also bore labels. A handwoven basket, for example, was "made in 1964, by Evelyn Stoner from Madagascar pine needles."

22 A bedroom drawer held important example of Grace's composition. She was especially proud of the black leather-covered dictionary she had begun in high school and added to throughout her life. It continued an alphabetical listing of unfamiliar words and definitions of each word in perfectly formed miniature print. Among those words are "accouchement," "*mulierbrile*," and, my favorite, "perspicacious." Snippets of paper throughout the house held words, some with definitions, awaiting inclusions in this marvelous collection. In that drawer also was a small blue notebook holding another list, begun in 1932 of handmade items given as gifts. One page begins, "1939, Mary, Christmas, yellow mittens w crocheted flowers." A folder of needlework in an adjoining cupboard held directions and a sketch of those mittens.

23 Accompanying nearly everything Grace had saved—photos, slides, handiwork, writings—were written explanation, labels, and entire scripts, all meticulously noted, identifying the item and giving pertinent information, which Grace surely knew because she had told it to me. Needlework items were labeled, grouped into labeled boxes, and placed on labeled shelves. Linens were identified by size, condition, and age. A walk-in closet housed two file cabinets filled with updated printed material dating from the early 1930s: bills and receipts; lists of household items with prices, places, and dates of purchase; appliance warranties and instructions; and articles from magazines.

24 Yet from years in the business world, Grace knew that she did not need to keep most of this material. She must have realized, too, that the labels told what she already knew. Ironically, it was as if her composing formed a discursive blueprint from which she could reconstruct and resume her life, should a catastrophe, like a stroke, occur. Certainly the linguistic display of her house epitomizes the extent to which discursive composition unified, constructed, and validated Grace and her way of life. Gerontologist tell us that old persons control death and assure remembrance by ordering their possessions, specifying gifts, composing value statements, or leaving visible examples of their life's work. I suspect that the addressivity of Grace's composition, a continuously constructed value statement, included the hope that readers would realize how much it revealed about a woman who never kept a diary because "someone might read it."

25   The two strokes Grace suffered, in October 1986 and March 1987, and her subsequent illness affected her composition and altered that life, which had been continually enlivened by discourse. Neither stroke, though, damaged areas of the brain most responsible for reading and writing processes. The lesions occurred in the right frontal lobe, which performs the high-level synthesis that coordinates, mediates, and integrates such processes (Gardner, 168, 275). These operations enable abstract thinking and spatial-temporal functions. Thus, despite left-side muscle weakness, Grace remained articulate and intelligent, but, while she could perform a delimited task, she displayed other poststroke difficulties, in relating goals to plans, discerning relationships and timing involved in making and executing plans, and recognizing when plans required change (Gardner, 270). The effects on her life were obvious; less obvious were its effect on her language use.

26   Since daily routines involve complex planning, Grace could no l longer live alone, and , like most childless widows needing assistance, she found herself in a nursing home (see Hess; Riley). Relocation a thousand miles from her home and personal belongings underscored the rupture in the life that composition had helped build. Following her strokes, the order Grace had obtained through composing no longer provided control. Grace composed no jottings, since the world she had used them to order was gone. "I had a place for everything, kept track of it all, but that's all gone. "I had a place for everything, kept track of it all, but that's all down the drain." Gone, too, was Grace's belief that she had any world control. "You live in someone else's world here, and abide by their rules," she wrote. Finally, strokes had short-circuited her ability to plan or dream, in Gardener's word (269). Less able to employ that simple yet profound complex skills, Grace had difficulty grasping a picture of her life big enough to require jottings.

27   This loss had also disrupted the continuity of her relationships (Cassell, 44). Carol Gilligan notes that being old sick and a woman is especially difficult, since women "define themselves in context of human relationships and judge themselves in terms of ability to care" (171). Not only had Grace's personal support shrunk to Mary and me, but her social interaction with other patients was severely limited. Nearly every patient was hearing impaired, deaf to Grace's quiet voice, and most had greater cognitive impairment than she. Territorial claims of long-term patients also thwarted her efforts to socialize (Hooyman and Kiyak, 368). "The first roommate wouldn't talk to me, said I didn't belong in her room. Now, this one can't hear me and insist I'm plotting against her. All I want is to be heard so I can converse with someone who lives here."

28   The nursing home afforded Grace few opportunities to compose or to participate in literacy events. These events were often for lower-functioning patient, although Grace did attend the monthly poetry reading and recitals. Understandably, she enjoyed literacy events employing various forms of composition, since she herself was an accomplished pianist, an avid photographer who had developed her own work, and, despite being color blind, an expert at several forms of needlework. At one such event, Grace and Mary gave a slide presentation of their trip to Germany using material Grace had prepared some before. Hesitant about this public display, Grace was also pleased. She and Mary decided that she would read for about five slides. Two of the five were out of order, but Grace did not notice the first and was unable to adjust her response to the second. However, she did supply unwritten information about other slides, telling, for example, about the autobahn.

29   "All this makes me wonder if who I have always thought I was is who I am" Grace confided. Since her strokes, besides language use, she had retained only the ability to

write shorthand and to tat. "Thank God," she added immediately, her voice vigorous. "I can still read and write." When I asked if she did those as well as before her stroke, she nodded happily. "Hm, hm, sure. Except for my handwriting which is awful, so small and cramped." Looking up, she asked, "What would I do if I couldn't read or write?" "I can't tell you how much I miss my friends. They've been my day-to-day family since my sister died four years ago, you know." Even in illness, Grace continued to correspond with over a hundred persons "because communication is the only means I have now of relating with my friends and family." In fact, difficulty formulating, altering, and executing elaborate plans necessarily affects complex processes like composing (Gardner 365). Both Grace's reading and her writing evidenced stoke effects. She was less selective about what she read, always beginning short-story collections, for example, with the first piece. Often not able to recall the contents of an article, she could tell from its title whether she had read it. In general, her letters during her illness became shorter and less developed and exhibited problems with sequence, organization, and conventions.

30   Yet Grace was unaware that her language skills were affected, because right-hemisphere strokes inhibit the patient's awareness of her illness effects and their implications. For Grace to have been cognizant of such deficits, she needed the very synthesizing ability the strokes had affected. In ordinary terms, Grace had more trouble getting things through her head than hold them there. Reading difficulties, then, were less a problem of recall than an inability to synthesize complexity with the rapidity required for the kind of material she read. The strokes, the illness context, and Grace's fluctuating health accounted for the differences between previous work and her illness writing, differences that became more noticeable over the nine months during which I observed Grace's discourse practices. However, fairness to her composing requires acknowledging that these factors alone do not account for the considerable variation existing among her illness writings. For example, except for handwriting, several pieces equal the quality of retirement letters. While most letters of this quality occurred early in her illness and while most letters with unmistakable impairment effects were written near the end of the study, this progression is not absolute. Sometimes only a day separated a "healthy" letter from a stroke letter.

31   Given the complexity of the human experience, including that of the human brain, medicine, can identify only some of the factors impinging upon impairment and illness. Two additional factors bear mentioning. First, the human factor was incalculable. The encouragement of the two persons who accepted Grace's dissonance while affirming her integrity—what Sacks calls existential medicine (248-51)—helped to bridge the stroke-related disruption in integrity: they sought to reflect to Grace the strength and wholeness she processed but could neither see nor confirm in herself without such mirroring. Second, Grace had maintained the cognitive ability to access writing schema culled for long-term, extensive, conscious use of discourse. This allowed her to use language tacitly, that is, to run partly "on automatic" after her strokes impeded access to explicit knowledge. Tacit skills undoubtedly contributed to those textual features of her writing that showed little impairment, for example, word choice, phrasing, and audience awareness. It is fortunate that Grace's tacit skills were well developed, given the complexity of composing and the nature of her impairment. Composition is, after all, so complex that psychology avoids its study. In fact, this is why few have studied stroke writing beyond such sentence dyads as question/answer or two- person conversation, and virtually no one has related composing to right-hemisphere stroke.

32   Grace had little difficulty with either word choice or phrase formation. Some examples—"bring me up to date," "you might want to," "thank you profusely," "I'm sure Ellen would add her thanks," "I too, would like to"—are only standbys, occurring often

in previous writing. Other phrasing examples, like "safely ensconced," gourmet-style meal," "arrived like a whirlwind," or "exchange pleasantries," indicate an accessibility to word choice and phrasing, as does, "I went today to a book review on Bess Truman which was quite worthwhile."

33 We may safely assume, likewise, that tacit skills contribute to the high degree of audience awareness maintained in Grace's illness writing. However, there were also indications that Grace directed conscious attention to this effort. Often she sat with the letter being answered in her lap for quick reference. Still very attuned to the events and people in her friends' lives, she asked Helen about her daughter, reminded Ellen of Mary's birthday, and commiserated with Dolly over her husband's death. In addition, her self-references were often audience-specific. To her traveling companion Lucille, for example, Grace wrote about missing her car, her freedom, and her travel. However, since Aileen, Grace's Florida neighbor, "wouldn't understand because she doesn't drive, and was home with her husband," Grace wrote about missing her home and playing cards.

34 Of course, diminished capacity to plan had the most noticeable effect on Grace's writing. Planning relates to spatial-temporal functions and to diminished duration of cognitive engagement. Because short-circuited planning abbreviates the duration of cognitive engagement, persons like Grace tend to be more easily disengaged, more given to impulse: that is, they become more easily distracted and spontaneous and less attuned to appropriate behavior or established protocol. These planning-related features of composing and behavior are reflected in problems of sequence, organization, and development and with attention to conventions. Grace's prestroke writing has privileged specific detail, description, and factual information, but in her illness writing, she often provides less development for topics and had difficulty organizing material. We can see this deprivation of topic and development in a letter to a cousin. Although each of its eight paragraphs deals with a single topic, six contain only one sentence; the other two each have two sentences. In another letter, several unrelated topics occur in a single paragraph. These problems with development and organization affect coherence, as, for example, when a letter of four paragraphs contains a paragraph of ten sentences with seven different topics or when an entire letter is a single paragraph of twenty-three sentences covering seven topics, only two consecutive pairs of which are related.

35 Organization is further affected by Grace's tendency to repeat a topic, reintroducing it elsewhere in the letter. For example, having written, "Mary is so good to me" near the beginning of one letter, seven sentences and five topics later, she reintroduces it with "Mary visits whenever she can." Sometimes, in a single letter, Grace returns three times to the same topic. Those topics to which she consistently returns were, of course, those that most concerned her: the thoughtfulness of her niece, Mary; her own lack of improvement; her new friend, Myrna; and her loss of lifestyle, personal surroundings, and social interaction. The stroke had made Grace less attentive to linguistic and genre conventions and to the general appearance of items she prepared for mailing. For example, she was less deliberate in her selection of paper, often beginning a letter on the same paper on which she had already jotted down a small segment of something she had overheard, like a bit of conversation, or an item from a television show. When *I* pointed this out once, Grace registered surprise, "Where'd I get that?" Toward the bottom of that letter, she unwittingly includes two sentences of a conversation betracted by the angry tone of the conversation or engrossed in her own letter, but she did not recall she had written those two sentences.

36 In contrast to prestroke discourse, these letters illustrate some difficulty with usage and genre conventions. Occasionally, misspellings such as "geriatrik," "enuff," and "allways" occur, this form a woman who found facility's spelling bee boring because, "Who

75

doesn't know how to spell 'ukulele'?" Finally, Grace often addressed envelopes upside down or, after folding the letter itself into thirds, wrote the address on a folded portion of the letter. Previously meticulous about observing protocol, Grace was less aware of convention and, at those times she was aware, less concerned about the following its directives. The few times she seemed to notice those problems addressing letters, she never related them to protocol: she never questioned their being mailed.

37   Difficulty with spatial relations affected Grace's handwriting. Once small, neat, and uniform, it had become tiny, cramped, and unevenly spaced. Because her visual awareness was affected, the left margin of each written page grew wider as in meandered down the page. Spatial deficits accounted, too, for misplaced genre conventions: greeting, closing, and signature sometimes appeared at unconventional places on the line. Grace also had consistent difficulty addressing envelopes, because placement in an open space burdens visual representation in stroke victims. This inability to relate things spatially explains why she could not follow patterns, even those whose steps she had explained to me.

38   A few months before she died, I observed Grace writing three letters at the same time. This fascinating episode epitomizes the role and the power of composing in her life. Grace had started a letter to a niece when she paused to glance at things on her desk; focusing momentarily on a newspaper article sticking form a book, she reached for a pink pad and began writing. She worked alternately on these two pieces for a bout fifteen minutes---writing reading what she had written and occasionally looking out the window. Then, reaching for a card her niece had sent, she noticed, picked up, and read another card, which prompted her to reach for a second pink pad and to begin her third letter. When I asked later if she usually did "that," Grace replied, "What? Get right to it and write? Yes, usually if I'm alone and don't get distracted. You're not a distraction." When I specified her writing three letters at once, she said she didn't "usually do that, but ideas came, so I dashed them off." Those letters were among the "healthy" group mentioned above. Incredibly, each was two full pages developed, coherent, and contained different contents. Two, though, do mention the papal visit occurring at the same time. The article that had prompted the second letter was about the pope's stop in Detroit; remembering a friend who had seen the pope in Miami, grace decided to write to her.

39   This episode illustrates Grace's skill at composing, though not it the obvious ways her previous writing suggest. Her stroke writings lack the controlled skill we recognize in her bound books, the intricacy of the black work composition now hanging in Mary's home, and the complexity of a multiple composition like the script, music, and marionette now safely stored in a glass case on videotape. This episode, in fact, reveals impulse intruding as distraction and raises questions about her control. Yet neither impairment nor tacit knowledge can account for the important element of this episode, namely, the underside of impulse, only rarely seen in a positive force – intense, though impermanent, concentration and deep, though not comprehensive, thought. For neither Grace composing nor the letters themselves evidence of impulsiveness. Grace showed no signs of being agitated, fluster, or fidgety; her actions were deliberate, their steady rhythm quickened briefly as she took up additional paper. In fact, she sat with composure and gave every evidence of concentrating on what she was doing, even to ignoring my presence.

40   Her composing that day made visible the lithe, brilliant execution of balance which all her writing necessarily had become, between the limits and unsteadiness of impairment and the assets are still available to her – conscious, tacit, and relational. For Grace, the stakes of composing were high: to lose balance would have been to lose "the living 'I'" (Sacks, 251). It would have been to lose reflection, the compliment to the composing experience that defined her. It is impossible to overestimate the role of language in Grace's life, a role radicalized by her illness. For her, everything else about being sick was disappointment and frustration. Yet each time I observed her reading or writing and each time we talked about language use, she was at ease, helpful, articulate, and content. Her satisfaction and pleasure increased, of course, when we talked about her own practices or those of her niece. She "couldn't even remember [having been] more proud than when Mary honored [their] family by writing a book." "Her life is also filled with writing, "Grace affirmed.

■ Though her composing skills were limited as result of the strokes, Grace's continued ability to write affected her experience of illness. Because she lacked sufficient synthesizing ability to make sense of her illness, Grace had to live in a more-or-less permanent state of disease. Implicated in loss, of course, was everything about Grace. Relatively unable to compose in the sense of bring together, of constructing and integrating meaning, her composing had become a necessarily less complicated, her constructions partial, and her meanings less adequate. Yet, within these constraints, composing and construction had been possible. For Grace, discursive composition, especially writing, had remained an enactment of literacy, of ordered experience, and of maintained relationships. While stroke effects prevented Grace from composing herself or her illness world, her acts of composition, being dramatic in nature, composed – however tenuously, inadequately, temporarily—what otherwise would have remained in centrifugal and fragmented. While composing could not com-pose her life to the degree it had before, it remained the greatest force for empowering, validating, and affirming grace and her self-worth. It allowed her to maintain a modicum of control and provided a means of salvaging her life and herself from an otherwise unbearable situation.

Credit

Harrienger, Myrna. "Writing a Life: The Composing of Grace" by Myrna Harrienger from *Feminine Principles and Women's Experience in American Composition and Rhetoric*, edited by Louise Wetherbee Phelps and Janet Emig, Copyright © 1995. Reprinted by permission of the University of Pittsburgh Press.

The Sticky Embrace of Beauty

ANNE FRANCES WYSOCKI

1 On some formal relations in teaching about the visual aspects of texts

2 The avant garde's response to the cognitive, ethical, and aesthetic is quite unequivocal. Truth is a lie; morality stinks; beauty is shit. And of course they are absolutely right. Truth is a White House communiqué; morality is the Moral Majority; beauty is a naked woman advertising perfume. Truth, morality, and beauty are too important to be handed over to the political enemy.

—Terry Eagleton, *The Ideology of the Aesthetic*

3 One more "thought"—I have a conviction that the design, registered in the human face thro years of life and work, is more vital for purposes of permanent record, tho it is more subtle, perhaps, than the geometric patterns of lights and shadows that passes in the taking, and serves (so often) as mere photographic jazz.

—Lewis Hine

My writing on these pages starts with two compositions.

4   The first composition is one you'll have to construct inside wherever you do your imaginative constructions, for it's a composition to take from words. My essay's title took shape for me as I was reading one of Carl Hiassen's novels about the political and cultural degradation of Florida's natural environment and beauty: in Stormy Weather Hiassen describes a minor (and unsavory) character's inability to escape the "sticky embrace of the BarcaLounger." I'd like for you to have that image of two (apparently) different orders of being—a heavy fleshy body and humanly constructed structure—uneasily and sweatily creased into each other as I shift your attentions to the second composition, one constructed of formed markings on paper.

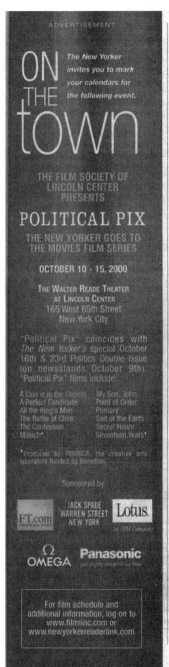

ciations of this kind were widespread among intellectuals in that fermenting period of Depression and the rise of Fascism in Europe. In Chicago, Saul Bellow and Isaac Rosenfeld were in an identical fever of radical world-upheaval. "Politics was everywhere," Rosenfeld recalled, looking back. "One ate and drank it." Trilling was quicker than most to fall away.

But when he advised the liberals of the forties to turn from "agencies, and bureaus, and technicians," and to cultivate instead a "lively sense of contingency and possibility," and when he was troubled by his complacent students of the fifties who glibly accepted antithetical ideas without resistance or perturbation—who were, in fact, bored by the subversive and the antisocial—how could he have foreseen the riotous campus demonstrations of 1968? In connecting politics with literature—"the politics of culture," he called it—he was unwittingly entering the vestibule of the politicization of literature, a commonplace in today's universities. Unwitting or not, Trilling was bemused to see how the impulse of unrestraint that inflamed the modern masters—Conrad, Mann, Lawrence, Kafka, Nietzsche—was beginning to infiltrate, and finally take over, popular thought and style. These writers, he pointed out, with all their relentless counterminings, asked "every question that is forbidden in polite society." By the nineteen-seventies, no question remained that was forbidden in polite society, and no answer, either; there was little left of the concept of polite society altogether. What was liberty for Lawrence became libertinism in the streets. The bold contrariness of the moderns had succeeded so well that Trilling starchily named its dominance in the country at large "the adversary culture." Babbitt and H. L. Mencken's booboisie were routed. Conrad's heart of darkness—the instinctual storm that had once been the esoteric province of modernist high art—had gone public. The Cossacks were astride the politics of culture.

Such were Trilling's ultimate convictions, hidden under the ornate historical scaffolding of "Sincerity and Authenticity," the Charles Eliot Norton Lectures he delivered at Harvard, in 1970. In language grown more and

THE NEW YORKER, OCTOBER 2, 2000   123

5   To the left [above] is a page out of the October 2, 2000 New Yorker, showing a column of text (which is working to bring Lionel Trilling back to life), and two advertisements. I'd like to draw your attentions (although I probably don't need to) to the advertisement on the right. When I received this New Yorker, I did what I usually do: 1 flipped through the pages to get a sense of what's going on, what I might want to read—and this page stopped me. I think this advertisement is a lovely piece of work, but it also angers me.

When I experience pleasure and offense so mixed, I know I have a good opening into critical work—no matter where it leads me or how strange.

6   On the following pages I use resources from the fields of visual composition, graphic design, and visual communication to try to work out what gives rise to my seeing beauty and feeling angry. My inability to come to a satisfactory accounting leads me to consider how notions of beauty, developed in the late eighteenth century, have been used in attempts to hold together two different orders of being and—by our time—have failed. I do this not to raise issues of aesthetics for specific consideration, but rather to communicate what I've learned in trying to understand my responses to this layout: I'll be arguing that approaches many of us now use for teaching the visual aspects of texts are incomplete and in fact, may work against helping students acquire critical and thoughtful agency with the visual, precisely because these approaches cannot account for a lot of what's going on in the Peek composition.

7   • What I came to understand when I turned to what's already published in the areas of visual composition, graphic design, and visual communication is that these approaches most often only partially explain my pleasure and none of my offense with the Peek composition: not only do these approaches assume a separation of form from content, but they emphasize form in such a way that "content" can be unremarkably disembodied—a very bad thing when the "content" is a particular body.

8   • Concurrently, by so emphasizing form, they propose that the work of shaping texts visually is to result in objects that stop and hold sight; I would rather that what we make when we shape the visual aspects of texts is reciprocal communication.

9   In my writing space here, then, I'm going to look at some present approaches to teaching the visual aspects of texts in order, grumpily, to argue the existence of the shortcomings I've just described. I will then turn back to eighteenth-century definitions of beauty and aesthetic judgment because they not only help me understand the shortcomings but because they also help me see grounds for shaping how we teach visual composition so that form does not override content, so that form is, in fact, understood as itself part of content, so that, finally, I better understand how to support students (and myself) be generously and questioningly reciprocal in our designings.

A FIRST FORMALITY
OVERLOOKING BODIES AND HISTORY

10   If I were to turn to a very popular little guide for teaching about page arrangement (and one I do use in my teaching), The Non-Designer's Design Book, by Robin Williams, I'd find rules for explaining— and explaining pretty well—how my eyes travel through the Peek layout.

11   Williams offers four "design principles"—contrast, repetition, alignment, and proximity—for visual arrangement. By applying her rules, it is possible to say why (at least in part) my eye starts (or stops) here ▬ ▬ ▬ ▬ ▬ ▬ ▬ ▬ ▬ ▬ ▬ ▬ ▬ ⌐

12   It is because of contrast: this is the lightest thing in this design and the only large round shape. The principle of repetition, meanwhile, says this design has harmony because the shapes of the text blocks repeat the shapes of the body; the size and proportions of the body repeat in the size of the ad itself, and the tones of grey repeat in photograph and typeface. As for alignment: the line of the body creates the line to which the other elements attach within the overall central alignment of the tall vertical shape of the layout. Proximity is at work here, following Williams' description, because similar words—the ordering information, for example—are all put close together.

13   Williams's principles allow for the creation of a clear visual hierarchy of elements in this layout, indicating what we are intended to see as most visually important in the layout. These principles do go a long way towards explaining why this layout seems

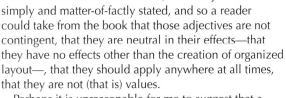

"professional, organized, unified," the values Williams, in the first pages of her book (11), holds up for all layout along with, later, the value of "consistency."

14 The orderly—analytic and analyzable—arrangement of this layout must certainly contribute to the pleasure I take from it.

15 But Williams gives no grounds for the values she lists. Instead, those adjectives are simply and matter-of-factly stated, and so a reader could take from the book that those adjectives are not contingent, that they are neutral in their effects—that they have no effects other than the creation of organized layout—, that they should apply anywhere at all times, that they are not (that is) values.

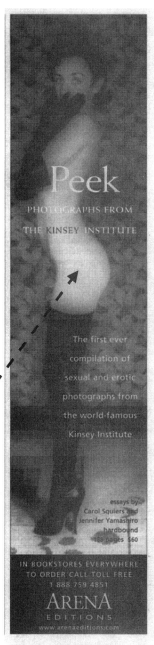

16 Perhaps it is unreasonable for me to suggest that a thin, inexpensive, introductory handbook for visual composition should be self-critical. After all the principles given in The Non-Designer's Design Book do allow me— and people in the classes I teach—to talk analytically about design; they do help us see how visual layout is not magic but is instead rationally organized and can be formally analyzed. But those principles, because they are presented without context or comment, also make it seem, as I have mentioned, that they are neutral and timeless.

17 **Instead, the values that underlie Williams' principles have both history and consequences.**

18 Johanna Drucker, for example, while describing how the field of graphic design took professional shape in the years and industrialization following World War I in the west, has argued that the values of organization and consistency inherent in most modern design are inseparable from ongoing pushes toward rationalization and standardization in industry, and thus inseparable from pushes toward shaping the standardized workforce necessary for industry to flourish. But rationalization and standardization became worthwhile in this process because something else is more essentially sought: that something else is efficiency—little wasted time or capital—in material production, but also efficiency in the production of workforces and of consumers for the material products. Graphic design, becoming a profession in this setting, gets shaped to be an efficient process for disseminating entwined information and desire. Implicit in Williams' principles and their underlying values, then, is the more essential goal that visual arrangement will make easy one's access to what is most important in a layout, that the arrangement will sieve out what is unnecessary or not to the point and will instead streamline the direction and speed of one's sight to hone in on . . . a woman's lovely in-soft-focus-so-as-to-almost-glow white ass, in this particular case.

19 We know from Joel Katz's writing about German

memos from World War II some particulars of what can happen when efficiency is the value placed above—or used to mask—all others: it is possible for many people to forget or be unable to see, under such circumstances, that other people are having their lives horribly and finally shaped to destruction through and behind the finely-carved information passing over a desk. It is always a suspect rhetorical move to align one's arguments (especially when they are about such ephemera as a one-time advertisement on thin paper in a weekly magazine) with others that address the horrors of Nazism; I apologize for having made the alignment here, but it is hard not to think of Katz's arguments whenever efficiency is an unquestioned value at work in one's textual composition. I do believe that teaching Williams' principles "as is" can quietly encourage us to forget—they certainly do not ask us to see—that there is someone's body in this layout. At best, Williams' principles allow us to talk about this body (as I did above) as yet another—as only another—formal aspect of this layout.

When form is treated as though it is abstract—unconnected to time and place—as it is in texts like *The Non-Designer's Design Book*, then, bodies and history are not called to sight or to question. And what is most valued, then, **is** form. Under such conditions, we are encouraged to look at the Peek layout as something well arranged, something without time or place, something therefore to contemplate: the layout is an object on which we can place and move our eyes pleasurably, with the pleasure that comes from believing that our viewing is without social or other consequences—without, also, then, the consequences of us somehow being shaped by the viewing.

20 We are not encouraged to ask about the woman in the ad as a woman, only as a shape.

21 Although, as I have written, *The Non-Designer's Design Book* does give us helpful vocabulary for analysis and composition of visual texts, it is—I am arguing—limited and limiting in what it gives us. Its approach does not help o encourage us to think about how we might have visual composition practice that helped us try out other, less abstract, forms, forms that support practice other than those of
standardly efficient production and consumption.
It does not help us think about pleasures
other than those of isolated,
private
looking-at-objects.

A SECOND FORMALITY
OVERLOOKING STILL BODIES AND HISTORY

22 I incorporate other principles for understanding visual composition in my classes to try to flesh out the abstract formality of Williams' ungrounded principles; these additional principles do not allow me yet to explain fully my pleasure and anger with the Peek ad, but they do help me further articulate my concerns about how we help our students learn about the visual aspects of texts. These other approaches come out of the writings of Rudolf Arnheim, who does—almost literally—ground his ways of seeing: Arnheim uses our bodily experiences of moving over the earth to shape principles for analyzing and creating visual compositions. What Arnheim offers helps me talk, in classes, about aspects of visual compositions that Williams' principles do not address; unfortunately, what Arnheim offers me—as with the Williams—only helps me consider part of the pleasures I take from the Peek advertisement.

23 In his book *The Power of the Center* Arnheim gives these grounds for principles of visual composition:

24 When I look at the open landscape before me, my self reaches out to the horizon, which separates the lake from the sky. Turning around I see at a shorter distance the woods and the house, and even more close by the ground beneath my feet. All these sights are experienced as being seen from the seat of my self, and they group themselves around it in all directions.

[...]

25 The foregoing is a distinctly egocentric way of experiencing the visual environment. It is, however, the primary way suggested spontaneously by what our eyes see. The world we see before our eyes exhibits a particular perspective, centered upon the self. It takes time and effort to learn to compensate for the onesidedness of the egocentric view; and throughout a person's life there persists a tendency to reserve to the self the largest possible share of the power to organize the surroundings around itself at the center. (4-5)

26 Arnheim's principles of visual arrangement develop, then, out of this sense of a self in a body, a self both looking out from the body and experiencing the body as it is subject to the "cosmic" forces of the universe: "Physically, the world of our daily activities is pervaded by one dominant force, the force of gravity" (10). Arnheim uses these grounding observations to analyze how art—paintings and sculpture—makes meaning, primarily in the west. He thus writes, for examples, that

27 To give tangible presence to the reference point of orientation facilitates the task of both draftsman and viewer. Elementary visual logic also dictates that the principal subject be placed in the middle. There it sits clearly, securely, powerfully. At a more advanced level, the central object is promoted to heading a hierarchy.

28 Through the ages and in most cultures, the central position is used to give visual expression to the divine or some other exalted power. [...] In portrait painting, a pope or emperor is often presented in a central position. More generally, when the portrait of a man shows him in the middle of the framed area, we see him detached from the vicissitudes of his life's history, alone with his own being and his own thoughts. A sense of permanence goes with the central position.

[...]

29 Since the middle position is the place of greatest importance, the viewer attributes weight to whatever he finds in that position. (72-73)

30 Before I say more about how I apply Arnheim's observations to the Peek layout, let me add to his writing, by drawing on another book, by a different author, that grows out of a course in "picture structure" (xi) for children and adults as well as out of Arnheim's groundings for "visual logic" (the book contains an introduction by Arnheim). Molly Bang's book Picture This: Perception & Composition steps a reader through building the story of Little Red Riding Hood by using abstract shapes—triangles, rectangles, circles— and then lays out for the reader "principles" of how we make meaning out of the shape and placement of objects on a flat surface. Bang's principles develop directly out of Arnheim's observations about our sense of body in a gravity-heavy world:

31 1. Smooth, flat, horizontal shapes give us a sense of stability and calm.

[...]

32 2. Vertical shapes are more exciting and more active. Vertical shapes rebel against the earth's gravity. They imply energy and a reaching toward heights or the heavens. [...]

33 4. The upper half of a picture is a place of freedom, happiness, and triumph; objects placed in the top half often feel more "spiritual" [...]

The bottom half of a picture feels more threatened, heavier, sadder, or more constrained; objects placed in the bottom half also feel more "grounded."

[...]

34 7. We feel more scared looking at pointed shapes; we feel more secure or comforted looking at rounded shapes or curves. [...]

What do we know of that is formed from curves? Rolling hills and rolling seas, boulders, rivers—but our earliest and strongest association is with bodies, especially our mothers' bodies, and when we were babies there was no place more secure and full of comfort. (56; 58; 76-78; 98)

35 What Arnheim and Bang give us, then, are explanations for why elements placed in a visual composition can take on (some of) the meanings they do for us: we experience the world through the effects of directioned gravity on our bodies and so we call upon those experiences when we see them visually recreated on the two-dimensioned space of page (or screen). We can thus understand the black box at the bottom of the Peek ad as making solidly present the ground on which the layout—and the woman—stand. The woman's buttocks are given visual weight not only because of contrast (which is how the principles in The Non-Designer's Design Book allow us to talk of them) but also because they are at the center of the layout. The overall visual proportions of the layout, repeated in the upright stance of the woman, "imply energy and reaching toward heights"—they give the layout a vitality that would not be present were the woman laying down.

36 But how well do other of Arnheim's and Bang's observations apply?

37 For example, are we meant to see this layout aligned with the portraits of popes and men of power—and of men in general—that Arnheim discusses, so that we are to see the woman in the Peek ad "alone with [her] own being and [her] own thoughts"? Are we to see her, centered in the layout, as "detached from the vicissitudes of [her] life's

history"? Such judgments are only possible if we pull in knowledge and experience that goes beyond how our bodies live with gravity. And given what we know about the articulations among women, sex, nudity, advertising, facial expressions, coffeetable books, and black thigh-high boots, I don't think any of us will judge the Peek ad as being about a woman alone with her own thoughts.

38   Another response to the possibility that we are meant to see this woman as alone with her thoughts comes from Bang, from her suggestion that I have the pleasure I do in seeing the curves of this woman's body because they are a sweet memory of maternal security and comfort. If we understand the body in the Peek layout through memories of losing ourselves into the curvy maternal body, then we are of course being given a body presented not as thinking or as even present to herself, in contrast to Arnheim's description of how we are likely to understand a centralized male figure. Instead, under this logic, this Peek body exists only for others, an unthinking natural being like the hills and rivers with which Bang associates it. Under this conception, how then can we understand the centrality of the body in the Peek layout as a formal presentation of a person "alone with [her] own being and [her] own thoughts"?

39   Even so, I do not think the woman in the Peek layout is being presented as an archetypal Mom, which is the only category offered in Bang that at all addresses the use of a gendered body in visual composition. I do not think that it is simply because Bang's book includes children in its audience that Bang does not discuss what is usually counterpointed to the perfect, unspeaking, warmly fleshed Mother, that is, the archetypal Prostitute, even though this latter figure can also be found being celebrated for its warm, generous, and curving comforts. To offer up this other figure would require acknowledging— among other cultural categories and structures with which the figure of the generalized Prostitute articulates—gender and gender relations, sexual orientation, the particularities of culture practice, relations and movements of capital and property, and so on. To offer up this other figure, in addition, with its complexities, would mean also necessarily bringing into this mix the complexities of the notion of Mother: when one body is acknowledged to be the result of multiple articulations, then all must be.

40   But that also means the body outside the layout, the viewing body on which these principles are based, must also be acknowledged in its complexity. In the passages I have quoted, Arnheim acknowledges that his approach is "egocentric"—and even though he writes that this ego-centeredness can be overcome, he does not describe in The Power of the Center what such an overcoming might entail or look like. Instead, the approaches laid out in that book—presented straightforwardly later as principles in the Bang book— reinforce a notion that anyone who regards the world visually (through a sight that is 'spontaneous') makes sense of the world and of human artifacts primarily by "reserv[ing] to the self the largest possible share of the power to organize the surroundings around itself at the center." And what sort of self is at that center? In the telling of Arnheim and Bang, it is an almost character-less self, looking out from a body whose actions are constrained only by gravity. This is a body without culture, race, class, gender, or age. This is a body with ten fingers and toes, able legs and arms, good strong posture, no genitalia; this is a body born to a mother remembered as nothing but soft and warm curves, a body that simply opens its eyes to see with unmediated understanding. This is the body that so many have written about since the latter part of the twentieth century, the body so many want to complicate and particularize, the body that exists nowhere but in abstraction, the body whose seeing—and understanding of what is seen—is now understood to be as constructed as any other cultural practice.*

41   A consequence of the generalized body being at the ground for what Arnheim and Bang write is that the pleasures of seeing—of looking at something like the Peek ad— are the pleasures of seeing one's apparently most essential self and experiences made visible. In this telling, **form** comes from one's egocentric experiences and one takes pleasure in seeing those experiences comfortably inscribed in other objects. I do not deny the physical necessity of gravity, and because, then, the elements of the Peek layout conform to my generalized experience of gravity, I can take some comfort in them: I can find pleasure in the layout's adherence and lack of resistance to a bottom-line physical, experiential, necessity that I experience daily. Following Arnheim and Bang, if I were to diagram my process of looking at the Peek layout, then, the diagram would show an arrow going in one direction: I look at the layout to see if its form matches what I know; the layout certainly does not look back at me, has no effect on me, my thinking, or my habits. I have argued that Williams' principles emphasize the layout as object, as container of abstract efficient form, as something to contemplate that has no effects on us as we contemplate; in parallel, I argue that Arnheim's and Bang's principles emphasize the layout equally as object, but now that object is a container of the form I experience as an abstracted body.

42 In neither case is the designed object conceived as something to establish relations between me and others; in neither cast object conceived to exist in a circuit of social and cultural relations.

43 As with Williams' principles, Arnheim's and Bang's principles—based in a conception of the gravity of abstract bodies—do help me explain some of my pleasure in the Peek layout, as I have described. I do not, therefore, want to discard immediately the approaches of any of these writers—but it ought to be clear from my inability to use these approaches to speak with any complexity about my responses of pleasure (much less my anger) to the Peek ad, or about the specific body in the layout, or about any relationship between the body or the words printed over her, or about how this layout articulates to wider social and cultural practices, or about how this layout asks me to learn about women or suggests possible relations I have with others, that I am not at all comfortable in using these approaches as they come, by themselves, unchanged.

TURNING TO THE FORM OF BEAUTY...

44 If it were simply that the formal approaches to the visual I've described so far are neutral, that they don't discuss gender (or race or class or culture or economies or...) because they have nothing to do with the constructions of gender (or race or class or culture or economies or. . .), I could stop writing here. All I'd need do is recommend that we don't teach students formal vocabulary and principles for visual analysis and production unless we also consider the visual aspects of texts through the lenses of specifically gendered (and so on) material lives. That is, we could teach contrast and repetition and centering and other formal terms that show up in other texts about visual design and visual grammar, and then augment our teaching with texts that help students and us question how photographs (at least) teach us about gender and race and class and...There are certainly plenty of such texts available.*

45 But the principles and guidelines that I've discussed for analyzing and giving visual form to texts are not neutral or universal, as I've started to argue in my initial discussions of them. They too arise out of and then in turn help shape our senses of who we are and what we are capable of doing (or not) in the world. They too need to be examined as choices, as actions that we take—when we produce texts that have any visual component—to build shaping relations with others and our selves. Several pages earlier I sketched out an argument about the development of graphic design in the twentieth century, for example, an argument that aligns the values behind many of the formal principles taught in the texts I've discussed (values such as unity, efficiency, and coherence) with the political and economic structures of industrialization, structures many of us find problematic. How, for example, do the evenly repeated—and endlessly repeated—regularly and rectangularly structured lines of the academic page function both to reflect and to teach us the visual pattern of (and so taste for) standardized linear order, such as we find on assembly lines, in parking lots, and in the rows of desks in classrooms? All these are sites for the production of regulated and disciplined workforces— sites to which I would then add the standard academic page.

46   I need to argue then that teaching about the visual aspects of texts in our classrooms can't be a simple matter of teaching about form (teaching the Williams or the Bang or the Arnheim, for example) supplemented by teaching about content (gendered and raced bodies, for example). Form is itself always a set of structuring principles, with different forms growing out of and reproducing different but specific values.

47   I want to make that last claim more specific now by turning to a point in our academic history when the separation of form from content was given a specific—and specifically gendered—inflection. I want—and need—now to turn back to the writings and judgments of Kant, to show how the separation of form from content can be, has been, gendered and abstracted. It is this particular way of constructing what form and content are, and how they relate, that leads particularly to my pleasure—and anger—in response to the beauty of the Peek ad but that also leads generally to recommendations I want to make for how we can teach carefully critical approaches to the analysis and production of visual texts of all kinds.

...A VERY FORMAL BEAUTY
KANT'S *CRITIQUE OF JUDGMENT*

48   I turn to Kant's aesthetics because his approach has been the dominant conceptual ground for the aesthetic conceptualizing of painters, designers, and other philosophers and theorists in the last two centuries; it has been the ground for understanding how our material bodily sensations entwine with our conceptual abilities, as in the sections I have quoted from Arnheim. I am not, obviously, going to do justice by Kant in these few pages (or in any number of pages or amount of hubris) but I turn to Kant because it is the structural—formal—nature of his analysis of knowledge, and so of beauty, that I believe has given rise, over the past two centuries, to the abstract approaches to visual composition, to the specific separation of form from content, about which I have been grumbling. But I also believe that Kant's analysis of what gives rise to judgments of beauty can be taken in other directions, directions that could give rise to alternative, less abstract and more socially-tied, understandings of the pleasures and complexities of visual compositions.

49   I will then, first lay out my understanding of the development of Kant's aesthetics— based primarily on the terminology and explanations in the Critique of Judgment—and then show the line of thought coming out of the form of the aesthetic that gives rise to what I've been discussing up to now in this chapter. Then I will lay out an alternative line of thought, in order to talk, finally, of different, more reflexive and reciprocal, approaches to visual composition.

50   Kant's aesthetics are integral to his understanding of the objects of philosophic inquiry, and so I need to sketch his understanding of the divisions of philosophy in order to show how aesthetic judgment serves an overarching function. Kant gives three divisions to the proper study of philosophy, corresponding to the three divisions—the cognitive, the ethical, and the aesthetic—used by Eagleton in the quotation that heads my essay: there are for Kant

51   the study of nature
         the study of morals
         the study of taste or aesthetics

52 Kant's first major work, the Critique of Pure Reason, considers how we can know Nature—the first area of human inquiry for him—and Kant builds a three-part structure of explanation:

understanding

sensation   **concepts**
                  categories used by the understanding
                  to shape sensation

53 On the one side are the formless sensations we have from being bodies in Nature; think back, for example, to Arnheim's descriptions of our sensations of gravity. On the other side are the categories or concepts that provide shape from inside us to the formless sensations. It is the faculty of the understanding that brings the sensations and the formal categories together, allowing us to have thoughts about the world at all: sensations without concepts to shape them have no form, and hence cannot be discussed, considered, or even thought; to have concepts without sensations to apply them to is like having a pair of scissors but nothing that can be cut.

54 What is important for me to note here is the role of form: we cannot control having sensations—the having of sensations is simply a given, necessary because humans are in Nature—but for Kant we exercise what is most human in us when, as our faculty of understanding functions, we apply formal conceptual categories to the sensations so that they can have any meaning at all.

55 In the Critique of Practical Reason, Kant structures our moral faculties following the formal structure from the Critique of Pure Reason:

reason

sense of duty   **concept of freedom**

56 Here, in parallel to the bodily sensations that function in the understanding, Kant works with a sense of duty that he believes is inherent in us: when, for example, we see an older person struggling to cross a street, we (Kant believes) naturally sense that we might do something. But what gives shape to the observation—what allows us to form the sensation into a reasonable action— is for Kant the concept of freedom: in the same way that the concepts of the understanding are structures—such as causality or quantity— that shape inchoate sensation so that we can think about and act on what comes to us through our bodies, so the concept of freedom contains "morally practical precepts" (9) that allow us "to extend the sphere of the determination of the will" (7). As with the structures of understanding, what is most human for Kant within the structures of reason, and hence most important, is our ability to give reason-full shape to what comes to us necessarily out of our nature.

57 If you were to take the two diagrams I have used to lay out the formal structure the first two Critiques, and put them next to each other, I hope you can see how they repeat the structures of the individual critiques. In each of the Critiques what is given by nature is subordinated to what (for Kant) are universal concepts of human thought (through, first, understanding and, then, reason); the result, for Kant, is that in each of the two Critiques "nature is harmonized with our design" (23): in each of the Critiques, particular sensations are brought under the realm of universal thought. But the first Critique concerns, overall, "the realm of natural concepts" (15) whereas the second concerns, overall, human moral decision-making—so, again, there is Nature on the one hand

and the forms of human intellectual work on the other. Kant thus needs, formally and conceptually, a third critique that can show how the natural focus of the first critique is brought in alignment with the free workings of reason in the second critique so that, once again and overall, nature is harmonized with human intellectual design. This is where judgment—taste, an appreciation of beauty—enters, to take on this general structure:

judgment

understanding   **reason**

58 In the third critique, then, the Critique of Judgment, Kant argues that, when we have a sense of pleasure, the faculty of judgment is what allows us to join the pleasure of the realm to universal design. This is not to say that we somehow judge or reshape the pleasure and somehow make it fit the design; instead, "the attainment of that design is bound up with the feeling of pleasure" (23): when we see what gives us pleasure, the pleasure, for Kant, comes when we recognize—judge—that the feeling is showing us how the particulars of our experience fit what is universal:

59 something in our judgments upon nature [...] makes us attentive to its purposivenvess for our understanding—an endeavor to bring, wherever possible, its dissimilar laws under higher ones [...] —and thus, if successful, makes us feel pleasure in that harmony of these with our cognitive faculty... (24).

60 Let me put this another way, using the words of Ernst Cassirer, who places this movement on Kant's part—what may seem to us an odd move from reason and understanding to aesthetics—in the context of the "concrete historical origins of metaphysics" (275). Cassirer steps from Socrates to Plato to Aristotle to Plotinus, tracing through those thinkers morphing notions of relations between the particular to the universal, the real to the ideal, with the end result, in Neoplatonism, being that (if we consider this relation from the perspective of a working artist):

61 the IDEA, which originally is encountered only as something mental and thus an indivisible unity, is extended into the material world; the mental archetype carried by the artist within himself commands matter and turns it into a reflection of the unity of the FORM. The more perfectly this is carried out, the more purely the appearance of the Beautiful is actualized. (278)

62 That is, under this telling, the Beautiful is (to quote Cassirer again) a "resonance of the whole in the particular and singular" (318), and the aesthetic is then "a type of contemplation that participates equally in the principle of empirical explanation of nature and in the principle of ethical judgment" (286). Aesthetic judgment is thus the awareness of a harmonious and interpenetrating relation between the parts of Kant's analysis, between the necessity of nature and the freedom of reason. For Kant, nature and the laws by which we think and act are not separate, and when we see an object in which nature and law are harmonized, it is beautiful. When we see an object that is formed according to universal structures, then the particular and the universal are harmonized, and beauty is created. The faculty of judgment can thus, I think, be schematized more finely:

judgment of beauty

feeling of pleasure   **concept of the
purposiveness of Nature**

63 There are several aspects to such judgments of beauty that I want to emphasize here. Notice, first, that what gives rise to a judgment of beauty—whatever the object is (and Kant discusses people, buildings, music, animals, clothing, gardens, poetry)—is implied in this structure: a judgment of beauty starts with the object, but quickly moves to an appreciation of the formal relations suggested by the object.

64 Second, when (in Kant's view) we make judgments of beauty, they are not personal. Instead, judgments of beauty apply universally. Kant writes that

65 it would be laughable if a man who imagined anything to his own taste thought to justify himself by saying: "This object (the house we see, the coat that person wears, the concert we hear, the poem submitted to our judgment) is beautiful for me" For he must not call it beautiful if it merely pleases him. Many things may have for him charm and pleasantness— no one troubles himself that—but if he gives out anything as beautiful, he supposes in others the same satisfaction; he judges not merely for himself, but for everyone, and speaks of beauty as if it were a property of things... (45, emphasis in the original)

66 Or, as Kant puts it later, "the beautiful is that which pleases universally" (54)— because, if a judgment of beauty is a judgment that finds universal design in a particular object, the quality recognized in the object must necessarily be universal. Eagleton describes Kant's position in this way:

67 Given the nature of our immutable faculties, Kant holds, it is necessary that certain subjective judgments elicit the universal consent of others, since these judgments arise from the sheer formal workings of capacities we have in common. (96)

68 Because, that is, we all (for Kant) think in the same formal ways, we will find beautiful objects in which the forms of our thinking are made visible.

69 Finally, for similar reasons for Kant, anyone who makes a judgment of beauty must be disinterested in the judgment. Although the feeling one finds in a judgment of beauty brings what Kant calls "satisfaction," such satisfaction cannot make the judger lose himself in the object of the judgment. Instead, one must not care whether the beautiful object exists:

70 We easily see that, in saying it is beautiful and in showing that I have taste, I am concerned, not with that in which I depend on the existence of the object, but with that which I make out of the representation in myself. Everyone must admit that a judgment about beauty, in which the least interest mingles, is very partial and is not a pure judgment of taste. (39, emphasis in the original)

71 A judgment of beauty for Kant, then, is a disinterested and universal judgment that finds universal form in the form of some particular object or person.

A FORMAL DISCONNECTION

72 Here is one way to summarize what I have just laid out about the structures of beauty in Kant's approaches to knowledge:

73 • For Kant, we are always to shape the particulars of emotion and bodily sensation according to universal principles.

74 • When we shape emotion and bodily sensation in accord with those principles, our motivations are not directed towards ourselves or others; instead, we are to act with disinterest, to act on judgments that could be (ought to be) made by everyone, everywhere.

75 • When we judge something to be beautiful, it is because beauty is formally inherent in the object.

76 In *Venus in Exile: The Rejection of Beauty in Twentieth-Century Art*, Wendy Steiner examines these statements within the context of Kant's time; she argues that Kant's approach to aesthetics has led us to conditions in our time that we might want to work against, conditions inseparable from the approaches to visual composition I have earlier described.

77   Steiner's arguments implicitly ask us to acknowledge that Kant's own philosophizing cannot be disinterested, in at least one way: from the beginning and throughout, Kant's philosophizing is gendered. That is, Kant's philosophizing—his certainty in the possibility of universal intellectual conditions— cannot be separated from how his sense of the world and its functioning grew out of his ability as a man of his time and place to look upon his experiences as being, necessarily, the experiences of all others. None of that, of course, enters Kant's Critiques. Steiner shows, however, how those conditions are stated explicitly by others: for example, she cites Arthur Schopenhauer stating that "Women are, and remain, thoroughgoing philistines, and quite incurable" (22). In Schopenhauer's thinking women are by nature incapable of true aesthetic feeling, just as they are incapable of the rigors of philosophic thought: because they are so tied to their bodies and emotion, they cannot approach the world intellectually, they cannot have the universal judgments Kant describes. Against such a cultural understanding of what a woman is and is capable of doing, it is not difficult to see Kant's philosophizing—the act of philosophizing as well as his philosophy's continual emphasis on formal abstract thought over what comes to us through our particular bodies—as a turn against aspects of life that have been and still often are culturally read as womanly.

78   Steiner quotes Mary Wollstonecraft's arguments that these womanly incapacities and inferiorities are not natural or inherent but rather the result of the limited lives, educations, actions, and positions that were (and are still) given to women; these inferiorities, Steiner writes, are what, "according to Mary Wollstonecraft, made women slaves to sensation" (23) because they had little or no access to the education that leads to abilities to perform (or a taste for) Kantian abstract intellectualizing. But precisely because Kant's philosophizing works continually to place and universalize understanding, reason, and judgment over bodily and other sensation, it abstracts body and sensation: body and sensation must be the same for all if thinking is to be the same—and so if someone appears incapable of thinking in the ways Kant has described thinking (as understanding, reasoning, and judging universally) it must because she is inherently incapable; there is no place in this structure for seeing, much less taking into consideration, how the particularities of one's material conditions shape one's structures of experience and thinking.

79   Against this background of necessary universals, Steiner delineates a reading of Mary Shelley's Frankenstein as a response to Kant's aesthetics. For Steiner, Shelley's writing— Frankenstein's monster and all that he wreaks—is a detailed teasing out of what happens when one acts with the disinterest required of the Kantian moral actor; the book is a way for Shelley to point out (according to Steiner) the "irony" in the aesthetics: "that in providing supposedly the most human of mental states, freedom, it utterly disregards love and family and pleasure, which have at least as much claim as freedom to define 'the human'" (13). But such disregard is never neutral; when we wish to indicate that something is not worthy of regard, when we diss what we regard, we make it so by making it not worthy of our sights. And so Steiner writes that

80   If Kant wanted to detach aesthetic experience from self-concern, [Shelley] shows that this detachment leads to a devaluation and indeed dehumanization of the feminine and the domestic leading to the direst of consequences: war and political oppression. (14)

81   How are war and oppression—and all the deaths of women and children in Frankenstein—a result for Shelley of Kant's particular form of aesthetics? In a Kantian aesthetic judgment a particular sensation is brought under the form of the universal, and away from any truck with one's own self or body; one is thus distanced from the embodied object that gave rise to the judgment. Steiner thus writes that "the purity of Kantian beauty is a deprivation that inevitably evokes the enmity of the perceiver, who wants to punish it for it inaccessibility and distance," and so, "When woman is the embodiment of that beauty, she is at risk" (17).

82   Steiner carries her arguments out of Frankenstein and through late nineteenth and into twentieth century art and literary practices. She does this by quoting, for example, Leo Tolstoy's writing about the beauty of women as the live their lives, have children, and age—

83   is this "beauty" real beauty? Of what use is it? [... T]hin and grizzled hair, toothless, wrinkles, tainted breath; even long before the end all becomes ugly and repellant; visible paint, sweat, foulness, hideousness. Where then is the god of my idolatry? Where is beauty? (36)

84   —to argue that Tolstoy found women "disastrous as symbols of artistic beauty, which must be universal, transcendent, safe from vicissitude and death" (36). She quotes Georges Braques saying, in 1910, that because he was incapable of depicting the full beauty of women he must

85   create a new sort of beauty, the beauty that appears to me in terms of volume line, of mass, of weight, and through that beauty interpret my subjective impression. [...] I want to expose the Absolute, and not merely the factitious woman. (44)

86   She quotes Apollinaire, who writes that "the modern school of painting"

87   wants to visualize beauty disengaged from whatever charm woman has for man, and until now, no European artist has dared attempt this. The new artists demand an ideal beauty, which will be, not merely the proud expression of the species, but the expression of the universe, to the degree that it has been humanized by light. (48)

88   Steiner also quotes Pound, Mayakovsky, D.H. Lawrence, Marinetti, and Joyce and she concludes that

89   As the avant-garde dodged the pathos of existence with their Promethean abstraction, they denounced sentiment and sensuality and stressed the purity of form and the self-containment of the aesthetic experience. (48)

                    [...]

90   In short, modernist artists turned the viewer's attention from subject matter to form, and symbolized this switch by subverting or eliminating the image of woman. In the process, they made the work a fetish, valuable in itself, compelling, a formal compensation for a problematic reality. (55)

91   If we agree with Steiner's arguments—if they help us make sense of, for example, paintings of women by de Kooning or Picasso (two more of Steiner's many examples)—then we have this as one possible legacy of a Kantian notion of beauty:

92   we receive in our time a notion of form that considers itself timeless and universal and disinterested, inhering in objects for us to look at rather than placed there by our learned habits and tastes. We receive a notion that form is about pulling away from what is "factitious," what is particular, what is messy and domestic and emotional and bodily and coughs and sweats and bloats and wants to talk back and even sometimes touch. We receive a notion of form that not only allows to pull away from all that, but that expects us to pull away, that instructs us—visually, by what it emphasizes—that we are supposed to pull away, be distant, be in our selves away from others, from Others.

93   What results, in this telling, are the two connected consequences I described earlier in response to Williams and to Bang and Arnheim.

94   • On the one hand, the object of art and design is formalized the abstraction, to the point where when I see it I can look at it as though it has no other qualities than the formal: beauty is contained in it, but only as form.

95 • On the other hand, my sense of my self is also reduced as I am separate from what gives me (formal) pleasure; in the telling of Arnheim, for example, a self is important here solely because its experience is guided by gravity, that most Newtonian and formal of forces.

Such a formal beauty has nothing to do with me or with you.

YES, BUT... IT DOESN'T HAVE TO BE ART TO GIVE PLEASURE

96 But the Peek layout isn't art, you may say: that body has not been taken over by rough lines as in the de Kooning drawing; it has not been made into several circles hanging off a thin stem. But, well, hasn't it? Isn't the body on the Peek layout dissolving into abstract shape? The body is softly focused, fading into the background: we are not being shown this body so as to see any dry and flaking skin on its elbows or to see any monthly bloating or any scars. Instead, we see unblemished flat white skin abstractly rounded—as though the body were a blank page on which we can put what we want: the gloves and boots are like paper-doll or refrigerator-magnet-doll clothing, pieces to take on and off at whim. We see the body as shapes made to be in tune with the shapes of type and with the layout itself, as I wrote earlier when I applied the principles Williams and Arnheim and Bang to the layout.

97 I want to argue that the body in the Peek layout has been made into form, has been departicularized: when we see this body, we are seeing a body only through the distant, universalized, formality that I have argued is well-seating in Kant's notion of aesthetic judgment and that we have inherited in much of our uncritical and uncriticized practices with and around the visual. And certainly my pleasure in looking at the body is, to some extent, formal, as I have written earlier: it must necessarily be so, because I have grown up into these formal approaches, I have been trained into—learned the vocabularies and the ways of seeing of (whether I can articulate them out loud or not)—this formal approach to beauty. I find pleasure in the Peek layout precisely because it is all abstracted, perfected, pulled out of the day-to-day, formalized.

OR ANGER...

98 And the anger that I feel, the anger I have been trying to understand since first seeing the layout, is inseparable from the pleasures I have been describing.

99 I've not spoken so far specifically of that anger, except to mention it at the beginning of this chapter, because I can only articulate it now, after having tried to understand my pleasure and how my pleasure is tied to Kant's formal aesthetics. It is easy to articulate a particular and well-known kind of anger about the Peek layout, about the layout being just one more in the endless pile of painted, photographed, and drawn representations of women shown as only sexual and also now used for selling, so that we all—men and women—are pushed to see women only as sexual objects, as objects serving as the means to the ends of others. **But what my analysis here shows me is that we should see this objectification—and the violence against women that can follow from it— as inseparable from the formal approaches we have learned for analyzing and making visual presentations of all kinds.**

100 The particular approach to form we have acquired through Kant asks us to think of form as separate from the content of the senses. It then asks, as we work with anything we wish to see or make as aesthetic, for form to take what is messy and particular and to abstract it and generalize it and universalize it. We have learned to think that form should do this, and we have learned to expect that form should do this, whether we are working with visual representations such as photographs or with the visualities of type on a page. When we see what is not so formally ordered, when we see what does not have beauty as an apparently inherent quality and that does not therefore live up to our formal

expectations, we denigrate it, or try to lay (or force) perfect form upon it, or try to erase it.

[101]   And a result of this formal approach, then, is that women—like anyone else subject to this formalizing—are "at risk," as Steiner claims and as her quotations from artists demonstrate: first, when women and other Others are subjected to this aesthetic formalizing, they are made distant, objects to be observed, not people to live with; then, when we see them in all their particularities and compare them to aestheticized representations, they are judged as lacking of that form and so in need of being perfected (often through self-discipline—think anorexia or Michael Jackson) or of being taken out of the realms of formal judgment, sometimes violently.

[102]   My anger is that I see the Peek ad, and the woman in the Peek ad, as beautiful only because I cannot see the particularities of either. The Kantian formal conceptions of good form into which I—probably just like you—have grown up teach me to see in a way that doesn't value the particular and the messy. It isn't that I learn to objectify and simplify women simply because I see so many magazine covers or advertisements or movies or TV shows with abstractly perfected, airbrushed women; it is also that I have learned to believe that what is well-formed must be formally abstracted and perfected. **My very (learned) idea of what is beautiful, of what is well-formed, is dangerous for women and any aestheticized Others.**

[103]   This desire for abstract formality we have learned—the Kantian universal formalism embodied in the layout of the Peek ad as well as in the vocabularies of Williams, Arnheim, and Bang—separate us from our histories and places, and hence from each other. If we believe that to be human is to be tied to place and time and messiness and complexity, then, by so abstracting us, this desire dehumanizes us and our work and how we see each other. This is dangerous.

[104]   We should look on these formal approaches with anger, and we should be working to change them.

STRETCHING TO FIND, THEREFORE, PARTICULAR BEAUTY

[105] If we want to change how we see women, then, or if we want to change how we see any group of people who are treated unfairly by our visual practices, it is therefore not enough to push for magazine covers and advertisements and catalogues and TV commercials that show (for example) women with fleshy and round and imperfect and aged flesh. We also have to criticize and rethink the formal categories we have inherited for making the visual arrangements that we do; we need to try new and different formal relations in our layouts and we need to learn to appreciate formal arrangements and practices that do not abstract and universalize.

[106]   Steiner, for example, in response to the analysis I've summarized on earlier pages, writes that perhaps "our aesthetic socialization is a good thing, every touch with beauty amounting to an all too rare experience of community and shared values" (xvii), but this is possible only if we see beauty

[107]   as a kind of communication. We often speak as if beauty were a property of objects: Some people or artworks "have it" and some do not. [... Instead,] Beauty is an unstable property because it is not a property at all. It is the name of a particular interaction between two beings, a "self" and an "Other": "I find an Other beautiful." (xx-xxi)*

               And

[108]   In our gratitude toward what moves us so, we attribute to it the property of beauty, but what we are actually experiencing is a special relation between it and ourselves. We discover it as valuable, meaningful, pleasurable to us. (xxiii, emphasis hers)

[109] If we see beauty as a quality we build, rather than one we expect to discover, then we can potentially see beauty — and other aesthetic qualities like coherence or unity or

balance — as shared values we can both celebrate and question. These are the values (and there could be others) that shape the material communication we build for each other and that thus shape how we see each other through what we build.

110 What if we were to build communications that, instead of seeking after the universal and abstract, sought after the particular? What if, instead of formal distance from others, we worked to figure out what visual forms might embody generosity toward others, or patience, or pleasure in the particular, or … ? What if, that is, we were to conceive as form as itself particular and temporal, tied to where and when and how we live, a set of structures for both representing and shaping how we see and experience each other?

ONE WAY TOWARD A FORMAL RECONNECTION

111 How then might we develop a taste for the different—the particular—sense of beauty I've just suggested? How might we develop senses of beauty and pleasure that allow us to see that beauty is something we construct together, that it is a way we can reciprocally share with each other the pleasures of being with in the world together, of appreciating what is particular about our lives?

112 I am going to present here one approach that might help us understand judgments of beauty as the recognition of reciprocal relationship instead of as distancing; I am trying to build (and to test through my teaching) approaches that see form as this kind of recognition, tying us to others and to our times and places. To do that I am going to return, quickly, to Kant, in order to tell an alternate lineage for the aesthetic's ability to articulate the particular and the universal, necessity and freedom; I want to bring necessity and freedom more closely together than Kant's formal search for universals allowed, so that we see them necessarily entwined, not separable and separated. In order to do this, I need to move in my own way from Kant into the 20th century, as necessity becomes social and freedom gets strange.

113 I do not think I am limb-walking when I say that Kant's notion of the mediation of the senses gets socialized, in some lines of thinking, beginning in the late 19th and through the last century. For Kant, we have no immediate access to the real; there is instead always the mediation of the intellectual categories between us and our sensations— and those intellectual categories are, for Kant, as I've described, universal, the same categories for everyone everywhere. That is, with Kant, we are to understand our bodily responses and tastes as being the same as everyone else's because the categories we use for creating understanding out of sensation are not tied to time or place. But if we look at this structure of understanding through Bourdieu, for example, I think we can understand Bourdieu's notions of habitus and taste as giving social groundings to the categories of the understanding: that is, what is "necessary" in Kant's schematism of the aesthetic—in our time—becomes (through Bourdieu) what we have learned to take for granted by having grown up into our particular times and places and the shared values that Steiner argues we can see when we are moved by or attracted to a composition. When we experience gravity, that is, we can only experience it because we have a term "gravity," which carries with it whatever we have learned (or not) about Newton, the apple, and the solar system. When we experience weight, a result of gravity, we only experience it through the value-weighted forms gendered bodies can take in our time and place. In all those Kantian schema I laid out several pages ago, then, we can understand what Kant labels as necessary—our bodily sensations—as being social before we ever can experience them. The web of social and cultural practices in which we move give us the words and concepts, as well as the tastes, for understanding what we sense. This is the necessary—and necessarily social—grounding structure of the day-to-day, of all that we share as we move in our particular circles and lives.

114 How then might we learn to appreciate—see the beauty of, take rich pleasure in—the particularities of our experiences and those of others within this shared day-to-day? I believe that various particularities can be made at least temporarily special, can be made to stand out against but still (necessarily) within the background of the day-to-day. This is one way to consider how freedom could function in those Kantian schema I presented on earlier pages, if we look at freedom through the Russian formalists and Brecht, through their appeals to "strangeness"—or through Heidegger's naming of the uncanny: freedom could be manifest in that part of any aesthetic experience that encourages us, momentarily and pleasurably, to see and understand how the shared, necessary, quotidian rhythms of our lives are built out of numberless and necessary particularities. Victor Shklovsky, for example, argues that

115 art exists that one may recover the sensation of life; it exists to make one feel things, to make the stone stony. [...] The technique of art is to make objects "unfamiliar." [...] Art removes objects from the automatism of perception. (12-13; emphasis his)

116 There are problems with this approach, which can do exactly what Steiner describes by putting our attention not on the full particularity of what stands out aesthetically but by instead putting our attention on "strangeness" itself. If we learn to recognize, however, that what is strange can only be so within the context of the shared day-to-day, then the strange and the social stay linked; the social does not get forgotten so that the strange then seems to possess some inherent, universal property.

117 It is possible then to understand that the existence of the strange—our ability to make things strange so that they can stand out as worthy of thoughtful and respectful attention—both heightens our awareness of the necessity of the day-to-day as well as shows us the freedom we have relative to it: the one is not possible without the other. Something like this is at work in Sonja Foss's arguments about "the construction of visual appeal in images":

118 A novel technical aspect of the image violates viewers' expectations; the violation functions both to sustain interest in the image and to decontextualize it. Connotations commonly associated with the technical aspect then provide an unexpected but familiar context in which to interpret the image. (215)

119 For my purposes here it is not important to focus on Foss's use of "technical," but it is important for me to state that I think her arguments go beyond "images": what Foss describes—what Shklovsky describes—is a process by which we can change relations we build with each other through the communications we make for each other. If we think of beauty (which I have now made strange) as what can result when some expected day-to-day particular is made to stand out against the background of the larger realm of steady social practices, then we can develop not only strategies for teaching about it but also for how we might go about making change in the formal approaches to lives and detached bodies about which I have been—am—angry.

120 I flip Cassirer's explication of Kant here, a bit, because I'm speaking of the "resonance of the particular and singular in the whole" for this beautiful strangeness, but Kant's basic structure is still at work—although I have attached new words to the structure. Under what I am arguing, aesthetic experiences allow us to participate equally in the necessity of the social and in the freedom of pushing against—making strange—that social so that we can appreciate its particularities. We can create aesthetic experiences— visual compositions, for the purposes of my teaching—for each other where we use the expected social constructions of form just enough to hold onto what audiences expect, but where we can then also make visible the particularities of our own lives and experience and hence make visible the limitations of the forms we have been asked to grow into but, if we are to be safe and fully respected, cannot.

WHAT THEN IS NEEDED

121 If we think of the experience of beauty as coming out of the day-to-day necessities of our social existence—an "experience of community and shared values" to use Steiner's words—when particularities of that existence are made to stand out, then I think we can see direct strategies of approach for teaching. There is no question that there is a certain necessity to effective visual composition because a design must fit a viewer's expectations if it is to make sense... but if design is to have any sense of possibility—of freedom—to it, then it must also push against the conventions, the horizons, of those expectations.

122 I want people in my classes, then, to learn the social and temporal expectations of visual composition so that they can, eventually, perhaps, change some of the results of those expectations. I do not start my teaching with design principles, then, but rather by asking people in classes to collect and sort through and categorize compositions of all kinds, to try to pull "principles" out of those compositions and their experiences. One result is that, after looking closely at telephone book ads for lawyers, for example, they can see the limitations and contingencies of (for example) Williams's design principles: an accident-and-injury lawyer who wants to come across as strong and willing to do everything on your behalf does not do well presented through rules aimed at harmony, clarity, and restraint. But, also, when people in these classes then make their own visual compositions, they understand that there are principles and why they need to follow them (in order to fit with the learned expectations of their audiences, not because there are universal, neutral forms) but they are also then aware that they can—and often should—push against the principles. They see how the visual compositions they make embody particular aspects of themselves, that what they make are not objects for contemplation by others but rather reciprocal communications, shaping both composer and reader and establishing relationships among them.

123 But there is more to our discussions than how to make compositions for narrowly specific rhetorical situations: as students make their collections, we talk about how different compositional strategies shape us by asking us to view, read, and respond in the terms of the form on the page or screen. When students are the audiences of design, they see how designs work to shape and naturalize the necessity of their day-to-day worlds. When they produce their own compositions, they consider their visual strategies as having real and expansive effects—because they see their work as fitting into, reproducing but also trying to make strange, the necessary but contingent principles that underlie how we live with each other. They see the work as reciprocal, shaping themselves as well as those for whom the work is made. They also then see the stickiness of beauty as it—like any other value giving form to what they make—binds form and content, composer and audience, together.

124 We come to see visual composition as rhetorical, as a series of choices that have much broader consequences and articulations than visual principles (as I've argued here) suggest. After such a course of activities students see themselves able to compose effectively with the visual elements of different texts for different rhetorical circumstances... but I also hope that they see themselves capable of making change, of composing work that not only fits its circumstances but that also helps its audiences—and its makers—re-vision themselves and try out new and more thoughtful relations between each other.

Credit

Wysocki, Anne Frances. "The Sticky Embrace of Beauty." From *Writing New Media: Theory and Applications for Expanding the Teaching of Composition* by Anne Frances Wysocki, et al. Copyright © 2004 by Utah State University Press. Reproduced by permission of the Utah State University Press, an imprint of University Press of Colorado, in the format Textbook via Copyright Clearance Center.

Materiality and Genre in the Study of Discourse Communities

AMY J. DEVITT, ANIS BAWARSHI, and MARY JO REIFF

1 Over the past two decades the concept of discourse community has been one of the most hotly contested notions in the field, subject to the range of by now well-known critiques that claim it is too utopian, hegemonic, stable, and abstract. Abstracted from real social situations, discourse communities may appear stable to advocates and critics assuming an imaginary consensus and a shared purpose that do not reflect real experience within communities. The concept of discourse community as stable and utopian has been, to some, so seductive that it both conceals the language and the social practices that take place within it and distracts researchers from examining how its internal workings may be recognized and studied. As a result, the concept of discourse community remains of limited pedagogical value.

2 To make communities tangible and their discourse actions palpable to students, writing teachers have begun to use ethnographic research, which, while valuable in locating the study of discourse within the behaviors of real communities, can be difficult to implement in the classroom. According to Beverly Moss, "When ethnographers study a community as outsiders, they must spend a significant amount of time gaining access to the community and learning the rules of the community well enough to gather and eventually analyze the data" (161). The process of sifting through the massive quantities of information gathered and attempting to stake out some analytical claims can present a major hurdle, particularly for student ethnographers. How do ethnographers connect what community members know and do with what they say and how they say it—their language practices? Genre analysis has been responsive to such questions and links patterns of language use to patterns of social behavior, reflecting the composition researcher's "narrower concern with communicative behavior or the interactions of language and culture" (Moss 156). Genre study allows students and researchers to recognize how "lived textuality" plays a role in the lived experience of a group. Teaching students how to analyze genres can provide discipline and focus to the study of discourse communities.

3 During the last half-century, genre theory has been reconceived by literary and rhetorical theorists as, among other things, "sites of social and ideological action" (Schryer 208)—as parts of all social environments. Language genres in these contexts become less transparent and more constitutive, less the means of classifying texts and more the sites at which language's social character can be understood. In this sense language and its genres are as material as the people using them. As sites of social action, genres identify the linguistic ecology of discourse communities, making the notion of community more tangible for teachers and students.

4 In the three connected essays that follow, we use the idea of genre to study discourse communities. We examine several contexts of language exchange in which the use of genre theory may yield insight into teaching, research, and social interaction: legal practice, medical practice, and classrooms. Illustrating how genres can sometimes restrict access to communities, Amy Devitt examines jury instructions as a genre, considering how the genre affects the interactions of jurors in ways that inhibit the successful execution of their duties. Anis Bawarshi suggests how a specific textual genre, the patient medical-history form, works in and provides critical access into doctors' offices. Mary Jo Reiff discusses how the combination of ethnography and genre analysis can give teachers, researchers, and students clearer ways to understand their classrooms.

5 Together, the essays suggest how genre analysis contributes to the use of ethnomethodology as a research technique that focuses on language and society and that is especially eligible to contribute to the pedagogy of text-dependent subject matters.

Whether we are studying academic, professional, or public communities, genres, considered as material entities, enable us to enrich the idea of a discourse community by giving discipline and focus to the study of the unities of language and society.

6   **Amy J. Devitt** is professor of English and Conger-Gabel Teaching Professor at the University of Kansas, where she teaches courses in writing and writing theory and English language studies. She is the author of *Standardizing Written English: Diffusion in the Case of Scotland 1520–1659*, articles on genre theory in *College English* and *CCC*, and two forthcoming books, a theoretical study of writing genres and a genrebased textbook for first-year writing courses (coauthored with Anis Bawarshi and Mary Jo Reiff).

7   **Anis Bawarshi** is assistant professor of English at the University of Washington, where he teaches courses in rhetoric and composition. His book *Genre and the Invention of the Writer* (forthcoming) examines the relationship between genre and subject formation and what that relationship means for the study and teaching of writing. He has recently coedited, with Sidney I. Dobrin, *A Closer Look: The Writer's Reader*.

8   **Mary Jo Reiff** is assistant professor of English and the director of the composition program at the University of Tennessee, where she teaches courses in rhetoric, writing, and technical communication. She has published articles in *WAC Journal, JAC, Issues in Writing*, and *Writing on the Edge*, and is currently completing a book on theories of audience.

WHERE COMMUNITIES COLLIDE: EXPLORING A LEGAL GENRE
— Amy J. Devitt —

9   Contemporary genre analysis focuses on the actual uses of texts, in all their messiness and with all their potential consequences. Genre analysis also ties that use to actual language, to the smaller bits of language that alert analysts to underlying ideas, values, and beliefs. Such analysis often reveals the conflicts between communities that use a genre, conflicts often invisible to analysis that looks at discourse in terms of its communities alone. This essay analyzes some genres, particularly jury instructions, that are created within one professional community to be used by nonmembers of that community. While their purposes seem to be inclusive, to give nonmembers access to the community's knowledge, genre analysis strongly suggests that the specialist and nonspecialist users have different beliefs, interests, and purposes as well as levels of knowledge. The consequences for both the professional communities and the larger society are significant, potentially drawing the boundaries around professional communities even more tightly. In order to keep from substituting one abstracted concept for another, to keep from idealizing and homogenizing the realities of genres, students should also see the messiness and especially the exclusiveness of genres.

10   Because genres represent their communities, they effect and make consequential the communities' interests. But it is when genres encompass participants beyond a narrow community that the effects of those interests become most troublesome. Surprisingly, many genres are designed within one specialist community for functions to be filled by nonmembers of that community. Tax forms are designed by the IRS, but they are supposedly meant to be used by people who may know little of tax regulations. The fact that so many people hire specialists to complete their tax forms merely confirms the difficulty of the task of translating specialists' knowledge into laypersons' actions. An especially significant recent example is the ballot, both the propositions on it and the physical construction of it. Ballots are created by politicians but are completed by citizens. Ballots contain propositions that voters vote on, but the propositions are written by lawyers and knowledgeable proponents of an issue. To have our votes count, as we learned in the United States so vividly so recently, we must not only feel informed enough to be willing to walk into the voting booth (not always an easy task as the issues become ever more complicated and our politicians' explanations ever more simplified into sound bites); we must also be able to understand the ballot once we are in the

booth. The genre of the ballot question makes it difficult to understand what is at issue. Typical ballot questions combine explanatory statements with legislative amendments, but the explanatory statements can rarely explain enough to enable the voter to understand the amendment. Even the physical layout of the ballot, we have learned, entails specialized but unstated knowledge, and good citizens must decipher where to punch, mark, and pull, and with what definiteness and strength. To mark a ballot seems a simple thing, but the community of election commissioners actually brings specialist knowledge to the interpretation of those ballots—knowledge not explained in the ballot genre. The specialists know what a chad is, for one thing, and understand what the machines will and will not count, how much must be punched for a vote to register. The specialists know that drawing a line through one candidate's name will render that ballot invalid, while the good citizen might know only that drawing such a line is a known way to register displeasure. Even without getting into the language of provisions, often unintelligible to even the most educated voters, the ballot as a genre includes complications and presumptions that serve the interests of the specialist creators but not of the nonspecialist users.

11 In fact, much of our civic lives involves genres that come out of a community of specialists, whether lawyers, legislators, or government employees. Doing our civic duty depends as much on our ability to understand and use genres accurately as it does on our willingness to be good citizens. Yet the difficulty remains of community- embedded genres producing action by nonmembers of that community. Although the borders of communities are more permeable and fluid than the community metaphor suggests, clashes of knowledge and perspective still result when specialists and nonspecialists meet, clashes that have consequences in terms of how participants interact, perform their actions, and produce certain effects in the world.

12 The inclusion of nonspecialists is vital to the U.S. judicial system, with the usually final decisions made not by all-knowing judges but by everyday citizens. Instructions to juries are designed to explain enough of the law so that a jury of peers can render an appropriate verdict. But jury instructions are written by lawyers, with their details hammered out by lawyers and the judge arguing privately, away from the ears of the jurors who must use them. By the time the judge gives a jury instructions, those instructions contain presumptions, implications, specifications known well by the law community but unknown to the unsuspecting jury members. The genre thus has a significance for the legal community that it does not have for the jurors. As a result, juries do not and cannot interpret the genre the way its creators intended, as lawyers would, and cannot render verdicts that follow those instructions fully and accurately, thus resulting in significant consequences, particularly for defendants.

13 One recent example turned on a single word (see Mathis). Michael Sharp was convicted of child endangerment in 1999 after he held on to his three-week-old daughter while police were trying to arrest him on an outstanding warrant. His girlfriend and a police officer testified that he seemed to be holding the baby carefully. Before long, Sharp handed the child to officers. At his trial, the judge in the case instructed the jury to find Sharp guilty if they found he had put the girl in a situation where her "body or health might be injured or endangered." The jury rendered a verdict of guilty. The problem, according to Sharp's lawyer and an appeals court, is that the word "might" has a different meaning in law than in common usage. The word has a different weight to each party; it is material in different ways. Courts define "might" as saying an action was probable, not merely possible. Since the jury instructions did not explain the court's meaning of "might," the appeals court overturned the verdict and ordered a new trial. As the appeals court judge wrote in his decision, "There is a very real possibility, especially under the facts of this case, that the jury would have returned a different verdict had the term 'might' been properly defined" (qtd. in Mathis). With the community of lawyers defining "might" differently than do nonmembers, can instructions to a jury ever specify the law sufficiently to let the jury do its job according to that law? The genre of jury instructions has a perhaps insurmountable task in needing to tell citizens unaware of legal technicalities how to follow the relevant law in making their decision, a task of making community members out of nonmembers, of getting nonmembers to enact and reproduce the agendas of a specialist community.

14   This difficulty is especially troubling in the particular jury instructions I have examined in detail, the instructions to a jury in the sentencing phase of a capital case—instructions to a jury deciding whether to sentence a defendant to death. Originally called in to examine potential bias in the pattern of instructions (a set of approved jury instructions that judges commonly use), I eventually worked to rewrite those instructions in order to make them clearer to an ordinary jury. What I discovered is that no matter how much I elaborated, no matter how many assumptions I made explicit, I could not capture in those instructions all the information that the lawyers considered relevant to the jury's task. Clarifying for the jury's purposes clashed with adhering to legal purposes. What seemed a reasonably straightforward genre when I began proved to be a genre mired in its specialized community's expectations and potentially misleading to its nonspecialized users. What was material to me and to juries was not material to lawyers and judges, and vice versa.

15   Part of the difficulty when specialized communities write to nonspecialist users lies in technical language, a difficulty commonly recognized and often addressed through defining key terms, but most of the difficulty comes from differences of interest and value that definitions cannot control. In capital cases, two key terms are "aggravating" and "mitigating," for juries must weigh aggravating and mitigating circumstances. These terms are so central to the law as well as to the task at hand that no definition or rewording could capture the full technical meaning of these terms to the courts. In addition, each potential juror may have a private sense of the value of these terms. But even greater difficulties arise from the use of common terms to serve specialist interests. The list of aggravating circumstances from the *Pattern Instructions* for the state of Kansas (a set of instructions modeled on existing instructions from other states) itemizes eight possible aggravating circumstances. Some of those circumstances appear to be matters of fact, though surely still contestable: that the defendant authorized someone else to commit the crime, that the defendant was imprisoned for a felony at the time, or that the defendant committed the crime for money, to avoid arrest, or to silence a witness. Other possible aggravating circumstances, though, require jurors to assess not only whether facts were proven but also the degree of seriousness of the crime: that the defendant previously "inflicted great bodily harm, disfigurement, dismemberment, or death on another," that the defendant knowingly "created a great risk of death to more than one person," or that the defendant "committed the crime in an especially heinous, atrocious or cruel manner." "The term 'heinous,'" the instructions continue, "means extremely wicked or shockingly evil; 'atrocious' means outrageously wicked and vile; and 'cruel' means pitiless or designed to inflict a high degree of pain, utter indifference to, or enjoyment of the sufferings of others." The list of aggravating circumstances is full of gradable words with no standard of comparison: "great" bodily harm and risk of death, "serious" mental anguish or physical abuse. Mitigating circumstances similarly depend on judgments of "significant" histories, "extreme" disturbances or distress, "relatively minor" participation, or "substantial" domination and impairment.

16   When I asked about providing some standard or clarifying what is legally defensible, I was told that there is no legally tested standard and so none could be provided.

17   In fact, the greatness or seriousness of the crime is precisely what the jury is being asked to evaluate. Yet nowhere do the instructions say that. Rather, the jury instructions follow the legal community's need for events to be based in fact rather than value, so circumstances are treated as either existing or not existing. That perspective appears explicitly in the next instruction about burden of proof: the State must prove "that there are one or more aggravating circumstances and that they are not outweighed by any mitigating circumstances." In fact, however, to decide whether an aggravating circumstance exists requires deciding whether the action was great, serious, or, in perhaps the most notorious language, "heinous." For a jury to decide that a crime was "especially heinous" and thus that an aggravating circumstance exists, the jury is told to define "heinous" as "extremely wicked or shockingly evil." Here in the courtroom, in the setting of this specialized community based in logic and reasoning, a jury of peers is told to "determine" and "consider" "evidence" that will allow them to decide "beyond a reasonable doubt" that a crime was "extremely wicked or shockingly evil." The clash of specialized standards with common values produces a very confused genre, not to mention jury. The material language of the genre produces material consequences, for the defendant as well as for the jury's actions and the legal community's use of those actions.

18   One final example from these jury instructions reveals the subtle form this clash between members and nonmembers of specialist communities can take and how it materializes in actual practices, languages exchanges, and relations. In the instruction just examined, the jury is to decide that "there are one or more aggravating circumstances and that they are not outweighed by any mitigating circumstances." The jury is not told how to weigh these circumstances but rather how not to weigh them:

19   In making the determination whether aggravating circumstances exist that are not outweighed by any mitigating circumstances, you should keep in mind that your decision should not be determined by the number of aggravating or mitigating circumstances that are shown to exist. (*Pattern* 56.00-F)

20 The negatives in these several instructions and the ones that follow compound, to a point that I believe most jurors would have difficulty interpreting: their decision rests on doubting (but not by counting) that some circumstances are not outweighed by others so that the defendant will not be sentenced to death. When I tried to rewrite these instructions to clarify and simplify them, though, I found that those negatives contained vital specialist presumptions. At one point, I suggested the wording, "In determining whether mitigating circumstances outweigh aggravating circumstances you should not decide by counting the number of mitigating or aggravating circumstances that you believe exist." That revision failed to capture several legal details. Of course, it is not a matter of the jurors believing circumstances exist; they have to be shown to exist, though elsewhere jurors can be persuaded that they exist. (Note again the insistence on circumstances simply existing or not, without acknowledging that the jury must evaluate the severity of the act.) Most seriously of all, the lawyers told me, I had changed the burden of proof. The prosecutors must show that aggravating circumstances exist, first of all, and second that they are not outweighed by mitigating circumstances. The defense does not have to prove that mitigating circumstances outweigh aggravating circumstances. To serve their own purposes, jurors might well begin deliberations by weighing mitigating against aggravating (being careful now not to count), without realizing that they were shifting the burden of proof. Because the materiality of any language depends on how different communities are invested in it, language is considered to be transparent both by jurors and by judges and lawyers. Written by lawyers, the language of jury instructions assumes that the jurors will, like the lawyers, know what is important and know what to do, that the genre will enable nonmembers to behave as members would.

21   No amount of explication, definition, or simplification can capture the specialized legal knowledge required for a just and fair decision, as defined by the court system. The legal community—and our society—needs these distinctions, established by law and precedent, to be maintained. The genre of jury instructions is meant to guide jurors in following that law. Yet the complexity of the law, the technical nature of its precedents, and, in short, the embeddedness of the genre in its community make it impossible for nonspecialists to understand fully as a specialist would, no matter how well-written, detailed, or rhetorically sophisticated the jury instructions.

22   Leading to the linguistic and technical complexity of jury instructions is the rhetorical complexity of the situation. Lawyers and judges are in the position of maintaining the law while needing to achieve their goals through the actions of others, the relatively ignorant jurors. Jurors are in the position of deciding another human being's fate based on society's values, while being told to disregard their instincts unless they conform to the law, a law they do not fully understand. The genre of jury instructions attempts to enact those behaviors, but, like all genres, its effects depend on the actions of politically and morally interested people. Jurors must somehow address or respond to the jury instructions, giving those instructions material consequence, but jurors can respond by acting against those instructions. This reality is revealed most explicitly in the concept of jury nullification, in which individual jurors vote not according to the evidence and the law but according to their beliefs about the rightness of the law, the oppression of the defendant's group, or other beliefs and values not represented in the jury instructions or the facts of the case. Even without such explicit political motivation or deliberateness, jurors often decide in ways that may or may not match even the jurors' understanding of the instructions they received. The most immediately significant genre in a capital case is the verdict, a genre with real consequences. Jury instructions try to influence that verdict, but their effectiveness depends not just on the legal community's ability to convey important specialist information but also on the jury's ability and willingness to conform to their expected role. Jury instructions also try to influence future legal actions, whether appeals of this particular case or future similar cases. The material effects of the genre for the legal community cannot be captured in the jury's actions or the verdict alone. Although designed to transcend the narrow interests of the legal community, jury instructions also return to that community, becoming another potential precedent and more specialist knowledge.

23   Tax forms, ballot questions, jury instructions—all genres designed precisely to bring specialist and nonspecialist communities together—all function in complex linguistic, informational, and rhetorical situations. All genres exist through and depend on human action, so these community-spanning genres, too, depend on the cooperation of participants from multiple communities, on people accepting the roles the genres assign to them and on being able to carry out the tasks expected of them. Since people in fact often have conflicting interests and motivations, the effects of such genres may be unpredictable. Lawyers and judges, for example, surely want a fair and just verdict, but their community's values also emphasize winning, not being overturned on appeal, and building reputations as well as bank accounts. The general populace from which jurors come also wants a fair and just verdict, but that desire interacts with popular notions of fairness and rightness and with individual moral differences, ideas about social injustices, and experiences with the legal system, as well as with concerns for a speedy return to jurors' regular lives and paychecks.

24   The communal agendas of those who create genres may conflict with the interests of those who use them—users who would ideally reproduce the ideologies and agendas of the legal community, but who do not. To say that the genre of jury instructions— and other similar genres—simply cross community borders is to simplify the complex interaction of individuals and groups, motives and agendas, and to ignore the conflicting consequences of one genre serving different groups. To understand more fully these genres is to understand more fully how the generic materialities are their uses-in-contexts, with serious effects on people's lives.

USING GENRE TO ACCESS COMMUNITY:
THE PERSONAL MEDICAL HISTORY GENRE AS "FORM OF LIFE"
— Anis Bawarshi —

25 As Bruce Herzberg describes it, the concept of discourse community is based on the assumption that "language use in a group is a form of social behavior, that discourse is a means of maintaining and extending the group's knowledge and of initiating new members into the group, and that discourse is epistemic or constitutive of the group's knowledge" (qtd. in Swales 21). Hence the idea of discourse community is built on the premise that what we know and do is connected to the language we use. Such an understanding acknowledges the materiality of language, but does not necessarily give us access and insight into the complex motives, relations, commitments, and consequences that accompany the use of language to get things done in specific situations, as Devitt's examination of jury instructions describes.

26 Analyzing genres within their lived contexts reveals to students, teachers, and researchers the material strength of those communities and their power over members and nonmembers alike. Whether examining legal, medical, or pedagogical genres, genre study gives us specific access to the sites of language use that make up communities, in all their complexity. When we use genre analysis as ethnomethodological technique, we not only gain access into communities, but also begin to recognize how "lived textualities" interact with and transform "lived experiences." Such recognition becomes especially significant when we are teaching students how to use language to participate more knowledgeably and critically in various sites of language use. Using the genre of the Patient Medical History Form as an example, I demonstrate how genre analysis gives access to the workings of discourse communities in a way that renders the idea of a discourse community a more tangible, helpful concept for teachers, students, and researchers.

27 Attention to the Patient Medical History Form (PMHF), a commonly used medical genre, suggests how focusing on a specific textual genre helps us to identify a discourse community by relating it to a specific site of interpersonal activity that most of us have experienced. The PMHF is a good way to understand something about how doctors function and how they treat us as patients. At the same time, it also serves to show that the community is not just a backdrop to language behavior, but a growing, moving environment that includes texts and speech as its constituents, just as people are its members. We compose our discourse communities as we write and speak within them. And genre is a key part of this process.

28 The idea of genre, despite the work of scholars in literary and rhetorical studies over the last few decades, is still more often than not understood as a transparent lens or conduit for classifying texts. The word *genre*, borrowed from French, means "sort" or "kind," and to study sorts or kinds of things is not thought to be as substantial as to study the things themselves. Genres appear to be transparent when they are understood as ways of classifying texts. But recent scholarship in genre theory has tried to dispel this view by stipulating genres to be language forms that have identifiable and changing roles in interpersonal relations and in larger collective contexts. One of the roots of the word genre is the Latin cognate *gener*, meaning to generate. This etymology suggests that genres *sort* and *generate*. Genres organize and generate the exchanges of language that characterize what we are referring to in this essay as discourse communities.

29 Carolyn R. Miller has defined genres as typified rhetorical ways of acting in recurring situations (159). Following Miller, Charles Bazerman defines genres as social actions. He writes:

30 Genres are not just forms. Genres are forms of life, ways of being. They are frames for social action [, . . .] locations within which meaning is constructed. Genres shape the thoughts we form and the communications by which we interact. Genres are the

> familiar places we go to create intelligible communicative action with each other and the guideposts we use to explore the unfamiliar. (19)

31 To claim that genres are environments within which familiar social actions are rhetorically enacted is to understand them as language practices. David Russell calls them *"operationalized* social action[s]" (512) within which communicants come to know specific situations as they enact them in language practices. The extent to which genres organize and generate discourse communities appears vividly in the example of the physician's office. A physician's office might be considered a local discourse community and part of a wider one insofar as its members share language practices and have comparable purposes. These purposes are enacted in social relations that are partly marked by the PMHF, a genre that within the medical profession is one of its Wittgensteinian "forms of life." As patients we recognize this form on our first visit to a physician as one that solicits information regarding our physical data (sex, age, height, weight, and so on) as well as medical history, including prior and recurring physical conditions, past treatments, and a description of current physical symptoms. Included in the genre is also a request for insurance carrier information and then a consent-to-treat statement and a legal release statement, which patients must sign. The form is at once a patient record, a legal document, and an element in a bureaucracy, helping the doctor treat the patient and presumably protecting the doctor from potential lawsuits.

32 But these are not the genre's only functions. The PMHF also helps organize and generate the social and rhetorical environments within which patients and doctors speak to one another. For example, the fact that the genre is mainly concerned with a patient's physical symptoms suggests that one can isolate physical symptoms and treat them with little to no reference to the patient's state of mind and the effect that state of mind might have on these symptoms. This genre assumes that body and mind are separate and also helps to perpetuate this belief. In so doing, the PMHF reflects Western notions of medicine, notions that are rhetorically naturalized and reproduced by the genre and that are in turn embodied in the way the doctor recognizes, interacts with, and treats the patient as a synecdoche of his or her physical symptoms. For example, it is not uncommon for doctors and nurses to say "I treated a knee injury today" or "The ear infection is in room 3" when referring to patients. The PMHF is at work on the individual, urging the conversion of a person into a patient (an embodied self) prior to his or her meeting with the doctor at the same time as it is at work on the doctor, preparing him or her to meet the individual as an embodied "patient." In this way, the genre is a site for the exchange of language within which participants influence one another and identify their discourse communities.

33 The mental state of patients may not be considered *material* to the injury or illness; conversely, the form tends to discourage patients' reporting of mental or emotional circumstances of injury and illness, with the result that they may be incompletely or inaccurately treated.

34 The PMHF is one of several related genres that constitute a community one could call "the physician's office." Each of these genres—which could include greetings, oral symptom descriptions, prescriptions, referrals, physical gestures, and explanatory metaphors—is a form of life that is part of other social practices (relations between doctors and patients, nurses and doctors, doctors and other doctors, doctors and pharmacists, and so on), all of which add up to what Amy Devitt has called "genre sets." As such a set, the physician's office is a multigenre community constituted by several interconnected genres, some of which may represent conditions of social conflict. Members of this community "play" various language games: they have multiple ways of identifying themselves and relating to others within the community. In this way genres help counter the idealized view of discourse communities as discursive utopias constituted by homogeneity and consensus. As Bazerman notes, "[G]enres, as perceived and used by individuals, become part of their regularized social relations, communicative landscape, and cognitive organization" (22). These social relations, communicative landscapes, and cognitive organizations, however, are always shifting, always multiple, as they are enacted by individuals within different genres. We can think of genres as the operational sites of discourse communities.

35 Teachers, students, and researchers gain ethnomethodological access to discourse communities through genre analysis, which enables them to observe how and why individuals use language in specific settings to make specific practices possible. Recognizing the presence of genres helps us to recognize the palpability and complexity of our discourse communities, to reduce their abstract, symbolic status, thereby making discourse communities more visible and accessible to ethnographic inquiry.

36 The following example, from the research of Anthony Paré, suggests the materialization of genre and its value for ethnographic inquiry. Paré records a portion of a conversation between a social work student, Michael, and his supervisor. The supervisor is responding to Michael's draft of an assessment report, a typical social work genre:

37 That's right. So you wrote here, "I contacted." You want to see it's coming from the worker, not you as Michael, but you as the worker. So when I'm sometimes in Intake and [working] as the screener, I write in my Intake Notes "the screener inquired about." . . . So it becomes less personal. You begin to put yourself in the role of the worker, not "I, Michael." [I]t's a headset; it's a beginning. And even in your evaluations . . . the same thing: as opposed to "I," it's "worker," and when we do a CTMSP for placement for long-term care, "the worker." So it positions us, I think. It's not me, it's my role; and I'm in the role of professional doing this job. (67)

38 In this example, we notice the extent to which the genre becomes the site for the exchange of language and social interaction. The student, Michael, is learning to "play a language game," the genre of the "assessment report." This exchange between social work student and supervisor takes place within the genre, a genre that constitutes the social roles and material relations of social workers—roles as impersonal observers and "professionals"—thus constituting, in part, the community of social work.

39 It is in the sum of exchanges such as this one, exchanges constituted by the various and sometimes conflicting genres used in different settings, that individuals compose in and compose discourse communities.

ACCESSING COMMUNITIES THROUGH THE GENRE OF ETHNOGRAPHY:
EXPLORING A PEDAGOGICAL GENRE
— Mary Jo Reiff —

40 In "The Life of Genre, the Life in the Classroom," Charles Bazerman describes genres as the "road maps" that student writers consult as they navigate "the symbolic landscape" (19). As typical responses to repeated social situations, genres are rhetorical maps that chart familiar or frequently traveled communicative paths and provide guideposts as writers adapt to unfamiliar academic terrain and study parts of society beyond the classroom. Thus understood, genre analysis is well suited for use in ethnographic approaches to writing pedagogy. Exploring the implications of genre for rhetorical instruction, Carolyn R. Miller observes, "For the student, genres serve as keys to understanding how to participate in the actions of a community" (165). Since genres embed and enact a group's purposes, values, and assumptions, they can illuminate a community's discursive behaviors; however, the question of how students gain entrance to and participate in this discursive landscape remains a source of debate.

41 Taking up the issue of genre analysis in writing instruction, Aviva Freedman poses the following question: "Can the complex web of social, cultural and rhetorical features to which genres respond be explicated at all, or in such a way that can be useful to learners?" (225). Freedman objects to studying genres outside the contexts in which they are found, abstracting them from living situations. Her concern is shared by David Bleich, who argues that genres—like all language use—are not eligible for study once they are considered to be independent of their contexts of use: "[T]he process of study lies always *within* the language-using society. There is no sense in which the language one tries to understand can be thought of as located outside the living situation in which the thinker (who is all the while using the language) is working" (122). Studying genres within the actual contexts of their use— within real human groups—requires "insider" research (Freedman 234), a type of research that can be carried out through the use of ethnography. With its emphasis on participant/observation and on hands-on attention to communities, ethnography enables students to examine communicative actions within living situations and to see first-hand how communities use genres to carry out social actions and agendas.

42   To understand genres as situated actions, Miller has advocated an ethnomethodological approach, one that "seeks to explicate the knowledge that practice creates" (155)—knowledge rooted in the materiality of circumstances and conditions of actual use of genres. Similarly, Bazerman has argued that "[b]y forging closer links with the related [enterprise] of [. . .] ethnomethodology, genre analysis can play" a major role in investigating communication within social organizations (23). I consider how ethnomethodology as an academic research method and ethnography as a genre of writing that is particularly useful in writing pedagogy can provide more authentic language tasks in classrooms and can give students better access to contexts of language use beyond the classroom.

43   Certainly ethnography has become an increasing presence in composition as a research method and a pedagogy. However, Wendy Bishop and others distinguish between the general research method of ethnography and the more focused ethnographic writing research, which usually explores particular sites of literacy or particular literacy practices. Clarifying this distinction, Beverly Moss notes, "While ethnography in general is concerned with describing and analyzing a culture, ethnography in composition studies is [. . .] concerned more narrowly with communicative behavior or the interrelationship of language and culture" (156). Ethnography in composition, particularly as a pedagogical approach, is concerned with the general as well as the particular: with the lived experience or behavior of a culture (as in anthropology or sociology) and with the way in which this behavior manifests itself rhetorically.

44   If ethnographies are understood as studies of communities and their social actions and genres taken to be rhetorical manifestations or maps of a community's actions, then genre analysis is an especially helpful path in ethnographic methodology. In order to investigate a community's social motives and actions, student ethnographers can examine the uses of language associated with these actions (the group's spoken and written genres) by gathering samples of the genre and analyzing what the rhetorical patterns reveal about the community—its purposes, its participants, and its values, beliefs, and ideologies. Ethnography is both a genre (a research narrative) and a mode of genre analysis—a research methodology used to grasp cultural beliefs and behaviors, often through the examination of genres, which are "frames for social action" (Bazerman 19). In "Observing Genres in Action: Towards a Research Methodology," Anthony Paré and Graham Smart propose how ethnographic inquiry and genre analysis work together. Understanding genre as "a rhetorical strategy enacted within a community," they say that "a full appreciation of the part that [social] roles play in the production and use of generic texts can only be gained by observing an organization's drama of interaction, the interpersonal dynamics that surround and support certain texts" (149). Ethnographic observation of a community that foregrounds genre analysis allows researchers to explore more fully the complexity of the group's social roles and actions, actions that constitute the community's repeated rhetorical strategies, or genres.

45   While students don't have extended periods to carry out ethnographic studies, they
can carry out what Bishop has labeled "mini-ethnographies," smaller-scale studies
that explore particular literacy events or local phenomena in a community. Marilyn
Chapman, in an essay on the role of genre in writing instruction, lists three main
teaching interests with regard to genre: "_learning genres_, or widening students' genre
repertoires; _learning about genres_, or fostering awareness [. . .] and _learning through
genres_ , or using genres as tools for thinking and learning in particular situations" (473).
Using ethnography in the classroom would address these goals and would have students
learn one research genre (ethnography), while they simultaneously use ethnographic
techniques to learn about and through other genres. As a result, incorporating
ethnography into the classroom ensures that all three of the above interrelated goals are
met, giving students access to the material practices of both the classroom community
and communities beyond the classroom.

46   With regard to the first goal, when students are assigned ethnographies, they learn
a new genre to add to their repertoire, a research genre that carries with it particular
purposes, participants, and agendas. According to Moss, the main purpose of this genre
is "to gain a comprehensive view of the social interactions, behaviors, and beliefs of a
community or a social group" (155). This purpose casts student researchers, as users of
the genre, into dual roles as both participants in the community and observers of the
community's interactions. Moss compares the ethnographer to a photographer who both
"takes pictures of the community" and is "in the picture at the same time" (154). The
process of inquiry and firsthand participant-observation entailed by this genre requires
that students engage in several rhetorical strategies: critical and reflective thinking (when
deciding upon what actions and artifacts to capture through pictures); what Clifford
Geertz called "thick description" (when developing the pictures so that the details
are vibrant and the images come to life); an awareness of the multiple audiences who
will view the pictures; and, as someone who is also "in the picture," development of
an ethos as an expert or producer of knowledge. These rhetorical strategies related
to purpose, audience, and persona give rise to a number of rhetorical features and
conventions. In order to address an audience and create a credible ethos, writers might
include a description of the data-collection methods, an explanation of the data, and a
discussion of their implications. To create a representation of lived experience, students
might incorporate details, dialogue, and direct quotations from community participants.
Students learn a new genre as they employ patternings of language and rhetorical
strategies to create an empirically grounded representation of social realities.

47   The second goal, learning about genres and fostering genre awareness, is also
accomplished through the use of ethnography. Since the main goal of an ethnographer,
according to Moss, is to gain "increased insight into the ways in which language
communities work" (170), it follows that the oral and written genres of groups will play a
central role in the investigation of the social context of language use.

48   Geertz defines ethnographies as "interpretations of interpretations" (9), meaning that
students must study the genres that community members use to interpret their contexts in
order to fully understand and themselves interpret the community.

49   For example, Susan, a pre-law student in my advanced composition class, carried out
a mini-ethnography on the law community. In order to find out how novice members
of the community become socialized to the values, beliefs, and knowledge of the
community, Susan considered genres such as opinions, wills, deeds, and contracts; she
focused her study on the genre of case briefs. She collected samples of constitutional
law briefs, which, she recognized, "illustrated the legal community's shared value of
commitment to tradition, as well as the need for a standard and convenient form of
communicating important and complex legal concepts." While

50   Susan also conducted interviews and observed lawyers in a small local firm, the genre analysis was the focus of her study, which helped to teach others about the habits and traditions of the law community. She learned about the generic features of case briefs, such as the technical terminology, rigid format, and formal style, and she became more aware of how these formal practices reflected and reinscribed the goals of the community. Recognizing that all the briefs follow the same format of presenting sections labeled "case information," "facts of the case," "procedural history," "issue," "holding," and "court reasoning," she surmised that "[e]ven the rigid structure of the format can help with our analysis by suggesting the community's emphasis on logic and order, which are two esteemed values of the profession." For students like Susan, using genre as a site for ethnographic inquiry cultivates a consciousness of the rhetorical strategies that characterize the daily work of a specific kind of professional community. By learning a community's language through its genres, students then have a more realistic sense of what it is to be a member of the community.

51   The third genre-related teaching interest is learning through genres, using genres to think about and understand particular situations. Ethnography gives students experience with genre analysis and with how research processes change received genres of reporting knowledge. As ethnographers seek to describe a community, they use various genres for research. Before beginning the study, students may write letters to seek permission to observe groups, or they might write proposals for their research or research plans and agendas. During the research, they use several genres such as field notes, journals or activity logs, project chronologies or summaries, progress reports, interview transcripts, even maps. When the research is completed, they may try to write in other genres that the situation warrants, like thank-you notes, self-assessments, peer assessments, or abstracts. Class time might be spent discussing the genre of the interview or the different purposes of descriptive versus analytic field notes. These genres are resources for supporting or extending thinking. Students learn a research genre that depends on genre analysis; they also learn to use, adapt, and possibly change a variety of genres during the different processes of inquiry.

52   When students carry out ethnographies, they become researchers who are also active social figures participating in and observing how people integrate their language genres with their wider collective purposes. Shifting the usual teacher/student relationship, students assume the role of investigators who are learning to speak from their own authority as researchers. As a result, classrooms become, in part, research sites at which all members are investigating, teaching, and learning. The research genre of ethnography creates a culture of inquiry, with language and genre the foci that lead to combined knowledge of rhetoric, collective values, and the broader purposes of different communities.

53   Students in these classrooms also help to create their own community while observing "meaningful discourse in authentic contexts," thus accomplishing what Freedman defines as the necessary criteria for learning genres: "exposure to written discourse" combined with "immersion in the relevant contexts" (247). Student ethnographers are able to study the uses of language and genre within real contexts, situations in which "speakers are alive, functioning, changing and interacting" (Bleich 120). Because ethnography is both a research genre (which functions for academic communities) and an approach to genre analysis (which explores communicative actions in groups outside the classroom), ethnographic work in class enables students to compose communities while composing in communities.

Credit

Queer Texts, Queer Contexts

HARRIET MALINOWITZ

1 *I have come increasingly to recognize that most learning in most settings is a communal activity, a sharing of the culture. It is not just that the child must make his knowledge his won, but that he must make it his own in a community of those who share his sense of belonging to a culture. It is this that leads me to emphasize not only discovery and invention but the importance of negotiating and sharing – in a word, of joint culture creating as an object of schooling and as an appropriate step en route to become a member of the adult society in which one lives out one's life.*
        Jerome Bruner, Actual Minds, Possible Worlds

2 *Axiom 1: People are different from each other. It is astonishing how few respectable conceptual tools we have dealing with this self-evident fact.*
        Eve Kosofsky Sedgwick, Epistemology of the Closet

3 *While taking a writing course several semesters ago, I was inhibited about writing any pieces involving gay subject matter which would then have to be read to the class. I believe all gay and lesbian writers confront this in their writing and in writing workshops, and at times compromise. However, it is the act of compromising that is lethal to the writer. It stunts our growth and maturity as writers. In this class, I hope to continue searching for the voice I have spent years trying to develop and allow the person I kept stifling to grow.*
        Student in a lesbian/gay writing class

4 *I want to be able to express myself as a gay man without fear of ridicule (or physical violence) by fellow classmates.*
        Student in a lesbian/gay writing class

5 *We're here. We're queer. Get used to it.*
        Queer Nation chant

6 In the last few years, there has been a subtle but persistent change in the classroom climate around the subject of sexual orientation. It's not that students have suddenly and universally become emphatic and comfortable with lesbian and gay existence; but they do seem to regard the issue itself with much less suspicion or surprise than they used to. In fact, students often introduce the subject themselves, either in classroom discussions or essay topics. Although five years ago, for instance, participants at the Conference for College Composition and Communication (CCC) were arguing for the "inclusion" of lesbian and gay issues in the writing classroom, teachers now are recognizing that lesbian and gay issues are already in the writing classroom – because they have become a part of our students' collective consciousness.

7   Like the eighteenth-century narrator of Laurence Sterne's *Tristram Shandy* – who could not write his autobiography fast enough because, while he attempted to recount the events of this past, the present continuously heaped more material upon him which itself had to be recorded – I have found that writing of this book couldn't keep up with the rapid pace of the lesbian and gay movement in the world outside of my study. I began, three years ago, intending to create a classic argument for "inclusion" based on widespread lesbian and gay invisibility in composition and its contexts, academy and society. Yet in the ensuring time, the mainstream media, responding to various social forces, have produced dramatically different coverage of the lesbian and gay issues than they ever did before, changing the conceptual landscape for everyone. At one time the absence of lesbian and gay issues or existence in news periodicals, literature, academic texts, television, film, and other media was a source of chronic cynical observation by lesbian and gay people; right now it is unlikely that a day will go by in which a lesbian- and gay- themed news story does not appear in, say, the *New York Times* – and there is an excellent chance that it will appear on the front page. The 1992 presidential race propelled lesbian and gay existence onto the front lines of campaign rhetoric and nation discourse; Pat Buchanan's speech at the Republican convention, Ross Perot's declaration (later reconsidered) that he would not place lesbian or gays in Cabinet posts, and the candidate Bill Clinton's ill-fated promise to end the ban on lesbians and gays in the military all provoked massive pollster activity in which the opinions of "people in the street" and citizens randomly selected by telephone were relayed to a public deciding how to position itself. Lesbians and gays moved quite abruptly from the problems and "invisibility" to a dazzling and confusing new "visibility."

8 We are now in what many activists, lobbyists, journalists, and profiteers have enthusiastically dubbed the "gay nineties." Nineteen ninety-three was certainly a watershed year for visibility. The National March on Washington for Lesbian and Gay Rights, the largest civil rights march in history, was carried live fro seven hours on C-SPAN and was picked up as a headline news item by virtually all major print and electronic media. Debates about lesbian and gays in the military involved the courts, the Cabinet, and the Congress, and brought gay activists to the White House for an unprecedented chat with the president. Lesbians were called "chic" for the first time in anyone's memory and graced the covers of magazines like *Newsweek*, *Vogue*, *New York*, and the "Style" section of the *New York Times*; even *Cosmopolitan* and *Redbook* scrambled to ride the trend.

9 At the same time, the issue of gays in the military developed to the point where the mantra "Don't ask, don't tell" mandated the hypocrisy of silence as federal policy. "Chic" lesbians still grappled with unemployment discrimination, inadequate healthcare, violence, and loss of child custody (Acey 1993). And referenda appeared on ballots around the country in record numbers to ban the deployment of sexual orientation as a protected civil rights category. Some of these explicitly insisted that homosexuality be discouraged in school – including state-funded higher education – as perverse, abnormal, and wrong. Spurious nomenclature such as "community standards" and "traditional family values" was (unsurprisingly) invoked, as it has been in past incarnations of reaction to bending the rules of gender and sexuality, and groups gave themselves names such as "American Family Association" and "Oregon Citizens Alliance" (Goldberg 1993) to smooth a patina of warmth and populism over their efforts to ensure democratic, ratified pop up frequently in classroom discourse, it was still the contestedness of lesbians' and gays' claim to "rights" that primarily framed the discussion – not people's complex experience as citizen-subjects. As one gay student of mine commented ironically, "I love hearing the question of whether or not I should be allowed to exist tossed around in a 'lively debate.'"

10 In the writing class, the reduction of lesbian and gay existence to a polarized "rights" debate may be of interest to teachers who are longtime fans of capital punishment and abortion as topics for infinite argument. But for many others in the composition community, helping student find their place in the sphere of academic and public discourse has come to be seen as something far more complex than the liberal tradition of argument would allow. As the editors of a landmark anthology of essays on postmodern rhetoric put it, "Language is a way of contending, in all senses of the word, with the processes through which discourse shapes human thought and social relations in a context of change and struggle" (Harkin and Schilb 1991, 6.) for this reason, questions about who our students are, about who we are as teachers of language, and about the diversity of variables involved in helping diverse people to write and learn have become important in composition. A prodigious literature has in fact emerged, the aim of which is to reshape our consciousness of how different groups of people make meaning in a multiliteracied environment.

11 Yet even within this new way of thinking about writing – one which knows the importance of recognizing students' gender, race, and class identities because they are the sites in which subjectivities (and, inescapably, knowledge) are produced – the complexities of sexual identity are rarely brought into the picture (except, perhaps, in those instances when one is reeling off a list of identity-markers that teachers ought to "consider"). In fact, while lesbian and gay studies curricula have proliferated in colleges around the country (and even, in rare cases, high schools), and lesbian and gay scholarship is now being published copiously across the disciplines, remarkably little critical examination of homophobia and lesbian and gay reality has penetrated the generally flexible borders of the self-consciously interdisciplinary field of rhetoric and composition. In the last few years, anecdotal accounts of pedagogical experiments have surfaced at conferences and in carefully selected "multicultural" anthologies. Yet our understanding of lesbian and gay subjectivities – and of the role of sexual identity in producing discourse generally – remains quite limited.

12 I am proposing, quite simply, that the field of composition find out about its lesbian and gay students. The wave of national publicity currently surrounding lesbian and gay people has done little to reduce them from the abstractions they have always been. In an essay about teaching a freshman composition class whose theme was AIDS, Peter Bowen (1993, 153) hilariously and poignantly captures many heterosexual students' distilled notions of gay people when he describes an assignment in which they were asked to imagine being gay for a few hours:

13 [J]ust as some students strategically evade the assignment, others completed it by evasion as the modus operandi of homosexuality. "It's easy to hide it," one student's narrative journey began, while another simply wished she "could just be open about who and what" she was. Devoid of any sense of pleasure, desire, or romance, there "gay" narratives construct their protagonists as guilty, shame-ridden fugitives, who, when they were not "looking over" their "shoulder" to avoid detection, were looking forward with dread and shame to the prospect of coming out to family and friends. So intensely did students connect homosexuality with concealment that at least two women came out as gay men in their journal entries. While such testimonials, which were often disqualified in the last line ("but thank God, I'm not gay"), frequently empathized with repression of gay people, they also preserved that oppression through their spectacular reconstruction of the closet.

14 If this is a common conception of the back rooms of ordinary citizens, rich and famous lesbians and gays don't seem to round out the picture, either. Though superstars such as Martina Navratilova, k. d. lang, and Ian McKellen, for example, are now "out," the sheer factuality of their lesbian and gay existence is remarkably satisfying to a public habituated to consuming the detailed "meanings" of its idols' lives. The risks that artists and athletes (as well as virtually all other lesbians and gays in our society) take in coming out, the rewards that motivate and enable them to come out, the ways they calculate those risks and rewards, the factors that position them to negotiate that calculation, the ways they locate and define and propel themselves within the master narratives of hegemonic heterosexual culture, the communities and identities they form within and in opposition to that culture – all of these things produce particular sorts of relationships to the world that have everything to do with who they "are." these are the sorts of things that teachers of writing need to know about if they are to help their students "contend" with that world through language.

15 Creating an academic environment in which the complexities of lesbian and gay subjectivity can enter public discourse will, first of all, entail "outing" realms of experience, fear, feeling, and prejudice that have not been substantively dealt with in our classes and departments before. Of course, this won't be easy, or it would have been done already. Behind the media glitz and hype, most academic institutions and the communities that contain them are *still* homophobic enough to discourage teachers and students from coming out of even speaking out strongly for change. Many schools and colleges still lack policies against discrimination based on sexual orientation.1 And social visibility and political progress produce backlash; gay youth who are "out" in school have long faced verbal abuse and physical violence, raising their truancy and dropout rates (Tracey 1990; Comstock 1991), and anti lesbian and antigay violence continues to escalate. In *The Women's Review of Books,* Felice Yeskel (1992) described the "increasingly organized and vocal" backlash on her University of Massachusetts campus after organizations and services for lesbian, gay, and bisexual students were put in place: homophobic graffiti, harassment, and intimidation impeded efforts to deliver a gay-affirmative quality of education and campus life. Various attempts to curb lesbian and gay art and scholarship get launched periodically, such as Jesse Helms's war on funding criteria at the National Endowment for the Arts, the fracases that erupted around Robert Mapplethorpe's' work at the Smithsonian in Cincinnati, and mass ad hominem attacks like the Briggs Initiative, which a decade and a half ago tried to ban lesbians and gays from teaching in California schools. (It was defeated after a concerned statewide mobilization of the gay community.) lesbian and gay scholarly work still has dubious cachet on a resume – outside of a cadre of avant–garde institutions are departments it can, in fact, render a job applicant unemployment in many cases2 – and has only barely begun to be suggested as a category of proposal or submission for conferences, journals, or other professional publications in composition and rhetoric, even when their theme is "multiculturalism" or "diversity." On a broader scale, people don't speak out when it might mean coming out because aside from jobs, they risk losing homes, children, and legal rights, as well as community, friendship, and respect. Many lesbians and gay men have been estranged and disowned by parents and siblings in what may strike some as primitive rites of ostracism which are yet frequently practiced in otherwise "close" and "liberal" families.

I have been involved with lesbian and gay activism, performance, and writing for more than fifteen years. Yet I am also a lesbian teacher who, until four years ago, hesitated to come out to my students en masse and to many of my colleagues – except in protected parts of the "ivory closet" (Escoffier 1990), such as women's studies programs. I did come out to individual students, usually those I perceived to be gay or progressive. I believed in the political importance of being out, because closeted gay people contribute to the conspiracy of lies that render the false impression that species we call people is generically heterosexual. So I asked myself what I had to lose by coming out to my students. In my relationship to them, wasn't I the one with the greater amount of power? Of course, the worst scenarios I could image, should the students homophobic ally rebel, involved violence. Other retributive acts I envisioned were ones which I was reported for obscenity in the classroom or otherwise harassed. I surmised that the New York City colleges in which I then taught part-time were less likely than some others to support the actions of students who did such things, though I had no clearly articulated bedrock of safety upon which to rest this hopeful conjecture. If these school did have antidiscrimination policies including sexual orientation, they certainly had not been publicized adequately to ally my own fears or the fears of others – faculty or students – in the same position. But besides the fear of such concrete reprisals or even violence, I feared something else, and that was the loss of the warm, open, supportive relationship I liked to have with my students, even if it was shakily based on false premises.

I can hypothesize that the closeted gay students in my classes remain silent out of some of the same fears. Although a number of students have come out to me privately, or have implicitly come out to the class, only one student out of all of the mainstream classes has ever explicitly come out publicly (and that was done hesitantly, as a gesture of solidarity after *I* came out). However, many students have had occasion to make or write about their dislike of gay people. Those times when I have asked them to read and discuss a gay-themed article or essay, there have usually been at least some students who have either laughed, expressed hostility (such as, recently, "Gay people are getting too bold these days"), or, when challenged by an idea or a fact they hadn't know, become defiantly skeptical. This has happened even in classes that have talked and written about a variety of other social issues and oppressions – classes of students who have expressed their outrage about racism, sexism, ageism, anti-Semitism, and other isms, from rhetorical positions ranging from the political to the sentimental. Usually, they will attempt to mitigate their own anger and derision by citing ostensibly liberal rationales: sexual orientation is "private," "nobody's business"; they don't mind what people do in their homes, they just don't like to see two men holding hands or kissing on the street or in the subway; they just don't like to see boys dressed or acting like girls; they have known a gay person at work, in school, or in the community, and "accepted" the person just like anyone else as long as the person kept quiet about his or her sex life. Some of them are anxious to make it clear that they are not "prejudiced," and frequently deflect attention away from their homophobic feelings about gay people in general by invoking images of transvestites, transsexuals, and pederasts. By overlaying the actual discussion with what in usual social terms is a hyperbolized one, they seem to feel that their negative reactions are justified, in that they target what are generally perceived as extreme cases of sickness and absurdity. Others frankly acknowledge their antigay feelings and beliefs, secure that cultural precedent has rendered them understandable and acceptable. A *New York Times* article on homophobia cited research which demonstrated that "[antigay] hostility is far more accepted among large numbers of Americans than in bias against other groups," and that "white teenagers surveyed were reluctant to advocate open bias against racial and ethnic groups, they were emphatic about disliking homosexual men and women. They are perceived 'as legitimate targets which can be openly attacked'" (Goleman 1990). Within composition, David Bleich (1989) has written about the results of a writing assignment he gave that asked students to describe a conversation with someone about homosexuality. He provides excerpts from the student texts that illustrate the majority feelings – about 60 percent – that "homosexuality was disgusting and gross – the most frequently used adjectives – and many men who did not actually advocate either extermination or gay bashing felt it was excusable to either beat up gays or 'throw them out the window' if one of them made a sexual proposal to them." Bleich found, however, a strong and correlation between sexist and heterosexist forms of domination and belief: only one woman said she would react violently to a proposed sexual encounter, and "no women advocated mass extermination, though one said that bisexuals (who spread AIDS) 'don't deserve to live'" (23). Clearly, this sentiment extends far beyond the classroom: lesbians and gays are virtually the only group left facing mass discrimination with no federally mandated civil rights protection, despite such a painfully obvious need for it. And as gay legal scholar Richard Mohr (1988) has pointed out, in the absence of that protection, complaining of discrimination can simply compound it, since the voicing of the problem publicly identifies the complainant as a stigmatized person and enlarges the sphere of vulnerability.

18   The focus of multicultural curricula has evolved in recent decades not as an abstract need to make education itself more diverse, but rather in the context of political developments and liberation movements in the nation and the world. Our society's gradual extrication from the mythical notion of itself as monocultural is probably more the result of the dialectic between academia and activism than of anything that has happened strictly in one or the other of those realms. As various groups have resisted social marginalization and disenfranchisement, they have also argued for the importance of representation in academic texts, syllabi, policies, and programmatic

agendas. Divisiveness within the academic community about the appropriateness of such inclusion has largely emerged from divergent notions of the place of ideology itself in the classroom. In composition, the argument at its surface level has been about whether or not ideology belongs in a writing class; at a deeper level, it is about *which* ideology belongs in a writing class, since new historicists, deconstructionists, social constructionists, and liberatory and critical pedagogues have repeatedly shown that culture is never neutral, unmediated, or value-free. Academicians who resisted idealogy just at that moment which is ceased to be white, male, and Western were really fighting not just academic, but vast social and political change. By the same token, writing instructors who exclude lesbian and gay existence from the sphere of knowledge and inquiry drawn upon every semester are, consciously or not, enacting resistance to a form of social reconceptualization that threatens to erode yet another set of borders which have heretofore demarcated comfortably recognizable zones of insiders and outsiders.

The Idea of a Lesbian and Gay Culture

19 Often, when lesbian and gay existence is discussed at all, it is consigned to the category of "personal identity." Yet given that a new constituency literally had to form and mobilize itself in order to challenge a society staunchly safeguarding homogenously heterosexual constructions of itself in its media, its government, its arts, its advertising, its military apparatus, its religious and educational institutions, and its notions of the family – with exceptions labeled "deviant" – to insist on interpreting that difference individualistically as a matter of "personal identity" promotes an amplified form of disempowerment. What is probably most notable about the late twentieth-century lesbian and gay liberation movement is that by creatively using the new "social space" afforded by contemporary work and domestic arrangements (D'Emilio 1983a, 1983b) and usurping the imperative silence of closetedness, it has made possible the emergence of what some would call a new "culture."

20 Much has been at stake for lesbian and gay people, not only in coming together and mobilizing *as* a group, but in promoting a sense of this group as a group to the society at large. In "Beyond Tolerance" (1965), Robert Paul Wolff argued that pluralistic democracy is limited by its tolerance only for established social groups that it *already* recognizes as coherent, even if somewhat odd, configurations; tolerance does not extend to idiosyncratic individuals. "One might expect," he reasoned, "that a society which urges its citizens to 'attend the church or synagogue of your choice' would be undismayed by an individual who chose to attend no religious service at all" (37). Similarly, "agnostic conscientious objectors are required to serve in the armed forces, while those who claim even the most bizarre religious basis for their refusal are treated with ritual tolerance and excused by the courts" (41). Society, he said, is willing to extend the tolerance of pluralism only to groups it can distinguish as legitimate because they already conform in some recognizable way to dominant social principles; those that are "beyond the pale" are "treated as crackpots, extremists, or foreign agents" (44). Pluralist theory grants every "genuine" social group a chance to partake in democratic decision making and to receive its rightful piece of pie: "Any policy urged by a group in the system must be given respectful attention, no matter how bizarre." Yet, "[b]y the same token, a policy or principle which lacks legitimate representation has no place in the society, no matter how reasonable or right it may be" (45). Almost uncannily foretelling what would happen when a lesbian and gay political constituency would manifest itself thirty years later, Wolff wrote, "With bewildering speed, an interest can move from 'outside' to 'inside' and its partisans, who have been scorned by the solid and established in the community, become presidential advisers and newspaper columnists" (44).

21 For lesbians and gays, then, as for other groups (such as, for example, deaf people or speakers of Black English), self-definition as a social community or "culture" has been instrumental in gaining access to recognition and entitlements. For instance though virtually everyone agrees that federal civil rights bill protecting lesbians and gays are fighting prominently for such a bill locates them within the familiar tradition of other groups, such as women and African Americans, whore long struggles for equality are well known and oft recited within popular lore. It is this familiarity that engenders enough public sympathy to produce local gains such as custody victories, domestic partnership benefits, bereavement leave, survivor tenancy rights, lesbian and gay studies courses, and occasional spots on sitcoms.

22   Anthropologists have attempted in various ways to define culture though they have never reached absolute consensus. Most contemporary definitions suggest that a culture is a repository of shared ideas, systems, and meanings that find expression in patterns of behavior and custom within a particular social group. It is the *ideational* component that defines the culture: what the people *learn* more than what they *do*, though it is quite probable that they will have in common certain things that they do insofar as they arise from their common knowledge. The linguist M. A. K. Halliday (1978) describes a culture as "an edifice of meanings – a semiotic construct" and maintains that "language *actively symbolizes the social system, representing metaphorically in its patterns of variation the variation that characterizes human cultures*" (5-3; emphasis his). Arthur C. Danto (1990, 33) describes the way cultures become conscious of themselves:

23   A culture exists as a culture in the eyes of its members only when they perceive that their
          practices are seen as a special in the eyes of other cultures. Until the encounter with the
          Other, those practices simply define the form of lice the members of the culture live,
          without any particular consciousness that it is just one form of life among many.

24   Halliday's and Danto's constructs suggest ways of conceptualizing "lesbian and gay culture," and in fact, this conceptualization has taken on wide currency. Lesbians and gays in the twentieth century have lived with an acute sense of difference within, and the definition by, the culture of the Other, and have shared meanings in some loose form at least since communities based on sexual orientation began forming in the U.S. in the 1940s (D'Emilio 1983a, 1983b). This sense of difference was for a long time based largely on exclusion and negative representation: existing outside familiar, legal, and religious sanctions, popularly portrayed as immortal and predatory, homosexuals when they met at all constituted a largely underground "culture" prior to the Stonewall uprising of 1969 that marked the beginning of mass resistance and liberation. Since then, an extensive network of cultural machinery has proliferate: there are gay and lesbian bookstores, churches, periodicals, plays and theatre companies, comedy clubs, books and presses, film festivals, resorts and cruises, legal and medical practices, political groups, parties, caucuses, and openly gay candidates, social organizations, families, artificial insemination centers, marches, sporting events, and academic programs.

Problems with "Identity" and the Construction of "Community"

25   Although many cite this boom in the artifacts of lesbian and gay identity as evidence of "culture" – or, as it is more widely called, "community" – we happen to be living in a time and place where the very notion of community based on shared identity is being heavily interrogated. The lesbian and gay community, along with the women's community, communities of color, and other communities of affinity is torn between those who posit a sense of group coherence based on one shared characteristic and those who deconstruct the premise of coherence, insisting that identity is multiple and fragmented and that "communities" predicted on identification alone are illusory, and thus fragile and doomed on implosion. They are fragile not only because the multiple threads of our identities intersect in exceedingly complex and unpredictable ways,

and one simple strand may very well be an unreliable basis upon which to forge sociopolitical alliances – but also because the meanings of even seemingly singular parts of our identities are unstable and evade consensus. For instance, when I asked several undergraduate students who call themselves lesbian or gay what they meant when they described themselves that way, some explained that it meant being *attracted to* the same gender, others that it meant *identifying with* the same gender, others meant a felling of "Otherness" or difference from those who conformed to gender roles, and so on. In a graduate seminar populated mainly by lesbian and gay students, some said they felt their gayness was something they had been born with while others said it was something they had chosen; some chose it because of same-gender attraction, some because it felt more "natural," and others – particularly women – because they felt that heterosexuality was an oppressive institution; and some saw it was a lifelong state, while others saw it as a ephemeral or situational state. This variety of definitions seems to be fairly typical of the "lesbian and gay community" at large: people may share a word with which they define themselves, but the condition signified by that word does not seem to be shared.

26   These two ways of viewing "identity" – as something that can be a basis for community formation and liberatory social change, on the one hand, and on the other hand as a construction so particularized and idiosyncratically realized that the notion of a "group identity" becomes diminished to the level of a wistful fiction – have been weighted against each other recently – primarily in academic, but also in activists, spheres. The debate rages not only between opposing camps, but also intrapersonally. If, for example, we accept that the category "woman" doesn't really exist but has been first a patriarchal, and then a feminist, falsely unitary invention – as postmodern feminist theorists such as Judith Butler (1990), Julia Kristeva (1986), and Nancy Fraser, and Linda Nicholson (1990) contend – must we concomitantly accept forfeiting proactive strategies such as the fight for safe and legal abortion, birth control, and equal pay, and the fight against rape, sexual harassment, battering, and social inequity? If "woman" doesn't exist, can any feminist agenda exist? Similarly, what happens to the category "lesbian and gay" – a category in which membership has at various points through out the twentieth century meant risking police raids and imprisonment, street violence, incarceration in mental institutions, expulsion from jobs, families and religious institutions, loss of child custody, dishonorable discharge from (or prohibition from entering) the military, McCarthyite inquisitions, disqualification from employment in education or government, and general social pariahhood – when we attempt to dissolve it? What does it mean in 1994, when the lesbian and gay rights movement is experiencing unprecedented political power and the notion that the group is entitled to "rights" is being argued and even accepted to a far larger degree than ever before, to say that to call even accepted to a far larger degree than ever before, to say that to call oneself a "lesbian" or a "gay man" is a totalizing and ultimately meaningless fiction? In other words, how can we destabilize a category without also abandoning our claim to material and social entitlement and our repudiation of marginalization and prejudice? Or, as feminist theorist Susan Bordo (1990, 153) has put it, "Most of our institutions have barely begun absorbing the message of modernist social criticism; surely, it is too soon to let them off the hook via postmodern heterogeneity and instability."

27   Yet on the other hand, what does it mean to cling to old, comfortable identity categories for certain pragmatic reasons when we have deconstructed them precisely *because* in crucial ways they really weren't working, even for the communities built upon them? The lesbian and gay "community" has experienced the contestation and disruption of the very "affirmative" meanings with which it attempted to usurp old, homophobic ones. For example, many lesbian feminists in the 1970s felt that lesbianism was a matter of political choice and commitment in which gender, rather than sexuality,

was the fundamental unifying factor; many gay men in the 1970s felt that gayness was most aptly expressed by sexual liberation; and many lesbians in the 1980s and 1990s have likewise claimed same-sex attraction and freedom of sexual expression as definitive properties of lesbian existence, and depicted 1970s-style lesbian feminism as an antisex, repressive regime. People of color and members of other ethnic groups have said that white gays and lesbians built a false, solipsistic, and racist image of "community" based on a gay-versus-straight opposition that was reductionistic of their personal and political experience. Many gay civil rights activists and professionals have been called "assimilationists" by radicals, while radicals have been called "extremists" and "too confrontational," and have been accused of tarnishing an otherwise improved public image for lesbians and gays. Many gays yearn for the right to marry (mass weddings have been performed at each March on Washington, as spectators wept and applauded); others have found spiritual redemption in milieux of radical promiscuity. Separatists and nationalists have been criticized for promoting hatred and reverse bigotry, while they in turn have accused others of self-denigration, limited vision, and misguided fear of militancy. Many have felt that they acceptance of lesbians and gays into the military would be an important political step, while others – particularly those affiliated with feminist and leftist politics – have disparaged that goal for its implicit endorsement of a reactionary institution. Some feel that the all-inclusive word "queer" accurately describes anyone, regardless of their sexual behavior, who wants to reject the norm of heterosexual conformity by claiming the appellation, while others feel it is politically essential to distinguish between those who are "lesbian or gay" and those who are "straight," or to register the unequal status of lesbians and gay men in a movement that has not eradicated male privilege. Bisexuals have claimed that their existence inherently problematizes such binaries and that insistence on polarization has left their needs and perspectives ignored, while gays and straights have respectively attempted to rein scribe bisexuals as "real" denizens of specific identity categories.

28   In short, these countless other arguments have not only divided the "community," but have led to the production in the gay press, at rallies, in course, and in social situations of ongoing metanarratives about the community's fragmentation. When queer theorist Ed Cohen (1991, 71-72) began his title of a rumination on gay identity and community with the question "Who are 'We'?" he was voicing an undercurrent of unease with absolute definitions that by the late 1980s ran like a fault line beneath much "community" work and activity. He writes in his first paragraph:

29   I often leave [gay and lesbian studies] meetings wondering how these people ended up in the same room with each other, thinking it's a miracle that any mutual understanding exists, and trying to figure out what in the world we have in common. . . . I mean, I'd like to have the feeling – as one reading group participant recently characterized his feeling about gay bars in the 1970s – that gay and lesbian studies was a place where we didn't have to explain to anyone "who we are." However my visceral response belies this characterization: the most often I find myself at these collocations, the more often the nausea in my stomach seems to tell me that "I" have no idea "who 'we' are."

30   Writing this book from 1993 to 1994, I too have lost the certainty about "who 'we' are" that at one point galvanized my choice of a dissertation topic. Originally, I conceived this theme rather simply: lesbians and gays were a group still neglected in academia's movement toward inclusiveness of diverse social groups and particularly in composition's interest in "multiculturalism." I believe that an argument pointing out this exclusion and its debilitating effects on students would lead to the filling in of a gap. Today, I still partly believe that only my concept of what I started out calling "lesbian and gay reality" has shifted away from something pertaining to a collection of identifiable bodies with clearly marked and recognizable ways of knowing and experiencing.

Instead, I imagine a more amorphous condition that anyone might have, and that might be had or interpreted in myriad ways – though some do seem to feel that they experience it in ways that are shared by others. Partly because of this new way of thinking about who "we" are and partly for other reasons which I will discuss later, the meaning of "inclusion" as a goal has been thrown into question.

31   My conceptual shift probably started when I began to read about essentialism and became convinced that much of my political development – which was heavily rooted in identity politics – had been based on assumptions that one must be able to effectively generalize about a group in order to make meaning and bring about change regarding its numbers' experiencing and conditions. I can, in fact, remember many times when, faced with the contradictions of feminist (which was my generative political experience), I groped in a panic for resolving explanations, rather than admit – let alone embrace – the fact that there were significant "truths" to be learned from the contradictions themselves. For instance, when someone would sincerely ask me to explain what "feminism" actually was, I would feel overwhelmed at my perceived task of amalgamating the many feminist perspectives I knew into coherent statement which suggested a clear common denominator. The task was especially difficult since I was alternately around feminists who refuted Freud's idea that biology is destiny; feminists who maintained that women's gentle and antiviolent "nature" was superior to men's natural aggression; feminists who thought that gender differences were entirely the result of cultural constructs; feminists who thought that gender differences were the most organic, significant, and intractable feature of civilization; feminists who wanted social parity with men; feminists who wanted total separation from men; feminists who saw economics as the root of women's oppression – etcetera. Yet it never occurred to me in those days to simply say that "feminism" was not just one thing, but a plethora of things, all which had to do with ways of rethinking meanings of gender – even though I had to rack my brains, and always unsuccessfully, to find a way around that simple and, one would think, obvious fact.

32   I remember a time in the summer of 1980 when my family visited me at the country house where I lived while I was in a creative writing program. We were going out for a walk and it had gotten chilly; my stepfather had not brought a jacket, so I offered to lend a sweater. My mother instantly became anxious at the idea of him wearing what she felt was a "woman's" sweater, but knowing of my feminism and anticipating a polemical reaction, she defended herself by remarking sardonically, "I suppose you're going to say there's really no difference between men and women." "Actually," I answered, "I think there are enormous differences between men and women. I just don't think there are big differences between sweaters." I thought it was a clever answer that undercut what I perceived as her "conventional" anxiety about maintaining proper gendered order and her lampooning of my feminism. Yet what I think actually happened was that, calculating that I couldn't possibly dent her bipolar notions of gender, I automatically relocated my defense to another "feminism" which I presented as a sort of "bottom line." In other words, she made her move based on her belief that "feminism" was one thing; I made my countermove by conveying that assumption that it was another thing altogether, and in such a way as if to say, "Where did you ever get that idea?" Yet in truth, both of our notions of "feminism" came from prominent discourses of the time, and I just easily could have argued from hers if it had promised to be effective. Nevertheless, even beyond the parameters of our argument I blotted out consciousness of the multiplicity of meanings that were clearly contained under that umbrella heading "feminism," as if surrendering the certainty of a singular position would leave me – us, feminists – desperately vulnerable, unpositioned and unequipped to answer what felt like (but, in fact, wasn't) the singular force of patriarchal oppression.

33   Just as "feminism" seemed to need to be reduced to a single unifying principle (though that principle shifted remarkably often) in order to feel useful, so did the category "woman." I remember many maxims from my early feminist days: the feminist teacher who iterated that "women always apologize" (yet seemed uncomfortable when I or other female students expressed our views assertively); the ecofeminists who said that "men rape the earth" while "women nurture"; my straight feminist friends who reported their relationships problematic amazingly opposite insights into gender roles in conversation: "men dominate conversations, women listen" and "men don't know how to talk, they're so taciturn, while women take all the responsibility for communicating." What is interesting to me, looking back at that time, is not just the fact that those generalizations painfully oversimplified, and only held up by simply bracketing out any information that threatened to puncture them, but moreover the fact that we so badly *needed* to generalize in the first place.

34   Generalizing was critically important; it was, for instance, key in the process known as "consciousness raising." Consciousness raising required each woman in a group to tell her story of a particular kind of experience – for example, her experience of sexuality, of violence, of having been raised and schooled as a female. What was discovered in consciousness-raising groups of the sixties and seventies was that experiences previously believed to be "unique" or fundamentally "personal" because they had been privatized were in fact widespread – and thus "political" or "social" – phenomena. If, for example, virtually every woman in the room reported that she had at some time in her life been sexually molested or that such an attempt had been made, one could make the highly useful generalization that sexual assault was not a story of an occasional lone "pervert" and an unlucky "victim," but rather of an event endemic to our society that was veiled way inscribed upon its notion of normal – rather than deviant – social conduct. Similarly, as each woman reported her frustration at having sole or primary responsibility for domestic work, even if she worked as many hours as her male partner did, that frustration ceased to be characterized as the mark of eccentricity or personal anomie and was recast as a systemic, and therefore political, problem. Thus, "the personal is political" meant that personal experience is *not* only particular and individual; it is symptomatic and illustrative of social beliefs, practices, and discourses. In this sense, generalizing enabled the formation of analyses, alliances, public discourses, and mass actions that produced liberating social change.

35   Yet a generalization outlives its usefulness at the point at which it reifies itself by ignoring the disruptive voices at its margins. Those voices don't only threaten to disrupt it; they are also disrupted *by* it, which is usually why they have gotten noisy to begin with. A classic example of such a voice at the margin is Sojourner Truth, the abolitionist and former slave who in her famous 1851 speech at a women's rights convention in Akron, Ohio, overcame white feminists' attempts to silence her rebuttal to an antisuffrage remark by a clergyman. He had claimed that women shouldn't have the vote because they were essentially weak and helpless – "women" in this care obviously meaning "white women" to all concerned – and Sojourner Truth interjected the following:

36   The man over there says women need to be helped into carriages and lifted over ditches, and to have the best place everywhere. Nobody ever helps me into carriages or over puddles, or gives me the best place – and ain't I a woman? Look at my arm! I have ploughed and planted and gathered into barns, and no man could head me – and ain't I a woman? I could work as much and eat as much as a man – when I could get it – and bear the lash as well! And ain't I a woman? I have born thirteen children, and seen most of 'em sold into slavery, and when I cried out with my mother's grief, none but Jesus heard me – and ain't I a woman? (Flexner 1959] 1975, 91-92)

37 Almost a century and a half ago, Sojourner Truth in effect deconstructed the category "woman," and in the process of forcing its reconfiguration to include those arbitrarily consigned to its outskirts she ineluctably altered what was possible for those embraced – or locked – within it. Her articulation of her experience made possible the revision of "We believe women aren't so fragile that we need to be helped into carriages and lifted over ditches; in a better world you would see that we are competent enough to vote" to read instead, "Women have *already* proved – have, in fact, been forced to show – that we can work as competently as men, and therefore obviously deserve the vote." White women generalized about their condition, and mobilized to change it; a Black women punctured their "we" with her "I," rendering their generalization obsolete and propelling the movement beyond its limiting parameters.

38 In 1984 Adrienne Rich (1986) wrote an essay called "Notes toward a Politics of Location" in which she took a critical and revisionist stance toward her own former reliance on generalizing as a tool of political analysis and praxis. Here are some excerpts from that text:

39 I wrote a sentence just now and x'd it out. In it I said that women have always understood the struggle against free-floating abstraction even when they were intimidated by abstract ideas. I don't want to write that kind of sentence now, the sentence begins "Women have always. . . ." We started by rejecting the sentences that began "Women have always had an instinct for mothering" or "Women have always and everywhere been subjugation to men." If we have learned anything in these years of late twentieth-century feminism, it's that that "always" blots out what we really need to know: When, where, and under what conditions has the statement been true? (214)

40 Perhaps we need a moratorium on saying "the body." For it's also possible to abstract "the" body. When I write "the body," I see nothing in particular. To write "my body" plunges me into lived experience, particularity: I see scares, disfigurements, discoloration, damages, losses, as well as what pleases me. Bones well nourished from the placenta; the teeth of a middle-class person seen by the dentist twice a year from childhood. White skin, marked and scarred by three pregnancies, an elected sterilization, progressive arthritis, four joint operations, calcium deposits, no rapes, no abortions, long hours at the type writer – my own, not in a typing pool – and so forth. To say "the body" lifts me away from what has given me a primary perspective. To say "my body reduces the temptation to grandiose assertions. (215)

41 *The difficulty of saying I* – a phrase from the East German novelist Christ Wolf. But once having said it, as we realize the necessity to go further, isn't there a difficulty of saying "we"? *You cannot speak for me. I cannot speak for us.* Two thoughts: there is no liberation that only knows how to say "I"; there is no collective moment that speaks for each of us all the way though.

42 And so even ordinary pronouns become a political problem. (224)

43 I quote at length from Rich because I feel that in this essay she very eloquently articulates a shift that has been felt by many people involved in identity politics. "Location" is a concept whose metaphoric value hinges on a literal truth: our epistemological location can be charted, to an overwhelming extent, according to the specific juncture at which the various axes along which we are positioned in the world converge. If I am a "lesbian," its meaning for me must certainly have something to do with the fact that I am Jewish, a New Yorker, forty years old in 1994, highly educated, middle-class, with a history of political activism, with friends who have died of AIDS and friends who are now HIV positive, from a socially and politically conservative family, etc. I know, from extensive reading, how different it would have been to have been that ostensibly same thing – a "lesbian" – in Nazi Germany, in the U.S. during McCarthy years, in Natalie Barney's salon in early twentieth-century Paris, as a poor small-town girl counting on the military as the only way out, as a Native American growing up on a reservation, as a working-class bar dyke, as a Salvadoran immigrant, as an elementary-school teacher in the Bible Belt, as a nun. And I know that in prior eras some of the feelings that I now call "lesbian" would have been instead attributed to "inversion," "romantic friendship," or perhaps to nothing at all; there might have been no words to describe this experience, and perhaps, as a result, no experience that I could mentally formulate (Foucault 1990; D'Emilio 1983a, 1983b; Faderman 1981).

Lesbian/Gay Identity and Composition

44 If my sense of what it means to be a "lesbian," then, is so bound up with these specific features of my own life, what does it mean to suggest that composition consciously address itself to, and in some ways reconfigure itself around, the needs and interests of "lesbian and gay" students? In other words, who are these people? What needs and interests might they have in common? On behalf of whom, and within what framework, am I advocating curricular change? These questions leave me feeling that I am tumbling down the slippery slope of social construction theory in a way that Carole Vance described in her keynote address at the 1987 "Homosexuality, Which Homosexuality?" conference in Amsterdam (1989, 21-22)

45 [T]o the extent that social construction theory grants that sexual acts, identities and even desire are mediated by cultural and historical factors, the object of study-sexuality-becomes evanescent and threatens to disappear. If sexuality is constructed differently at each time and place, can we use the term in a comparatively meaningful way? More to the point in lesbian and gay history, have constructionists undermined their own categories? Is there an "it" to study?

46 Amazingly to me now, it hardly occurred to me to wonder about these questions when I proposed two courses in two different New York City colleges, one called Writing About Lesbian and Gay Experience and the other called Writing About Lesbian and Gay Issues, both of which ran in the spring of 1992. At the end of those courses, I recruited students to be interviewed for this study, and it was only after interviewing them and closely reviewing their responses and the texts they had produced that I realized the extent to which (1) I had created generalizations in my mind about the issues lesbian and gay students faced in mainstream writing classes, and (2) I had *needed* to believe in "general rules" about lesbian and gay students, so that they would be presented wholesale to an academy that would have a clear mandate to change its policies and assumptions.

47 What all the students did have in common was the awareness that they lived in homophobic world, and that homophobia affected them in some way. However, the ways in which they seemed to be affected, as well as the ways they manifested responses to that homophobia is their writing acts, varied greatly. For some, homophobia had had a silencing effect on their writing, whereas others drew what they characterized as perverse sort of inspiration from homophobia and eagerly rose to the challenge of writing *against* an oppressive social discourse. Some, after years of frustration with schools that obliterated lesbian and gay existence from the sphere of knowledge, wanted to write about nothing *but* being gay; others had become convinced that gay life was not appropriate academic material and that to write about it was "selfish" or "self-indulgent"; while still others saw their experience with homophobia as a useful conduit to apprehending other forms of social disenfranchisement, such as racism or sexism. Some saw our class as a way to "come out," or to come out in a new way-perhaps in an academic way, or a more deeply theorized way; some used it to find courage or language to come out to their families, to come out in their artistic work (often in the context of theatre), or literally to come out of a purely privatized experience of sexuality and into the realm of political activism and public discourse; other said they had never had a problem with being out; one student said that the class had, ironically, helped him to come out as a Hispanic, which he had experienced as a more denigrated part of his identity and which he had kept more hidden than his gayness; and one student, inadvertently "outed" to his father and thrown out of his house in midterm, was so numbed that he withdrew officially from the course but continued to sit in on it as – as he put it – the only "therapeutic" environment he knew.

48 Predictably, age, gender, race, and class locations of students positioned them differently regarding the ways they interpreted lesbian and gay experience as well as specific texts about that experience. Several heterosexual students probed the meanings of their heterosexuality in new ways, writing analytical papers which decentered an identity whose constructedness and power relationship vis-à-vis other identities they had never before considered. The heterosexual students also brought varied experiences to the class: one decided during the course that she was bisexual, and after the course began to call herself a lesbian; one, the child of divorced parents, had been alternately raised by her lesbian mother in an interracial household in New York and her father in a Klan stronghold in the South, and wrote about "the gay family" from an unusual standpoint; the daughter of a liberal Jewish family used course material about gays in the Holocaust to reread years of Hebrew school training and family discussions, wondering why the story of Nazi Germany had always been portrayed as a singularly anti-Jewish event.

49 Ultimately, sexual identity emerged – in some sense, for all the students, though usually most urgently for the lesbian and gay students – as an important epistemological context and social location in which writing acts were situated. Though the students' experiences and even the bases of their self-definitions were quite diverse, the totality of them resisting neat encapsulization, they were no more and no less so than than one would expect the experience and definition of any other identity component to be. In fact, the complexity and centrality of sexual identity in their meaning-making processes appeared so much to resemble those of other features of identity that the dearth of attention given it in writing classes struck me anew as an egregious omission. The students, for their part, in their interviews and in texts that they wrote in class expressed this view virtually unanimously.

50 Yet the reason for this omission was a mystery to no one. Leaving sexual identity out of the classroom is not an accident; it is an expression of institutionalized homophobia, enacted in classrooms not randomly but systematically, with legal and religious precedents to bolster it and intimidate both teachers and students. Consider, for example, the first paragraph of a recent memorandum written by a tenured, full professor of English at Cosmopolitan University, one of the sites of my study, in response to a letter argueing for domestic partner benefits for university employees:

51   I and other members of the Faculty council have received a letter from Professor S., a member of the Association of Lesbian and Gay Faculty, Administration, and Staff, complaining that the absence of provisions for domestic partner benefits for their same or opposite sex couples is a serious failing. I do not believe that serious attention should be given to this complaint. Such liaisons have no standing in law or religion. If they are sexual relationships, they are widely regarded as immoral, they may be illegal in many states, and they will be thought offensive by the vast majority of faculty, staff, students, and their parents. In my view cosmopolitan University should not appear to condone or endorse such relationships by providing special benefits to them. (Memo to Faulty council Benefits Committee, November 25, 1992)

52 If, as this professor contends, homosexual relationships are "thought offensive by the vast majority of faculty, staff, students, and their parents," what does it mean for lesbian or gay students to approach writing assignments that ask them to do such things as to reflect upon the "self," to narrate personal events, to interpret texts in ways that reveal the subjectivity of the writer, and to write research papers on topics that are "of interest to them"? Think of how they are told to be aware of issues of audience, subject, and purpose, and to claim textual authority. Then consider the convoluted dimensions these rhetorical issues take on when lesbian and gay writers inevitably have to choose between risking a stance from an outlaw discourse or entering into the familiarly dominant discourses of heterosexuality.

53 Sexual identity is a component of personal and social identity highlighted for lesbians and gay men because homophobia in the culture makes it problematic. Because lesbians and gay men must constantly assess the consequences of being out and negotiate the terms of disclosure, often necessitating elaborate monitoring of what is said and even though ("internalized homophobia"), a particular complication woven into their processes of construing and constructing knowledge. Even for those who are most out, acts of making meaning involve constant confrontations with many of the premises and mandated of the dominant culture – creating an epistemological condition roughly equivalent to what W.E.B. Du Bois ([1953] 1961) called "double consciousness." Lesbian and gay writers do not have to be familiar with reader-response theory, the transaction between a heterosexual reader and a homosexual text can yield explosive meanings.

54 Sexual identity informs heterosexuals' epistemologies, too, though in ways that may be less immediately apparent to them – just as most socially dominant or validated identities are more dimly perceived as players in people's meaning-making operations than are the identities of Others. Heterosexuals, like white people, insofar as that part of their identity is not regularly challenged or scrutinized, are free to not regard it as a significant fact demarcating their selfhood; it is possible for them to experience it instead as part of a seamless garment of "humanness"-which is to say, they frequently do not "view" or "see" it until it is touched by the discourse of the Other. Yet, as a number of queer theorists have pointed out, the homo-hetero opposition is firmly entrenched in Western dualistic though, and although homosexuality is popularly viewed as a transgression against the norm of heterosexuality, it can perhaps more accurately be seen as a corequisite for it, without which there would be no pairing and "heterosexuality" as an identity could not exist. The fact that heterosexuality, as a culturally normative position, usually sidesteps met discourse and self-realization in a way that homosexuality does not doesn't mean that it is not a solid fixture in the interpretive and expressive process of heterosexual student writers.

55 Tugging against the legacy of academy-endorsed homophobia is the precedent of CCCC, which for its 1993 convention included the category "Gay and Lesbian concerns in the Profession" for the first time as an "area to be emphasized" in its program proposal form. This inclusion should in fact not be surprising, since the field of composition has increasingly come to recognize and research the vast significance that writers' locations within particular communities and social conditions have for their writing acts. One section of the proposal form read as follows:

56 We have . . . acknowledged that merely studying writers and writing – stripped from their personal, social, and political contexts – is insufficient as a way of coming to know the things that are important to us. Recent conventions with themes such as "Strengthening community through Diversity" and "Contexts, Communities, and Constraints: Sites of Composing and Communicating" have highlighted the growing pains that any cross-disciplinary group endures. We are in search of what Adrienne Rich called "a dream of a common language." while at the same time we are trying to allow room for new idea, growth, and change – the essential characteristics that make us cross-disciplinary in the first place. (Lilian Bridwell-Bowles, 1993 program Chair)

57 This statement of an organization's thinking-in-progress illustrated that multicultural awareness has come to be regarded by rhetoricians not simply as an ideal of fairness, but as a fundamental attribute of effective pedagogy. Sites of identity and affinity are undergoing rigorous scrutiny as shapers of students' epistemologies, language, and semiotic constructions. The spheres of most frequent analysis are those involved in racial-, gender-, and class-identity formation. I was arguing that sexual identity is inscribed in discursive acts in ways that both parallel and overlap with the effects of those other identities, and that including sexual identity in our consideration of diverse identities is a necessary component of legitimate composition research and practice. The fact that "lesbian and gay" may be an amorphous category and its meaning indeterminate is no reason to drop the whole enterprise, since genders, races, and classes are equally amorphous when probed beyond their surface coherence.

58 My primary purpose in this book is to illustrate some of the complex dimensions of how lesbian and gay experience in composition classes. This involves exploring the forces of work for lesbian and gay student writers in the social act or writing, which will hopefully suggest the need for the recognition of lesbian and gay discourses among the multiple discourses that composition theory sees as the site of its work. Composition is a field whose structures have begun to reflect the premise that the social roles of writers are inscribed upon their writing acts. Given that composition is rapidly evolving within a social constructionist theoretical framework, it would appear inappropriate for composition to ignore the way that sexual identity – like race, gender, and class – is constructed through language.

59 In addition to social construction theory, my work is informed by related work that has been done on liberatory, or critical, pedagogy. Critical pedagogy has had wide applications in writing classes. Critical pedagogy asks students to analyze conditions in their lives not only to cultivate academic forms of expression and interpretation, but also to promote consciousness of the world outside the classroom, the ways socially constitutive and transformative force. Critical pedagogy sees education as a key agent of social change, rather than as simply a route to personal improvement or mobility. It posits itself as emancipatory rather than assimilationists in that it asks students to read against hegemonic social discourses rather than with or into them. As lesbian and gay students *must* read against the hegemonic discourse of homophobia in order to come out – personally, academically, politically, publicly – critical pedagogy seems like an inevitable component of any gay-affirmative classroom practice.

60 Narratives by and about lesbian and gay students who have taken one or the other of my gay-themed writing classes, along with samples and analyses of their work, are at the heart of this book. I have included excerpts from my interviews with them, texts they produced in my class, in some cases texts they produced in prior writing classes, and reflective pieces that they wrote in my class. By illustrating what can happen to lesbian and gay student writers in a queer centric environment, I hope to expose some of the ways that composition might better serve lesbian and gay student writers and overcome some of its heterosexist premises. I also hope to demonstrate the homophobia in the classroom actually undermines composition's broader intentions, and that incorporating lesbian and gay studies into the framework of its thinking will benefit the field as a whole. I hope that my work will impel composition theorists and practitioners to reconsider some of the shape and substance and application of our discipline – that which at the least may be seen as adversely affecting a significant group of our whole society. Such reflection should have additional benefits to composition, in that it may provoke the imagining of new structures relevant to other communities whose Otherness also refuses conventional wisdom about the act of writing.

A Few Words About Classification and Definition

61 Of course, my language reaffirms the very polarity that I at least half-regard as fictive. If I acknowledge that the homo-hetero opposition is the product of dualistic thinking, and if I wish to puncture the rigid taxonomies and prejudices that have produced homophobia, it seems paradoxical that I nevertheless divide the students in my field of vision into "homosexuals" and "heterosexuals." Furthermore, such a division seems to beg the question of how people qualify for these categories in the first place. What is a "homosexual," anyway? Is it someone who *has sexual relations with* same-sex partners? Is it someone who *desires* same-sex partners? What if someone has sexual relations with the opposite sex but desire same-sex paring? What if someone has sexual relations with members of the same sex, rejecting sexual desire for the opposite sex as not to be acted on (as was the case with some 1970s lesbian feminists)? What if someone has sexual relations with/desires both sexes? Or switches sexual object-choice in midlife? To what extent does the definition have to do with gender-appropriateness as determined by cultural norms? To what extent does it have to do with self-definition, for whatever reason? What if we are all really, as Freud claimed, polymorphous perverse?

62   I believe that each of these criteria has some claim to detinition. However, I am going to fall back on the very schism that many in the field of gender studies are seeking to dismantle, not because I feel it reflects any underlying "truth" about human identity, but rather because I *do* feel it reflects a "truth" about our culture. Recognizing that the categories we exist within (and in fact our entire sense of "self") are social constructions should not lead us to a perception of these things as somehow lesser in their effects than we would have them be if we viewed them as springing from some essential source. However constructed, the products of our collective social imagination receive particular rewards, punishments, license, restrictions, affirmations, and violations in the social world. For present purposes, suffice it to say that many people indeed experience their sexuality in fluid or inconsistent ways, yet are likely to claim (or be assigned) particular sexual identities because our society in the twentieth century is disposed to file people in such ways in order to make sense of them. Because this system of classification has a significant impact on how people see themselves, and how people see themselves has a lot to do with how they behave and negotiate social meanings and how and what they write, I will use the categories "lesbian/gay" and "heterosexual" in my investigation. My only criteria for inclusion in each category are people's self-descriptions (or self-perceptions). (By "people" I refer to both specific subjects in my study and to hypothetical students I may theorize about-i.e., when I use the term "lesbian student" I mean a student who feels that that term describes her.) I will include bisexuals in the category "lesbian/gay" was suitable for them if less precise than "bisexual."

63   The contemporary term "queer," used mostly by younger activists and artists, conveys in popular jargon the basic idea of a broad category embracing a spectrum of those who deviate from the heterosexual norm. I will occasionally use that term because, though colloquial at this time, it is more inclusive, and thus often more accurate, than any term currently in our formal language. In addition, the prodigious body of theoretical work in lesbian and gay studies now emerging from academic presses has broadly come to be known as "queer theory," and it is from that new canon of information that much of my own thinking has developed.

64   I have encountered a problem similar to that which I have had with "lesbian and gay" with the word "community." at times in this book I use the multiple form "communities" to suggest that "the lesbian and gay community" is in fact not monolithic, but is comprised of numerous groupings that identify themselves, and whose members identity themselves, in various ways. At other times I employ the singular term "lesbian and gay community" for lack of a less awkward alternative and in order not to divert my discussion to a self-conscious explication of what I "really" mean by it, I want to clearly establish that I am taking the liberty of using it as a deliberately imprecise abstraction which will suggest the many ways it is being interrogated and understood. In other words, I am not trying to signify a "real" community possessed of genuine shared

consciousness; I am trying to signify loose configurations whose members have believed in certain ways at certain times that they were in some manner connected by shared knowledge or experience.

65   I began this work with the premise that homophobia and the silencing of lesbian and gay discourse *do* have a significant impact on students who do not define themselves as lesbian or gay, insofar as the silencing or any social group creates cognitive gaps for the whole community. Furthermore, any taboo wields an imperative for all members of a society to consciously position themselves outside the sphere of culpability; in doing this, they are complicit in reaffirming the taboo and frozen in their assigned social locations. As Diana Fuss (1992, 3) has written:

66   To protect against the recognition of the lack within the self, the self erects and defends its borders against an other which is made to represent or to become that selfsame lack. But borders are notoriously unstable, and sexual identities rarely secure. Heterosexuality can never fully ignore the close psychical proximity of its terrifying (homo)sexual other, any more than homosexuality can entirely escape the equally insistent social pressures of (hetero)sexual conformity. Each is haunted by the other. . .

67   The defenses employed in self definition aren't unique to the realm of sexual identity. They work similarly to enforce racial demarcations, for example, as described by Toni Morrison (1992):

68   [I]t may be possible to discover, through a close look at literary "blackness," the nature – even the cause – of liberty "whiteness." What is it *for*? What parts do the invention and development of whiteness play in the construction of what is loosely described as "American"? . . . Black slavery enriched the country's creative possibilities. For in that construction of blackness *and* enslavement could be found not only the not-free but also, with the dramatic polarity created by the skin color, the projection of the not-me. (9, 38)

69   The presence of lesbian and gay discourses in the classroom, then, contributes significantly to our understanding of the ways that seemingly remote, autonomous identities are in fact deeply implicated in one another's existence – and of the ways that in writing we produce ourselves through our production of the other. Such notions suggest, too, that identity is not immutable and static, but rather may be reconstructed, repositioned, or redefined. The absence of a particular discourse may itself be a message. Michael Foucault ([1978] 1990, 27) has written:

70   Silence itself – the things one declines to say, or is forbidden to name, the discretion that is requited between different speakers – is less the absolute limit of discourse, the other side from which it is separated by a strict boundary, than an element that function alongside the things said, with them and in relation to them within overall strategies.

71   No one in Western culture exists outside the complex web of signification forged by homophobic discourse and silence about sexual difference. Eve Kosofsky Sedgewick (1990, 185-86) has used the term "homosexual panic" to describe the condition, beginning in the nineteenth century, of so-called heterosexual men who define themselves "*as against* the homosexual" in societies where the prescribed condition of intimate homological male bonding (as in, for instance, the armed forces or sports teams) and the prohibited reality of homosexuality so startlingly resemble one another – where privilege and pariahhood thus exist so perilously close to one another – that men are in a constant state of paranoia and manipulability. If we conceive of sexuality as a sharply partitioned dichotomy, then knowing about the "self" – something students are invariably asked to do in writing classes, in some form – certainly involves problematizing the schema wherein we achieve self-definition through vacancies created by others having taken up particular positions on the psychosexual map. Alternatively, Adrienne Rich (1982, 20) has written of a "lesbian continuum" which includes "a range – through each woman's life and

throughout history—of woman identified experience; not simply the fact that a woman has had or consciously desired genital sexual experience with another woman." if we conceive of sexual identity as existing along such a continuum, then we are all located on it—and writing about the "self" involves other forms of social knowledge. Whatever taxonomy of sexual identity we might choose to employ, the subject of queerness is not the province of some faceless Other, but rather has social and epistemological relevance for everyone.

Notes

[1] Such policies are increasingly being proposed and adopted, but they remain heavily contested. According to an article in the Chronicle of Higher Education, the nation Gay and Lesbian Task Force reported that by early 1992, "at least 150 institutions and metacarpus university systems had such policies." the article goes on to state that on some campuses. "proposals to add language on sexual orientation have led to heated debate" (Mooney 1992, A18).

[2] Twenty four states in the county and the District of Columbia still have sodomy laws on the books, they presence more acutely felt since the U.S. Supreme Court's Bowers v. Hardwick decision in 1986 upheld Georgia's sodomy law. Challenges to other states' statutes have subsequently been struck down, citing Bowers as a precedent. There is no national lesbian and gay civil rights ordinances protecting the civil liberties of lesbians and gays. Thus, in most areas of the country there is no protection for lesbians and gays from discrimination in either public or private employment. In 1992 the state of Colorado adopted strict legislation in the form of Amendment 2, designed to preempt any such protection and override local ordinances within the state. The amendment states; "Neither the State of Colorado, through any of its braches or departments, nor any of its agencies, political subdivisions, municipalities or school districts, shall enact, adopt or enforce any statute, regulation, ordinance or policy whereby homosexual, lesbian or bisexual orientation, conduct, practices or relationships shall constitute or otherwise be the basis of, or entitle any person or class of persons to have or claim any minority status, quota preferences, protected status or claim of discrimination." At the time of this writing, the constitutionality of the measure is being debated up the hierarchy of the courts. An even more virulently antigay measure was voted down at the same time in Oregon after a nationwide mobilization to defeat it. In 1993, nineteen antigay rights initiatives were proposed – and ultimately approved – at the local level around the country, and antigay groups composed primarily of fundamentalist Christians are attempting to place initiatives limiting the rights of lesbians and gays on the ballot in eight states in 1994. The two state initiatives in one year. Ultimately, then, there are no grounds for legally contesting religious or "moral" rationales for screening homosexuals from the employment as teachers in most parts of the United; it remains legal to fire a homosexual in all but seven states. (Mohr, 49; Goldstein, 24; Holmes, A17. Data on state law furnished by National Lesbian and Gay Task Force. Text of Amendment 2 furnished by the Equal Protection Campaign of Colorado.)

[3] For an illuminating discussion of "the sex hierarchy" – the vertical scale of social and acceptability on which forms of sexuality are measured- see Rubin (1989).

[4] Almost always, these responses change when I come out to a class. I am not suggesting that my students find me so engaging that this new knowledge wipes away all their homophobia, but that that a visible and audible lesbian "I" in the classroom alters the players in, and thus the terms of, the discourse. Students' panicked need to demonstrate what they are "not" diminishes markedly when I am available to be that "not" for them. At that point, they generally perform their heterosexual identities through friendly "interest," "curiously," "support," or at worst, polite dissention ("Because of my religion, I can't approve of the gay life-style, but. . . .").

[5] A prime spokesperson for such academicians is Maxine Hairston. See, for example, her article "Diversity, Ideology, and Teaching Writing," Also see James D. Williams's review essay "Politicizing Literacy."

[6] "Experience" was amended to "Issues" in the second course title at the suggestion of the department chair.

⁷ The name "Cosmopolitan University" is pseudonymous, as in the name of the other college in which I gathered data for this study.

⁸ "Queer" remains an emotionally contested word, not only because the borders of its meaning are in an ongoing process of negotiation, but because it evokes, particularly for older lesbians and gay men, vivid associations with humiliation and violence. A recent New York Times article compared the current reappropriation of "queer" by young radicals to young African Americans' use of the world "nigger," calling it "a defiant slap at an old slur" aimed to "demystify" and "strip" the word of its pejorative meaning (Marriott). In both cases, the generational splits on the acceptability of the linguistic appropriation seem deeply etched in divergent experiences. Those who recall being called "queer" or "nigger" at the time of an assault understandably find it impossible to cultivate the word as a term of empowerment. Those, on the other hand, for whom the word has symbolic or historical rather than personally experiential significance find it much easier to connotatively flip it and employ it without severe emotional distress.

Credit

"Isabel Serrano"

HARRIET MALINOWITZ

1   Isabel is a thirty-two-year-old English major at Municipal College, a first-generation U.S. mainland-born Puerto Rican returning student, who grew up in New York City in a devout family of Jehovah's Witnesses. She is close to completing a B.A. in the traditional four years, though she has worked full-time all along as a booking agent for musicians. She envisions no career benefits to her college degree and says that she is doing it "just for herself."

2   Till age eleven, Isabel grew up in the housing projects of upper Manhattan. Then her family moved to a neighborhood in one of the outer boroughs of the city where they were the first Hispanics, a place she describes as "a very narrow, bigoted environment." Her father was an elder in the church; as a child Isabel went to Witness meetings five times a week, took a review-like exam every five weeks, and canvassed door-to-door on weekends. Though both her parents had only grade-school educations, Isabel says that they were "self-taught" due to "reading and writing constantly because of the religion." Isabel feels that "religion was an addiction" for her parents, though she herself felt ambivalent about it even in childhood, frequently challenging her father's accounts of things with her own "close" readings of Bible passages and calling him a hypocrite. She says that the subjection of women always seemed wrong to her, and that the religion— which proscribed smoking, drugs, and fornication before marriage, and deemed homosexuality "unnatural" and therefore sinful—never felt fair. At the same time, though, she recalls being frightened enough at the idea of being separated from her brothers and sisters after death, of being excommunicated or marked (which would mean not being allowed to associate with followers), and of losing the approval of her parents to stay within the church until she reached the age of twenty-one. At that point, while she was practicing as a Bible teacher to youth, the combination of recognizing her sexual orientation and realizing that women who were being abused had no rights within church doctrine to fight back led her to unofficially break with the Witnesses by ceasing to attend meetings. She says that she still values certain humanistic religious principles, but that she now credits "the unique conscience of the individual to monitor behavior" as the guiding moral force in people's lives, and calls herself an agnostic.

3   Growing up, Isabel kept journals and she took several creative writing courses in school. She's not sure that she sees any sustained relationship between her lesbian identity and her writing—"I don't know that I write thinking I'm a lesbian"—though connections have appeared in unexpected circumstances, such as in a course where she was asked to write a paper about "how the music industry could cater to a person like me. So of course I have to mention it." She says that when it does come up, "I focus more on being gay *and* lesbian. Like the injustice, what we have to go through as a community, rather than just focus solely on *my* experience as a lesbian." She took her first college writing courses at another campus which she attended for a year, a technically oriented school where "everyone was outspokenly homophobic" and where she feels that more generally "I didn't have the freedom to voice what I think I voice at Municipal." She produced little there that felt of value to her, and she says that because of the much freer environment at Municipal "my writing changed drastically when I came here."

4   At Municipal, discussion of lesbian and gay existence arose in several courses; she cites a Virginia Woolf course, a course on women and the law, and a communications course as examples. Within this new social context, she found herself responding to individual homophobic remarks as stimuli rather than as restraints. "Nowadays what's happening is that when I find that people are uncomfortable with lesbian issues or gay issues, it makes me want to write about it. That's been happening in the past year." She finds that she is much more inspired to write about lesbian and gay issues when people express discomfort about them than when there is either an absence of such discussion at all or blatantly outspoken homophobia. The reason, she feels, is "because I'm getting really angry. I'm just getting really upset and tired of people misconstruing what is." When she feels the need to address lesbian or gay existence in a course, she says, "My first thought is always, should I say this? Then I say, the hell with it, and then I write it. But there's always been that question, thus far—do I *want* to say this?" She is always moved to actually write by realizing "of course I want to say it. I look at what I really want to say, and this is what I really *want* to say, and I say it. Because it should be said."

5   Isabel feels that often when she does take the plunge of writing or speaking about lesbian and gay issues, the response is "silence. Everybody stares." Yet she finds herself driven by a desire to "set the record straight" each time she encounters "the inaccurate perception, the *limited* perception, of what it is to be gay." In her communications class, she was part of a panel discussion in which her topic was "declaring Madonna a saint." She spoke about Madonna's celebration of sexuality and showed the performer's controversial "Justify My Love" video. When the instructor commented that the lesbian and gay community was angry at Madonna because she had not come out as a lesbian— an observation that Isabel felt to be false—she found it impossible to counter the charge without identifying herself. "I started saying I know a lot of lesbians. Well, of course I wasn't going to say I know a lot of lesbians and not say I was one! So I said it very casually. I just came out like I was talking about ice cream. I said, 'Well, I know a lot of lesbians, myself included. And we don't feel that way.' And then, you know, you feel that silence—like everyone cannot believe you just said that."

6   "I have three things going that I have to contend with," Isabel says. "I'm a woman, I'm Puerto Rican, and I'm a lesbian." One time in a class she announced these three facets of her identity as preface to further commentary in which, she says, "I just went in on a soapbox." Yet she emphasizes repeatedly that in response to the "stereotyping" and "stigma" that she feels is inscribed upon her by numerous others, "I find that I have to set the record straight."

7   Her first awareness of gayness came from her brother's caricatured imitations of gay men, her father's derogatory remarks, and frightening references to the "unnaturalness" of homosexuality in the Bible. Yet, she says, "I never viewed gays and lesbians as disgusting, as people in my religion did. I never had that sentiment at all. To me they were people. They were like me. The few people that I did know through school, and the ones at school that I did not know, I was always intrigued with the fact that they were so open about it." When I comment on the irony of her appropriation of the liberal tenet "They were people; they were like me"—expressions usually employed to reveal the discovery of an amazing similarity despite huge perceived differences, while she is talking about a group of which she literally *is* a part—Isabel says that until she was twenty-one, she simply didn't identify as a lesbian. "Whenever I had crushes on someone, I would fantasize that I was a boy in order for it to be OK." She also mentions "a little escapade" with an older woman during her teens that she "literally blocked out"—a curiously anomalous coping strategy for someone who, despite having been surrounded by negative discourses of homophobia, is sure that she "never had that sentiment at all."

8   Coming out began for Isabel through an act of writing. "I went to my sister's apartment; she was out of town, and I fed the dog. And I was staying there that night, and I was writing. This very quiet neighborhood in Queens was very conducive to writing. And then I just wrote about being a lesbian. And I remember that I just cried—not because I was sad, but because this was such a great realization." She realized that she was attracted to women, but was "still kind of lingering in and out of the religion. Not being an active member, but still being associated with it. Basically I kind of weaned myself out of it, till one day, probably a month or two after, I decided that there was no way I could be part of this." She still didn't come out to anyone else or act on her attractions to women, but she made lesbian friends and went with them to lesbian social spots such as Provincetown. A year later, she had her first lesbian relationship. Though she says "I was definitely ready," she also comments, "I felt as uncomfortable at the beginning saying I was a lesbian as I did saying I was a Jehovah's Witness to people that weren't Witnesses." She has never come out to her parents. Though they feel close to her lover of three years and have been to the one-bedroom apartment which the two women share, everyone has tacitly chosen to preserve the myth that Isabel and Julia are "friends." "My mom discounts [my not being married] by saying I'm very independent. The reason [she does this] is because I was officially baptized in the religion, and I was not excommunicated. Because it's not like they caught me sleeping with a woman. I just kind of disassociated myself by not attending. If they excommunicated me, that would mean that my parents would have to keep limited association with me. And I don't know that I could deal with it. It's not that I'm ashamed. It's simply that I don't know if I could take not talking to my parents."

9   Isabel rates herself "anywhere between seven to eight" on an "outness" scale of one to ten "because it fluctuates, depending on where I am. With my family I'm out in a sense even not talking about the relationship, because Julia's always, for the most part, there with me. At work I'm totally out. In the street I'm careful because I don't like being harassed."

10   When asked what it means for her to call herself a lesbian, her first response is to reflect on the instructive dimension of self-definition, casting the act in terms similar to that of her wish to "set the record straight": "The first thing that comes to mind is the word 'specific.' I want to be specific. Because I think lesbians are still very much a minority, and people don't know we exist, so I notice that lately I do say it sooner than I would a few years back. Because I want to let it be known that we exist." When pressed further—"But what makes you *consider* yourself a lesbian?"—she says, "It's because I really do have a strong identification with women—like emotionally, spiritually, physically. I understand a woman much better than I do a man. And vice versa. Many things need not be explained. There's a common ground there that's very strong."

The Joy of Discomfort

11   "Our class just made me think more of myself as a lesbian," says Isabel. "I was surprised at the class that being gay was an issue for a lot of people. It hadn't been for me—but I've realized that it is. I mean, I don't live a real closeted life. So I never came to terms with my anger. And there is some there, and I think this class kind of made me angry. I also think writing the paper on how 'out' a lesbian can be—it just occurred to me then that no matter how 'out' I strive to be, I can never be truly out. There will always be instances when I do have to conceal my sexual identity. And that realization, although it's a very simple one and probably everyone knew that in coming to the class, I was not dealing with it, or thinking about it. I think I'm really *thinking* about gay now, where before I was just *being* gay."

12   The first class meeting, in which the debate about over enrollment took place, scared her "because it was so polemical. I thought this was going to be a very *positive* class, and we were going to talk about the *good* stuff." A very outspoken lesbian feminist in the class initially alienated her—"I picked up on her anger right away, and thought, I'm not going to like this"—yet Isabel feels that ultimately she "understood" her and concluded "that she's right. She's right about women not being taken seriously. I understood what I considered her fanatical need to always be around women. In the end I was glad that

there [are] Veronicas in this world, because we need them. They're constantly reminding us that we still have a struggle. I've always had a very difficult time being around negative people. But I now understand that their experience is different, and this is the way they deal with it, and it's not necessarily bad." By the end, Isabel says, she not only accepted Veronica's difference, but also came to see her as not so different; she felt that she actually identified with her.

13   More broadly, Isabel's first take on the class was that "everyone was uptight about being gay. Being gay was an issue in their lives. It was something that they dealt with constantly, day to day. And I felt—I'm not like that." Yet as time went by, she felt "enlightened": "I feel now that I have the same thoughts, except I may not express them in such a vehement manner. But I have them, and what remains to be seen is how I'm going to deal with them." She says that being in the class she felt, for the first time, the need to come out to her parents, even while realizing that she doesn't have the courage to do it yet. As a result of the class, she says, "I feel that I'm tired of the misunderstanding that people have toward gays and lesbians. And I've become outspoken in all my classes. Not that I haven't been in the last semesters, but this semester it just came very naturally to me without any thought." She noticed that in those classes where she brought up the subject of lesbian and gay existence, "I was very emotional. I probably sounded like some students in our class." She acknowledges that in these classes, as in some earlier classes, the discomfort of the other students and sometimes of the teachers produced a responsive discomfort in her that she is on some level appreciative of, and which propelled her toward speech. She tries to account for the strange pleasure of her own discomfort: "It's forcing me to think about an issue that involves me, and that involves a lot of my friends, a lot of people I know, my community. And it's forcing me in a direction that I can't pinpoint at this point in time, but I think if I had to say it in one sentence, it's forcing me to set the record straight. And I suspect that it will come out in writing—in creative writing, articles. I have that need now—whereas before, it wasn't a compelling need. This class has made me more focused. It gave me the impetus, the clarity, to just go for it." She also says, "I feel I now give more deliberate thought to being gay, because I'm being asked to think about being gay. In another class, I wouldn't have been asked to think about that."

14   Certain course readings particularly shaped Isabel's focus. She credits Adrienne Rich's essay "Compulsory Heterosexuality" for jolting her from a habitual stance of conceptualizing "women as a whole" to recognizing the "more specific category" of lesbians. "In my other [women's studies] classes I never wrote about lesbianism. I wrote about women's rights. So that article was the beginning of a process that was subconsciously making me zoom in on lesbians." She also cites Amber Hollibaugh's "Writers as Activists" as an important influence because it suggests possibilities for human change. Hollibaugh writes of the use of the "oral tradition" in her working-class family, in which "you convince people with the power of your body and your voice." Hollibaugh opens by saying,

15   Writing is the most difficult thing that I do, and activism is the easiest. The first four or five years that I wrote anything at all, I constantly told everybody that I just put it down on a piece of paper—but I wasn't really a writer. ... I didn't know how to see that identity—of being a writer—in combination with the way that I had constructed my politics. (69)

16   "I identified with that," says Isabel, "because to this day I don't consider myself to be a writer. And she went from not being political at all to being so political. And I was wondering, how does one do that?"

17   Isabel describes with particular relish reading the assigned series of coming-out narratives. "What I really enjoyed was the level of discomfort that gays and lesbians

feel about being gay. It comes back to my not dealing with that aspect. That there *is* discomfort. And this is what I was feeling now—discomfort. Not with being gay—but with the fact that I can't be who I really am freely." Isabel feels that this discomfort is propelling her somewhere, though she's not sure exactly where. "It's nebulous now. You'll have to interview me six months from now, and I'll tell you." She is only clear now that "It makes me really mad." When asked why she seems so pleased about her fall from happiness, she speaks appreciatively of a greater sense of awareness and purpose. "I used to think about [homophobia], but I didn't give it time. It was just yeah, too bad. This stinks. Next! Whereas now, it's really with me, the discomfort." She says that now she wants to write letters to government officials and read texts produced by the gay press which had "annoyed [her] at one point in time" because she had assumed that they represented a univocal, angry perspective that she could not share. She says that the class changed her in the sense that "I probably think about being gay every day now. ... It made me think a lot about politics, about our government, about the way it's run. It made me question it a lot. It made me think about other groups, the way our system is, our society in general, our values. So many things came into the picture here."

[18]   Reiterating once more that the class has galvanized her desire, in her everyday life, to "set the record straight," Isabel clarifies that choosing appropriate contexts for corrective remarks is important to her. "I don't think I'll ever be a person that says, 'Hi, my name is Isabel. I'm a lesbian.' Just like I wouldn't say, 'Hi, my name is Isabel. I'm Puerto Rican.' It's just not my style."

[19]   Isabel says that as a consequence of our class's theme-based structure, her writing there was "much more focused" than her writing had been in other classes. "There's no hesitancy. I say what comes to me. A lot of times a lot came to me instantly that remained to be explored, so there was a lot of thinking in this class—but not a lot of editing, initially." By "editing," she says, she means "censoring," or what she calls "forethought." "I'm more impromptu now. My writing has im-proved as a result, because I zoom in on what I *want* to say." She explains that the kind of "forethought" that occurs for her in other writing situations often leads to aborted texts. "A very specific essay like 'Autohomophobia' I probably would never have written in another class, because I don't feel that another class would identify with the struggles of the community. I would find it a real difficult task to get that across, and I wouldn't have empathy from the audience." She explains that by inventing the word "autohomophobia" she was suggesting not "internalized homophobia," but "fear of someone in our community that appears different"—the "auto" drawing attention to the sense of identification that comes from the feared object's being a part of one's own community, the "homophobia" referring to the fact that the aversion is specifically to another gay person. She says that she would also be very hesitant to write "A Lesbian's Ongoing Endeavor" in another class because "It's very personal. It's very revealing. I think with these subjects I want immediate understanding."

[20]   Isabel feels that it would be a good idea to have more classes like this "because there *haven't* been any classes like this. And it helps in writing because you're discussing something that you really feel strongly about, and you really want to find out more about it because you're in that class, and it's—put this in quotes—a 'safe' environment. I think from the writing comes more writing, and probably better." She feels that mainstream writing classes should include an assignment on lesbian and gay life because it may afford "that opportunity for someone to come out and feel at ease to be out. And to contribute to the class."

Constructing Community

[21]   The texts that Isabel produced in the course seemed fairly consistently geared toward correcting what she perceived as errors in others' perceptions. Her primary objective

in writing does appear to be precisely that which she articulates repeatedly in her commentary: a need to "set the record straight." Her writing style could probably best be described as journalistic and inductive: she draws predominantly on countless examples of injustice and distorted logic, competently arranging them so that they provide a panoramic view of what is "wrong with the picture" of dominant heterosexist ideology. Her mode of challenging ideology is to juxtapose it against "truths" accessed from the public domain of gay culture which highlight mass culture's distortions. By inserting herself into popular gay discourses as they appear in the gay press, at rallies and demonstrations, and at community events, Isabel makes these "truths" her own. She is adept at appropriating them and organizing pieces of them into texts of her own whose purpose generally seems to be to expose and to persuade—by unraveling falsehoods and emphasizing alternative viewpoints, constructions, and interpretations. She is rarely exploratory herself. "Setting the record straight" seems to have less to do with using her own experience to deconstruct the maxims of mass culture than with aligning herself with a counterculture that has already spoken powerfully to her, that she has already recognized as a significant counter discourse in the world, and that she wants to promote and be a part of so as to add to its force.

22 For example, in an informal draft called "Observations on Social Construction," she comments:

23 I think social construction for women in general still dictates that they should be married at least by 30 years old. If they are not, it is for a reason other than free will; i.e., "She is a career woman, who puts her job before personal life" or "She's a bitch, no man will ever go near her." The thought of a woman willingly choosing not to marry or being a lesbian rarely enters the picture. Today, many people still think women become lesbians because they were abused as children, abused by men, or never had "the right guy." Moreover, our society has not accepted the notion of a significant other. With the exception of a handful of corporations, most organizations do not have a category for a relative or a gay lover to be listed as a beneficiary for insurance or medical benefits.

24 The mass media, in particular, perpetuates the notion that everyone is straight. Books, publications, music, cinema, theatre, television, advertising all cater to a straight crowd. When the subject of homosexuality is introduced, it is almost always negative. The gay person is usually depicted as a fucked-up individual who has a difficult time living a "normal" life.

25 If one adds more modifiers to a woman in our society it gets worse, i.e., Latina Lesbian Woman. A Latina lesbian woman has a much harder time living down stereotypes. As a Latina, she is expected to be "warm, loving, wild, sexy, and lovable and self-sacrificing to her man." If she happens to be gay, she is accused (a lot of the times by her own relatives and the Latino community) of trying to be "macho" like men.

26 Like many students trying to grasp what "social construction" actually means, Isabel envisions it from a rather liberal viewpoint: negative or restrictive dogma has enshrouded a particular identity, limiting the freedom of those bearing that identity. If we can just invoke basic logic to persuade employers, media, and the average person in the street to open their minds and see that that identity has been cast in an unfairly and irrationally pejorative light, a new valuation will supplant the old and liberation will occur. Of course, what is obscured in such a view is the complexity that is involved in prejudice making to begin with: values and beliefs are predated by other values and beliefs, and are entrenched in political structures that are not only produced *by* discourse, but also must produce it themselves if they are to continue to exist. The indignation in Isabel's text takes as its object symptoms, not the underlying structures that have manifested them. There is no indication here that there is any method in the madness of homophobia, racism, or sexism, any system larger than themselves that they seek to uphold. In its appeal to rationality and democratic apportionment of individual liberties, Isabel's argument overlooks what *is* rational in the uneven delegation of rights in a society desperate to preserve its hierarchies. As Shane Phelan writes in her book *Identity Politics: Lesbian Feminism and the Limits of Community:*

27   The acknowledgment that we are constituted, which is the first step away from an atomistic liberalism, must be followed by the question: By what or whom are we so built? The answer "language," or "culture," or "tradition," is hardly an answer unless it is followed by more questions: Who controls the language, culture, and tradition? What interests and purposes are served by the present constitution of the self? (1989, 145)

28   Isabel's focus on unfairness, stereotyping, and false representation is endemic in the mass lesbian and gay movement's struggle for civil rights, where a widespread goal is social assimilation and equality for people who are not heterosexual. The fact that the branches of the mass media "all cater to a straight crowd" has been widely pointed out and fought by popular organizations such as the Gay and Lesbian Alliance Against Defamation (GLAAD), articles in gay publications, empassioned letters to the editors of the mainstream press, and groups of friends who gather in skeptical hope, chronic frustration, and wry humor in front of made-for-TV movies and television shows "experimenting" with gay characters. That women become lesbians by default rather than "free will" and choice is also a popular maxim that has received popular debunking in the lesbian and gay community.[1] In fact, Isabel doesn't seem to feel that her use of quotations around statements representing homophobic social mythology require citations or documentation; they enclose remarks that are generally recognizable— both because of their prevalence in social discourse and, I would argue, because of the extent to which they have been highlighted and charged with absurdity in queer counter discourse. In this light, her argument can be seen not only as an enunciation of resistance to received wisdom, but simultaneously as a manifestation of received counter-wisdom. "Setting the record straight" is not a burden she sees herself having to shoulder alone. A movement has already produced useful countercultural critiques and objections to heterosexist commonplaces. Her task, it seems, is to be a responsible member of that movement, deploying these critiques wherever she collides with the falsified "record."

29   This is what I wonder over and over again as I read Isabel's work: She is writing about relatively "new" ideas, but are they *her* new ideas? They don't strike me that way, yet it seems to me that they *may feel to her* like "her" new ideas because she has only recently encountered them. If I buy a house, the house may not be new, but it is *my* "new house." Isabel's work, then, highlights for me the flimsiness of the line between what I would call "received wisdom" and what I would call "original thinking." If we reject romantic notions of a unique "self" capable of producing thought that is not derivative, that is not itself written by prior discourses, then what wisdom counts as "received," and what contrastingly counts as "original"? Is the dichotomy even a valid one? Rereading Isabel makes me think that it's not.

30   Take, for example, her essay called "Autohomophobia." She explains at the outset, "For the purpose of this essay, I am taking the liberty of inventing a new word, autohomophobia. Autohomophobia refers to homosexuals involved in their own existence who fear and neglect the virtue of the differences between themselves and their homosexual brothers and sisters." The subject of the essay (though not the word that supplies its title) is one that has been at the center of raging discussion in the lesbian and gay community for some time now, and the notion of "difference" or "diversity" within identity-based communities has been debated as well in other political movements and presses and throughout academia. Yet Isabel enters the discussion assuming that these social divisions need to be described before they can be redressed:

31 ...More often than not, we segregate ourselves. In more subtle ways or perhaps not so subtle, we socialize with those who look and think like us. Gays with gays, lesbians with lesbians, white middle-class gays socialize with the same, minorities with minorities from their respective backgrounds, etc.

32 Limiting ourselves to those like us not only results in derision but in the long wrong-run, jeopardizes our common goal of being integrated into one society. All of us want to be accepted for who we are and desire the same rights and benefits extended to heterosexuals. How can we, then, aspire to be accepted as part of the general public when we ourselves do not make an effort to know each other? Are we perhaps as guilty as the feminists in Adrienne Rich's essay "Compulsory Heterosexuality" (who failed to take into account Lesbianism as an innate propensity in women) of disregarding a segment of our community just because their experience is not ours? Converging once a year for Gay Pride Day is not enough to effectu- alize our mutual aim of being taken seriously in our quest for equality. In reality, this is an excellent example of what could really happen if we all met regularly and showed by our presence and mutual interaction that despite our different backgrounds and belief systems, we are able to coexist as a united group of people.

33 Having described the problem, Isabel alternately pushes toward Utopian solutions and pulls back from the overoptimlsm they require:

34 Admittedly, this is easier said than done. While it is, no doubt, much more comfortable to be in our own element with people of similar backgrounds, we can overcome our autohomophobia if we make a concerted effort to know about the respective struggles of different groups in our community. But, how does one begin to identify and fight for the struggles of another group when, in reality, all of us in the gay community (black, white, women, men, young, old, parents, etc.) have an ax to grind of our own?

35 As part of a minority group, we carry the great weight of living in a biased society. However, this weight is a common ground for all of us to get together and share with each other the experiences of our respective backgrounds and hence build a strong support system for the future. The question, however, remains. How can we do this and when do we start?

36 . . . We could form a version of the United Nations where all special-interest groups within the gay community meet regularly to voice their needs and struggles through their elected representatives. ACT UP, the Korean Lesbian and Gay Organization, Latino Gay Men of NY, GLAAD, SAGE, et al. could all convene at a forum and discuss how best to meet their individual needs with the cooperation of others. Doing so will create greater harmony in the community which will invariably allow us to be more effective in meeting our goals as a gay nation.

37 Before forming a United Gay Nation, we must overcome the fear that stems from believing that our individual problems will never be resolved if we take that of others. If we look at the big picture, we will be able to determine that we have enough in common (i.e., we have all been targets of homophobia) to build a strong support system that can help us cope with our personal strife. . . .

38 On an earlier draft—which was not substantially different from this draft—I had written to Isabel: Your essay is about, I think, one of the most urgent issues in the lesbian and gay community—the divisiveness that continually undermines and threatens the power we have when we are united in action. In this draft, I think you do a really good job of setting the reader up to regard this divisiveness as ludicrous and counterproductive. At the same time, I think dire problems exist for deeply rooted reasons. Prejudices and angers and fears are usually not simple. You ask many of your questions rhetorically—["Rather than condemning members of our community who engage in S&M, why don't we just accept it as a different expression of intimacy .. .?" "Instead of accusing lesbians of acting and dressing like men and accusing men of emasculating women, why don't we praise them for not falling prey to the dictates of convention?" "If we don't happen to be politically active, why make fun of those in our community who lobby for our rights . . . and stigmatize them as obsessive?"]—and maybe in your next draft you could try to dig for some of the answers. What always seems frustrating to me is that *most* of us (I think) ask these questions—just like I think most people pose questions like "Why can't there be world peace?" and "Why can't everyone love and respect one another?" with real wistfulness and sincerity, yet support wars and feuds and all forms of oppression—because particular circumstances seem to them to necessitate it, to be unfortunate obstacles to the harmony they crave. So I think you would be doing important work if you really tried to explore just why we *do* pick on each other so much, and resist the real unity that we all crave on some level and that could propel us collectively into the position in the world so many of us seem to be perpetually seeking.

39 What I was unsuccessfully suggesting was that Isabel backtrack from her incredulity and her plan for action to consider the real difficulties and tensions that divide the community. She is not atypical of student writers in her desire to invoke the closure of the happy family, the cohesive community, even if doing so requires creating a fairy tale in which the deeper grittiness of our prejudices and alienation from one another must be elided. Invisible here are the meanings of our memberships in other communities, the competing allegiances which produce different concepts of "identity"—and consequently, divergent notions of "community." Isabel is confident that the "big picture" reveals that "we have enough in common"—homophobia—to fuel the construction of a "United Gay Nation." She seems unaware, however, that this "Nation" is itself a heavily contested enterprise, and that some of its sharpest critics are those who resent having to subsume their ethnic, gender, or other identities to their sexual identity as the price of sustaining the harmony of the queer collective. Prejudices related to these identities are centuries-old; what magic tonic does the gay community possess that would so easily eradicate them at the moment of sexual liberation?

40 It is important to bear in mind that Isabel wrote this essay near the beginning of the course—a moment perhaps still within the era she was describing when she said, "I used to think about homophobia, but I didn't give it time. It was just yeah, too bad. This stinks. Next! Whereas now, it's really with me, the discomfort." It is the absence of this "discomfort," and of recognition of its sources, that seems to me to make this essay weak. As a reader who is both part of the lesbian and gay community and a consumer/observer of mass culture, I can't buy Isabel's defused, unproblematized renditions of S&M, gender bending, and political positioning.

41 Yet, looked at another way, the essay virtually rises out of other sorts of discomfort: discomfort with splitting, with the slow speed of social change, with internecine dislike and distrust. If I, as a reader, know that Isabel's Utopia has already failed, that doesn't necessarily mean that she should know it, or that her writing should reflect it. She is writing from her point of entry into one conversation, before yet reaching the threshold of a more interior one. Poised at that point, she adds her voice to the others lamenting that the "common goal of being integrated into one society" is threatened by "limiting ourselves to those like us." The ideal of a "common goal" or "common ground"—or, as Adrienne Rich put it, the "dream of a common language"—is something that one must perhaps actively yearn for and even strive for in order to fully appreciate its impossibility. It is legitimate, maybe even necessary, to reinvent the wheel.

42 Several of Isabel's other early texts, both formal and informal, have these qualities of apparent overreliance on "received wisdom" and coasting perhaps a bit too smoothly along a road ostensibly bound for heaven. But by the time she writes an informal draft called "Reflections on Outing" in the beginning of the second half of the term, she seems to be moving someplace new. In this case, she takes a side in a well-publicized, highly polarized debate, but also, for the first time, she is able to use material that might seem contradictory or nonaligned with the main thrust of her argument, rather than simply avoiding it as a potentially problematic disruption. For instance, she writes:

43 The mass publicity outing has received is reason alone to celebrate its birth. Articles on the subject have appeared throughout the nation and in all major papers and periodicals. Whether favorable or unfavorable articles, they have all contributed to gay and lesbian visibility.

44 In another section, she writes:

45 In her article [in the *Village Voice*] opposing outing, C. Carr writes, "I am still waiting for the news of Malcolm Forbes to improve my life." Yet because of the outing of this public figure she has had an opportunity to write a lengthy article about a gay and lesbian issue in a mainstream paper and talk about the existing homophobia. Hopefully, this article will be read by someone whose light bulb went off, and came to terms with another existence, that of the gay and lesbian community.

46 A formal essay later still, called "Being 'Out': A Lesbian's Ongoing Endeavor," reads initially like a feature article chronicling the difficulties of living as a lesbian. Many of the difficulties she cites are fairly predictable in that they have been widely discussed, though she elaborates them quite competently: no domestic partnership benefits, negative images (and nullifying absences) in the mass media, fear of disclosure in the workplace, harassment in the streets, strictures within the family. At the end, though, she adds something surprising:

47 Since our culture assumes heterosexuality to be a given, a lesbian is always faced with setting the record straight and consequently coming out over and over again. When a gynecologist inquires "what method of birth control do you use," we explain none and why; when someone we barely know assumes the significant other is a man, we correct them; when we are asked out on a date by men who don't take no for an answer, we educate them with another fact in life—lesbianism. The coming out process—no matter how accustomed we are to doing it—is never stress-free, for we are always confronted with the possibility of rejection and condemnation. Very often fear returns and we experience the same symptoms we did when we first came out. Our throat goes dry, our voice becomes low and we stumble for words to disclose our sexual identity.

48 Having to do something over and over can also create a sense of powerlessness. This sense of lack of control is a constant within our lives which we struggle to overcome every day in one form or another and that's the "catch": the perpetual coming out which interrupts the quest to live in peace with oneself and society.

49 The reason this section of her essay feels surprising to me is that it is not simply about an unfair material or social reality which can be changed by legal or educational reform. It is about a fundamental paradox of being out—that coming out is an act doomed to only briefly satisfy the need that provoked it. Being out is a "perpetual" and redundant process, requiring one to enter a stressful experience over and over again. One is only as out as one's last act of coming out; the refusal to do it on any given occasion throws into question one's entire status as an out lesbian or gay man. If one constantly has to redefine one's existence to the world, how out is s/he? And yet, if one doesn't do it, s/he's not out, either. Isabel calls attention to the feelings of "powerlessness" attached to maintaining a social identity which requires continually doing something threatening and risky that is nonetheless destined, each time, to undo itself. In this instance her willingness to engage with the contradictions inherent in the process of "setting the record straight" propels her beyond the closure either of Utopian resolution or of abandonment of the corrective project to a "catch" which, while frustrating, may function as a gateway to deeper theoretical exploration. No particular institution is responsible for this "catch"; therefore none can be enjoined to rectify it. There is no particular record to be set straight here, but rather a reckoning to be had with the immense complexity of identity. Judith Butler (1991) has written that "being 'out' must produce the closet again and again in order to maintain itself as 'out'" (16) because identity *is* nothing more than a string of linked performances: "How and where I play at being [a lesbian] is the way in which that 'being' gets established, instituted, circulated, and confirmed" (18). Heterosexuality itself, she says, "only constitutes itself as the original [sexual identity] through a convincing act of repetition" (23); and "if heterosexuality is compelled to *repeat itself* in order to establish the illusion of its own uniformity and identity, then this is an identity permanently at risk, for what if it fails to repeat, or if the very exercise of repetition is redeployed for a very different per- formative purpose?" (24; emphasis Butler's). One difference between Isabel and Butler—other huge differences notwithstanding—is that Isabel perceives only lesbian and gay identity (as opposed to heterosexuality) to be at "risk," presumably because the dominant society doesn't recognize it except for those moments when it is injected into existence through speech, whereas for Butler, the "risk" is inherent in the notion of identity to begin with. In any case, I read the end of "Being 'Out': A Lesbian's Ongoing Endeavor" as a new kind of theoretical moment for Isabel, her first excursion outside the administrative offices where "the record" is malproduced and straightened.

50   By the time she writes her final project called, "Is 'Outing' Ethical?"—an extended discussion of the subject she had touched on briefly in an earlier informal draft—Isabel has consolidated all the techniques that have worked for her over the course of the term. Once again, she proves herself extremely capable of amassing numerous facts, quotations, and arguments culled from a wide range of media and pitting them against one another, this time ultimately batting down the anti-outing side with the weight of her pro-outing logic which "sets the record straight." For example:

51   [T]he logical.. . question is "Privacy (i.e., sexual orientation), according to whom?" Why is it, for example, that we know all about Liz Taylor's past and present husbands but nothing is ever printed on openly gay Congressman Barney Frank's domestic partner, Herb Moses, who accompanies him to the White House and numerous work-related functions. Yet the mainstream press wasted no time in printing details of the Congressman's personal life when it was discovered that he had slept with a male prostitute years before. In their March issue of 1992, *New York Queer* notes, "Ten times as many articles about Frank's involvement with Gobie (the male prostitute) appeared in 1989 and 1990 than articles about Frank's work in other years."

52   Likewise, she rests her argument largely on her faith in the media's power to overhaul deep-seated social beliefs, should it ever be so benignly inclined:

53   The claim "blondes have more fun" is a myth created by the same society that insists heterosexuality is the only natural way to be. If, on the other hand, the mainstream press accepts and begins to depict homosexuality in the same matter-of-fact manner it treats heterosexuality, they will help remove the stigma they themselves perpetuate—that being gay is bad and should be kept private.

54   She also pursues her insight from "Reflections on Outing" that, in this controversy, the medium is the message:

55   By debating the very issue of "outing" everyone—whether they know it or not—is contributing to gay and lesbian visibility. When the media or the public argue that Pete Williams should not have been outed, they are in essence confirming that he is gay and hence, restating the position of outers.

56   Disappointingly to me, Isabel did very little in the end of what I interpret as "taking risks" or venturing out on a theoretical or even speculative limb. She rarely seemed to find ambiguity useful or compelling, and except occasionally, it was hard for me to get much of a sense that she was writing to learn. Her writing was proficient, yet seemed to me to lack the excitement of student texts that are themselves scenes of encounter with new ideas, texts that read as if they are in motion, taking their writers as well as their readers someplace new. Isabel almost always seemed to be writing about what she *already* knew,

and her project seemed to be to brandish that information in as persuasive a manner as possible in order to "set the record straight." She consistently challenged homophobic discourse by wielding popular counter homophobic discourse that was itself packaged as if beyond the question of resistance. Even when addressing issues on which the gay community has been divided—such as dealing with diversity or outing—she refrained from resisting or playing with the borders of the side she had chosen.

57   Nevertheless, it seems to me that something important did happen for Isabel in this class: she discovered discomfort and anger, and at the same time she found her place in a community challenging the hegemonic discourses that provoked these responses. Her writing, though from one perspective geared solely toward puncturing and refuting those discourses, is from another perspective an act of solidarity with a group that she perceives as championing her interests, challenging the narratives that have undermined her. "Our class just made me think more of myself as a lesbian," she says. "I'm really *thinking* about gay now, where before I was just *being gay.*" The time she spent there was a time of entering and solidifying the categories "lesbian" and "gay"; it was not a time to dismantle them. Across a wide range of academic and political circles, as I have discussed in Chapter 1, scholar/ activists are debating the very question of how to reconcile postmodern disassemblies of identity categories with the need to strengthen those categories in order to fight for social change. Questioning the meaning of those categories can be distressing for any activist, even one intellectually challenged and inspired to take up the enterprise; it can certainly seem altogether beside the point for someone just beginning to feel empowered by these categories, someone who is just starting to experience the comfort of membership in a "united" community battling the discomfort of oppression.

58   When Isabel self-mockingly says, "I just went in on a soapbox"— referring to her attempt to explain her identities as woman, Puerto Rican, and lesbian to another class—she seems to be implying that, on some level, she is using the familiar rhetoric of right and wrong that she grew up with in the Jehovah's Witnesses. She *is* perhaps a bit absolutist, perhaps a bit like the Bible in her deliverance of "truth" to the pagans of the world of identity politics; yet I also see extraordinary courage in her acts of giving language to her unfolding sense of self. From early childhood and, in relation to her family, into the present, she has lived with the knowledge that the "truth" about her sexuality, put into language, would sever her connections to people literally through excommunication. In Isabel's essays, her use of counterfacts and ideology from the lesbian and gay community to refute conservative social forces is fascinatingly reminiscent of her early challenges to her father in which she pointed out divergent meanings in Bible passages and his interpretation of Witness doctrine as it affected the environment of their household. As the recipient of absolutist thinking, she was imparted information that her own experience implicitly refuted, and yet the use of her experience as a counter narrative was forbidden. Instead, it seems that from a young age she used the approach of "setting the record straight" via the experience of others in order to crack the power of forces that controlled her agency. Later, she again put to use the strategy of rational correction she had tried on her father—this time the subject being sexual identity, and her audience, people to whom she had no close relationship, such as students in her other classes. In those situations she was finally able to more fully voice the "truth" of her own experience without huge personal penalty, hi our class, in which there seemed to be the greatest opportunity to use her own experience in original and exploratory ways, she didn't. Was it perhaps because, once again, she feared excommunication from a new ideological and affectional family? Interpreted within that context, Isabel's work and her intentions for the future—to "set the record straight" in the public sphere through writing—seem quite understandable. Her writing seems to be

Isabel Serrano

concerned not so much with deconstructing the lesbian and gay community as, literally, constructing it for herself—and constructing a place for herself within it.

Note

[1] Of course, the reverse is also true: The religious view of homosexuality as sin *does* posit it as a choice, and a segment of the lesbian and gay community debunks *this* by reclaiming the essentializing notion of inherent "orientation."

Credit _____

Malinowitz, Harriet. "Isabel Serrano." Reprinted with permission from *Textual Orientations: Lesbian and Gay Students and the Making of Discourse Communities* by Harriet Malinowitz. Copyright © 1995 by Harriet Malinowitz. Published by Heinemann, Portsmouth, NH. All rights reserved.

Constructing Consumables and Consent: A Critical Analysis of Factory Farm Industry Discourse

CATHY B. GLENN

1 People historically have used other animals as resources. From hunters in the New World tracking the gigantic woolly mammoth to Cheyenne tribes hunting buffalo and European settlers raising cows, pigs, and chickens, humans have viewed nonhuman animals as a natural resource for their use and consumption (Benton and Short 1999). The various discourses that surround this practice differ depending, in part, on how the humans in question conceive of their relationship to nature and, consequently, to the animals they view as natural resources (Spiegel 1996). For instance, the hunting practices and ritualistic use and sacrifice of revered and respected animals are aspects of a well-worn story about the spirituality of Native American cultures (Cheney 1989). Another familiar narrative concerns family farmers who settled the plains and raised domesticated animals on their small farms to use and consume for subsistence purposes (Fox 1999). Still another account recalls Inuits who—by eating, wearing, using as tools, and so on—ecologically made the most of all parts of the seals they hunted in order to survive the harsh Arctic climate (Fox 1999). At least one common thread weaves through this patchwork of tales. In these three narratives, the human animals are directly connected to the land and to the nonhuman animals they use and consume—they live with, hunt alongside, know, understand, and respect both the land and the other animals they exploit. While it is important to avoid the romantic tendency of overlooking these cultures' negative marks on the environment, it is also necessary to note that current discursive constructs surrounding the practices of using and eating other animals are unlike those in any other previous narrative. Moreover, with the recent advent of factory farming (also known as high-intensity farming)—and consequent criticism by those who insist the practice is inhumane and environmentally destructive (Adams 1990; Cockburn 1996; Dunayer 2001; Fox 1999; Krayna 2002; Miller 1988; O'Brien 2001; Rifkin 1994; Schmidt 2000; Spiegel 1996; Spira 1996; Williams 1998)—an assortment of corporate strategies have ensued that construct an image of a benevolently beneficial industry. And, despite significant concerns among environmentalists and activists, resistant strategies have brought about little, if any, change. Part of the reason for this ineffectiveness, I suggest, is the immense power of the discursive practices constructed to support the industry. In this article, I am concerned with how that construction is accomplished and how it contributes to the ways USAmericans[1] think about nonhuman animals confined on factory farms. In particular, I focus on two common and codependent corporate discursive strategies: (1) the widespread use of "doublespeak" to describe particular processes internal to the industry, and (2) the creation of "speaking" animals in advertisements to sell the products of those industrial processes.

2 *Discourse,* for the purposes of this article, denotes the production of knowledge and power through language, and *discursive practices* are those institutional formations (or epistemes) within which meanings of and between contradictory discourses are constructed. This meaning construction is the way that institutions establish particular orders of truth, or what becomes accepted as commonsense "reality" in a given society (Foucault 1978, 1981). *Doublespeak* is a style of discourse within factory farm industry discursive practices that—although descriptive—is intentionally misleading by being ambiguous or disingenuous. I argue, then, that doublespeak (alongside advertisements) promotes particular ways of knowing nonhuman animals: we take for granted that "farm" animals are objects for our use and consumption. Moreover, these discourses demonstrate and extend, respectively, William Cronon's (1996) ideas of "Nature as

Commodity" and "Nature as Virtual Reality" (p. 46). Ultimately, I argue that this factory farm industry discourse helps construct how USAmericans think about animals in ways that—tacitly and oftentimes unintentionally— endorse industry practices even in the face of serious concerns raised by environmental and animal advocates.

3 Communication scholars have focused on various sites of environmental controversy and the discourse that swirls around and constitutes them (Cantrill 1993; Killingsworth and Palmer 1995; Lange 1990, 1993; Moore 1993; Myerson and Rydin 1997; Oravec 1981, 1982, 1984; Patterson and Lee 1997; Peterson 1991; Peterson and Horton 1995; Renz 1992; Segal 1991). These studies, in their attention to vitally important environmental issues, demonstrate how the discursive strategies of both proenvironmental and antienvironmental forces serve to construct and/or frame those issues. My aim is to add to the discussion *factory farm industry discourse* in order to focus on an issue that has, as of now, gone unexamined in communication studies. This study offers a critical analysis of how particular overlapping discursive strategies constructed by the factory farming industry help create, sustain, and perpetuate a practice that is cruel and environmentally dangerous.

4 In the first section, I offer a theoretical discussion of Cronon's notions of Nature as Commodity and Nature as Virtual Reality, first discussing an historical lineage that made them possible and then suggesting their codependence (Cronon 1996). Next, I describe what I argue is a practice of doublespeak internal to the factory farm industry that manifests as a Nature as Commodity discourse. In the following section, I offer an analysis of the "Happy Cow" advertising campaign created by the factory farm-supported California Milk Advisory Board that, I argue, manifests as a Nature as Virtual Reality discourse. I conclude by suggesting various critical strategies for reading and resisting factory farm discourses.

Theoretical Considerations

5 To understand what Cronon means by Nature as Commodity and Nature as Virtual Reality in the context of this study, it is helpful to trace the roots of these metaphors. Before doing so, however, it is important to note that "nature" is understood here as being as much a cultural construction as it is something "out there" that can be discovered and used (Haraway 1991; Latour 1993). As Cronon (1996) puts it, nature

6 is a profoundly human construction. This is not to say that the nonhuman world is somehow unreal or a mere figment of our imaginations—far from it. But the way we describe and understand that world is so entangled with our own values and assumptions that the two can never be fully separated. (p. 25)

7 Lisa M. Benton and John Rennie Short (1999) theoretically follow suit when they acknowledge that we can understand the environment in positivist terms but that "the environment is also a product of our social institutions. The environment plays an active role in cultural representation, political discourse, and national identity. . . . [And] environmental truths are made rather than found" (p. 2). Nonhuman animals, then, as a part of nature or the environment, are included in this cultural construction and the way we think about and value them is less a matter of who and how they *are* than it is about how *we construct them to be*. That is to say, even though they exist as beings-in-the-world with their own purposes and value, it is through the lenses of human purposes and values that we construct a relationship with them. Understanding, then, how particular discourses have historically constructed how we view our relationship with nature and animals helps us to recognize how specific forms of that relationship are presently possible.

8 The lineage of nature being understood as a commodity can be traced back to a New World "technological metadiscourse" (Benton and Short 1999, 2) that constructed nature as a resource for human purposes and that continues to influence current discourses. The technological metadiscourse, influenced by colonial discourses, assumes that humans' relationship to their environment is one mediated by the use of technology to facilitate a consumerist approach to natural-resource exploitation. This relationship includes the assumptions that progress is enabled by "subduing [the] environment [and] improving or controlling nature," the "intense use of [the] earth's resources," and understanding that the "environment [is] important if 'use value' exists" (Benton and Short 1999, 3).

9   These elements of a technological metadiscourse set the stage for what would become the immense enterprise of factory farming. Cronon points out that the cumulative effect of commodifying nature during the westward expansion could be seen in industries related to changing animal populations (Cronon, in Benton and Short 1999, 55). Buffalos were hunted to near extinction and their disappearance was key to introducing and installing domesticated animals on farms of the settled plains. Moreover, the ascendance of capitalism and modern modes of production fortified the "Nature as a Commodity" discourse and promoted the discursive practices of contemporary factory farms. Although farm animals have been raised since Roman times in confined quarters to restrict their movement and, in turn, to fatten them, the current practices of factory farming are relatively unique. Late-stage capitalism, with its emphasis on technological innovation and efficiency, has enabled this industry to develop highly sophisticated and automated practices. In the 1950s, the cattle industry, in its packing practices, developed an assembly-line production mode that made the process more efficient and extended that mode of production to slaughtering practices. Contemporary practices are a direct offshoot of these with at least one significant difference: the scale at which these factory farms operate has increased tremendously in recent years (Adams 1990; Cockburn 1996; Rifkin 1994; Schmidt 2000; Spira 1996; Williams 1998).

10   The factory farming industry, I argue, is a particularly compelling manifestation of the Nature as Commodity discourse. Even though Cronon may not explicitly cite factory farms as such, his analysis clearly points in the direction of understanding this industry as a manifestation of this discourse. For instance, Jerry L. Pulley (1994) points out that the U.S. Department of Agriculture (USDA) has designated cows, pigs, and sheep "grain-consuming animal units" (pp. 271-74) that become commodities to be bought, traded, and sold in agricultural marketplaces as well as on Wall Street. In the next section, I extend Cronon's metaphor to include similar forms of doublespeak that pervade this industry's internal workings and that construct nonhuman animals as commodities.

11   Nature as Virtual Reality, for Cronon (1996), is a discourse that is closely related to Nature as Commodity and, I suggest, is also connected to Benton and Short's (1999) technological metadiscourse. As Cronon reasons, the creation of virtual nature (e.g., in computer simulations or technologically saturated nature parks like Sea World) often enables consumers to think of and, thus, buy nature as a commodity. That is, technologically created nature comes so "close to constructing an alternative reality" that even though we might conceive of nature as *the real* reality, "it is increasingly possible to inhabit a cultural space whose analogues in nature seem ever more tenuous" (Cronon 1996, 43-45). Put simply, what this technology mimics, it also tends to elide. However, Cronon suggests that this aspect of Nature as Virtual Reality, if attended to discursively, is useful in understanding how we talk (and think) about nature: "virtual can in fact serve as a powerful and rather troubling test of whether we really know what we're talking about when we speak of nature" (p. 45).

12   Cronon, throughout his analysis, is referring to computer-generated programs (e.g., artificial intelligence) that attempt to replicate natural processes, not to the "HappyCow" advertisements that I discuss later in this article. However, we can understand the technology used to create these advertisements as capable of creating an alternative

reality in which animals are constructed as able to "speak" for themselves in order to tell consumers that they are content and happily consent to being used as resources.

In sum, Nature as Commodity and Nature as Virtual Reality are particular discursive manifestations (or metaphors) of an overarching technological metadiscourse that influences how we think about nature and, by extension, other animals. In the next two sections, I offer examples of each metaphor within the context of factory farming.

Animal as Unit/Nature as Commodity: Discursive Strategies in Industry

Joan Dunayer, in her book *Animal Equality: Language and Liberation* (2001), offers a wide-ranging, contemporary collection of examples of language used by various human institutions to hide the inhumane treatment of animals. In this section, I employ Dunayer's data, collected from factory farm industry insider literature and reported from her firsthand experiences, and I argue that the language employed to neutrally describe various inhumane and cruel processes constitutes a powerful current example of doublespeak. As Richard M. Coe (1998) describes it, "Doublespeak techniques include the abuse of euphemism, nominalization, abstraction, presupposition, jargon, titles, and metaphor and other tropes as well as inflated language, gobbledygook, symmetrizing, stipulative definition, and ambiguity (weasel words)" (pp. 192-95). William Lutz (1987) notes that doublespeak is not so much the use of these techniques per se; rather, it is the intent to deceive by using these linguistic forms that constitutes doublespeak (pp. 383-91). An example of doublespeak is its use by the military:

> It's not a Titan II nuclear-armed, intercontinental ballistic missile with a warhead 630 times more powerful than the atomic bomb dropped on Hiroshima, it is just *a very Large, potentially disruptive re-entry system* , so don't worry about the threat of nuclear destruction. It is not a neutron bomb but a *radiation enhancement device* , so don't worry about escalating the arms race. It is not an invasion but a *rescue mission* , or a *predawn vertical insertion* , so don't worry about any violations of United States or international law. (Lutz 1987, 385-86, his emphasis)

Certainly, this is not a new discursive strategy, nor is it unique to the military or the government.

Dunayer points to numerous examples of factory-farming language that, I argue, constitute doublespeak, and each accomplishes the same objective: using sterile language to hide violence.

Dunayer begins by exploring the use of the euphemism *animal agriculture*, which has largely replaced *livestock industry*. Rather than calling their business enterprise a livestock industry, the National Cattlemen's Association (NCA) has urged those in the U.S. "cow-flesh[2] industry" to use *animal agriculture* (Dunayer 2001, 125). As Dunayer clarifies, *industry* could set off environmental warning bells, whereas *agriculture* is generally understood as a safe, natural practice. Moreover, instead of *factory or high-intensity farm*, the NCA has recommended using the euphemism *family farm*. Although a questionable phrase with respect to its accuracy because of the tremendous size of these corporations, this anachronism survives in current discourses: "Don Tyson's multi-billion dollar bird-flesh company—the world's largest— maintains the quaint façade of a 'family farm' (a label that confers tax, as well as PR benefits)" (Dunayer 2001, 125).

Most of us understand that the terms *beef, veal, pork, and poultry* are euphemisms employed by the industry to designate flesh from cows, calves, pigs, and birds such as chickens and turkeys. We recognize that such euphemisms are employed mainly for marketing purposes, and for the most part, we accept the practice without necessarily questioning its ethics. It is a recognizable discursive move that removes the "beingness" or subjectivity of animals and replaces it with aword that morphs a subject for its own purposes into an object for consumption. Put differently, the use of these euphemisms disguises the fact that the body parts we purchase and consume are the objectified remains of former subjects. It is a familiar example of nature (in this case, nonhuman animals) as commodities.

20   Moreover, government agencies follow suit in this commodification process. For instance, Dunayer (2001) points out that the Internal Revenue Service designates so-called farm animals as "'inventory' [and] 'items' that are *financed, capitalized, depreciated, invoiced, leased, and liquidated.*" The USDA also commodifies animals, calling them "grain- and roughage-consuming 'animal units'." These "units" are made up of "veal calves," "dairy cows," "beef cows," "feeder pigs," "breeder pigs," "layers," and "broilers" (p. 132). Clearly, the industry and the government that helps support it, understands "food" animals as no more than the products (meat, dairy, and eggs) that are eventually rendered from their short existences. Understood as objects intended to produce sellable products, then, animals on factory farms are commonly treated as such. However, this is a side of factory farming that the industry would rather not put on public display.

21   A current factory farming textbook, *Intensive Pig Production*, denotes sows' restricted living quarters as "individual accommodation[s]" (Dunayer 2001, 133). Moreover, the American Veterinary Medical Association (AVMA)—which, incidentally, promotes "animal agriculture"—reports that the sows in this housing situation appear to be "satisfied in their environment." Dunayer's description of a typical housing situation for pregnant sows merits quoting at length:

22   Sows endure each pregnancy isolated in a stall with iron bars and a concrete floor. The stall is so narrow that a sow has room only to stand up and lie down. If the stall is open in the rear, she also is chained to the floor by a neck collar or body harness. ...Typically, a sow reacts to tethering with violent escape attempts lasting up to several hours: repeatedly she yanks on her chain; screaming, she twists and thrashes; sometimes she crashes against the stall's bars before collapsing. After her futile struggle to break free, she lies motionless, groaning and whimpering, her snout reaching outward beneath the bars. Finally, she sits for long periods with her head drooping and her eyes vacant or closed. (p. 126) And even though she—housed in a crate while pregnant—"often develops sores from rubbing against the narrow crate or tears her nipples attempting to stand," the crate that restrains the pregnant sow is innocuously coined a "modern maternity unit" (p. 127).

23   Sows are not the only pigs who—during an entire lifetime in captivity— endure brutal conditions veiled by industry discourse. Piglets, if born too small, are called "runts" and are "euthanized." This involves, as Dunayer points out, holding a piglet by their back legs and slamming their head against the floor. Often, the piglets are still conscious after the first attempt to kill them. Although this is not a practice unique to factory farming, the point is that calling it euthanasia hides the violence and suffering inflicted on these animals behind a euphemism that renders the practice humane or sterile.

24   Hens also suffer immensely so that farmers can extract from them as many eggs as possible. One way to increase egg laying is to shock the hens into an artificial molting period:

25   Suddenly left in total darkness, the hens are denied food and, in many cases, water. Usually the water deprivation lasts one to two days, the starvation at least ten. Forced molting should increase profits, *Commercial Chicken Production* Manual authors Mack North and Donald Bell note—provided no more than 2 percent of the hens die. In an egg factory with a million hens, 2 percent is 20,000 individuals. (Dunayer 2001, 129)

26   This practice is dubbed "induced molting" (hiding the violence of force), "fasting" (as though it were voluntary), or "recycling" (which, while mimicking environmental discourse, only recognizes the additional egg-laying cycle while completely erasing the

bird).

27   Particularly disingenuous is the discourse—constructed for both industry insiders and public relations—surrounding the handling of calves whom the dairy industry discards and who are subsequently exploited as white veal. Housed in extremely narrow crates, the calves are partitioned off from other calves, frustrating their attempts to lick or nuzzle each other. They are fed only an iron-deficient formula and no roughage (to keep their muscle tissue white), and the formula is mostly water, powdered milk, and fat. These calves frequently have "chronic diarrhea (which is often fatal)" and suffer because of their diet, from ulcers, heat stress, and bloat (Dunayer 2001, 132). The housing situation, according to the industry, is for the calves' own protection: it keeps them from "running around a little bit too much" (p. 132). Calling the conditions merely "unaesthetic," industry insiders suggest that "each calf 'has its own private stall' that 'features' partitions for 'privacy.'" And, with respect to the extreme level of dietary deprivation, the industry disguises "what is artificial as natural" by calling the calves "milk-fed," "special-fed," or "fancy-fed" (p. 132).

28   The factory farming discourse hides vicious practices by constructing them as "natural," "accommodating," and "comfortable" for the animals confined in the factory. (Transportation and slaughtering practices are equally cruel; however, a discussion of those practices and the host of euphemisms that hide that violence is outside the scope of this article.) For the buying public, the animals' remains are simply consumable commodities. When questions are raised about possible mistreatment of animals, what the industry offers is the company line: of course, the animals are not abused; if they were, they wouldn't be producing or reproducing. Research of industry literature indicates, however, this is not necessarily the case:

29   Hens with deep, infected wounds or broken bones lay eggs at a normal rate, as do hens who have lost the ability to stand or even sit upright. Cows with foot disease produce abundant milk. Sows and ewes "crippled by lameness" reproduce. Pigs with pneumonia grow as desired. (Dunayer 2001, 133)

30   *Successful Farming* livestock editor Betty Freese visited a pig farm with a high rate of piglet birth and survival and found that pigs kept in horrendous conditions can still be commercially productive:

31   "[I saw sows] in gestation crates so narrow that when they laid down, their legs rested on their neighbor. In the crowded nursery, pigs had bleeding tail stumps and ulcerated holes in place of ears." She admits, "We've held up herd production figures and stated that abused animals wouldn't produce like this." (Dunayer 2001, 133-34)

32   For the factory farm, as in other corporations, the bottom line is profit. Animals' welfare can be traded off when production rates remain high regardless of the animals' poor health and living conditions. For Cronon (1996), this discourse would characterize a nonhuman animal "as a thing capable of being bought and sold in the marketplace quite apart from any autonomous values that might inhere in it" (p. 133).

33   However, living conditions and health (or at least the image of them) become valuable commodities in themselves when the discourse is public. That is, when it comes to advertising, positive images of animals' health and welfare become just as saleable as the products rendered from the animals, and the two discourses of industry doublespeak and public advertising can be seen as codependent. On one hand, internal discourse hides the violence, and on the other, advertisements create an alternative reality to take replace the actual reality. In the next section, using Cronon's Nature as Virtual Reality, I discuss a recent example of this discourse: the "Happy Cows" advertising campaign.

Animal as Speaking Subject/Nature as Virtual Reality:
Discursive Strategies in Advertising

34 Cronon's (1996) metaphor of Nature as Virtual Reality helps us understand how our own technological creation of an alternative nature can both elide nature in its actuality and, at the same time, test the validity of our discourse about nature itself. Here, I am interested in exploring how advertisements' representations of "speaking animals" who are selling the end "products" of the brutal processes they endure in the factory farm system serve, at least, a dual discursive purpose. The first purpose is to sell product, and the second role is somewhat trickier (and, I argue, unintended): to make the nonhuman animal victims disappear and replace them with animals functionally indistinguishable from humans. It is this last that, I contend, tests our discourse about nature. It is also, I believe, a discourse that tests the boundary between humans and other animals by explicitly erasing that boundary while tacitly reinforcing it.

35 The first function of speaking animals in advertisements is the obvious one: to sell product, in part, by selling us on the cute, clever, or pretty animal character. An effective approach to marketing and advertising is the use of a spokesperson who, through his or her particular appeal, can lend power to messages intended to be persuasive. Whether it is Charlie Tuna or the Foster Farms chickens selling themselves, the talking spokes-"person" for the industry is usually persuasive, in part, because he or she uses an appeal to emotion (e.g., both Charlie Tuna and the Foster Farms chickens were intended to be humorous). The use of speaking animals selling themselves is largely taken for granted and rarely questioned with respect to ethics. On December 11, 2002, however, the activist organization People for the Ethical Treatment of Animals (PETA) filed suit against the California Milk Advisory Board claiming that its "Happy Cows" advertising campaign is fraudulent and unethical. "Happy Cows" is a vastly popular advertising campaign that features television, radio, and billboard ads along with merchandise for adults (e.g., calendars and T-shirts) and children (e.g., coloring books and board games). These ads, I argue, sell an alternative reality created by the computer-generated "natural" environments of these virtual animals. The advertisements feature healthy, clever, and funny animals enjoying their easy lives and happily consenting to "contributing" their share to the "family" business. Moreover, the campaign—which started in October 2000 and continues through the present— is being credited in part for moving California's dairy industry ahead, in terms of profits, of Wisconsin's long top-seated dairy industry (Krayna 2002). In one television spot, an old-fashioned wooden barn lies in the middle of an empty green field with two cows inside on a bed of hay, awakening to the sound of a rooster. One yawns and sighs while the other says, "Morning. So what do you think then . . . get an early start on that alfalfa on the back forty?" The other responds, "What's the hurry, hit the snooze." As the rooster is kicked out of the barn, the following words appear in the foreground and a voice-over is heard speaking, "Great Cheese comes from Happy Cows. Happy Cows come from California. Real California cheese. It's the cheese" (quoted from the PETA lawsuit 2002b).

36 Another television ad plays with the stereotypical California obsession with health and fitness by featuring two bulls commenting on a cow's healthy appearance and lifestyle: In another grass-covered valley, one bull asks the other, "You're from back East, right?" "Huh?" asks the other. "Yeah, trust me on this one, man. The babes out here are different." The easterner asks, "How come?" "I don't know. All the sunshine, I guess. Clean air, good food, something. They just really take care of them . . ." Just then a dairy cow walks by, and as they spot her, they say, "Whoa." "Oh, yeah—hey, you work out?" As the shot widens to show more of the valley sparsely populated with grazing cows throughout, the same catchphrase is repeated: "Great Cheese comes from Happy Cows. Happy Cows come from California. Real California cheese. It's the cheese" (quoted from the PETA Federal Trade Commission complaint document 2002a).

37   What PETA argues in its lawsuit (and Dunayer has demonstrated in her research) is that these depictions do not reflect the actual conditions of animals confined on factory farms. They are usually raised in extremely crowded conditions, on high-intensity dry-lots where they often stand all day in an amalgamation of urine- and feces-saturated dirt (or mud, when it rains). They rarely graze on grass, and on the biggest California farms, cows never graze but are fed highly concentrated feed doctored with antibiotics aimed at staving off diseases (brought about partly by horrendous living conditions). They are not raised together in families; the cows are usually overworked by being kept pregnant so that they can be milked constantly; they live short lives (five to six years on average while the natural lifespan is twenty-five to thirty years); and they are not in control of when they eat, when they sleep, or whether they work (PETA2002a, 2002b; Dunayer 2001; Krayna 2002). Although this is the actuality of animals confined to factory farms, this campaign exemplifies Cronon's notion that, in a discourse of "Nature as Virtual Realty," the alternative reality can elide and replace the actual reality.

38   A related function of ads that feature speaking animals is reminiscent of an earlier cartoon featuring a virtual animal. The principles involved in creating a character that sells us on exploiting it for its products or killing and eating it is similar to an invented creature called a "schmoo":

39   The schmoo is a fictitious being invented by American cartoonist Al Capp. The schmoo delights in being eaten by humans, and indeed it desires nothing more.¡–We might, Michael Martin suggests, imagine real animals that, were they able to communicate with us, would express the same desire. (Fox 1999, 164-65)

40   As Fox reasons in his book *Deep Vegetarianism*, Michael Martin (an outspoken opponent of vegetarianism) creates a fantasy scenario that raises significant ethical questions about a number of issues. One of those is the possibility that genetic engineering could, in fact, create animals that "can neither suffer nor be aware in general of what is happening to their bodies . . . because they lack consciousness, or have limbs that shed themselves and regenerate" (Fox 1999, 165).

41   Fox reminds us that we are in an age of cloning and of technology that can radically change the way we relate to the environment and other animals. It may be possible to create animals with no reasons for existing except those selected by humans, machines that we can use and consume without thought. This scenario raises considerable ethical questions about how much, as human beings, we are willing to manipulate our environment and, as important, exploit other animals for gastronomical pleasure. Fox suggests that "making animals into sheer machines represents a throwback to Cartesianism of the past, another technological triumph over nature, a denial and cancellation of animals' independent congenital characteristics, and a grave form of our own alienation from the biosphere." He says these dominating and exploitive tendencies

42   will contribute (and arguably are now contributing) to our own species' self-destruction as well as to the devastation of the environment. And even if we somehow escape or postpone this fate, they may help to usher in a "brave new world" so repugnant in its artificiality none of us would wish to inhabit it. (Fox 1999, 166)

43   This last image, in particular, strikes me. The discourse of animal characters selling their own demise not only lends credence to the idea that they consent to being eaten, but it creates the conditions for the possibility that *when* it is possible to "make" animals for consumption, we will be discursively conditioned to take for granted the technological "breakthrough" of exploiting genetically engineered animal-machines.

44   Another related purpose that these virtual animals serve, I suggest, is to blur the line between human and other animals while encouraging a human behavior that tacitly reinforces the line. Robert Harrison (1996) writes,

45 It would be helpful to find an intermediary case between the human [animal] and the [nonhuman] animal, since it is our concept of the distinction between the two that we hope to clarify. Yet the mark of our exceptionality in the natural order is that intermediate species between the human and animal do not exist, *at least not in nature*. (p. 427)

46 I suggest that our creation of animals that are speaking subjects acts as that discursive intermediary between human and nonhuman worlds because they occupy a liminal space created in a virtual reality. As is so commonly accepted, an ostensibly key distinction between humans and other animals is our "exceptional" ability to speak. Since Descartes, we have prided ourselves on our rational abilities—the ability to consciously consider ourselves, enjoy an emotional sense, and possess language—all three characteristics that other animals allegedly do not possess.3

47 I The virtual creation of a speaking animal subject that represents another species as rational, feeling, and self-conscious renders the distinction between other animals and human ones hypothetically contestable. Surely, we don't believe that there are actual animals who exist like the ones in animatronic or animated television commercials (though, it would be an interesting future research project to learn how children view these images). However, without an actual connection to the animals being represented—those who are ill treated, sold, and killed—all we have is a connection to a simulacrum. These virtual speaking subjects are facsimiles that walk, talk, sing, and entertain us— and sell, over and over again, their own exploitation and slaughter for our pleasure. We trust these speaking subjects because they use the same tools to communicate that we do: words. And, as such, they seem just like us. As Harrison (1996) puts it, "If animals could speak they would no longer be animals but a species of humanity" (p. 427). In the virtual world, then, these speaking subjects are "humanimals" or "anihumans" (Minahen, 1997, 233-34).

48 In addition to this blurring of boundaries, the consequent behavior encouraged by these advertisements (e.g., buying, eating, and using of other animals' body parts) also, simultaneously, serves to tacitly reinforce the boundaries between human and nonhuman animals. It is our uniquely human exceptionality that Harrison suggests makes it impossible to ignore that there is no actual intermediary between human and nonhuman animals. Part of that so-called exceptionality is our ability to speak and reason: "Human identity is wagered entirely on the use of 'words,' while the animal body, with all of its inarticulate sounds, is relegated to a mechanical universe of automatons and chiming clocks" (Senior 1997, 62). By "giving" virtual animals the abilities to speak and reason and, *at the same time*, taking for granted that their only actual value to us is to be found in their body parts, the boundary between humans and other animals is once again distinct.

49 It is more than ironic that with one hand, we endow these virtual animals with exceptional human characteristics so that we might speak for (or through) them, while with the other hand, we take away their hypothetical ability to speak for themselves (at least through these virtual means). In essence, we have created a "subject" that is no more than an object—a subject without agency or the means to protect itself. Thus, we are left with a particularly painful paradox: nonhuman animals finally can speak to us and reason with us, but only from the perspective of an industry selling them to us, the consuming public. They are virtually gagged—they cannot language their actual pain or protest.

Some Concluding Thoughts

50 The evidence is overwhelming that factory farms are hazardous to the environment. This study has demonstrated that particular discursive strategies on the part of the industry—

doublespeak and advertisements—do much to distract from or veil those hazards. As important, the analysis points to the ways in which nonhuman animals are constructed in these discourses as objects and commodities whose only value is as product to be used or consumed by human animals. The discursive power manifest in the intertwined discourses of Nature as Commodity and Nature as Virtual Reality creates tremendous support for the factory farming industry. When nonhuman animals are viewed as resources, "languaged" as commodities, and treated as objects, advertising campaigns that function to supplant that actuality with a virtual reality support the conditions for the former. And when virtual reality becomes the primary source of knowledge about the actuality of animals confined on factory farms, the erasure of that actuality supports the virtual. Resisting these discourses, then, for those moved to do so, is a particularly challenging task.

51 Dunayer (2001) suggests that relanguaging objectified animals as subjects is one place to start. She also suggests relanguaging sterile-sounding practices related to our treatment of nonhuman animals in order to reflect their violent actuality, when necessary. She offers a vast resource of linguistic options in the form of "Style Guidelines" for writers who would like to follow in her footsteps and report conditions in graphic and affective (what she would argue is truthful) language. Also provided is a "Thesaurus of Alternatives to Speciesist Terms" that can be used by anyone who speaks about nonhuman animals and who would prefer to remove the speciesist assumptions embedded in many words and phrases.

52 My move in this study was to incorporate several of Dunayer's suggested language changes in order to emphasize the subjectivity (rather than constructed objectivity) of the nonhuman animals confined on factory farms. For instance, using *nonhuman animals* instead of simply *animals* in relation to human animals points to the false dichotomy set up when we write of "humans and animals." Changing "animals *that*" to "animals *who*" also resists the tendency to objectify other animals, a tendency that is reflected by and embedded in our language constructs. Concerned scholars and readers can adopt simple relanguaging strategies and their efforts can contribute in reinvesting "farm" animals with their subjectivity. At the very least, changing the way we talk about other animals may begin to help us think about nonhuman animals confined on factory farms as more than objects for our use and consumption.

53 Coe (1998) suggests that critical reading strategies be taught earlier and more often in the public schools so that children can learn to recognize and defend against doublespeak. Media literacy with respect to advertisements ought to also be a part of this strategy. Lutz (1987) suggests a similar strategy, adding that children and adults need to fall in love with the miracle of language, and following Charlton Laird, notes that language is

54 the most important tool man [*sic*] ever devised. . . . Language is (man's) [*sic*] basic tool. It is the tool more than any other with which he [*sic*] makes his [*sic*] living, makes his [*sic*] home, makes his [*sic*] life. As man [*sic*] becomes more and more a social being, as the world becomes more and more a social community, communication grows ever more imperative. (p. 391)

55 Certainly, Laird and Lutz are correct about language being an important means of constituting reality; it is, however, often used as a standard by humans at the expense of nonhumans (and some gendered individuals at the expense of others, as is ironically the case in the quotation above). As David Clark (1997) writes in this respect,

56 Language is the implacable human standard against which the animal is measured and always found wanting; but what if the "animal" were to become the site of an excess against which one might measure the prescriptive, exclusionary force of the *logos* , the ways in which the truth of the rational word muffles, strangles and finally silences the animal? (p. 191)

57 A strategy, then, that would begin to challenge factory farming discourses, in particular, and factory farming, in general, must include more than relanguaging.

58 Cronon suggests that we need to find a middle ground between nature as wilderness and nature as artifice in order to recognize and honor the Other:

59
> Learning to honor the wild—learning to remember and acknowledge the autonomy of the other—means striving for critical self-consciousness in all of our actions. It means that deep reflection and respect must accompany each act of use, and means too that *we must always consider the possibility of non-use* . (p. 89, emphasis added)

60 Because the use of factory farm animal products supports a clearly cruel and environmentally dangerous industry, choosing nonuse (that is, refusing to buy products associated with factory farming) is an ethically sound choice. Much like the refusal to purchase goods created by slave labor in developing countries sends a message to the offending corporation, the rejection of products from an industry that routinely inflicts suffering on nonhuman animals can also send a message. In Cronon's terms, then, alongside Dunayer, Coe, and Lutz, we can begin the process of critical self-reflection and consciousness by educating others and ourselves with respect to practices that exploit and abuse nonhuman animals. Moreover, by changing how we talk (and being aware of how we are talked to) about those practices, it is possible to begin *seriously* to consider the option of nonuse. My hope is that this article makes a contribution to those considerations.

Notes

[1] Although it is common to use the term *American* to signify those who were born and live in the United States of America, it is a term that positions the U.S. as "the" America and those who live here as "the" Americans. This is, of course, a misnomer given that South America and Canada are also a part of the Americas, and I use "USAmerican" to acknowledge this actuality. Moreover, I follow Malini Johar Schueller (1998) in adopting the term because it critically underlines "the imperialism inherent in the slippage between the terms [*American* and *USAmerican*]" (p. 207). I use the term *USAmerican* in contrast to *American*, then, to signify my resistance to a discursive practice that privileges the United States and, by extension, promotes a colonial imperialism. (For an in-depth discussion, see McCaig 2000.)

[2] Dunayer's own discursive move throughout the book is to juxtapose the sterile language of human industries with her own graphic and affective descriptions of the nonhuman consequences. Certainly, one could argue that her language moves beyond description and her explicit advocacy on behalf of animals, apparent in her language, presupposes a stronger discursive choice than "mere" reporting of conditions. In some ways, her strategy can be conceived as simply inverting language that hides by replacing it with loaded or emotionally laden language. On the other hand, if we read Dunayer as employing a narrative technique, one that unashamedly takes an affective stand for other animals who cannot speak for themselves (at least, not in away that can be easily understood by human animals), we can appreciate the approach as a critical move that seeks to connect with readers in ways that compel an acknowledgement of the conditions under which these animal subjects live for most of their lives. In the context of communication studies, then, it is possible to understand Dunayer's discursive style as performative writing: for examples and discussions of such an approach, see Miller and Pelias (2001); Pollock (1999); Menchaca (2002); Pelias (1998); Goodall (2000); and Bochner and Ellis (2002).

[3] Researchers in a number of different areas have challenged this premise. See Griffin (1992), Dawkins (1993), Masson and McCarthy (1995), and de Waal (1997).

Credit _____

Glenn, Cathy B. "Constructing Consumables and Consent: A Critical Analysis of Factory Farm Industry Discourse." *Journal of Communication Inquiry* (28:1), 63-81. Copyright © 2004 by SAGE Publications. Reprinted by permission of SAGE Publications.

Composing as a Woman

ELIZABETH A. FLYNN

1 It is not easy to think like a woman in a man's world, in the world of the professions; yet the capacity to do that is a strength which we can try to help our students develop. To think like a woman in a man's world means thinking critically, refusing to accept the givens, making connections between facts and ideas which men have left unconnected. It means remembering that every mind resides in a body; remaining accountable to the female bodies in which we live; constantly retesting given hypotheses against lived experience. It means a constant critique of language, for as Wittgenstein (no feminist) observed, "The limits of my language are the limits of my world." And it means that most difficult thing of all: listening and watching in art and literature, in the social sciences, in all the descriptions we are given of the world, for silences, the absences, the nameless, the unspoken, the encoded-for there we will find the true knowledge of women. And in breaking those silences, naming ourselves, uncovering the hidden, making ourselves present, we begin to define a reality which resonates to us, which affirms our being, which allows the woman teacher and the woman student alike to take ourselves, and each other, seriously: meaning, to begin taking charge of our lives.

—Adrienne Rich, "Taking Women Students Seriously"

2 The emerging field of composition studies could be described as a feminization of our previous conceptions of how writers write and how writing should be taught.[1] In exploring the nature of the writing process, composition specialists expose the limitations of previous product-oriented approaches by demystifying the product and in so doing empowering developing writers and readers. Rather than enshrining the text in its final form, they demonstrate that the works produced by established authors are often the result of an extended, frequently enormously frustrating process and that creativity is an activity that results from experience and hard work rather than a mysterious gift reserved for a select few. In a sense, composition specialists replace the figure of the authoritative father with an image of a nurturing mother. Powerfully present in the work of composition researchers and theorists is the ideal of a committed teacher concerned about the growth and maturity of her students who provides feedback on ungraded drafts, reads journals, and attempts to tease out meaning from the seeming incoherence of student language. The field's foremothers come to mind-Janet Emig, Mina Shaughnessy, Ann Berthoff, Win Horner, Maxine Hairston, Shirley Heath, Nancy Martin, Linda Flower, Andrea Lunsford, Sondra Perl, Nancy Sommers, Marion Crowhurst, Lisa Ede. I'll admit the term foremother seems inappropriate as some of these women are still in their thirties and forties-we are speaking here of a very young field. Still, invoking their names suggests that we are also dealing with a field that, from the beginning, has welcomed contributions from women-indeed, has been shaped by women. The work of male composition researchers and theorists has also contributed significantly to the process of feminization described above. James Britton, for instance, reverses traditional hierarchies by privileging private expression over public transaction, process over product. In arguing that writing for the self is the matrix out of which all forms of writing develop, he valorizes an activity and a mode of expression that have previously been undervalued or invisible, much as feminist literary critics have argued that women's letters and diaries are legitimate literary forms and should be studied and taught alongside more traditional genres. His work has had an enormous impact on the way writing is taught on the elementary and high school levels and in the university, not only in English courses but throughout the curriculum. Writing-Across-the- Curriculum Programs aim to transform pedagogical practices in all disciplines, even those where patriarchal attitudes toward authority are most deeply rooted.

Feminist Studies and Composition Studies

3 Feminist inquiry and composition studies have much in common. After all, feminist researchers and scholars and composition specialists are usually in the same department and sometimes teach the same courses. Not surprisingly, there have been wonderful moments when feminists have expressed their commitment to the teaching of writing. Florence Howe's essay, "Identity and Expression: A Writing Course for Women," for example, published in *College English* in 1971, describes her use of journals in a writing course designed to empower women. Adrienne Rich's essay, "'When We Dead Awaken': Writing as Re-Vision," politicizes and expands our conception of revision, emphasizing that taking another look at the texts we have generated necessitates revising our cultural assumptions as well.

4 There have also been wonderful moments when composition specialists have recognized that the marginality of the field of composition studies is linked in important ways to the political marginality of its constituents, many of whom are women who teach part-time. Maxine Hairston, in "Breaking Our Bonds and Reaffirming Our Connections," a slightly revised version of her Chair's address at the 1985 convention of the Conference on College Composition and Communication, draws an analogy between the plight of composition specialists and the plight of many women. For both, their worst problems begin at home and hence are immediate and daily. Both, too, often have complex psychological bonds to the people who frequently are their adversaries (273).

5 For the most part, though, the fields of feminist studies and composition studies have not engaged each other in a serious or systematic way. The major journals in the field of composition studies do not often include articles ad-dressing feminist issues, and panels on feminism are infrequent at the Conference on College Composition and Communication.[2] As a result, the parallels between feminist studies and composition studies have not been delineated, and the feminist critique that has enriched such diverse fields as linguistics, reading, literary criticism, psychology, sociology, anthropology, religion, and science has had little impact on our models of the composing process or on our understanding of how written language abilities are acquired. We have not examined our research methods or research samples to see if they are androcentric. Nor have we attempted to determine just what it means to compose as a woman.

6 Feminist research and theory emphasize that males and females differ in their developmental processes and in their interactions with others. They emphasize, as well, that these differences are a result of an imbalance in the social order, of the dominance of men over women. They argue that men have chronicled our historical narratives and defined our fields of inquiry. Women's perspectives have been suppressed, silenced, marginalized, written out of what counts as authoritative knowledge. Difference is erased in a desire to universalize. Men become the standard against which women are judged.

7 A feminist approach to composition studies would focus on questions of difference and dominance in written language. Do males and females compose differently? Do they acquire language in different ways? Do research methods and research samples in composition studies reflect a male bias? I do not intend to tackle all of these issues. My approach here is a relatively modest one. I will survey recent feminist research on gender differences in social and psychological development, and I will show how this research and theory may be used in examining student writing, thus suggesting directions that a feminist investigation of composition might take.

Gender Differences in Social and Psychological Development

8 Especially relevant to a feminist consideration of student writing are Nancy Chodorow's *The Reproduction of Mothering*, Carol Gilligan's *In a Different Voice*, and Mary Belenky, Blythe Clinchy, Nancy Goldberger, and Jill Tarule's *Women's Ways of Knowing*. All three books suggest that women and men have different conceptions of self and different modes of interaction with others as a result of their different experiences, especially their early relationship with their primary parent, their mother.

9 Chodorow's book, published in 1978, is an important examination of what she calls the "psychoanalysis and the sociology of gender," which in turn influenced Gilligan's *In a Different Voice* and Belenky et al.'s *Women's Ways of Knowing*. Chodorow tells us in her preface that her book originated when a feminist group she was affiliated with "wondered what it meant that women parented women." She argues that girls and boys develop different relational capacities and senses of self as a result of growing up in a family in which women mother. Because all children identify first with their mother, a girl's gender and gender role identification processes are continuous with her earliest identifications whereas a boy's are not. The boy gives up, in addition to his oedipal and preoedipal attachment to his mother, his primary identification with her. The more general identification processes for both males and females also follow this pattern. Chodorow says,

10 Girls' identification processes, then, are more continuously embedded in and mediated by their ongoing relationship with their mother. They develop through and stress particularistic and affective relationships to others. A boy's identification processes are not likely to be so embedded in or mediated by a real affective relation to his father. At the same time, he tends to deny identification with and relationship to his mother and reject what he takes to be the feminine world; masculinity is defined as much negatively as positively. Masculine identification processes stress differentiation from others, the denial of affective relation, and categorical universalistic components of the masculine role. Feminine identification processes are relational, where as masculine identification processes tend to deny relationship. (176)

11 Carol Gilligan's *In a Different Voice*, published in 1982, builds on Chodorow's findings, focusing especially, though, on differences in the ways in which males and females speak about moral problems. According to Gilligan, women tend to define morality in terms of conflicting responsibilities rather than competing rights, requiring for their resolution a mode of thinking that is contextual and narrative rather than formal and abstract (19). Men, in contrast, equate morality and fairness and tie moral development to the understanding of rights and rules (19). Gilligan uses the metaphors of the web and the ladder to illustrate these distinctions. The web suggests interconnectedness as well as entrapment; the ladder suggests an achievement-orientation as well as individualistic and hierarchical thinking. Gilligan's study aims to correct the inadequacies of Lawrence Kohlberg's de-lineation of the stages of moral development. Kohlberg's study included only male subjects, and his categories reflect his decidedly male orientation. For him, the highest stages of moral development derive from a reflective under-standing of human rights (19).

12 Belenky, Clinchy, Goldberger, and Tarule, in *Women's Ways of Knowing*, acknowledge their debt to Gilligan, though their main concern is intellectual rather than moral development. Like Gilligan, they recognize that male experience has served as the model in defining processes of intellectual maturation. The mental processes that are involved in considering the abstract and the impersonal have been labeled "thinking" and are attributed primarily to men, while those that deal with the personal and interpersonal fall under the rubric of "emotions" and are largely relegated to women. The particular study they chose to examine and revise is William Perry's *Forms of Intellectual and Ethical Development in the College Years* (1970). While Perry did include some women subjects in his study, only the interviews with men were used in illustrating and validating his scheme of intellectual and ethical development. When Per-y assessed women's development on the basis of the categories he developed, the women were found to conform to the patterns he had observed in the male data. Thus, his work reveals what women have in common with men but was poorly designed to uncover those themes that might be more prominent among women. *Women's Ways of Knowing* focuses on "what else women might have to say about the development of their minds and on alternative routes that are sketchy or missing in Perry's version" (9).

13   Belenky et al. examined the transcripts of interviews with 1.35 women from a variety of backgrounds and of different ages and generated categories that are suited for describing the stages of women's intellectual development. They found that the quest for self and voice plays a central role in transformations of women's ways of knowing. Silent women have little awareness of their intellectual capacities. They live-selfless and voiceless-at the behest of those around them. External authorities know the truth and are all-powerful. At the positions of received knowledge and procedural knowledge, other voices and external truths prevail. Sense of self is embedded either in external definitions and roles or in identifications with institutions, disciplines, and methods. A sense of authority arises primarily through identification with the power of a group and its agreed-upon ways for knowing. Women at this stage of development have no sense of an authentic or unique voice, little awareness of a centered self. At the position of subjective knowledge, women turn away from others and any external authority. They have not yet acquired a public voice or public authority, though. Finally, women at the phase of constructed knowledge begin an effort to reclaim the self by attempting to integrate knowledge they feel intuitively with knowledge they have learned from others.

Student Writing

14   If women and men differ in their relational capacities and in their moral and intellectual development, we would expect to find manifestations of these differences in the student papers we encounter in our first-year composition courses. The student essays I will describe here are narrative descriptions of learning experiences produced in the first of a two-course sequence required of first-year students at Michigan Tech. I've selected the four because they invite commentary from the perspective of the material discussed above. The narratives of the female students are stories of interaction, of connection, or of frustrated connection. The narratives of the male students are stories of achievement, of separation, or of frustrated achievement.

15   Kim's essay describes a dreamlike experience in which she and her high school girlfriends connected with each other and with nature as a result of a balloon ride they decided to take one summer Sunday afternoon as a way of relieving boredom. From the start, Kim emphasizes communion and tranquility: "It was one of those Sunday afternoons when the sun shines brightly and a soft warm breeze blows gently. A perfect day for a long drive on a country road with my favorite friends." This mood is intensified as they ascend in the balloon: "Higher and higher we went, until the view was overpowering. What once was a warm breeze turned quickly into a cool crisp wind. A feeling of freedom and serenity overtook us as we drifted along slowly." The group felt as if they were "just suspended there on a string, with time non-existent." The experience made them contemplative, and as they drove quietly home, "each one of us collected our thoughts, and to this day we still reminisce about that Sunday afternoon." The experience solidified relationships and led to the formation of a close bond that was renewed every time the day was recollected.

16   The essay suggests what Chodorow calls relational identification processes. The members of the group are described as being in harmony with themselves and with the environment. There is no reference to competition or discord. The narrative also suggests a variation on what Belenky et al. call "connected knowing," a form of procedural knowledge that makes possible the most desirable form of knowing, constructed

knowledge. Connected knowing is rooted in empathy for others and is intensely personal. Women who are connected knowers are able to detach themselves from the relationships and institutions to which they have been subordinated and begin to trust their own intuitions. The women in the narrative were connected doers rather than connected knowers. They went off on their own, left their families and teachers behind (it was summer vacation, after all), and gave themselves over to a powerful shared experience. The adventure was, for the most part, a silent one but did lead to satisfying talk.

17   Kathy also describes an adventure away from home, but hers was far less satisfying, no doubt because it involved considerably more risk. In her narrative she makes the point that "foreign countries can be frightening" by focusing on a situation in which she and three classmates, two females and a male, found themselves at a train station in Germany separated from the others because they had gotten off to get some refreshments and the train had left without them. She says,

18   This left the four of us stranded in an unfamiliar station. Ed was the only person in our group that could speak German fluently, but he still didn't know what to do. Sue got hysterical and Laura tried to calm her down. I stood there stunned. We didn't know what to do.

19   What they did was turn to Ed, whom Kathy describes as "the smartest one in our group." He told them to get on a train that was on the same track as the original. Kathy realized, though, after talking to some passengers, that they were on the wrong train and urged her classmates to get off. She says,

20   I almost panicked. When I convinced the other three we were on the wrong train we opened the doors. As we were getting off, one of the conductors started yelling at us in German. It didn't bother me too much because I couldn't understand what he was saying. One thing about trains in Europe is that they are always on schedule. I think we delayed that train about a minute or two.

21   In deciding which train to board after getting off the wrong one, they deferred to Ed's judgment once again, but this time they got on the right train. Kathy concludes, "When we got off the train everyone was waiting. It turned out we arrived thirty minutes later than our original train. I was very relieved to see everyone. It was a very frightening experience and I will never forget it."

22   In focusing on her fears of separation, Kathy reveals her strong need for connection, for affiliation. Her story, like Kim's, emphasizes the importance of relationships, though in a different way. She reveals that she had a strong need to feel part of a group and no desire to rebel, to prove her independence, to differentiate herself from others. This conception of self was a liability as well as a strength in the sense that she became overly dependent on the male authority figure in the group, whom she saw as smarter and more competent than herself. In Belenky et al.'s terms, Kathy acted as if other voices and external truths were more powerful than her own. She did finally speak and act, though, taking it on herself to find out if they were on the right train and ushering the others off when she discovered they were not. She was clearly moving toward the development of an authentic voice and a way of knowing that integrates intuition with authoritative knowledge. After all, she was the real hero of the incident.

23   The men's narratives stress individuation rather than connection. They are stories of individual achievement or frustrated achievement and conclude by emphasizing separation rather than integration or reintegration into a community. Jim wrote about his "Final Flight," the last cross-country flight required for his pilot's license. That day, everything seemed to go wrong. First, his flight plan had a mistake in it that took 1 ½ hours to correct. As a result, he left his hometown 2 hours behind schedule. Then the weather deteriorated, forcing him to fly as low as a person can safely fly, with the result that visibility was very poor. He landed safely at his first destination but flew past the second because he was enjoying the view too much. He says,

24   Then I was off again south bound for Benton Harbor. On the way south along the coast of Lake Michigan the scenery was a beautiful sight. This relieved some of the pressures and made me look forward to the rest of the flight. It was really nice to see the ice flows break away from the shore. While enjoying the view of a power plant on the shore of Lake Michigan I discovered I had flown past the airport.

25   He finally landed and took off again, but shortly thereafter had to confront darkness, a result of his being behind schedule. He says,

26   The sky turned totally black by the time I was half-way home. This meant flying in the dark which I had only done once before. Flying in the dark was also illegal for me to do at this time. One thing that made flying at night nice was that you could see lights that were over ninety miles away.

27   Jim does not emphasize his fear, despite the fact that his situation was more threatening than the one Kathy described, and his reference to his enjoyment of the scenery suggests that his anxiety was not paralyzing or debilitating. At times, his solitary flight was clearly as satisfying as Kim's communal one. When he focuses on the difficulties he encountered, he speaks only of his "problems" and "worries" and concludes that the day turned out to be "long and trying." He sums up his experience as follows: "That day I will long remember for both its significance in my goal in getting my pilot's license and all the problems or worries that it caused me during the long and problem-ridden flight." He emerges the somewhat shaken hero of his adventure; he has achieved his goal in the face of adversity. Significantly, he celebrates his return home by having a bite to eat at McDonald's by himself. His adventure does not end with a union or reunion with others.

28   Jim's story invites interpretation in the context of Chodorow's claims about male interactional patterns. Chodorow says that the male, in order to feel himself adequately masculine, must distinguish and differentiate himself from others. Jim's adventure was an entirely solitary one. It was also goal directed-he wanted to obtain his pilot's license and, presumably, prove his competence to himself and others. His narrative calls into question, though, easy equations of abstract reasoning and impersonality with male modes of learning since Jim was clearly as capable as Kim of experiencing moments of exultation, of communion with nature.

29   Joe's narrative of achievement is actually a story of frustrated achievement, of conflicting attitudes toward an ethic of hard work and sacrifice to achieve a goal. When he was in high school, his father drove him twenty miles to swim practice and twenty miles home every Tuesday through Friday night between October and March so he could practice for the swim team. He hated this routine and hated the Saturday morning swim meets even more but continued because he thought his parents, especially his father, wanted him to. He says, "I guess it was all for them, the cold workouts, the evening practices, the weekend meets. I had to keep going for them even though I hated it." Once he realized he was going through his agony for his parents rather than for himself, though, he decided to quit and was surprised to find that his parents sup-ported him. Ultimately, though, he regretted his decision. He says,

30   As it turns out now, I wish I had stuck with it. I really had a chance to go somewhere with my talent. I see kids my age who stuck with something for a long time and I envy them for their determination. I wish I had met up to the challenge of sticking with my swimming, because I could have been very good if I would have had their determination.

31   Joe is motivated to pursue swimming because he thinks his father will be disappointed if he gives it up. His father's presumed hold on him is clearly tenuous, however, because once Joe realizes that he is doing it for him rather than for himself, he quits. Finally,

though, it is his gender role identification, his socialization into a male role and a male value system, that allows him to look back on his decision with regret. In college, he has become a competitor, an achiever. He now sees value in the long and painful practices, in a single-minded determination to succeed. The narrative reminds us of Chodorow's point that masculine identification is predominantly a gender role identification rather than identification with a particular parent.

32 I am hardly claiming that the four narratives are neat illustrations of the feminist positions discussed above. For one thing, those positions are rich in contradiction and complexity and defy easy illustration. For another, the narratives themselves are as often characterized by inconsistency and contradiction as by a univocality of theme and tone. Kathy is at once dependent and assertive; Joe can't quite decide if he should have been rebellious or disciplined. Nor am I claiming that what I have found here are characteristic patterns of male and female student writing. I would need a considerably larger and more representative sample to make such a claim hold. I might note, though, that I had little difficulty identifying essays that revealed patterns of difference among the twenty-four papers I had to choose from, and I could easily have selected others. Sharon, for instance, described her class trip to Chicago, focusing especially on the relationship she and her classmates were able to establish with her advisor. Diane described "An Unwanted Job" that she seemed unable to quit despite unpleasant working conditions. Mike, like Diane, was dissatisfied with his job, but he expressed his dissatisfaction and was fired. The frightening experience Russ described resulted from his failed attempt to give his car a tune-up; the radiator hose burst, and he found himself in the hospital recovering from third-degree burns. These are stories of relatedness or entanglement; of separation or frustrated achievement.

33 The description of the student essays is not meant to demonstrate the validity of feminist scholarship but to suggest, instead, that questions raised by feminist researchers and theorists do have a bearing on composition studies and should be pursued. We ought not assume that males and females use language in identical ways or represent the world in a similar fashion. And if their writing strategies and patterns of representation do differ, then ignoring those differences almost certainly means a suppression of women's separate ways of thinking and writing. Our models of the composing process are quite possibly better suited to describing men's ways of composing than to describing women's.[3]

Pedagogical Strategies

34 The classroom provides an opportunity for exploring questions about gender differences in language use. Students, I have found, are avid inquirers into their own language processes. An approach I have had success with is to make the question of gender difference in behavior and language use the subject to be investigated in class. In one honors section of first-year English, for instance, course reading included selections from Mary Anne Ferguson's *Images of Women in Literature*, Gilligan's *In a Different Voice*, Alice Walker's *Meridian,* and James Joyce's A *Portrait of the Artist as a Young Man*. Students were also required to keep a reading journal and to submit two formal papers. The first was a description of people they know in order to arrive at generalizations about gender differences in behavior, the second a comparison of some aspect of the Walker and Joyce novels in the light of our class discussions.

35 During class meetings we shared journal entries, discussed the assigned literature, and self-consciously explored our own reading, writing, and speaking behaviors. In one session, for instance, we shared retellings of Irwin Shaw's "The Girls in Their Summer Dresses," an especially appropriate story since it describes the interaction of a husband and wife as they attempt to deal with the husband's apparently chronic habit of girl-watching. Most of the women were sympathetic to the female protagonist, and several males clearly identified strongly with the male protagonist.

36   The students reacted favorably to the course. They found Gilligan's book to be challenging, and they enjoyed the heated class discussions. The final journal entry of one of the strongest students in the class, Dorothy, suggests the nature of her development over the ten-week period:

37   As this is sort of the wrap-up of what I've learned or how I feel about the class, I'll try to relate this entry to my first one on gender differences.

38   I'm not so sure that men and women are so similar anymore, as I said in the first entry. The reactions in class especially make me think this. The men were so hostile toward Gilligan's book! I took no offense at it, but then again I'm not a man. I must've even overlooked the parts where she offended the men! Another thing really bothered me. One day after class, I heard two of the men talking in the hall about how you just have to be really careful about what you say in HU 101H about women, etc. Why do they have to be careful?!What did these two really want to say? That was pretty disturbing.

39   However, I do still believe that MTU (or most any college actually) does bring out more similarities than differences. But the differences are still there-I know that.

40   Dorothy has begun to suspect that males and females read differently, and she has begun to suspect that they talk among themselves differently than they do in mixed company. The reading, writing, and discussing in the course have clearly alerted her to the possibility that gender affects the way in which readers, writers, and speakers use language.

41   This approach works especially well with honors students. I use somewhat different reading and writing assignments with non-honors students. In one class, for instance, I replaced the Gilligan book with an essay by Dale Spender on conversational patterns in high school classrooms. Students wrote a paper defending or refuting the Spender piece on the basis of their experiences in their own high schools. I have also devised ways of addressing feminist issues in composition courses in which the focus is not explicitly on gender differences. In a course designed to introduce students to fundamentals of research, for instance, students read Marge Piercy's *Woman on the Edge of Time* and did research on questions stimulated by it. They then shared their findings with the entire class in oral presentations. The approach led to wonderful papers on and discussions of the treatment of women in mental institutions, discrimination against minority women, and the ways in which technology can liberate women from oppressive roles.

42   I return now to my title and to the epigraph that introduces my essay. First, what does it mean to "compose as a woman"? Although the title invokes Jonathan Culler's "Reading as a Woman," a chapter in *On Deconstruction*, I do not mean to suggest by it that I am committed fully to Culler's deconstructive position. Culler maintains that "to read as a woman is to avoid reading as a man, to identify the specific defenses and distortions of male readings and provide correctives" (54). He concludes,

43   For a woman to read as a woman is not to repeat an identity or an experience that is given but to play a role she constructs with reference to her identity as a woman, which is also a construct, so that the series can continue: a woman reading as a woman reading as a woman. The noncoincidence reveals an interval, a division within woman or within any reading subject and the "experience" of that subject. (64)

44   Culler is certainly correct that women often read as men and that they have to be encouraged to defend against this form of alienation. The strategy he suggests is almost entirely reactive, though. To read as a woman is to avoid reading as a man, to be alerted to the pitfalls of men's ways of reading.[4] Rich, too, warns of the dangers of immasculation, of identifying against oneself and learning to think like a man, and she, too, emphasizes the importance of critical activity on the part of the woman student-

refusing to accept the givens of our culture, making connections between facts and ideas which men have left unconnected. She is well aware that thinking as a woman involves active construction, the recreation of one's identity. But she also sees value in recovering women's lived experience. In fact, she suggests that women maintain a critical posture in order to get in touch with that experience-to name it, to uncover that which is hidden, to make present that which has been absent. Her approach is active rather than reactive. Women's experience is not entirely a distorted version of male reality, it is not entirely elusive, and it is worthy of recuperation. We must alert our women students to the dangers of immasculation and provide them with a critical perspective. But we must also encourage them to become self-consciously aware of what their experience in the world has been and how this experience is related to the politics of gender. Then we must encourage our women students to write from the power of that experience.

Notes

[1] I received invaluable feedback on drafts of this essay from Carol Berkenkotter, Art Young, Marilyn Cooper, John Willinsky, Diane Shoos, John Flynn, Richard Gebhardt, and three anonymous CCC reviewers.

[2] The 1988 Conference on College Composition and Communication was a notable exception. It had a record number of panels on feminist or gender-related issues and a number of sessions devoted to political concerns. I should add, too, that an exception to the generalization that feminist studies and composition studies have not confronted each other is Cynthia Caywood and Gillian Overing's very useful anthology, *Teaching Writing: Pedagogy, Gender, and Equity*. In their introduction to the book, Caywood and Overing note the striking parallels between writing theory and feminist theory. They conclude, "[The process model, insofar as it facilitates and legitimizes the fullest expression of the individual voice, is compatible with the feminist re-visioning of hierarchy, if not essential to it" (xiv). Pamela Annas, in her essay, "Silences: Feminist Language Research and the Teaching of Writing," describes a course she teaches at the University of Massachusetts at Boston, entitled "Writing as Women." In the course, she focuses on the question of silence--"what kinds of silence there are; the voices inside you that tell you to be quiet, the voices outside you that drown you out or politely dismiss what you say or do not understand you, the silence inside you that avoids saying anything important even to yourself, internal and external forms of censorship, and the stress that it produces" (3-4). Carol A. Stanger in "The Sexual Politics of the One-to-One Tutorial Approach and Collaborative Learning" argues that the one-to-one tutorial is essentially hierarchical and hence a male mode of teaching whereas collaborative learning is female and relational rather than hierarchical.
She uses Gilligan's images of the ladder and the web to illustrate her point. Elisabeth Daeumer and Sandra Runzo suggest that the teaching of writing is comparable to the activity of mothering in that it is a form of "women's work." Mothers socialize young children to insure that they become acceptable citizens, and teachers' work, like the work of mothers, is usually devalued (45-46).

[3] It should be clear by now that my optimistic claim at the outset of the essay that the field of composition studies has feminized our conception of written communication needs qualification. I have already mentioned that the field has developed, for the most part, independent of feminist studies and as a result has not explored written communication in the context of women's special needs and problems. Also, feminist inquiry is beginning to reveal that work in cognate fields that have influenced the development of composition studies is androcentric. For an exploration of the androcentrism of theories of the reading process see Patrocinio P. Schweickart, "Reading Ourselves: Toward a Feminist Theory of Reading."

⁴ Elaine Showalter, in "Reading as a Woman: Jonathan Culler and the Deconstruction of Feminist Criticism," argues that "Culler's deconstructionist priorities lead him to overstate the essentialist dilemma of defining the *woman* reader, when in most cases what is intended and implied is a *feminist* reader" (126).

Credit

Flynn, Elizabeth. "Composing as a Woman." *College Composition and Communication* 39.4. Copyright © 1988 by the National Council of Teachers of English. Reprinted by permission.

Contextualizing "Composing as a Woman"
ELIZABETH A. FLYNN

1   Ideas that challenge received wisdom often need to be expressed with a minimum of qualification in order to overcome the considerable resistance that might accompany their introduction. Qualification usually comes later, after the ideas have circulated and been responded to. Thomas Kuhn's *The Structure of Scientific Revolutions* (1962) is a case in point. Kuhn explains in the preface to the first edition of the book that his exposure to the history of science radically undermined some of his basic conceptions about the nature of science and the reasons for its special success (v). The result was his development of the importance of "paradigms," "scientific achievements that for a time provide model problems and solutions to a community of practitioners" (vii). Kuhn is primarily interested, however, in those anomalous moments when the paradigm is disrupted and a revolution results (ix). Given that his conception of how scientific change occurs challenged existing explanations, he needed to make the strongest case possible. In a postscript to the second edition of the book written seven years later, however, he responds to his critics and refines his position. He acknowledges that the boundaries that separate scientific communities are considerably less rigid than he originally suggested (177) and that the change brought about by revolutions need not be large and need not be accompanied by crisis (181).

2   "Composing as a Woman" (1988), while hardly the equivalent of Kuhn's *The Structure of Scientific Revolutions,* was, like Kuhn's work, written at a transitional moment. It looks back to the time when feminism and composition studies had not yet engaged each other, and it looks forward to the emergence of feminist composition. Work that the essay draws on—Nancy Chodorow's *The Reproduction of Mothering,* Carol Gilligan's *In a Different Voice,* and Belenky, Clinchy, Goldberger, and Tarule's *Women's Ways of Knowing*—was written at a similar moment. Explanations of psychological and intellectual development by male researchers had ignored important differences between the processes of males and females because they had focused exclusively on the development of males. Chodorow, Gilligan, and the *Women's Ways of Knowing* collective needed to make clear that attending to women's different processes changes traditional findings in important ways. And they needed to establish that significant differences do exist. Qualification of their basic claim would have weakened their position and invited dismissal of their ideas.

3   Like Chodorow, Gilligan, and the *Women's Ways of Knowing* collective, I was introducing a relatively new idea into composition studies, the idea that the composing processes of male and female students may differ in important ways. To make the point, I selected especially good examples that demonstrated the usefulness of feminist work in other fields to the study of composition. Although the qualifications I provided have often been overlooked, I did make clear that my findings were provisional, that there were similarities as well as differences between the male and female writers, and that some student writing exhibited characteristics that contradicted the dichotomous descriptions I provided. I nevertheless was primarily interested in establishing, if only tentatively, that it would be productive for researchers in the field to attend to differences between male and female writers.

4   Fifteen years later we are at a considerably different moment within feminist studies in general and feminist composition in particular. The legitimacy of feminist approaches no longer needs to be established. They have been embraced to a greater or lesser degree in most fields in the humanities and the social sciences, and important work is being done in areas such as the sciences, law, and engineering. Within composition studies, feminism has emerged as an important area of inquiry, and numerous single-author and multiple-author books, journal articles, and book chapters have appeared in recent years. The biannual Feminism(s) and Rhetoric(s) conference has increased in size and significance, and numerous junior scholars are exploring rhetoric and composition from a feminist perspective. Some of this work continues to focus on differences between male and female writing strategies. As often, though, it challenges or qualifies the claims of earlier work, thereby providing refinement and the development of new research directions.

5   My recent work has moved far beyond the research questions addressed in "Composing as a Woman." For instance, in my book, *Feminism Beyond Modernism,* I defend postmodern feminism and distinguish it from modern and antimodern feminisms. A postmodern feminist approach, I argue, challenges conceptions of gender as an essence or a fixed category, seeing it, instead, as a dynamic process. I point out some of the limitations of modern feminist emphases on equality between men and women and of antimodern emphases on differences between men and women. Portions of the book are substantially reworked versions of essays I published in the 1990s. In some ways, however, "Composing as a Woman" has overshadowed these essays. It continues to be reprinted (this, I believe, is the seventh reprinting), and with each reprinting the disparity between the historical moment that gave rise to it and the present historical moment increases.

6   This is a good time, therefore, to point out some of my present discomfort with the essay. I must confess that even when I was writing "Composing as a Woman" I felt uneasy about dichotomous representations of the differences between males and females in the work I was drawing on and about assumptions that women's traditional roles were reproduced easily and readily because daughters identified with and emulated their mothers. In my family, class differences intersected gender differences in complex ways, and the accounts of neither Chodorow, Gilligan, nor the *Women's Ways of Knowing* collective seemed adequate to explain the conflicts between my parents or between my mother and me. My students, too, have made it clear that the families they come from often depart from the traditional nuclear family in which the mother is the primary parent. Many are raised by single parents, or their mothers work outside the home. I don't regret publishing "Composing as a Woman" when I did. But I hope, as it continues to be republished, that it will be seen in its historical context. It was important, in the late 1980s, to make a strong case for differences between men and women, even if we would later need to qualify, refine, and even contradict those claims.

Credit _____

Memoria Is a Friend of Ours:
On the Discourses of Color

VICTOR VILLANUEVA

A memory. Seattle, 1979.

1 She is a contradiction in stereotypes, not to be pegged. He likes her right off. She wants to go to Belltown, the Denny Regrade, to take photos. He wants to go along. He does, feeling insecure and full of bravado, slipping into the walk of bravado he had perfected as a child in Brooklyn. Stops into a small café at the outskirts of downtown, at the entry to the Regrade. It's a French-style café, the Boulangerie, or some such. To impress her, he speaks French.

2 *"Une tasse de café, s'il vous plait. Et croissants pour les duex."* Don't laugh. It's how he said it.

3 He's an English major, a senior, quite proud of having gotten this far in college. But he's insecure about what this will lead to (since he had only gotten as far as deciding to stay in college till he's finally in over his head). He tells her of a novel he will write someday. His description goes something like:

4 I've been thinking about a novel about a white Puerto Rican kid who buys into the assimilation myth, hook, line, and sinker. He does all the right things – learns the language, learns how to pronounce "r's" in words like "motherrr" and "waterrr" and how not to trill the "r" when he says "three," and does well in school. He's even a war hero. Does it all, only to realize that assimilation just can't happen. Yet he can't really be Puerto Rican. So maybe he goes to Puerto Rico to find out who he might have been and what he is tied to. I don't have it all worked out.

5 The plot line might not have been worked out, but this was the impulse nevertheless – to keep alive the memory of assimilation denied, a truism turned to myth, to try to hold on to, maybe even to regain, that which had been lost on the road to assimilation.

A Poem by Luis J. Rodriguez:

6 The calling came to me
While I languished
in my room, while I
whittled away my youth
in jail cells
and damp barrio fields.
It brought me to life,
out of captivity,
in a street-scarred
and tattooed place
I called body.
Until then I waited silently,
a deafening clamor in my head,
but voiceless to all around;
hidden from America's eyes,
a brown boy without a name.
I would sing into a solitary
tape recorder,
music never to be heard.
I would write my thoughts
In scrambled English;
I would take photos in my mind-
   plan out new parks,
   bushy green, concrete free,
   new places to play
   and to think.

> Waiting.
> Then it came.
> The calling.
> It brought me out of my room.
> It forced me to escape
> night captors
> in street prisons.
> It called me to war,
> to be writer,
> to be scientist
> and march with the soldiers
>   of change.
> It called me from the shadows,
> out of the wreckage
> of my *barrio* – from among those
> who did not exist.
> I waited all of 16 years
> for this time.
> Somehow unexpected,
> I was called.

7 *Memoria* calls and pushes us forward. *Memoria* is a friend of ours. We must invite her into our classrooms and into our scholarship.

A reminiscence:

8 That morning I had spoken with Ceci, my friend the Cuban English professor. Her husband had said something to me over the phone that I had to unravel quickly, immediate translation from my first language to my only language, slipping the Spanish into English to understand. Their baby, I'm told, used to translate into Spanish for her mother when someone spoke in English at home, translated the English into Spanish so that the English professor would understand. Cute. During that phone conversation, I tried to come up with a familiar Spanish saying about how Cubans and Puerto Ricans are two wings of the same bird. It was there: at the tip of the mind. But I could never. I said it in English. Ceci said it for me in Spanish. Quickly. Then again more slowly. I heard it. I understood it. I recognized it. I still feel unsure that I could produce it. My Spanish is limited to single sentences, never extended stretches of discourse. I can't. At least I don't believe I can. And I listen to salsa and mambo and bomba and plena – the music of my childhood. But I can't dance to it in front of anyone. And phrases from the CDs slip by me, untranslated. I am assimilated. I am not. So I was driving home from some chore or other on the afternoon of the morning, I had spoken to Ceci. And in the midst of a left turn I thought: "I'm fifty now, maybe a third of my life left, I wonder if I'll die without ever being fluent in the language that first met my ears." English is the only language I know, really. Yet Spanish is the language of my ear, of my soul. And I try to pass it on to my children. But I'm inadequate.

9 In some sense, the impulse of the book I had described twenty-one years ago gets worked out in *Bootstraps*, the assimilation myth explicit in the title; the story told then elaborated upon with research and with theory. It's an attempt to play out a kind of Freirean pedagogy: the political explored through the experiential. And it does more. It's

10 an autobiography with political, theoretical, pedagogical considerations. The story includes ethnographic research. The story includes things tried in classrooms. The story includes speculations on the differences between immigrants and minorities, the class system and language, orality and literacy, cultural and critical literacy, Freire, ideology, hegemony, how racism continues and the ways in which racism is allowed to continue despite the profession's best efforts. And in [so doing] the story suggests how we are – all of us – subject to the systemic. This is the personal made public and the public made personalized, not for self-glory nor to point fingers, but to suggest how, maybe, to make the exception the rule. (xviii)

11 I wrote that in 1992. Now some part of that first impulse reasserts itself, fictionalizing, telling the story, reaching back to the heritage that is at risk of passing away quickly. To the kids before my father died last spring:

12 Remember to call your grandpa abuelo. He'll like the sound of that, since none of my sister's kids have called him that. If you let him, he'll watch baseball day and night and not say much. Push him for the stories of Puerto Rico during his childhood. Ask him about catching shrimp with his hands, and the stories of how the neighborhood boys got a Model A Ford, about the revolutionary who hid out in the El Yunque, about his time in the Army. Ask about my grandfather, Basilio, and gardening, and working as a groundskeeper and gardener for the university. And ask about Tio Benito, the tall farmer, inland, on the coffee bills. "Inland" is important about knowing about being Puerto Rican, about Puerto Rico. I remember when I met him. A tall PR. Man, that was very cool. And he gave me sugar cane from his farm, and a coffee bean, and a lemon that he had cut a hole on the top of. And he told me to chew on the bean, squeeze lemon juice on the tongue, and chew on the cane. I wish I could give you that memory, mi'jitas.

13 Now, Mom is easier. She loves to talk. But she'd rather forget the past. And I don't want the past forgotten, so press her too.

A poem: Victor Villanueva y Hernándes

14

Triste lucha la del árbol con espinas	Sad struggle of the tree of thorns
Fuerte ardor que solo a su alma	Fierce feeling covered solely by
se cobija.	your soul
Vano empeño para el ser que vive,	Vain striving for he who lives,
En tratar de comprender su propia vida.	In trying to understand his own life.
Muy dulce es percivir de la noche	So sweet to see your caresses in
sus caricios;	the night
Pero es terrible saber	But so terrible to know
Que más tarde en la madrugada	That later in the light of day
Agonizando todos ellos quedan....	All the agonies remain....
Triste lucha del irbol con espinas	Sad struggle of the tree of thorns
triste lucha la del que ya un	sad struggle of that which is
poquito tarde,	already a little late,
Ni siquiera el más leve	Without even the lightest
suspiro	sigh
su alma alienta.	your soul's breath
Triste e interminable lucha	Sad and interminable struggle
esta que jamás se aleja	that which will never leave
¡Oh, que triste lucha ésta	Oh, how sad this struggle
que a mi pecho	Weighing so on my chest!
Tanto apena!	
¡Triste lucha... triste lucha!	Sad struggle...sad struggle!
-"En el pasado -	"In the past
versa tu presente"	turns the present"
19 de enero 1951	19 January 1951

15 The fiction, the *Bootstraps* retold and fictionalized, would have to begin back then, not quite a generation after the change of hands, when the Spanish colony was handed over to the United States, the changes seen by three generations – *Boricua* to Nuyorican to the middle class of color far removed from the cultural soil of either of the generations, maybe even a wheat field in Eastern Washington. It's important. The memory.

16 So many have said this so well, that it's hard for me to reiterate without breaking into the academic discourse of cite-and-quote – Adell, JanMohamed and Lloyd, Omi and

Winant, Saldívar, San Juan, Singh, Skerrett, and Hogan, Smorkaloff, and the "standards" like Anzaldúa or hooks – all have written about the connections between narratives by people of color and the need to reclaim a memory, memory of an identity in formation and constant reformation, the need to reclaim a memory of an identity as formed through the generations. And I'd say the need to reclaim and retain the memory of the imperial lords, those who have forcibly changed the identities of people of color through colonization.

17 Nelly, the department's graduate secretary, hands me a flyer for a meeting of the Pacific Islanders' group, inviting me to join the students, staff, and faculty (which includes two department chairs I work with often). We smile at each other. Her cultural ways – Filipina – and mine are so different really – except that we have two out of three imperial lords in common: Spain and the United States. It binds us. Our first imperial lord was there before the world got large, more local: the Japanese and the Caribes. We laugh, while others look and listen on with looks of wondering. It's not their memory.

18 Memory simply cannot be adequately portrayed in the conventional discourse of the academy.

19 I am grateful for the acknowledgement of perceptions that academic discourse provides, for the resources the conventions of citation make available, for the ideocentric discourse that displays inductive or deductive lines of reasoning, a way to trace a writer's logical connections.

20 Academic discourse is cognitively powerful!

21 But the cognitive alone is insufficient. It can be strong for *logas*. It can be strong for *ethos*. But it is very weak in *pathos*. Academic discourse tries, after all, to reach the Aristotelian ideal of being completely logocentric, though it cannot be freed of the ethical appeal to authority. A demonstration: Agustín Lao, in "Islands at the Crossroads: Puerto Ricanness Traveling between the Translocal Nation and the Global City," writes that

22 Puerto Ricans (like other racialized diasporas) function within multiple and ambiguous registers of race and racism. As colonized subjects, all Puerto Ricans are "colored" by colonial discourses. On the other hand, differential processes of racialization can either nominalize Puerto Ricans as "ethnic" and/or allow some light-skinned Puerto Ricans to "pass" as "white," [...] A single Puerto Rican "transmigrant" can be classified as *trigueña* on the island, black in Ohio, and Latina in New York. (178-79)

23 Now consider the rhetorical effect of Professor Lao's assertion (though with qualification) and a couple of stories from this light-skinned Puerto Rican. Both take place during the Summer of 2000:

24 He was picked up at the registration desk of the hotel in Iowa City. The limousine (really a van) driver walks up, a man in his late fifties or early sixties, buzz cut, thick build, surely one more accustomed to hard physical labor, a farmer, one would imagine, given the locale. Says at least the guest is on time, kind of so the person behind the registration desk, kind of to himself, maybe even to the guest. He goes on to say that the last guest he'd picked up had been fifteen minutes late, then didn't pay the fare.

25 Once in the van, the story of the deadbeat develops. It was a family of four, including an infant. No car seat.

26 "I could've had my license pulled, with no cat seat for the baby. Then he tries to pay me with a $100 travelers' check, like I carry that kind of money at five in the morning."

27 "Were they foreigners?" assuming the passengers would have overestimated the fluidity of travelers" checks.

28 "Who can know these days. The guy wore a turban. What are you?"

29 Internal soliloquy: he didn't say "rag head," so maybe this is more the condition of the international seaports flowing into the middle of America, the in-migration of the newest immigrants and those new immigrants from the 1930s, a land no longer completely owned by those of Scandinavian and German ancestry. But 1898 and 1917 really should mean something in a situation like this [NB: 1898: the U.S. acquisition of Puerto Rico; 1917: US citizenship conferred on all Puerto Ricans]

30 "Me? I'm American."

31 "Coulda fooled me!"

32 "Yeah, well. I'm from New York."

33 The conversation ends. The next passenger turns out to be a black man with a cruub coming out of an upper-middle-class home in the suburbs of Iowa City. Kind of felt sorry for the driver and his uncomfortable assumptions.

Second story:

34 It was another one of those receptions produced by the dean of the graduate school. This one was to welcome doctoral fellows in residence. Most were persons of color. I was there as a department chair and as one of the mentors to a couple of the fellows.

35 The scene: Back porch of the house, clusters of folks with drinks in the hand or paper plates with guacamole and chips, talking, smiling, overlooking cows grazing in the valley below and green soft rolling hills nearby, maybe three hundred yards away, where there will soon be wheat blowing beautifully in the wind.

36 A conversation ensures with one of the fellows, a woman who grew up in the black area of Boston, Roxbury. Listening in is an associate dean, originally from Central Asia, overly happy to be away from Russian bureaucracy. The conversation turns to race in the wheatland.

37 VV: "Around here folks don't know if I'm Spanish, Jewish, Italian, from the Middle East, or from South Asia."

38 Associate Dean: "I would have thought you were Italian."

39 Roxbury: "I don't know. He looks pretty Portorican to me."

40 Sure, she knows the hue, she sees the "niggerlips," one of those names I endured as a child, just like Martín.

Martín Espada:

41
Niggerlips was the high school name
for me.
So called by Douglas
the car mechanic, with green tattoos
on each forearm,
and the choir of round pink faces
that grinned deliciously
from the back row of classrooms,
droned over by teachers
checking attendance too slowly.
Douglas would brag
about cruising his car
near sidewalks of black children
to point an unloaded gun,
to scare niggers
like crows off a tree,
he'd say.
My great-grandfather Luis
was un negrito too,
a shoemaker in the coffee hills
of Puerto Rico, 1900.
The family called him a secret
and kept no photograph.
My father remembers
the childhood white powder
that failed to bleach
his stubborn copper skin,

and the family says
he is still a fly in milk.
So Niggerlips has the mouth
of his great-grandfather,
the song he must have sung
as he pounded the leather and nails,
the heat that courses through copper,
the stubbornness of a fly in milk,
and all you have, Douglas,
is that unloaded gun.

42 Professor Lao, I would contend, is not quite right. Those of us who are light-skinned don't pass for white; we're just not automatically sorted into the appropriate slot. But more to the point is that Lao's academic discourse (complete with scare quotes and nominalizations) is insufficient, lacks emotional appeal. And though Aristotle thought it not right to sway with emotional appeals, he knew that the greatest impact on listeners is in fact the emotional. The personal here does not negate the need for the academic, it complements, provides an essential element in the rhetorical triangle, an essential element in the intellect – cognition *and* affect. The personal done well is sensorial and intellectual, complete, knowledge known throughout mind and body, even if vicariously.

43 And for the person of color, it does more. The narrative of the person of color validates. It resonates. It awakens, particularly for those of us who are in institutions where our numbers are few. We know that though we really are Gramsci's exceptions – those who "through 'chance' […have] had opportunities that the thousand others in reality could not or did not have" – our experiences are in no sense unique but are always analogous to other experiences from among those exceptions. So more that narrating the life of one so that "one creates this possibility, suggests the process, indicates the opening," in Gramsci's terms (*Selections from Cultural Writing* 132), we remember the results of our having realized the possibility, discovered the process, found the opening, while finding that there is in some sense very little change on the other side. This is what Ellis Cose describes as *The Rage of a Privileged Class*. This is Luis Rodriguez's call, that we'll read below.

44 Ellis Cose, I've written before ("On Colonies"), explains, mainly by way of anecdote, the reasons African Americans in particular continue to be angry even after having crossed over to the other side. He explains the ways in which little slights continue to display the racism inherent in our society. Those "Dozen Demons" are

45
1. Inability to fit in.
2. Exclusion from the club.
3. Low expectations.
4. Shattered hopes.
5. Faint praise.
6. Presumption of failure.
7. Coping fatigue.
8. Pigeonholing.
9. Identity troubles.
10. Self-censorship and silence.
11. Mendacity.
12. Guilt by association. (57-68)

46 I haven't been called a "spic" in many years (except by others of color, perhaps, in fun, I hope). Yet little things happen that betray the underlying racism that affects us all, no matter how appalled by racism we might be. I read Anzaldúa or hooks or the poetry of Espada or Cruz or Esteves or any other writings of color, and I know I haven't become clinically paranoid. I know that I've been poked by one of the demons. Some of the slightest signified by Cose are self-imposed, instances of Frantz Fanon's internal colonialism. Some are externally imposed. All can be laid bare through the personal made public.

47 There's the story of the academics of color who wrote about the subtle ways in which they find themselves victims of some of Cose's demons – exclusion, expecting less, presuming failure, pigeonholing as "brown-on-brown" research rather than disinterested research (read: white and classical-empirical). Someone far away read the essay once published and files suit for slander. The authors had never heard of the person. This is a very funny story to people of color who have heard it – the laughter of verification and white guilt gone awry.

48 The converse:
"Man, I loved your book [or article or essay], I could relate. The same things have happened to me," something I've heard time and time again wherever I travel. Identity minus troubles among Cose's demons, associating guiltless, a new club formed.

49 Somehow, the spic does remain, despite all the good fortune and accolades, not only from within but from without. While a good academic piece would help me to remember, rich narrative does more for the memory.

50 And the precedent is old. *Memoria* was the mother of the muses, the most important of the rhetorical offices. Now rhetorics of writing seem to go no further than invention, arrangement, and style; when delivery is still there, it's the matter of "voice." But memory is tied in as well, surely for people of color. It's as if we have accepted Plato's prophecy that literacy would be the downfall of memory, leading only to remembrance. We have to remember Plato, because his writing is significant by virtue of its genre, an attempt at representation of dialogue, of storytelling, of the play. Plato's literacy took shape not as logocentric discourse but as a representation of discourse in action. Though folks like Volosinov have shown that all discourse, written as well as spoken, is dialogic. Plato is maybe the coolest of the philosophers because of the resonance of the dialogue, the possibility for humor, the clear presence of all three points in the rhetorical triangle and the often unspecified dimension which is context. I don't mean to be waxing Platonic, really, only to suggest that there's something to Plato's notion of memory as more that recollection and to his leaning on a written discourse that approximates orality as a means toward arriving at Memory. The narratives of people of color jog our memories as a collective in a scattered world and within an ideology that praises individualism. And this is all the more apparent for the Latino and Latina, whose language contains the assertion of the interconnectedness among identity, memory, and the personal. There is a common saying among Puerto Ricans and Cubans: *Te doy un cuento de mi historia*, literally rendered as "I'll give you a story about my history": me, history and memory, and a story.

51 A thousand years before the first Europeans arrived on Puerto Rico, the native people of the mainland and the lesser. Antilles migrated to Puerto Rico, where they could live in relative peace, able to fish and live off the fresh vegetation – pineapple and varieties of tuber that have no name in English. We don't know the names of the first inhabitants of Puerto Rico. Our history is the history told by the Europeans, who, conferring their values on the land, took the language of the local imperial lords. We only know the names given the first Puerto Ricans by their first colonizers, the first to raid them, the first to enslave them, the ones the Europeans honored by naming a region after them. These first colonizers were the peoples of Carib. And they named the people of the island Arawak and the culture of the Arawak was called Taino. And their island was named Boriquén.

52 Then came Columbus (or Columbo or Calón. I'm glad we've stopped translating people's names, or I'd have to walk around with the name Conqueror Newton). And then Ponce de León. Then the priests.

And when the slaves of Puerto Rico rebelled, slaves from Africa were brought in, and the Boricuas ran inland, away from the fortressed walls of El Morro, acquiescing to the Spanish yet surreptitiously trading with Dutch and English, French and Italian pirates who would find other ways to enter the island. This subversion became jaibería. So I understand Angel Rama, when he says that it is it the Caribbean that "the plural manifestations of the entire universe insert themselves" (qtd. in Smorkaloff vii). My mother's name is Italian (the line is never lost in the Spanish tradition: my father's mother – Herndádes and my mother becoming Maria Socorro Cotto de Villanueva, my father was thus Victor Villanueva y Hernádes and me Victor Villanueva y Cotto until we both were Americanized and I became "Jr.") My mother's name: Italian. The memory of that first Italian, whether family or slavemaster (which is how so many of the Tainos got their names, just like the African Americans of the mainland) – lost.

53 Centuries after the first Europeans later, I am Puerto Rican – a product of the first migrations of Puerto Ricans to New York in the late 1940s, though my mother arrived though what was euphemistically called "indenture servitude," what others called "white slavery," as if somehow more barbaric than the slavery of Africans. And I assimilate. And I don't. But I know how to seem to be – jaibería – and I have the memory – the memory provided by stories told. Memory does danger. And it's fed through the stories told.

54 I'm trying to figure this out, somehow: who I am, from where, playing out the mixes within. It isn't a question for me, whether public or private discourses. I am contradictory consciousness. The discourse should reflect that. I am these uneasy mixes of races that make for no race at all yet find themselves victim to racism. The discourse should reflect that. I am an American (in every sense – a boy from Brooklyn, jazz and rock 'n' roll, and from the Americas, with an ancestry dating back before the Europeans), an academic, a person of color – an organically grown traditional intellectual, containing both of Gramsci's intellectual formations, yet not quite his new intellectual. The discourse should reflect that as well. And I am in a wheatfield, attempting to pass on a memory as I attempt to gather one. Personal discourse, the narrative, the auto/biography, helps in that effort, is a necessary adjunct to the academic.

55 Looking back, we look ahead, and giving ourselves up to the looking back and the looking ahead, knowing the self, and, critically, knowing the self in relation to others, maybe we can be and instrument whereby students can hear the call.

Credit

Villanueva, Victor. "'Memoria' is a Friend of Ours: On the Discourse of Color." *College English* 67.1. Copyright © 2004 by the National Council of Teachers of English. Reprinted by permission.

Writing Autobiography

BELL HOOKS

1   To me, telling the story of my growing-up years was intimately connected with the longing to kill the self I was without really having to die. I wanted to kill that self in the writing. Once that self was gone---out of my life forever---I could more easily become the me of me. It was clearly the Gloria Jean of my tormented and anguished childhood that I wanted to be rid of, the girl who was always wrong, always punished, always subjected to some humiliation or other, always crying, the girl who was to end up in a mental institution because she could not be anything but crazy, or so they told her. She was the girl who sat a hot iron on her arm pleading with them to leave her alone, the girl who wore her scar as a brand marking her madness. Even now I can hear the voices of my sisters saying, "mama make Gloria stop crying." By writing the autobiography, it was not just this Gloria I would be rid of, but the past that had a hold on me, that kept me from the present. I wanted not to forget the past but to break its hold. This death in writing was to be liberatory.

2   Until I began to try and write an autobiography, I thought that it would be a simple task, this telling of one's story. And yet I tried year after year, never writing more than a few pages. My inability to write out the story I interpreted as an indication that I was not ready to let go of the past, that I was not ready to be fully in the present. Psychologically, I considered the possibility that I had become attached to the wounds and sorrows of my childhood, that I held to them in a manner that blocked my efforts to be self-realized, whole, to be healed. A key message in Toni Cade Bambara's novel *The Salt Eaters*, which tells the story of Velma's suicide attempt, her breakdown, is expressed when the healer asks her, "Are you sure sweetheart, that you want to be well?'

3   There was very clearly something blocking my ability to tell my story. Perhaps it was remembered scoldings and punishments when mama heard me saying something to a friend or stranger that she did not think should be said. Secrecy and silence---these were central issues. Secrecy about family, about what went on in the domestic household was a bond between us---was part of what made us family. There was a dread one felt about breaking that bond. And yet I could not grow inside the atmosphere of secrecy that had pervaded our lives and the lives of other families about us. Strange that I had always challenged the secrecy, always let something slip that should not be known growing up, yet as a writer staring into the solitary space of paper, I was bound, trapped in the fear that a bond is lost or broken in the telling. I did not want to be the traitor, the teller of family secrets---and yet I wanted to be a writer. Surely, I told myself, I could write a purely imaginative work---a work that would not hint at personal private realities. And so I tried. But always there were the intruding traces, those elements of real life however disguised. Claiming the freedom to grow as an imaginative writer was connected for me with having the courage to be open, to be able to tell the truth of one's life as I had experienced it in writing. To talk about one's life---that I could do. To write about it, to leave a trace---that was frightening.

4   The longer it took me to begin the process of writing autobiography, the further removed from those memories I was becoming. Each year, a memory seemed less and less clear. I wanted not to lose the vividness, the recall and felt an urgent need to begin the work and complete it. Yet I could not begin even though I had begun to confront some of the reasons I was blocked, as I am blocked just now in writing this piece because I am afraid to express in writing the experience that served as a catalyst for that block to move.

5   I had met a young black man. We were having an affair. It is important that he was black. He was in some mysterious way a link to this past that I had been struggling to grapple with, to name in writing. With him I remembered incidents, moments of the past that I had completely suppressed. It was as though there was something about the passion of contact that was hypnotic, that enabled me to drop barriers and thus enter fully, rather reenter those past experiences. A key aspect seemed to be the way he smelled, the combined odors of cigarettes, occasionally alcohol, and his body smells. I thought often of the phrase "scent of memory," for it was those smells that carried me back. And there were specific occasions when it was very evident that the experience of being in his company was the catalyst for this remembering.

6   Two specific incidents come to mind. One day in the middle of the afternoon we met at his place. We were drinking cognac and dancing to music from the radio. He was smoking cigarettes (not only do I not smoke, but I usually make an effort to avoid smoke). As we held each other dancing those mingled odors of alcohol, sweat, and cigarettes led me to say, quite without thinking about it, "Uncle Pete." It was not that I had forgotten Uncle Pete. It was more that I had forgotten the childhood experience of meeting him. He drank often, smoked cigarettes, and always on the few occasions that we met him, he held us children in tight embraces. It was the memory of those embraces---of the way I hated and longed to resist them---that I recalled.

7   Another day we went to a favorite park to feed ducks and parked the car in front of tall bushes. As we were sitting there, we suddenly heard the sound of an oncoming train---a sound that startled me so that it evoked another long-suppressed memory: that of crossing the train tracks in my father's car. I recalled an incident where the car stopped on the tracks and my father left us sitting there while he raised the hood of the car and worked to repair it. This is an incident that I am not certain actually happened. As a child, I had been terrified of just such an incident occurring, perhaps so terrified that it played itself out in my mind as though it had happened. These are just two ways this encounter acted as a catalyst, breaking down barriers, enabling me to finally write this long-desired autobiography of my childhood.

8   Each day I sat at the typewriter and different memories were written about in short vignettes. They came in a rush, as though they were a sudden thunderstorm. They came in a surreal, dreamlike style that made me cease to think of them as strictly autobiographical because it seemed that myth, dream, and reality had merged. There were many incidents that I would talk about with my siblings to see if they recalled them. Often we remembered together a general outline of an incident but the details were different for us. This fact was a constant reminder of the limitations of autobiography, of the extent to which autobiography is a very personal storytelling---a unique recounting of events not so much as they have happened but as we remember and invent them. One memory that I would have sworn was "the truth and nothing but the truth" concerned a wagon that my brother and I shared as children. I remembered that we played with this toy only at my grandfather's house, that we shared it, that I would ride it and my brother would push me. Yet one facet of the memory was puzzling---I remembered always returning home with bruises or scratches from this toy. When I called my mother, she said there had never been any wagon, that we shared a red wheelbarrow, that it had always been at my grandfather's house because there were sidewalks on that part of town. We lived in the hills where there were no sidewalks. Again I was compelled to face the fiction that is a part of all retelling, remembering. I began to think of the work I was doing as both fiction and autobiography. It seemed to fall in the category of writing that Audre Lorde, in her autobiographically based work *Zami*, calls bio-mythography. As I wrote, I felt that I was not as concerned with accuracy of detail as I was with evoking in writing the state of mind, the spirit of a particular moment.

9   The longing to tell one's story and the process of telling is symbolically a gesture of longing to recover the past in such a way that one experiences both a sense of reunion

and a sense of release. It was the longing for release that compelled the writing but concurrently it was the joy of reunion that enabled me to see that the act of writing one's autobiography is a way to find again that aspect of self and experience that may no longer be an actual part of one's life but is a living memory shaping and informing the present. Autobiographical writing was a way for me to evoke the particular experience of growing up southern and black in segregated communities. It was a way to recapture the richness of southern black culture. The need to remember and hold to the legacy of that experience and what it taught me has been all the more important since I have since lived in predominately white communities and taught at predominately white colleges. Black southern folk experience was the foundation of the life around me when I was a child; that experience no longer exists in many places where it was once all of life that we knew. Capitalism, upward mobility, assimilation of other values have all led to rapid disintegration of black folk experience or in some cases the gradual wearing away of that experience.

10   Within the world of my childhood, we held on to the legacy of a distinct black culture by listening to the elders tell their stories. Autobiography was experienced most actively in the art of telling one's story. I can recall sitting at Baba's (my grandmother on my mother's side) at 1200 Broad Street---listening to people come and recount their life experience. In those days, whenever I brought a playmate to my grandmother's house, Baba would want a brief outline of their autobiography before we would begin playing. She wanted not only to know who their people were but what their values were. It was sometimes an awesome and terrifying experience to stand answering these questions or witness another playmate being subjected to the process and yet this was the way we would come to know our own and one another's family histories. It is the absence of such a tradition in my adult life that makes the written narrative of my girlhood all the more important. As the years pass and these glorious memories grow much more vague, there will remain the clarity contained with the written words.

11   Conceptually, the autobiography was framed in the manner of a hope chest. I remembered my mother's hope chest, with its wonderful odor of cedar, and thought about her taking the most precious items and placing them there for safekeeping. Certain memories were for me a similar treasure. I wanted to place them somewhere for safekeeping. An autobiographical narrative seemed an appropriate place. Each particular incident, encounter, experience had its own story, sometimes told from the first person, sometimes told from the third person. Often I felt as though I was in a trance at my typewriter, that the shape of a particular memory was decided not by my conscious mind but by all that is dark and deep within me, unconscious but present. It was the act of making it present, bringing it into the open, so to speak, that was liberating.

12   From the perspective of trying to understand my psyche, it was also interesting to read the narrative in its entirety after I had completed the work. It had not occurred to me that bringing one's past, one's memories together in a complete narrative would allow one to view them from a different perspective, not as singular isolated events but as part of a continuum. Reading the completed manuscript, I felt as though I had an overview not so much of my childhood but of those experiences that were deeply imprinted in my consciousness. Significantly, that which was absent, left out, not included also was important. I was shocked to find at the end of my narrative that there were a few incidents I recalled that involved my five sisters. Most of the incidents with siblings were with me and my brother. There was a sense of alienation from my sisters present in childhood, a sense of estrangement. This was reflected in the narrative. Another aspect of the completed manuscript that is interesting to me is the way in which the incidents

bell hooks

describing adult men suggest that I feared them intensely, with the exception of my grandfather and a few old men. Writing the autobiographical narrative enabled me to look at my past from a different perspective and to use this knowledge as a means of self-growth and change in a practical way.

In the end I did not feel as though I had killed the Gloria of my childhood. Instead I had rescued her. She was no longer the enemy within, the little girl who had to be annihilated for the woman to come into being. In writing about her, I reclaimed that part of myself I had long ago rejected, left uncared for, just as he had often felt alone and uncared for as a child. Remembering was part of a cycle of reunion, a joining of fragments, "the bits and pieces of my heart" that the narrative made whole again.

Credit _____

The Politics of Teaching Literate Discourse
LISA DELPIT

1 I have encountered a certain sense of powerlessness and paralysis among many sensitive and well-meaning literacy educators who appear to be caught in the throes of a dilemma. Although their job is to teach literate discourse styles to all of their students, they question whether that is a task they can actually accomplish for poor students and students of color. Furthermore, they question whether they are acting as agents of oppression by insisting that students who are not already a part of the "mainstream" learn that discourse. Does it not smack of racism or classism to demand that these students put aside the language of their homes and communities and adopt a discourse that is not only alien, but that has often been instrumental in furthering their oppression? I hope here to speak to and help dispel that sense of paralysis and powerlessness and suggest a path of commitment and action that not only frees teachers to teach what they know, but to do so in a way that can transform and subsequently liberate their students.

Discourse, Literacy, And Gee

2 This article got its start as I pondered the dilemmas expressed by educators. It continued to evolve when a colleague sent a set of papers to me for comment. The papers, authored by literacy specialist James Paul Gee ("Literacy, Discourse, and Linguistics: Introduction" and "What Is Literacy?"), are the lead articles of a special issue of the *Journal of Education*[1] devoted solely to Gee's work. The papers brought to mind many of the perspectives of the educators I describe. My colleague, an academic with an interest in literacy issues in communities of color, was disturbed by much of what she read in the articles and wanted a second opinion.

3 As I first read the far-reaching, politically sensitive articles, I found that I agreed with much that Gee wrote, as I have with much of his previous work. He argues that literacy is much more than reading and writing, but rather that it is part of a larger political entity. This larger entity he calls a discourse, construed as something of an "identity kit," that is, ways of "saying-writing-doing-being-valuing-believing," examples of which might be the discourse of lawyers, the discourse of academics, or the discourse of men. He adds that one never learns simply to read or write, but to read and write within some larger discourse, and therefore within some larger set of values and beliefs.

4 Gee maintains that there are primary discourses, those learned in the home, and secondary discourses, which are attached to institutions or groups one might later encounter. He also argues that all discourses are not equal in status, that some are socially dominant - carrying with them social power and access to economic success - and some nondominant. The status of individuals born into a particular discourse tends to be maintained because primary discourses are related to secondary discourses of similar status in our society (for example, the middle-class home discourse to school discourse, or the working-class African-American home discourse to the black church discourse). Status is also maintained because dominant groups in a society apply frequent "tests" of fluency in the dominant discourses, often focused on its most superficial aspects - grammar, style, mechanics - so as to exclude from full participation those who are not born to positions of power.

5 These arguments resonate in many ways with what I also believe to be true. However, as I reread and pondered the articles, I began to get a sense of my colleague's discomfort. I also began to understand how that discomfort related to some concerns I have about the perspectives of educators who sincerely hope to help educate poor children and children of color to become successful and literate, but who find themselves paralyzed by their own conception of the task.

6   There are two aspects of Gee's arguments which I find problematic. First is Gee's notion that people who have not been born into dominant discourses will find it exceedingly difficult, if not impossible, to acquire such a discourse. He argues strongly that discourses cannot be "overtly" taught, particularly in a classroom, but can only be acquired by enculturation in the home or by "apprenticeship" into social practices. Those who wish to gain access to the goods and status connected to a dominant discourse must have access to the social practices related to that discourse. That is, to learn the "rules" required for admission into a particular dominant discourse, individuals must already have access to the social institutions connected to that discourse - if you're not already in, don't expect to get in.

7   This argument is one of the issues that concerned my colleague. As she put it, Gee's argument suggests a dangerous kind of determinism as flagrant as that espoused by the geneticists: instead of being locked into "your place" by your genes, you are now locked hopelessly into a lower-class status by your discourse. Clearly, such a stance can leave a teacher feeling powerless to effect change, and a student feeling hopeless that change can occur.

8   The second aspect of Gee's work that I find troubling suggests that an individual who is born into one discourse with one set of values may experience major conflicts when attempting to acquire another discourse with another set of values. Gee defines this as especially pertinent to "women and minorities," who, when they seek to acquire Status discourses, may be faced with adopting values that deny their primary identities. When teachers believe that this acceptance of self-deprecatory values is *inevitable* in order for people of color to acquire status discourses, then their sense of justice and fair play might hinder their teaching these discourses.

9   If teachers were to adopt both of these premises suggested by Gee's work, not only would they view the acquisition of a new discourse in a classroom impossible to achieve, but they might also view the goal of acquiring such a discourse questionable at best. The sensitive teacher might well conclude that even to try to teach a dominant discourse to students who are members of a nondominant oppressed group would be to oppress them further. And this potential conclusion concerns me. While I do agree that discourses may embody conflicting values, I also believe there are many individuals who have faced and overcome the problems that such a conflict might cause. I hope to provide another perspective on both of these premises.

Overcoming Obstacles To Acquisition

10   One remedy to the paralysis suffered by many teachers is to bring to the fore stories of the real people whose histories directly challenge unproductive beliefs. Mike Rose has done a poignantly convincing job of detailing the role of committed teachers in his own journey toward accessing literate discourse, and his own role as a teacher of disenfranchised veterans who desperately needed the kind of explicit and focused instruction Rose was able to provide in order to "make it" in an alien academic setting.[2] But there are many stories not yet documented which exemplify similar journeys, supported by similar teaching.

11   A friend and colleague who teaches in a college of education at a major Midwestern university, told me of one of her graduate students whom we'll call Marge. Marge received a special fellowship funded by a private foundation designed to increase the numbers of faculty holding doctorates at black colleges. She applied to the doctoral program at my friend's university and traveled to the institution to take a few classes while awaiting the decision. Apparently, the admissions committee did not quite know what to do with her, for here was someone who was already on campus with a fellowship, but who, based on GRE scores and writing samples, they determined was not capable of doing doctoral-level work. Finally, the committee agreed to admit Marge into the master's program, even though she already held a master's degree. Marge accepted the offer. My friend - we'll call her Susan - got to know Marge when the department head asked her to "work with" the new student who was considered "at risk" of not successfully completing the degree.

12 Susan began a program to help Marge learn how to cope with the academic setting. Susan recognized early on that Marge was very talented but that she did not understand how to maneuver her way through academic writing, reading, and talking. In their first encounters, Susan and Marge discussed the comments instructors had written on Marge's papers, and how the next paper might incorporate the professor's concerns. The next summer Susan had Marge write weekly synopses of articles related to educational issues. When they met, Marge talked through her ideas while Susan took notes. Together they translated the ideas into the "discourse of teacher education." Marge then rewrote the papers referring to their conversations and Susan's extensive written comments.

13 Susan continued to work with Marge, both in and out of the classroom, during the following year. By the end of that year, Marge's instructors began telling Susan that Marge was a real star, that she had written the best papers in their classes. When faculty got funding for various projects, she became one of the most sought-after research assistants in the college. And when she applied for entry into the doctoral program the next fall, even though her GRE scores were still low, she was accepted with no hesitation. Her work now includes research and writing that challenge dominant attitudes about the potential of poor children to achieve.

14 The stories of two successful African-American men also challenge the belief that literate discourses cannot be acquired in classroom settings, and highlight the significance of teachers in transforming students' futures. Clarence Cunningham, now a vice chancellor at the largest historically black institution in the United States, grew up in a painfully poor community in rural Illinois. He attended an all-African-American elementary school in the 1930s in a community where the parents of most of the children never even considered attending high school. There is a school picture hanging in his den of a ragtag group of about thirty-five children. As he shows me that picture, he talks about the one boy who grew up to be a principal in Philadelphia, one who is now a vice president of a major computer company, one who was recently elected attorney general of Chicago, another who is a vice president of Harris Bank in Chicago, another who was the first black pilot hired by a major airline. He points to a little girl who is now an administrator, another who is a union leader. Almost all of the children in the photo eventually left their home community, and almost all achieved impressive goals in life.

15 Another colleague and friend, Bill Trent, a professor and researcher at a major research university, told me of growing up in the 1940s and 1950s in inner-city Richmond, Virginia, "the capital of the Confederacy." His father, a cook, earned an eighth-grade education by going to night school. His mother, a domestic, had a third-grade education. Neither he nor his classmates had aspirations beyond their immediate environment. Yet, many of these students completed college, and almost all were successful, many notable. Among them are teachers, ministers, an electronics wizard, state officials, career army officers, tennis ace Arthur Ashe, and the brothers Max and Randall Robinson, the national newscaster and the director of Trans-Africa, respectively.

16 How do these men explain the transformations that occurred in their own and their classmates' lives? Both attribute their ability to transcend the circumstances into which they were born directly to their teachers. First, their teachers successfully taught what Gee calls the "superficial features" of middle-class discourse - grammar, style, mechanics - features that Gee claims are particularly resistant to classroom instruction. And the students successfully learned them.

17 These teachers also successfully taught the more subtle aspects of dominant discourse. According to both Trent and Cunningham, their teachers insisted that students be able to speak and write eloquently, maintain nearness, think carefully, exude character, and conduct themselves with decorum. They even found ways to mediate class differences by attending to the hygiene of students who needed such attention - washing faces, cutting fingernails , and handing out deodorant.

18   Perhaps more significant than what they taught is what they believed. As Trent says, "They held visions of us that we could not imagine for ourselves. And they held those visions even when they themselves were denied entry into the larger white world. They were determined that, despite all odds, we would achieve." In an era of overt racism when much was denied to African-Americans, the message drilled into students was "the one thing people can't take away from you is what's between your ears." The teachers of both men insisted that they must achieve because "you must do twice as well as white people to be considered half as good."

19   As Cunningham says, "Those teachers pushed us, they wouldn't let us fail. They'd say, 'The world is tough out there, and you have to be tougher.'" Trent recalls that growing up in the "inner-city," he had no conception of life beyond high school, but his high school teachers helped him to envision one. While he happily maintained a C average, putting all of his energy into playing football, he experienced a turning point one day when his coach called him inside in the middle of a practice. There, while he was still suited up for football, all of his teachers gathered to explain to him that if he thought he could continue making Cs and stay on the team he had another thing coming. They were there to tell him that if he did not get his act together and make the grades they knew he was capable of, then his football career would be over.

20   Like similar teachers chronicled elsewhere, these teachers put in overtime to ensure that the students were able to live up to their expectations. They set high standards and then carefully and explicitly instructed students in how to meet them. "You can and will do well," they insisted, as they taught at break times, after school, and on weekends to ensure that their students met their expectations. All of these teachers were able to teach in classrooms the rules for dominant discourses, allowing students to succeed in mainstream America who were not only born outside of the realms of power and status, but who had no access to status institutions. These teachers were not themselves a part of the power elite, not members of dominant discourses. Yet they were able to provide the keys for their students' entry into the larger world, never knowing if the doors would ever swing open to allow them in.

21   The renowned African-American sociologist E. Franklin Frazier also successfully acquired a discourse into which he was not born. Born in poverty to unschooled parents, Frazier learned to want to learn from his teachers and from his self-taught father. He learned his lessons so well that his achievements provided what must be the ultimate proof of the ability to acquire a secondary dominant discourse, no matter what one's beginnings. After Frazier completed his master's degree at Clark University, he went on to challenge many aspects of the white-dominated oppressive system of segregation. Ironically, at the time Frazier graduated from Clark, he received a reference from its president, G. Stanley Hall, who gave Frazier what he must have thought was the highest praise possible in a predominantly white university in 1920. "Mr. Frazier ... seems to me to be quite gentlemanly and mentally white."[3] What better evidence of Frazier's having successfully acquired the dominant discourse of academe?

22   These stories are of commitment and transformation. They show how people, given the proper support, can "make it" in culturally alien environments. They make clear that standardized test scores have little to say about one's actual ability. And they demonstrate that supporting students' transformation demands an extraordinary amount of time and commitment, but that teachers *can* make a difference if they are willing to make that commitment.

23   Despite the difficulty entailed in the process, almost any African-American or other disenfranchised individual who has become "successful" has done so by acquiring a discourse other than the one into which he or she was born. And almost all can attribute that acquisition to what happened as a result of the work of one or more committed teachers.

Acquisition And Transformation

24 But the issue is not only whether students can learn a dominant secondary discourse in the classroom. Perhaps the more significant issue is, should they attempt to do so? Gee contends that for those who have been barred from the mainstream, "acquisition of many mainstream Discourses ... involves active complicity with the values that conflict with one's home and community-based Discourses." There can be no doubt that in many classrooms students of color do reject literacy, for they feel that literate discourses reject them. Keith Gilyard, in his jolting autobiographical study of language competence, graphically details his attempt to achieve in schools that denied the very existence of his community reality:

25 I was torn between institutions, between value systems. At times the tug of school was greater, therefore the 90 .2 average. On the other occasions the streets were a more powerful lure, thus the heroin and the 40 in English and a brief visit to the Adolescent Remand Shelter. I.. .saw no middle ground or more accurately, no total ground on which anomalies like me could gather. I tried to be a hip schoolboy, but it was impossible to achieve that persona. In the group I most loved, to be fully hip meant to repudiate a school system in which African-American consciousness was undervalued or ignored; in which, in spite of the many nightmares around us, I was urged to keep my mind on the Dream, to play the fortunate token, to keep my head straight down and "make it." And I pumped more and more dope into my arms. It was a nearly fatal response, but an almost inevitable one.[4]

26 Herb Kohl writes powerfully about individuals, young and old, who choose to "not-learn" what is expected of them rather than to learn that which denies them their sense of who they are:

27 Not-learning tends to take place when someone has to deal with unavoidable challenges to her or his personal and family loyalties, integrity, and identity. In such situations there are forced choices and no apparent middle ground. To agree to learn from a stranger who does not respect your integrity causes a major loss of self. The only alternative is to not-learn and reject the stranger's world.[5]

28 I have met many radical or progressive teachers of literacy who attempt to resolve the problem of students who choose to "not-learn" by essentially deciding to "not-teach." They appear to believe that to remain true to their ideology, their role must be to empower and politicize their most disenfranchised students by refusing to teach what Gee calls the superficial features (grammar, form, style, and so forth) of dominant discourses.[6] Believing themselves to be contributing to their students' liberation by deemphasizing dominant discourses, they instead seek to develop literacy *solely* within the language and style of the students' home discourse.

29 Feminist writer bell hooks writes of one of the consequences of this teaching methodology. During much of her postsecondary school career she was the only black student in her writing courses. Whenever she would write a poem in black Southern dialect, the teachers and fellow students would praise her for using her "true authentic voice" and encourage her to write more in this voice.[7] hooks writes of her frustration with these teachers who, like the teachers I describe, did not recognize the need for African-American students to have access to many voices and who maintained their stance even when adult students or the parents of younger students demanded that they do otherwise.

30 I am reminded of one educator of adult African-American veterans who insisted that her students needed to develop their "own voices" by developing "fluency" in their home language. Her students vociferously objected, demanding that they be taught grammar, punctuation, and "Standard English." The teacher insisted that such a mode of study was "oppressive." The students continued venting their objections in loud and certain tones. When asked why she thought her students had not developed "voice" when they were using their voices to loudly express their displeasure, she responded that it was "because of who they are," that is, apparently because they were working-class, black, and disagreed with her. Another educator of adults told me that she based her teaching on liberating principles. She voiced her anger with her mostly poor, working-class students because they rejected her pedagogy and "refused to be liberated." There are many such stories to recount.[8]

31   There are several reasons why students and parents of color take a position that differs from the well-intentioned position of the teachers I have described. First, they know that members of society need access to dominant discourses to (legally) have access to economic power. Second, they know that such discourses can be and have been acquired in classrooms because they know individuals who have done so. And third, and most significant to the point I wish to make now, they know that individuals have the ability to transform dominant discourses for liberatory purposes - to engage in what Henry Louis Gates calls "changing the joke and slipping the yoke,"[9] that is, using European philosophical and critical standards to challenge the tenets of European belief systems.

32   bell hooks speaks of her black women teachers in the segregated South as being the model from which she acquired both access to dominant discourses and a sense of the validity of the primary discourse of working-class African-American people. From their instruction, she learned that black poets were capable of speaking in many voices, that the Dunbar who wrote in dialect was as valid as the Dunbar who wrote sonnets. She also learned from these women that she was capable of not only participating in the mainstream, but redirecting its currents: "Their work was truly education for critical consciousness ... .They were the teachers who conceptualized oppositional world views, who taught us young black women to exult and glory in the power and beauty of our intellect. They offered to us a legacy of liberatory pedagogy that demanded active resistance and rebellion against sexism and racism."[10]

33   Carter G. Woodson called for similar pedagogy almost seventy years ago. He extolled teachers in his 1933 *Mis -Education of the Negro* to teach African-American students not only the language and canon of the European "mainstream," but to teach as well the life, history, language, philosophy, and literature of their own people. Only this kind of education, he argued, would prepare an educated class which would serve the needs of the African-American community.

34   Acquiring the ability to function in a dominant discourse need not mean that one must reject one's home identity and values, for discourses are not static, but are shaped, however reluctantly, by those who participate within them and by the form of their participation. Many who have played significant roles in fighting for the liberation of people of color have done so through the language of dominant discourses, from Frederick Douglass to Ida B. Wells, to Mary McCloud Bethune, to Martin Luther King, to Malcolm X. As did bell hooks' teachers, today's teachers can help economically disenfranchised students and students of color, both to master the dominant discourses and to transform them. How is the teacher to accomplish this? I suggest several possibilities.

35   What can teachers do? First, teachers must acknowledge and validate students' home language without using it to limit students' potential. Students' home discourses are vital to their perception of self and sense of community connectedness. One Native American college student I know says he cannot write in Standard English when he writes about his village "because that's about me!" Then he must use his own "village English" or his voice rings hollow even to himself. June Jordan has written a powerful essay about teaching a course in Black English and the class's decision to write a letter of protest in that language when the brother of one of the students was killed by police.[11] The point must not be to eliminate students' home languages, but rather to add other voices and discourses to their repertoires. As bell hooks and Henry Gates have poignantly reminded us, racism and oppression must be fought on as many fronts and in as many voices as we can muster.[12]

36 Second, teachers must recognize the conflict Gee details between students' home discourses and the discourse of school. They must understand that students who appear to be unable to learn are in many instances choosing to "not-learn" as Kohl puts it, choosing to maintain their sense of identity in the face of what they perceive as a painful choice between allegiance to "them" or "us." The teacher, however, can reduce this sense of choice by transforming the new discourse so that it contains within it a place for the students' selves. To do so, they must saturate the dominant discourse with new meanings, must wrest from it a place for the glorification of their students and their forbears.

37 An interesting historical example is documented by James Anderson. Anderson writes of Richard Wright, an AfricanAmerican educator in the post-Reconstruction era, who found a way through the study of the "classical" curriculum to claim a place of intellectual respect for himself and his people. When examined by the U.S. Senate Committee on Education and Labor, one senator questioned Wright about the comparative inferiority and superiority of the races. Wright replied:

38 It is generally admitted that religion has been a great means of human development and progress, and I think that about all the great religions which have blessed this world have come from the colored races - all. .. I believe, too, that our methods of alphabetic writing all came from the colored race, and I think the majority of the sciences in their origin have come from the colored races . . .. Now I take the testimony of those people who know, and who, I feel are capable of instructing me on this point, and I find them saying that the Egyptians were actually wooly-haired negroes. In Humboldt's Cosmos (Vol. 2, p. 531) you will find that testimony, and Humboldt, I presume, is a pretty good authority. The same thing is stated in Herodotus, and in a number of other authors with whom you gentlemen are doubtless familiar. Now if that is true, the idea that the negro race is inherently inferior, seems to me to be at least a little limping.[13]

39 Noted educator Jaime Escalante prepared poor Latino students to pass the tests for advanced calculus when everyone else thought they would do well to master fractions. To do so, he also transformed a discourse by placing his students and their ancestors firmly within its boundaries. In a line from the movie chronicling his success, *Stand and Deliver*, he entreated his students, "You *have* to learn math. The Mayans discovered zero. Math is in your blood!"

40 And this is also what those who create what has been called "Afrocentric" curricula do. They too seek to illuminate for students (and their teachers) a world in which people with brown and black skin have achieved greatness and have developed a large part of what is considered the great classical tradition. They also seek to teach students about those who have taken the language born in Europe and transformed it into an emancipatory tool for those facing oppression in the "new world." In the mouths and pens of Bill Trent, Clarence Cunningham, bell hooks, Henry Louis Gates, Paul Lawrence Dunbar, and countless others, the "language of the master" has been used for liberatory ends. Students can learn of that rich legacy, and they can also learn that they are its inheritors and rightful heirs.

41 A final role that teachers can take is to acknowledge the unfair "discourse-stacking" that our society engages in. They can discuss openly the injustices of allowing certain people to succeed, based not upon merit but upon which family they were born into, upon which discourse they had access to as children. The students, of course, already know this, but the open acknowledgment of it in the very institution that facilitates the sorting process is liberating in itself. In short, teachers must allow discussions of oppression to become a part of language and literature instruction. Only after acknowledging the inequity of the system can the teacher's stance then be "Let me show you how to cheat!" And of course, to cheat is to learn the discourse which would otherwise be used to exclude them from participating in and transforming the mainstream. This is what many black teachers of the segregated South intended when they, like the teachers of Bill Trent and Clarence Cunningham, told their students that they *had* to "do better than those white kids." We can again let our students know that they can resist a system that seeks to limit them to the bottom rung of the social and economic ladder.

42   Gee may not agree with my analysis of his work, for, in truth, his writings are so multifaceted as not to be easily reduced to simplistic positions. But that is not the issue. The point is that some aspects of his work can be disturbing for the African-American reader, and reinforcing for those who choose - wrongly, but for "right" reasons - not to educate black and poor children.

43   Individuals *can* learn the "superficial features" of dominant discourses, as well as their more subtle aspects. Such acquisition can provide a way both to turn the sorting system on its head and to make available one more voice for resisting and reshaping an oppressive system. This is the alternative perspective I want to give to teachers of poor children and children of color, and this is the perspective I hope will end the paralysis and set teachers free to teach, and thereby to liberate. When teachers are committed to teaching all students, and when they understand that through their teaching change *can* occur, then the chance for transformation is great.

Notes

1   *Journal of Education,* special issue: *Literacy, Discourse, and Linguistics: Essays by James Paul Gee* 171.1 (1989).

2   Mike Rose, *Lives on the Boundary* (New York: Free Press, 1989).

3   Anthony M. Platt, *E. Franklin Frazier Reconsidered* (New Brunswick, N.J.: Rutgers University Press, (1991), p. 15.

4   Keith Gilyard, *Voices of the Self* (Detroit: Wayne State University Press, 1991), p. 160.

5   Herbert Kohl, *I Won't Learn from You! The Role of Assent in Education* (Minneapolis, Min.: Milkweed Editions, 1991).

6   Gee's position here is somewhat different. He argues that grammer and form should be taught in classrooms, but that students will never acquire them with sufficient fluency to gain entry into dominant discourses. Rather, he states, such teaching is important because it allows students to gain "meta-knowledge" of how language works, which in turn "leads to the ability to manipulate, to analyze, to resist while advancing" (*Journal of Education,* special issue 171.1, p.13).

7   bell hooks, *Talking Back* (Boston: South End Press, 1989), p. 11.

8   See, for example Carlos Yorio, "The Other Side of the Looking Glass," *Journal of Basic Writing* 8.1 (1989).

9   Henry Louis Gates, Jr., quoted in Reginald Martin, "Black Writer as Black Critic: Recent Afro-American Writing," *College English* 52.2 (Feb. 1990), p. 204.

10   hooks, *Taking Back.,* p 50.

11   June Jordans, "Nobody Means More to Me Than You and the Future Life of Willie Jordan," *Harvard Educational Review* 58.3 (1988).

12   hooks, *Talking Back*; and Henry Louis Gates, Jr., *Race, Writing, and Difference* (Chicago: University of Chicago Press, 1986).

13   James D. Anderson, *The Education of Blacks in the South,* 1960–1935 (Chapel Hill, N.C.: University of North Carolina Press, 1988), p. 30.

Credit

"God Don't Never Change": Black English from a Black Perspective

GENEVA SMITHERMAN

1 Ain nothin in a long time lit up the English teaching profession like the current hassle over Black English. One finds beaucoup socio-linguistic research studies and language projects for the "disadvantaged" on the scene in nearly every sizable Black community in the country.[1] And educators from K through grad. school bees debating whether: 1) Blacks should learn and use only standard white English (hereafter referred to as WE); 2) Blacks should command both dialects, i.e., be bidialectal (hereafter BD); 3) Blacks should be allowed (??????????) to use standard Black English (hereafter BE or BI, for Black Idiom, a more accurate term). The appropriate choice having everything to do with American political reality, which is usually ignored, and nothing to do with the educational process, which is usually claimed. I say without qualification that we cannot talk about BI apart from Black Culture and the Black Experience. Nor can we specify educational goals for Blacks apart from considerations about the structure of white American society.

2 Both Black and white critics of American society have dealt extensively with the rather schizophrenic nature of the American politico-social sensibility, caused by the clash of the emphasis on class flexibility and individualism with the concomitant stress on class conformity and group status. It is interesting to note the way this class consciousness neurosis is reflected in the area of language.

3 A quick look at the tradition of schoolroom grammars and the undergirding ideology of early English grammarians reveals that the current "national mania for correctness" has been around a long time. You see, from the Jump, the English language itself, didn't command no respect, for Latin was the lingo of the elite. (Outside thought: if WE wasn't given no propers, you know BI wouldn't be given any.) What those grammarians did was to take note of the actual usage of English only for the purpose of denouncing and reforming that usage. Clearly these grammarians was comin from a position that English could and must be subjected to a process of regularizing, based on a Latin/Classical model On the British side, there was Bishop Robert Lowth *(Short Introduction to English Grammar,* 1763), who conceptualized his grammar in terms of giving "order and permanence" to the "unruly, barbarous" tongue of the AngloSaxons: "The English language, as it is spoken by the politest part of the nation, and as it stands in the writings of our most approved authors, often offends against every part of Grammar." The continuity of this line of thinking in the American sensibility is best exemplified by Lindley Murray *(English Grammar,* 1795). Now Murray was really a deep dude cause, see, his book, was not gon simply introduce the proper method of English usage among the young, but inculcate in them all the morals and virtues commensurate with correct English. Dig it, now, here what he say:

4 The author of the following work [referring to himself, like they always did, in the ridiculous third person] wishes to promote the cause of virtue as well as of learning; and with this view, he has been studious, through the whole of the work, not only to avoid every example and illustration, which might have an improper effect on the minds of youth, but also to introduce on many occasions such as have a moral and religious tendency.

5 By the Twentieth Century, the individual norm had been replaced by a group norm. According to Charles C. Fries *(American English Grammar* 1940), the job of the public schools was to teach

6   the type of English used by the socially acceptable of most of our communities [since] in the matter of the English language, it is clear that any one who cannot use the language habits in which the major affairs of the country are conducted, the language habits of the socially acceptable of most of our communities, would have a serious handicap.

7   Obviously this didn't make things no better for the common folk. It was just substituting one linguistic authority for another—the individual Latinate standards of a Lowth or Murray for the group Anglican standards of middle America. Both authorities and norms is based on race and class position and is simply attempts to make the "outsiders" ta1k like the "insiders." This superimposition of a dialect norm has little to do with language power, linguistic versatility, or variety of expression and everything to do with making what one grammarian labeled the "depraved language of common people" (*The Art of Speaking,* 1668), and by extension, the common people themselves, conform to white, middle-class society. Thus nowadays, "nonstandard" dialect is that which "deviates" from the collective language of the majority culture. For example, it is now all right to use the contracted form (which offended the idiosyncratic sensibilities of those early grammarians like crazy), so it is acceptable to say *It's that way* for *It is that way.* Similarly, we can, without causing too much consternation, use the objective case after copula, as *It is me* for *It is I.* The point is that both examples represent forms regularly used by middle-class and white Americans. But dig now, in no way, do the new language pacesetters accept *It bees that way* (a popular BI statement; an expression of Black existentialist reflection and thought; used by Nina Simone as the title of a hit recording). See, an idiomatic phrase like this comes from a "lower-class" dialect (and a people) that is given no respect.

8   On the one hand, then, the denigration of BI is but a manifestation of white America's class anxiety. After all, as Baldwin says, in a country where everybody has status, it is possible that nobody has status. So Americans, lacking a fixed place in the society, don't know where they be in terms of social and personal identity. For this reason, it has been useful to have nigguhs around, so at least they always knows where the *bottom* bees. On the other hand, then, the pejorative attitude toward BI is a manifestation of white America's racism (undergirded by or coupled with class elitism). I shall cite three examples reflecting racism in the area of linguistics.

9   Toward the end of the last century, Ambrose Gonzales collected stories from the Gullah (or, as we called it down in Tennessee, "Geechee") region of the Carolina Coast and published these in *Black Border.* Speaking about the language of the Gullah Black folk, Gonzales contended:

10   The [Gullah] words are, of course, not African, for the African brought over or retained only a few words of his jungletongue, and even these few are by no means authenticated as part of the original SCant baggage of the negro slaves… S1ovenly and careless of speech, these Gullahs seized upon the peasant English used by some of the early settlers and by the white servants of the wealthier colonists, wrapped their clumsy tongues, about it as well as they could, and, enriched with certain expressive African words, it issued through their flat noses and thick lips as so workable a form of speech that it was gradually adopted by the other slaves and became in time the accepted Negro speech of the lower districts of South Carolina and Georgia. With characteristic laziness, these Gullah Negroes took short cuts to the ears of their auditors, using as few words as possible, sometimes making one gender serve for three, one tense for several, and totally disregarding singular and plural numbers.

11   (Outside thought: such absurd nonsense was validly challenged by Black historian-turned-linguist Lorenzo Dow Turner in his *Africanisms in the Gullah Dialect,* 1949.)

12   In 1924, in an article titled "The English of the Negro," and again in 1925, in his *English Language in America,* George Philip Krapp discussed Black speech patterns

throughout the South. (Outside thought: his discussion is appropriately titled by his last name.) In reconstructing the evolution of this dialect, Krapp argued that there were "no African elements …in the English of negroes [sic]"; rather this dialect reflected "archaic survivals" of English which had lingered because the "negro, being socially backward, has held onto many habits which the white world has left behind." Finally, Krapp dismissed Black speech by concluding that "negro English… is merely a debased dialect of English, learned by the negroes from the whites."

13　Well, even though Gonzales and Krapp were writing in what my fifteen-year-old son terms the "olden days" ain't nothin changed. In a recent record, *The Dilect of Black Americans,* distributed for educational purposes by Western Electric, we are told of Joseph, a recent Black high school graduate, who was refused a job because "his speech carries no respect. In fact it generates negative attitudes, and the middle-class Black must be careful of the language he uses—or which language he uses." Sound familiar? Sure, just another variation on the linguistic purist/ class anxiety theme of Lowth, Murray, and Fries; and the linguistic ethnocentricism and rampant racism of Gonzales and Krapp. (Outside thought: still at 1763 and it's 1973.)

14　In conceptualizing linguistic performance models for Black students, our contemporary objectives must be informed by such historical socio-political realities as I have touched upon here. They must also be informed by accurate, comprehensive descriptions of BI. Both kinds of information are so highly interrelated as to be virtually inseparable. Let me proceed, then, to discuss this latter point in some detail.

15　Most linguists and educators currently belaboring the "problem" of what has come to be popularly termed "Black English" have conceptualized the dialect in very narrow, constricting, and ultimately meaningless terms. Depending on the "scholarship" consulted or the rap sessions overheard in teachers' lounges, one finds 8-10 patterns of usage labeled BE. For example: zero -s morpheme in sentences such as *He work all the time, Those scientist inventing many thing, My mother name Mary;* copula deletion as in He a hippie (also in the preceding example); multiple negation as *Can't nobody do nothin in his room;* and, of course, that famous and oft-quoted use of be as finite verb, as in *They be slow all the time.* And so on and so on. The point is that such a list contains only a very small ultimately unimportant set of *surface* grammatical features. One searches in vain for any discussion of surface vs. deep structure significance in the so-called "scholarly" literature on BI. I'm talkin bout deep structure in the Chomskian sense of the term. What, after all, is the underlying semantic differentiation between *He work all the time* and *He works all the time?* Or even between *My mother's name is Mary* and *My mother name Mary?* But this is logical. because if BI were really deep structurally different from WE, then there would be a situation of mutual unintelligibility. Oh, yeah, white folks understand BI speakers, it ain't a question of communication. Whites might not like what they hear, but they bees hearin and comprehendin every bit of it. Just as white speakers from one region of the country understand whites from another region. As a matter of fact, though I doubt if many white folks would admit it, they have far greater difficulty with British English than with BI. Yet British English commands great prestige in this country. (Outside thought: since America was once a British colony, this is what Frantz Fanon might call the "colonized mentality.")

16　This "much ado about nothing" is what led to the accusation by a Brother, at a recent Black professional meeting, that the research on BI was bogus scholarship, pseudo-intellectual attempts to create a field of knowledge or a discipline out of nothing. He was not misled, as, unfortunately, many English teachers are, by the overcomplexification, linguistic jargon, and statistical paraphernalia-i.e., scholarly trappings that make some of the articles on BI almost unreadable, and the linguists themselves nearly unintelligible. (Dig it, "zero -s morpheme" is just another way of saying that the kid left off an "s.")

The dire consequence of this whole business to the English teaching profession can be illustrated by the case of a Black freshman at Wayne State, who submitted the following:

17 [TEACHER'S, ASSIGNMENT: Take a position on the war in Viet Nam and present arguments to defend your position.]

18 I think the war in Viet Nam bad. Because we don't have no business over there. My brother friend been in the war, and he say it's hard and mean. I do not like war because it's bad. And so I don't think we have no business there. The reason the war in China is bad is that American boys is dying over there.

19 The paper was returned to the student with only *one* comment: "Correct your grammar and resubmit." What sheer and utter nonsense!

20 Now, my advice to teachers is to overlook these matters of sheer mechanical "correctness" and get on with the educational business at hand. Don't let students get away with sloppy, irresponsible writing just because it happen to conform to a surface ion of correctness. Yeah, that's right, there is such a thang as sloppy "correct" writing-writing, for instance, where every statement is generalized comment without any specific, supporting details; or where the same modification structures or sentence patterns are used with tedious repetition; or where the student uses one simple kernel structure after another instead of combining and condensing. While *zero -s* and *-ed morphemes* may be easier "issues" for the already overworked English profs to deal with, I would warn such teachers not to abdicate their *real* responsibility: that of involving students in the totality and complexity of the communication process. And I would denounce as futile and time-wasting the attempts to move Black students from, for example, "He tired" to "He is tired" or from "They sold they house" to "They sold their house." Not only are such ventures misuses of important educational time, they are perhaps, albeit subtly, racist because such goals involve only lateral moves and Black folks need (upward) vertical moves. That what we mean when we sing with Curtis Mayfield "We movin on up," *Up,* not sideways.

21 None of this has been to assert that there is not a distinctive verbal style that characterizes contemporary Black American speech. But it is to reiterate a point I've made many times heretofore: it's *style, not language per se,* in which the uniqueness of Black expression lies. This style must be located in the situational context, in the Black Cultural Universe. And anybody who *knows* anythang about BI knows that that's where it's at.

22 (Outside thought: emphasis on *knows,* cause like my daddy the preacher say, everybody talking bout Heaven ain't goin there.) I'm talking bout the Black Lexicon, and bout the rhetorical devices and unique patterns of communication found in what Richard Wright called the "Forms of Things Unknown." Such stylistic/language forms are an indigenous part of the Black historical past and are rooted in the Black Cultural sensibility. They achieve a dynamism of meaning which emanates from a shared sense of oppression, and they represent, perhaps, the continuity of our African sensibility. in the New World. Although older Black writers used these forms only sporadically in they works (even Richard Wright himself), the new Black writers, the poets especially, are hip to the significance of these patterns from our Oral Tradition and have appropriated them with maximum power and poetic effect. I shall cite a few illuminating examples. Don Lee effectively uses items from the Black Lexicon when he describes Malcolm X as being from "a long line of super-cools/ doo-rag lovers/revolutionary "pimps."[2] He employs Capping, Signification, and Black Rhythmic Pattern in his poem denouncing the self-styled Black revolutionary, who is all talk and no action-dig on the title alone: "But he was cool or: he even stopped for green lights."[3] Black prison poet Etheridge Knight does a poetic variation of the Toast in his poem about the Black prisoner Hard Rock, a super-bad dude, about whom there is a "jewel of a myth that Hard Rock had once bit/A screw on the thumb and poisoned him with syphilitic spit."[4]Maya Angelou plays the Dozens on both Blacks and whites in her companion poems "The Thirteens."[5] The ritualistic barbershop scene in John Oliver Killens' novel *Cotillion*[6] is shot through with a secular version of the Call-Response Patern. And Richard Wright's own "Fire and Cloud,"[7] a short story about a militant Black minister, contains one of the most effective prose renditions of the sacred manifestation of this basic pattern.

23   Why is it that these substantive features of BI are never included in the descriptive monographs of "Black English"? Why is it that only the superfluous features of usage are extrapolated and dealt with in "language programs for the disadvantaged"? And isn't it interesting that these Superficial features of BI are easily translatable into WE? Whereas ain't no way in the world you can transform the "Forms of Things Unknown." Methinks there is some insidous design afoot to cut off Black students from they cultural roots, from, according to Frantz Fanon, "those they left behind," to create a new class of super-niggers, nouveau-white Blacks, who will rap in the. oppressor's dialect, totally obliterating any knowledge or use of BI-2 form of language firmly imbedded in the African-American past. Because, you see, the plain and simple fact is that language does not exist in a vacuum but in the socio-cultural reality. And with this broad view of BI, a view informed by cognizance of our historical past and political present, *even* those surface features take on a different meaning. As Baraka says:

24   I heard an old Negro street singer last week. Reverend Pearly Brown, singing, "God don't never change!" This is a precise thing he is singing. He does not mean "God does not ever change!" He means "God don't never change!" The difference... is in the final human reference... the form of passage through the world. A man who is rich and famous who sings, "God don't never change," is confirming his hegemony and good fortune... or merely calling the bank. A blind hopeless black American is saying something very different. ...

25   Being told to "speak proper," meaning that you become fluent with the jargon of power, is also II part of not "speaking proper." That is the culture which desperately understands that it does not "speak proper." or is not fluent with the terms of social strength, also understands somewhere that its desire to gain such fluency is done at a terrifying risk. The bourgeois Negro accepts such risk as profit. But does *close-ter* (in the context of "jes a close-ter, walk wi-thee") mean the thing as *closer*"? Close-ter, in the term of its user is, believe me, exact. It means a quality of existence, of actual physical disposition perhaps in its manifestation as a *tone* and *rhythm* by which people live, most often in response to common modes of thought best enforced by some factor of environmental emotion that is exact and specific. Even the picture it summons is different, and certainly the "Thee" that is used to connect the implied "Me" with, is different. The God of the damned cannot know the God of the damner, that is, cannot know he is God. As no Blues person can really believe emotionally in Pascal's God, or Wittgenstein's question, "Can the concept of God exist in a perfectly logical language?" Answer: "God don't never change."[8]

Credit _____

Smitherman, Geneva. "'God Don't Never Change': Black English from a Black Perspective." *College English* 34.6. Copyright © 1973 by the National Council of Teachers of English. Reprinted by permission.

Transgender Rhetorics: (Re)Composing Narratives of the Gendered Body
JONATHAN ALEXANDER

1 This essay attempts to demonstrate how transgender theories can inspire pedagogical methods that complement feminist compositionist pedagogical approaches to understanding the narration of gender as a social construct. By examining sample student writing generated by a prompt inspired by transgender theories, the author's analysis suggests how trans theories might usefully *expand* and *extend*—for both instructors and student—our analysis of the stories we tell personally, socially, and politically about gender. Ultimately, the author argues that trans theories and pedagogical activities built on them can enhance our understanding of gender performance by prompting us to consider gender as a material and embodied reality.

---

2 As a queer feminist compositionist, I have given a lot of thought to the relationships among narrative, identity, gender, and the teaching of writing. I have asked myself and my students to think critically about how we compose ourselves as men, women, masculine, feminine, and even gay, straight, or bi. To this end, I have frequently organized my writing courses around issues of gender or sexuality, using textbooks focused specifically on issues of gender, such as Anna Katsavosa and Elizabeth Wheeler's *Complements*, which offers numerous essays inviting students to consider and assess gender roles, social norms and the intersections between gender and politics. More recently, though, transgender and transsexual activists and theorists have inspired me to think with students a bit more provocatively about the "story" that we—individually and collectively, in specific cultural spaces and at a national level—tell about gender.

3 Let me give you an example.

4 On the first day of a writing-intensive honors course on "Contemporary Masculinities," I brought in for discussion a couple of recent essays by Patrick (formerly Pat) Califia-Rice entitled "Family Values" and "Trannyfags Unzipped." In these articles, Califia-Rice discusses his transition from female to male, his relationship with another FtM transsexual, and their decision to have a child together. As can be imagined, the essay sparked much discussion among this group of intelligent, mostly white, mostly straight college-aged students from largely middle-class backgrounds. Califia-Rice's life seemed strange to them, even as they applauded his willingness to undergo hormone treatments and suffer the taunts and harassment of those who do not understand his life.

5 Throughout our discussion, we kept returning to a deceptively simple set of questions: What is a man? Is Patrick Califia-Rice a "real" man? How can we tell? The majority of students – all but one – was willing to accept Califia-Rice as a man, despite his long history as a self-described dyke. Part of what students focused on in supporting their claim that Califia-Rice is indeed a man is Califia-Rice's own writing about his body. He writes both movingly and provocatively about his transition from a female to a male body:

6 I am going through my own metamorphosis. My hips are smaller, my muscle mass is growing, and everyday it seems like there's more hair on my face and body. My voice is deeper, and my sex drive has given me new found empathy with the guys who solicit hookers for blow jobs. When I think that I can continue with this process – get chest surgery and pass as male – I feel happier than at any other point in my life. And when I think that something will stop me, I become very depressed. (" Family")

7 Given such a description, such self-narration about a highly conscious and purposeful self-fashioning, students felt compelled to accept that Califia- Rice is indeed a man.

In the process of the discussion, though, we had to puzzle over how gender comes to be defined in relation to biology, cultural norms, social roles, and even political assumptions about the organization of the species.

8   Such questioning, often prompted by the writing of trans theorists and activists such as Califia-Rice, cuts to the core of the relationship among gender, bodies, and politics. For instance, trans activist and author Leslie Feinberg, in *Transgender Warriors*, wonders, "Why is the categorization of sex a legal question at all? And why are those categories policed? Why did these laws arise in the first place?" (62). I think these are good questions that ask student – and instructors – to trace the genealogy of gender as a disciplinary construct of power and knowledge in our society. And, as I've considered the work of other trans theorists and writers, I have been shifting my consideration of gender and its composition not only to include trans voices, but in many ways to ground my discussion of gender with my students in trans theories. The result, as I hope to show in this essay, is an approach to thinking about gender that is invigorating, critical, and insightful – one that opens up new vistas for students in considering the intersections among gender, the body, and the body politic.

9   To unpack in the following pages the usefulness of trans theories to the teaching of writing about gender, I want to review composition approaches to teaching about gender as a narrativized social construction, consider what transgender theorists and activists can offer us as compositionists in thinking about such narrations, and recount a pedagogical experiment in which I attempted to take advantage of some "trans thinking" to spark in my students more provocative reflection on the construction, articulation, and representation of gender. My goal in this essay is twofold: first, to demonstrate how transgender theories can inspire pedagogical methods that complement feminist compositionist approaches to understanding the narration of gender as a social construct; and, second, to suggest how such theories might usefully expand and extend – for ourselves and for our students – our analysis of the stories we tell about gender. In general, I want to approach a deceptively simple question – *What is the story we tell about gender?* – and then discuss some of the possibilities that trans theorists bring us and our students for understanding that story in some provocative and complex ways. More specifically, I want to argue that trans theorists and pedagogical activities inspired by them can remind us to complement our understanding of gender performance with a sense of gender as a material and embodied reality.

Pedagogies Of Possibility: Some Feminist Rhetorics Of Gender

10   Over the last three decades, numerous composition scholars who have been influenced by feminism have undertaken an examination of how gender is a multivalent construct whose identity- and community-shaping power needs interrogation in our classrooms, our teacherly performances, and our students' writing. And while I cannot in these pages offer a full accounting of the impact of feminism on and within our field, I would like to suggest here some general trends that seem particularly noteworthy as prelude to thinking about what trans theorists have to contribute to this rich discussion.[1]

11   In "Feminism in Composition: Inclusion, Metonymy, and Disruption, "Joy S. Ritchie and Kathleen Boardman take a long, historical view of feminism in composition, and they note that "[t]he explicit recognition of composition's lack of attention to women's material lives has led women in anger, frustration, and recognition to tell the stories of their coming to awareness"(17). In a great many ways, telling the *story* of women's experience has been at the heart of many feminist projects in composition. A significant number of early feminist compositionists worked in this vein, asking whether men and women *fundamentally* write the stories of their lives in differently gendered ways. Elizabeth A. Flynn's landmark essay, "Composing as a Woman," originally published in *CCC* in 1988, asked a seemingly straightforward question: "Do males and females compose differently?" (245). Seeking to extend and complicate this discussion, Patricia A. Sullivan addressed a number of related issues in her 1992 essay, "Feminism and Methodology in Composition Studies," such as "considering the influence of gender on the composing process" (125), "tak[ing] issue with the assumption that discourse is gender neutral"(126), and "seek[ing] to generate new knowledge about the relationships between gender and composing that can help us counteract the androcentrism that leaves women's modes of thinking and expression suppressed and undervalued"(132). Sullivan's work thus argued that gender is a multivalent force that has an impact on composing in both subtle and profound ways, and she maintained that we should turn our attention to an examination of that impact.

12 To demonstrate and even play with some "women's modes of thinking and expression:' Terry Myers Zawacki wrote "Recomposing as a Woman-an Essay in Different Voices," an experimental piece interweaving narration and analysis. Zawacki's writing in this essay is clearly designed to open up spaces for women to explore – safely, productively, and challengingly – the insights they have into gender, its construction, and its representation in writing: "If I situate myself in the context of other voices, if I write about experiences and feelings, if I choose not to get to the point, it's not because I am a woman, but rather because I want to discover the possibilities for representing a gendered self in writing" (319). Seeing writing as possibility for representing gender, as opposed to a *revealing* of a fundamental gender, is a significant shift in thinking about the composition of gender. Zawacki states, "Instead of trying to discover what makes a written voice distinctly a woman's, or a man's, I want to focus on how language can be manipulated to make readers believe that there is a gendered self contained in the margins" (318). For Zawacki, it's insufficient to suggest simply that men and women write differently; rather, our experience of gender and the use of language are wrapped up in the politics of manipulation and marginalization based on socially constructed gender differences, and we need new ways to use language to explore that relationship.

13 Subsequent feminist scholarship in composition has picked up on this theme of possibility and examined a variety of pedagogical strategies for understanding and interrogating with students the ways in which gender functions in our lives, both personally and politically. In the opening pages of "Genders of Writing," published in 1989, David Bleich discusses homophobic responses among students, and he links such responses to the privilege that men in general have in our society: 'All authoritative social roles are held by men – in politics, medicine, law, religion, science, art, and, of course, the academy. It should come as no surprise that the style of thought developed by these men in the name of all people should correspond with the structure of social relations that sustains their social privileges" (13). At the same time, Bleich counters such privilege with the assertion that "[neither] I nor anyone else can actually advocate some fixed taxonomy of gender. What I and many others do think, however, is that the flexibility and permeability of gender boundaries must be recognized and accepted by all" (13). For Bleich, recognizing the potential "permeability of gender boundaries" might help weaken the connection between a perceived sense of unassailable maleness and corresponding "social privileges."

14 How to question, interrogate, understand, and critique that connection has been the subject of more recent feminist scholarship in composition. For instance, Susan Romano's "On Becoming a Woman: Pedagogies of the Self" is a rich essay in which Romano looks at a number of pedagogical practices, including pseudonymous online discussion. For Romano, the goal in using such practices is clear; she is invested both "in expanding the range of students' discursive options, and in producing equitable discursive environments [...]" (453). In a similar vein, Gail Hawisher summarizes even

more broadly what she sees as the common goals of much feminist-inspired composition pedagogy:

15   [E]ven as we disagree as to the forms a feminist pedagogy might take, the goals of that pedagogy remain remarkably similar. They seek to elicit in students a critical awareness of that which was once invisible – to provoke in students through reading, thinking, writing, and talk a sense of agency, a sense of possibility. They aim to forward, through teaching, a feminist agenda that probes the dominant discourses of sexism, gender preference, and [...] racism and classism. (xvii)

16   The emphasis here is on creating spaces in writing classrooms for women's stories to be told and their voices to be heard, considered, and appreciated-with the ultimate goal, perhaps, of both (1) engaging a "critical awareness" of the relationship between gender and the sociopolitical matrix, and (2) promoting agency among those who wish to undertake such an analysis.

17   Most recently, composition scholarship in this vein has grappled with issues not only of gender but also of sexuality, recognizing that sexuality intersects with and complicates our understanding of gender. In a sociocultural matrix in which heterosexuality is the normative default, gender expectations for men and women are often figured as binary and complementary: men and women form discrete pairs of "opposites" appropriately attracted to each other, each displaying the appropriate gender characteristics of its half of the pairing. Lesbians and gays "transgress" this binary pairing, potentially casting the gender dichotomy upon which heterosexuality is based into disarray or at least question. As a result, lesbians' and gays' experiences of gender may often be different from those of heterosexuals. Harriet Malinowitz's groundbreaking 1995 book, *Textual Orientations: Lesbian and Gay Students and the Making of Discourse Communities*, uses a wide variety of methodologies and points of reference, including feminism, ethnography, and critical pedagogy, to argue for a more careful consideration of the composing practices of lesbian and gay students. Specifically, she argues for a pedagogy that would respect the critical insights about both sexuality and gender brought to our classrooms by those, namely lesbian and gay students, who have been subject to marginalization, who have existed outside the norm:

18   The sort of pedagogy I am proposing would entail thinking about the ways margins produce not only abject outsiderhood but also profoundly unique ways of self-defining, knowing, and acting; and about how, though people usually want to leave the margins, they do want to be able to bring with them the sharp vision that comes from living with friction and contradiction. (251-52)

19   Put another way, our students' identities, informed by prevailing, politicized, and personal definitions of gender and sexuality, can have a significant impact on their participation in class, their sense of themselves as learners and knowledge producers, and, by extension, their engagement with writing as a mode of exploration, communication, invention, and discovery. Opening up spaces in our classrooms to allow and encourage students to undertake such explorations not only empowers them and promotes their own agency but also potentially extends critical awareness to all students of how writing can be used to explore the intersection between the seemingly personal (a sense of gender, a sense of sexuality) and the political (sociocultural expectations of appropriate gender and sexual behavior).

20   Some scholar-teachers have suggested that such identity interrogation along the axes of sexuality and gender is important for both students *and instructors*. In "Bi, Butch, and Bar Dyke: Pedagogical Performances of Class, Gender, and Sexuality," Michelle Gibson, Martha Marinara, and Deborah Meem suggest that instructors themselves need to be critically aware of the identities – and the stories that compose such identities – they bring into the classroom with them if they are to be sensitive to the many different stories that *students* bring into the classroom:

21
> Compositionists committed to creating classrooms in which traditional academic power structures are problematized and critiqued must also commit themselves to interrogating their own positions in those classrooms. We must think seriously about the identities we bring with us into the classroom, remain conscious of the way those identities interact with the identities our students bring, and insert ourselves fully into the shifting relationships between ourselves and our students at the same time that we resist the impulse to control those relationships. (486)

22 Again, the emphasis on creating spaces in which difference is not simply interrogated but appreciated is a crucial dimension of feminist-inspired composition pedagogies.

23 Gibson and I have recently attempted to extend this discussion in our own essay, "Queer Composition(s): Queer Theory in the Writing Classroom," in which we argue that "queer theory asks us to question, at the most fundamental levels and in the most essential ways, the nature of authorship, representation, and the process of coming into being through language" (7-8). Specifically, in its questioning of the essentialist nature of identities based on sexual orientation, queer theory can be used to highlight for *all* students how our identities are shaped and communicated through a variety of intersecting social processes. For instance, how we understand ourselves as gay or straight – our "personal" identities – is socially inflected by labels that, on one hand, stigmatize certain behaviors and, on the other hand, reify others. Homophobic taunts, for example, show how language use intervenes in the composing of socially acceptable identities; having one's actions, mannerisms, or interests labeled "gay" can force a reexamination of how one narrates his or her "story" – both to him – or herself and to others.[2]

24 In general, though, while this recent work has borrowed productively from the emerging fields of sexuality studies and even queer theory, paying particular attention to the experiences of gays, lesbians, and even bisexuals as writers and subjects of writing, only minimal attention has been paid to transgendered or transsexual students and the "sharp vision[s]" about gender that they may bring to composition classrooms. Two very recent works (2004) include "The Transgendered and Transgressive Student: Rhetoric and Identity in Trans- Queer Ethnography: " by Lindsey Larkin and Marshall Kitchens, and "Boy? You Decide/Girl? You Decide: Multimodal Web Composition and a Mythography of Identity" by Brian R. Houle, Alex P. Kimball, and Heidi A. McKee – both appearing in a special issue of *Computers and Composition Online* entitled "Sexualities, Technologies, and Literacies." In both pieces, authors use multimedia formats to describe, in the words of Houle, Kimball, and McKee, how "multi-media enabled (or hindered) potentially transgressive expressions of and understandings of gendered and sexual identities" (par. 1). Larkin and Kitchens pose the fundamental question about representing transgendered identities, in either multimedia or more traditional formats: "What difficulties does a student encounter when constructing a text that transgresses binary notions of gender typically held by classmates in a computer-mediated writing classroom?" (abstract). Such work is crucial in, at the very least, becoming aware of the presence of transgendered students in our classrooms and in learning how to respect those presences.

25 At the same time, however, next to no scholarly work addresses directly how transgender or transsexual *theories* might inform a feminist composition pedagogy. We strive to expand our sense of respect for the many diverse voices coming into the classroom, but another question begs to be asked: how can we use the "sharp vision[s]" of transgendered experience to extend and complicate *all of our students'* – and our own – understanding of *the construction and narration* of gender? Malinowitz suggests that paying attention to gay and lesbian students might offer us insights into "profoundly unique ways of self-defining, knowing, and acting:" Gibson and I agree. I cannot help wondering if paying closer attention to transgendered ways of being and knowing might offer us profoundly different ways of understanding gender and its rhetorics. In the following section, I describe what I think are some relevant trans theories and begin to make connections between them and their potential usefulness in the writing classroom.

Possibilities Of/For Gender: Some Trans Theories

26 In many ways, trans theorists, activists, and writers are equally invested in engendering in others a "critical awareness" about gender and in opening up a "sense of agency, a sense of possibility" about what gender means – and *could* mean – as a construct that is simultaneously deeply personal and profoundly political. Granted, transgender is a tricky word to define, and it is often used as a "catchall" category for a range of those who "play with" or "transgress" gender norms, including cross-dressers, gender-fuckers, transvestites, drag kings/ queens, and transsexuals.[3] But the aims of many self-identified trans activists and theorists are to create cracks in the monolithic structure of gender identity and to search for wiggle room in what William Pollack has aptly termed the "gender straitjacket" (40-43). Feinberg says in hir[4] book *Trans Liberation* that the transgender movement is one of "masculine females and feminine males, cross-dressers, transsexual men and women, intersexuals born on the anatomical sweep between female and male, gender-blenders, many other sex and gender-variant people, and our significant others. All told, we *expand understanding* of how many ways there are to be a human being" (5, emphasis added).

27   How does such "expansion" take place? Feinberg argues that we need to acknowledge both the presence and the material lives of those who are not born either specifically male or female *and* understand, more generally, the restrictive nature of concepts such as male/female and masculinity/femininity for *all* people. First, speaking of hir experience as a transgendered individual, Feinberg reminds us that

28   Millions of females and millions of males in this country do not fit the cramped compartments of gender that we have been taught are "natural" and "normal." For many of us, the words *woman* or *man, ma'am* or *sir, she* or *he* – in and of themselves – do not total up the sum of our identities or of our oppressions. Speaking for myself, my life only comes into focus when the word *transgender* is added to the equation. (7)

29 Acknowledging the presence of the transgendered is useful not only for understanding those who are differently gendered or whose presentation or experience of gender falls outside our "norms":'but also for helping us interrogate the constructs of gender that we often take for granted as "natural" or "normal." Specifically, Feinberg notes that "[j]ust as most of us grew up with only the concepts of woman and man, the terms feminine and masculine are the only two tools most people have to talk about the complexities of gender expression" (8). Part of the transgender project, then, is not just to alert others to the presence of differently gendered people or those who experience their gender in ways other than strictly masculine or feminine, but also to examine critically how gender limits our potential sense of self: "Our struggle will also help expose some of the harmful myths about what it means to be a woman or a man that have compartmentalized and distorted your life, as well as mine. Trans liberation has meaning for you – no matter how you define or express your sex or your gender" (5).

30   Many trans theorists have been inspired to think along such lines after considering the work of queer theorist Judith Butler, whose notion of gender performativity has been a useful if contentious approach to thinking critically about gender.[5] Butler argued in *Gender Trouble*, are consideration of feminism's critique of gender, that "[t]here is no gender identity behind the expressions of gender; [...] identity is performatively constituted by the very 'expressions' that are said to be its results:' (25). The result of such

performances for Butler is the denaturalization of "gender" a s a category; gender is not necessarily an essential and natural given, but rather a sociocultural construct whose repeated performances – as masculinity and femininity – have come to appear and seem natural. David Gauntlett summarizes well how many activists and writers, including some trans theorists, have appropriated Butler's notion of performativity to envision expansive possibilities for challenging the norms of gender:

31
> Butler calls for subversive action in the present: "gender trouble "– the mobilization, subversive confusion, and proliferation of genders – and therefore identity. Butler argues that we all put on a gender performance, whether traditional or not, anyway, and so it is not a question of whether to *do* a gender performance, but what form that performance will take. By choosing to be different about it, we might work to change gender norms and the binary understanding of masculinity and femininity. (Pars. 9-10)

32 Along such lines, Kate Bornstein, a prominent and popular trans activist and writer, argues in numerous texts, such as *My Gender Workbook and Gender Outlaw*, that gender identity is a construct in need of deep – and playful – questioning. Her *Workbook* offers a delicious parody of the self-help genre to encourage readers to query the conventional ways in which they think of gender. Specifically, she claims as her goal the following:" Providing the public discourse with the possibility of subjective proof that gender is neither natural nor essential, but rather the performance of self-expression within any dynamic relationship" (21).

33 Some feminist compositionists have found Butler's work useful as well. For instance, in her book *Feminism beyond Modernism*, compositionist Elizabeth Flynn describes Butler's understanding of gender performativity as a "'doing: hence calling into question foundational conceptions of gender that see identity as prior to and determinative of action" (137). This conception parallels Bornstein's assertion above, that gender is "neither natural nor essential" but rather performative. Flynn's and Bornstein's goals in using Butler to underscore the performative nature of gender is not to do away with it, but rather to open up spaces of thinking more expansively of gender. As Flynn notes, Butler's "postmodern feminist perspective results in a problematizing of traditional gender categories rather than in a dismissal of them" (39-40). Such formulations are useful in the composition classroom to help students question naturalized and normative constructions of gender that students might take as assumed givens, thus dictating behavior. For instance, we can help students question behavioral and attitudinal differences between men and women, which may clearly exist, as arising not from a biological imperative but from sociocultural experiences of sexism and privilege.

34 While Butler's is a compelling argument about gender, some trans theorists have offered a substantial critique of how "performance" doesn't quite capture the interweaving of gender, identity, and the body, or a sense of the *embodied*-ness of gender identity. Jay Prosser, in *Second Skins: The Body Narratives of Transsexuality*, critiques "the equation 'camp = queer = performativity = transgender' that per-vades [queer theory]" in that it "not only misrepresents reality but ignores the important 'narrative' of *becoming a biological* man or woman" (qtd. in Dickemann 463). Transsexual activist and theorist Susan Stryker too directly takes on Butler and performativity as explanatory trope of the narration of gender:

35
> Gender in the Butlerian paradigm is strikingly cinematic – any stability of gender identity's visual image is due solely to the incessant, unvarying repetition of its chosen signs over time.[...] Signs of gender that we change relatively effortlessly like our clothes or relatively painlessly like the length of our hair have received the bulk of critical attention simply because they are more easily mobilised, their capacity for movement more readily perceived. [...] [T]he flesh can be all too easily perceived as part of the fixed landscape against which gender performs itself, rather

than as part of the performance itself.[.. .] Transsexuality offers a dramatic instance of the temporal in stability of the flesh. It sets embodiment in motion. (593)[6]

36 Similarly, in Henry Rubin's *Self-Made Men: Identity and Embodiment among Transsexual Men*, in which Rubin carefully recounts and examines narratives of female-to-male transsexuality, he states that "The lives of transsexual men highlight the cultural significance of the body. Through FTM experience, we can see the modern relationship between sexed bodies and gendered identities. [.. .] We view bodies as the reflection of a gendered self" (180). Given these critiques, "performativity" seems at times too loose as a trope, too much like changing our clothes or cutting our hair, to explain how transsexual theorists understand the narration of gender and its inscription *both in the psyche and on the body*.

37 To promote and even provoke this critique, some trans activists employ pedagogical techniques, as Bornstein does in her My Gender Workbook. Their goals are, ultimately, similar to those of many feminist composition pedagogues: they seek an expansive notion of gender that prompts us to question restrictive norms and categories, understand how gender is used as a politically and personally normalizing category, and develop a deeper consciousness of the embodied nature of gender identity. To highlight the pedagogical dimension of trans activism, Pat Califia (pre-sex change) concludes her powerful book, *Sex Changes: The Politics of Transgenderism*, with a series of provocative questions about gender – questions that I argue can challenge our students', as well as our own, sense of gender and its personal and political power:

38 If you could change your sex as effortlessly in reality as you can in virtual reality, and change it back again, wouldn't you like to try it at least once? W ho do you think you might become? What is that person able to do that you don't think you can do now? What would you have to give up to become oppositely sexed? What would change about your politics, clothing, food preferences, sexual desires, social habits, driving style, job, body language, behavior on the street? Are you able to imagine becoming a hybrid of your male and female self, keeping the traits that you value and abandoning the ones that are harmful?(2 77)

39 Such writing has prompted me to ask students comparable questions, to help them explore and interrogate the sociocultural articulation of gender, as well as its connection to the sociopolitical matrix in our culture – a subject to which I turn in the following section of this essay.

Trans pedagogy: An experiment in transition

40 Originally, when considering using trans-related materials in my composition courses, I introduced students to several trans-themed Web sites, such as Leslie Feinberg's homepage, Transgender Warrior. Such sites offered quite a bit of useful fodder for discussion with students, for a number of reasons. First, trans sites frequently deconstruct the male/female binary-one of the most pervasive modes of meaning making in our culture. Second, in deconstructing this binary, trans sites powerfully reveal gender as a social construction-as a narration that rhetorically, and politically, uses gender to maintain categories, roles, and knowledges that delimit and police our bodies and identities. Further, in examining the stories that trans activists tell about themselves, we witness the construction of counternarratives, alternative modes of identity construction, and a number of creative rhetorical moves that show how narratives of personal experience can be used to query a variety of personal and sociopolitical issues. For instance, in telling a story about something as seemingly simple as using a public restroom, trans writers such as Feinberg reveal how "clear-cut" our social expectations of gender performance are; gender-ambiguous individuals often face significant harassment, even bodily harm, if they are perceived as using the "wrong" restroom, which are almost exclusively designated "male" or "female:'

41   In many ways, though, I found this approach – exposure to and discussion of trans-related Web sites – to be critically limited and thus pedagogically unsatisfying. It seemed easy at times for students to "dismiss" trans people as pretty much wholly "other," their concerns, insights, and critiques unrelated to those of my "traditionally" gendered students. Who cares if a few freaks have trouble using public toilets? Given such responses, I wanted a more pro-vocative way to challenge our understanding of the composition of gender. Feinberg writes that "gender is the poetry each of us makes out of the language we are taught" (*Trans Liberation* 10); with such a thought in mind, I wanted to work with students to examine that language a bit more carefully, a bit more deeply. Moreover, I wanted to work with students on exploring, as trans theorists and feminist compositionists advocate, a sense of agency and possibility with respect to gender; or, as Feinberg puts it, "we need more language than just feminine/masculine, straight/gay, either/or. Men are not from Mars and women are not from Venus" (28).

42   The pedagogical question I posed myself, then, was how do we find such language? To capture some of the critical "gender poetry" that Feinberg talks about, I took a clue from Califia's comments about virtual gender switching, and I designed an in-class writing exercise in which students were prompted to write from the perspective of another gender.[7] In concocting this exercise, I sensed that I was in risky territory, potentially opening up not new possibilities for thinking about gender, but a much more sexist and stereotypical can of worms. But I wanted to know, and I wanted to examine with students, some possible answers to Califia's questions – as well as metacritically reflect on the process of gender/sex switching, even if only virtually, and what it might tell us about the narration and construction of gender in our society. So, to approach Califia's questions, I decided to use some creative freewriting as a way to help students think about the questions in an engaging, enjoyable, and, ideally, insightful manner. Indeed, I've found that, in composing creative works, students often write more openly, willingly, and even critically about issues that concern and interest them, and I hoped to use some of this creative and critical energy to think with them about gender.

43   Specifically, I adapted Will Hochman's "paired fiction writing," in which pairs of students collaboratively construct fictional stories through a series of teacher prompts.[8] In the original exercise, the instructor asks a pair of students to compose, separately, the setting for a story. After a set time of freewriting (perhaps ten to fifteen minutes), the pair exchange writing (or swap seats at a computer terminal) and are then instructed to write about characters for the settings that their partners composed. The students compose directly in their partners' drafts, creating one text with two authors. After another switch, students have to concoct a dilemma or crisis for the character in the setting, and then, after one final switch, students have to resolve the conflict. My particular "twist" on paired fiction writing involved having students in a second-quarter first-year writing course compose their stories from what they perceived to be the experiences and assumptions of someone of a different gender. I began by pairing students by gender; men worked with men, and women with women. About twenty students participated, producing ten complete narratives. All students were visibly traditionally gendered, and none identified himself or herself as transgendered or transsexual.

44   I used this particular creative writing assignment for several reasons. First, the resulting stories are almost always fascinating and generally very clever; students are surprised that they are able to enter into one another's texts with great ease, and they frequently find the challenge of posing and resolving fictional crises challenging but fun. Besides introducing students to some of the basic dimensions of narrative and storytelling, this activity often reveals for students some of the stereotypes, clichés, and familiar tropes upon which many narratives depend for their intelligibility and accessibility to a variety of audiences.

45 Further, I decided to use a narrative-based exercise because many feminist compositionists have argued, persuasively, that examining narrations of experience, even fictionalized experiences, can be quite revealing about gender constructs and their connections to larger sociocultural and political matrices. In fact, analyzing experience- its contents, its narration and representation, its genealogy-has been a central pedagogical practice of many feminist-inflected approaches to composition, often prompting students to produce and analyze their own experiences through personal narratives." Reading and Writing Differences: The Problematic of Experience," by Min-Zhan Lu, has been a particularly inspiring essay for both its theoretical sophistication and its lucidity in showing what a feminist analysis can bring to examining narrations of experience. Lu maintains that "[t]he feminist dictum that the personal is political has taught us to recognize the centrality of the gendered experience in the production of knowledge" (241), and she argues that inviting students to consider carefully and critically the content of their own "gendered experience" plays a crucial part in developing their understanding of the relationship between gender and "knowledge," or the creation of socially sanctioned and enforced norms. For Lu, the pedagogical task at hand is to design writing prompts that will invite and encourage students to undertake this work:

46 We need assignments that ask students to explore the analytic possibilities of experience by locating the experience that grounds their habitual approach to differences; by sketching the complex discursive terrain out of and in which the self habitually speaks; by investigating how that terrain delimits our understanding of differences along lines of race, class, sex, and gender; and by exploring personal and social motivations for transforming one's existing self-location in the process of rereading and rewriting. (243)

47 The result, Lu hopes, is that "experience should motivate us to care about another's difference and should disrupt the material conditions that have given rise to it" (239). With this theoretical backdrop, Lu then traces in her essay how she has attempted to craft such assignments, teaching and having students write about provocative texts by Sandra Cisneros and Gloria Anzaldúa by filtering the issues raised in those texts through students' own "personal history" (247).[9]

48 Similarly, in working with this exercise, I hoped to explore the following with my students:

49 1. I wanted to evoke some of Feinberg's gender poetry, to see the uses to which my writing students were putting their developing language skills in the construction of gender. If virtually transsexed, even if only for an hour, what stories would my students tell? What poetry would they make out of the language of gender they had been taught?

50 2. I wanted to "test" with students Butler's notion that "[t]here is no gender identity behind the expressions of gender; [...] identity is performatively constituted by the very 'expressions' that are said to be its results" (25). This is nearly a commonplace in gender and queer studies, but I wanted to probe with my students what such a formulation actually means. Specifically, does "performativity," as a concept, capture the complex set of representations, identifications, projections, subjectifications, and even immiserations that "gender" encompasses?

51 3. And, finally, I was curious to see whether anyone would or could, in Califia's words, "imagine becoming a hybrid of your male and female self." If so, if choosing to be *different* about gender, perhaps "we might work to change gender norms and the binary understanding of masculinity and femininity."(277)

52 How did students respond to the exercise? They nearly unanimously found it "fun," "easy," and "great." Comments collected immediately after completing the exercise are intriguing:

53   It wasn't really weird writing from another gender's point of view (F). I like writing fiction because you can go wherever you want to with the stories. There [are] no limits or anything holding you back. (F).

54   [...] the story is always moving in some new direction. (M).

55   While I agree that it was "fun," some of the most pedagogically interesting dimensions of the exercise opened up in the reflective discussion following it. As we read aloud and discussed some of the stories as a class, we began to see some dominant trends in how students composed (and composed *about*) gender—trends that suggest both a reliance on rather sexist stereotypes in thinking about gender *and* a sense that gender is much more than just a sense of role or "performance"; rather, like many trans theorists, the students' stories reveal a complex if intuitive sense of gender as *embodied*. Such insights, as I will argue below, suggest that this trans-inspired pedagogy opens up some exciting ways for thinking with students about gender and its composition. With that in mind, let's examine some of the stories to unpack some of these directions and insights.[10]

Gender Poetry: Students Writing, Students Transiting

56   Two stories, "Unsafe" and "Mr. Football," deploy some of the more simplistic yet pervasive gender stereotypes in our culture—feminine insecurity and masculine idiocy. Indeed, my earlier use of quotation marks around "women" and "men" indicates that students were clearly composing in stereotypes—often broad ones—and that they were reliant upon clichés of gender and broad assumptions about masculinity and femininity in the crafting of their narratives. For instance, in "Unsafe," written by two young men, Sarah is a new student at Berkeley who is "terrified of large cities" and who has been told that her "beautiful looks can get [her] anywhere [she] want[s]." She's lonely, having a hard time adjusting, and feels that she "will always feel unsafe in [her] home," despite the new security system installed by her landlord. In contrast, the most distinguishing feature of "Mr. Football," written by two young women, is that he has "a great 8-pack and well-defined muscles." He's a stereotypical jock with the requisite low IQ; in the story, which is mostly a portrait of a college-aged jock, he finds himself spellbound by the beauty of a jellyfish, only to be stung by it, resulting in an injury that will, fantastically, take all summer to heal. And heal he must, for "[i]f he doesn't play football he won't be able to afford school. His scholarship pays for all of his school need." With such stereotypes, the male authors in the former story depict a young woman as frightened and helpless, and the female authors in the latter story poke fun at the muscle-bound idiocy of a "macho" man. As you can imagine, just reading and discussing these stories in class prompted quite a consideration of how stereotypes of gender persist and circulate in our culture; such stereotypes are generally tied to narrations of gender with which these students are obviously familiar. Rehearsing them, particularly having the "other gender" acknowledge them in their stories, sparked much recognition of how trivializing, pernicious, and even damaging such gender narrations can be.

57   Two other stories, a bit longer and more detailed, are noteworthy for their commonality, specifically their deployment of an "innocence punished" trope—a more complex yet still stereotypical narration of female gender. "Scarlet," written by two young men, is set in a dance club, and the primary drama revolves around Scarlet's decision to try crack, offered to her by an undercover cop. She takes the crack, begins confessing to a life of crime, and is promptly arrested and hauled off to prison. "Amanda," also written by two young men, depicts a young woman struggling to stay in college. She can only afford a "ghetto" apartment, and she ends up adopting some of the nastier habits of her neighbors, such as drug abuse and crime. In both stories, the young women depicted are originally every bit as "innocent," even naïve, as Sarah in the earlier story, "Unsafe," but Scarlet and Amanda compromise their original innocence to "fit in." They become, at

least to the outside world, more than the little girls they are originally on the inside, and they are duly punished—in often horrifying ways, including prison time and violence: Scarlet has been involved in an underworld of drugs and murder, while Amanda, in order to finance her college education, becomes a drug dealer. In a way, their "performances" in these stories are a masking of their original innocence so they can enter the supposedly (and stereotypically) dangerous world of men:

58   [Scarlet] is a very intimidating woman and she is afraid that if she does not step up to the challenge with this attractive man that she is very fond of, then she will be looked at differently.

59   Amanda came to one realization during her time in the ghetto; you only survive if you can fit into a society.

60   The performances of toughness, though, fail, and both suffer profound loss—perhaps as a result of their gender transgression: they hide and betray their feminine innocence. While we can certainly read these stories as instances of misogyny, even an interlocking mix of sexism and racism in the case of "Amanda," I would also suggest that these are stories about their authors' masculinity, or sense of being "male." For instance, the men in the stories (drug dealers and the like) are hardly models of success. But, more tellingly, I think we can detect a bit of projection in the writers' crafting of their female characters: the main characters, for instance, fear not fitting in, not being "tough enough." As such, perhaps the young men's writing is actually a reading of the impossibility of masculinity, of achieving an identity as a "real man."

61   Two final stories, "The Little Dream Girl" and "Turnabout," are, I think, among the most sophisticated. Some stereotyping persists, but it is put to different and more complex uses. "The Little Dream Girl," written by two young men, depicts a rather strong, independent-minded high school female athlete, Ashley, who breaks out of the feminine mold set by Sarah in "Unsafe." The opening description of Ashley reveals toughness and determination:

62   Ashley is the star forward of Edgewood high's girls' basketball team. She is a senior at the school and she hopes to someday win a scholarship to play in college. Since her family doesn't have too much money, and she has 3 brothers and a baby sister, she needs this scholarship to further her goal of becoming an English professor and free lance writer. She enjoys writing fiction, mostly impromptu fiction, as it is a great strength to her just like basketball is. She spends her days practicing basketball, reading, writing, and just being a normal high school teen. She is 6 feet tall, with curly blonde hair to her shoulders.

63   She's bold, tries hard, faces failure, but never gives up. For instance, as a basketball player, she takes a momentary setback (a lost game) and goes on, vowing to try harder next time. Hers is ultimately a story of success. That would be fine—if the narrative weren't also a thinly veiled reading and critique of my course. You can hear the metacritique in the narrative through its references to "impromptu writing" exercises and a writing assignment on feminism, which the students were working on at the time. In fact, the male writers target the writing of a "paper about feminism" as the source of Ashley's potential unhappiness with just settling down with a man; she'll want a career instead: "Because after she wrote a paper about feminism, she sees herself as wanting an impressive career." I think we can easily read some anxiety about feminism here, particularly in the snide tone that pops up here and there in the narrative ("All went well for the little dream girl from Edgewood, Nebraska"). But, to the writers' credit, they allow Ashley to succeed—even if she is only a "little dream girl."

64   The other story, "Turnabout," written by two young women, is a wonderful revenge fantasy, in which a selfish young man (written by two young women) battles within himself about how to break up with his clingy girlfriend, on whom he is cheating with

her best friend. He muses to himself as follows:

65   I decide that I'm going to tell her what happened and tell her that "we" aren't
      working anymore. I know she's going to assume that I'm breaking up with her to be
      with her best friend, and I hate when girls do that. They just flip out over something
      that doesn't even exist. And this isn't fair to me because I'm putting myself in a bad
      situation. So I decide to call her up and discuss what we need to talk about.

66   In a surprise twist at the end of the story, however, we find out that the clingy girlfriend
      has been cheating on him! The female authors read (and write) the clingy girlfriend as
      a *man's* mistaken deployment of a stereotype that comes back to surprise him—and us.
      The boy muses, "I don't want to break her heart but I don't care much for her anymore
      either"; but, by the end of the narrative, we discover, with the narrator, that the girlfriend
      "also had something to tell me ... she slept with my best friend as well." Both stories
      parody the stereotypes they narrate, creating, I believe, some intelligent criticism along
      the way. What do such stories suggest about the narration of gender among these
      students? First, all of the stories deploy significant stereotypes, which shouldn't be
      surprising. In some ways, the writing situation—creation of "on-the-spot" narratives—
      called for stereotypes, familiar tropes, even clichés. I do not think it is a leap, though, to
      suggest that these gender stereotypes represent significant ways in which and through
      which students know, approach, and attempt to understand one another. That being
      the case, pointing out the more vicious or insidious stereotypes can be enlightening
      to them, and we had productive discussions about the stereotypes deployed in these
      stories. Indeed, many students were surprised at how consistently, even misogynistically,
      they performed unflattering characterizations of one another, based solely on gender. In
      many ways, I think this exercise was beneficial in that it *highlighted* for students the very
      stereotypical attitudes they might harbor about one another. Flynn writes the following
      about the pedagogy of addressing gender issues in the classroom:

67   [...] gender is often invisible. Students do not always see that gender is at the root
      of a powerful ideological system of inequality and sociality that affects all aspects
      of their lives. They do not necessarily recognize their own gendered behavior or
      attitudes or those of their friends or individuals who hold authority over them.
      Making gender visible often involves initially making productive use of their
      resistances to it. (*Feminism*150)

68   By taking on the supposed "role" of the other gender, each author has the opportunity,
      upon reflection, to see the limitations of those roles.

69   Some students, for instance, displayed a willingness to read the stereotypes critically,
      working the norms, as it were, to create resistant readings—and performances—of self
      and other. A story such as "Mr. Football," for all of its clichés of the dumb, muscle-
      bound, hypermasculine jock, may be signaling some not unjust revenge, a bit of critical
      "reverse stereotyping." The dumb blonde meets the even dumber jock—a meeting made
      more intriguing if you know that the two authors of "Mr. Football" are intelligent young
      women who just happen to be blonde. Similarly, in "Turnabout," the two female writers
      craft a story in which a man is surprised to find out that his girlfriend has been cheating
      on *him*. The female authors compose a male character who seems to believe that
      cheating is typically the domain of male behavior; however, in this case, his girlfriend is
      also cheating, suggesting that she is as every bit as interested in exploring and expressing
      her sexuality as he is. Moreover, his sexist assumption—that *men* cheat, perhaps
      because they are more "sexed"—is proven false. In a way, then, "Turnabout" becomes
      a story about sexual empowerment for young women, even as it pokes fun at men who
      think that *they* are the ones who are more typically nonmonogamous because of their
      supposed sex drive. In writing and then examining the narratives, I was asking students to
      interrogate the "performativity" of gender—and we did.

70   Flynn's point about how "[m]aking gender visible often involves initially making productive use of their resistances to it" is also well taken in light of the stories my students produced. "Little Dream Girl" worries over the construction of a "politically correct" gender performance: the strong, independent woman. The story queries both this emerging stereotype and, in performing it a bit snidely, attempts to critique my perceived agenda in calling it forth, or inviting it to be performed in these narratives. While the story might resist my perceived agenda, it nonetheless offered us a vision of womanhood—the strong woman, pursuing success in typically masculine fields such as sports—for consideration and discussion. More provocatively, it allowed us to discuss not only this version of womanhood but also the male writers' snide crafting of it in their portrait. What motivated their mild derision? How are changing gender roles threatening, both to women and men? Such questions were productively fostered by this exercise, and our reflection on the stories was often rich and rewarding.

Transgender And Rhetorics Of Embodiment

71   As I have thought more about the exercise and my students' stories, I have focused a bit more on the "transition" that I asked students to perform—the shift they undertook in writing from a differently gendered perspective. Certainly, in no way am I suggesting that my students experienced what it is like to be transsexual or that their narrations remotely approached the lived experience of making the transition as a transsexual— in body and psyche—from one gender or sex to another. Virtually assuming another gender's perspective, or what you *think* is another gender's perspective, for one hour in a classroom may be instructive about many things, but it does not a transsexual make. Nonetheless, I believe the exercise opened up a space in the classroom to talk not only about the performance of gender but also about the *embodiment* of gender—and how normalizing constructs of gender are inscribed on both mind *and body*.

72   We know the stereotype of transsexuality: a woman or man feels trapped in the "wrong body" and thus seeks sexual-reassignment surgery to correct nature's "mistake." Recent writing about transsexuality, though, offers a much more complex understanding of the phenomenon and process, as well as useful insights into the ways in which the performance of gender is *embodied*. In "Transsexuality: The Postmodern Body and/as Technology," Stryker argues that

73   [t]he transsexual body as cyborg, as a technologization of identity, presents critical opportunities similar to those offered by the camera. Just as the camera offers a means for externalizing and examining a particular way of constructing time and space, the transsexual body—in the process of its transition from one sex to another—renders visible the culturally specific mechanisms of achieving gendered embodiment. It becomes paradigmatic of the gendering process, functioning, in Sandy Stone's words, as "a meaning machine for the production of ideal type." (592; emphasis added)

74   I think we can see such "embodiment" in my students' "cyborg" narratives. The "culturally specific mechanisms of achieving gendered embodiment" abound in their tropes, in their "production of ideal type[s]." Granted, these are the imagined bodies of imagined others, but the perception and composition of gender as *embodied* needs attention in our discourses about gender, as trans theorists argue.

75   For instance, in moving from the opening paragraph's describing a setting to the second paragraph's inscribing a character into that setting, a distinct "gendering process" occurs. Look at "Unsafe" as an example:

76   In this place you can see that is very big, crowed, full of lights, and people. This place is place is huge it is full of tall buildings, cars it is crowed everywhere you go. There are some very dark street where nobody walks by, restaurants that nobody is willing to eat in because there nasty smells, but there are places out there that are beautiful with nice flowers around, big gardens and nice smells.

77   I, Sarah, am terrified of large cities. They are big and smelly, but I have to live in one because I am going to school at Berkley University. The changes that I have had to make are huge for me and they are hard to deal with every day. My goal everyday is to survive to the next day. I have lived in a little town my whole entire life and I loved it there. Everyone knew everyone and in the city nobody knows who you are. I feel so lost and lonely. The only way I can cope living in this city is by talking to my friends back at home. They tell me not to worry and that my beautiful looks can get me anywhere I want.

78   The first scene-setting paragraph is generic, even ambiguous, with some things good, some bad. The introduction of Sarah, a stereotypically insecure young woman, highlights the city's negativity, contrasting it to the innocence and security of a "little town." It is as though Sarah's feminine innocence is so powerful that it genders the landscape, pitting her insecurity and naiveté against the "big and smelly" dangerous (masculine?) city.

79   A similar, perhaps even more pronounced, gendering occurs in "Scarlet":

80   Setting: An 80s pop dance club in Soho. Everyone is beautiful and wild hair and funky outfits are seen under the lights. The theme of this popular haven is black and white cubism. The waitresses wear white and black spandex and the drinks are never colored. The building is very dimly lit, and usually packed with pretty people in bright colors, to exhibit their individualism and self-gratification which was popular in the 80s. Many young people and one 75-year-old man flock to the dance floor, bars, and few VIP rooms to live it up. In the back, there are "drug rooms" where many people experiment with white and black cocaine powder. The room usually smells of expensive perfume, cigarette smoke, and alcohol. The walls are 2 to 3 stories high, and a large projector screen shows silent movies from old science fiction B movies. The doorway has a receptionist desk and coat area filled with black and white plants, and an aquarium with black, white, and trans-parent fish. The only art or d6cor of the building is found in the comfy furniture in wild shapes and the interesting dance floor design of cubist black and white shapes.

81   Main Character: her name is Scarlet Weathers or that is what people know her as, she is a very mysterious woman. When she walks into the bar everyone stops and looks to her. All the guys begin to swarm her. She wears a bright red sequin dress, unlike many of the others in the club who wear black and white and insanely bright colors like yellow. She seems rich, like no other woman in the club. No one really knows her age because she is very mysterious. She always has a lit cigarette, but rarely puts it to her mouth. She is always the center of attention when she walks into a room.

82   Scarlet is the only splash of red in the club, and she rather deliciously performs, in the second paragraph at least, a film noir femme fatale. Her distinctly gendered presence lends the landscape its only real color. In many ways, we're witnessing here a powerful "performance" of gender roles and stereotypes, as Butler describes in *Gender Trouble*: a reiteration, in narrative after narrative, to reify certain norms to the point of naturalness. Scarlet's clothing and demeanor, for instance, her red sequined dress and the dangling lit cigarette—these are some of the performed signifiers of her gender, culturally legible and understandable to everyone in the room as obvious, even "natural."

83   But some aspects of the stories, to my mind, point to more than just gender "performance," as it has been articulated by queer theorists like Butler. Indeed, of all the things my students could have imagined in(to) their narratives, the *body*—the *gendered* body—is something that several of them chose (consciously or not) to highlight in their construction of the "other" gender. Let's look again, for instance, at "Mr. Football" with Stryker's comments in mind. Our beach-loving jock is "very athletic in many different sports. He has a great 8-pack and well-defined muscles. He's around 6'4" and weighs around 210 (pure muscle)." Compellingly, much of the gender performance here is written *on the body*, and, moreover, this masculine-gendered body is a *sculpted* body, not a "naturally" occurring one. And in another narrative we can see a bit more body sculpting to discipline the body in the performance of a gender. In "Turnabout," two female students have their male protagonist state, "As I come home from classes I go straight to Bally Total Fitness to manage, part time. It's an easy job, and it allows me to get in shape while being paid." Clearly, these female students feel that the pursuit of the "buff body" is a desired (and perhaps desirable) trait among males. To my mind, such embodiments seem slightly beyond the "performative"; they seem more "transsexual"— the literal crafting of the body to meet certain "ideal types" of gender "performance."

84 The male writers, too, narrated bodies that "speak" to particular assumptions about what gendered bodies are supposed to look like. In "Unsafe," the female narrator has been told by others "not to worry and that [her] beautiful looks can get [her] anywhere [she] want[s]." In this case, a specific kind of female body is seen by the male students *as itself having agency*. The woman is seemingly only as strong as her physical attractiveness. We see a similar dynamic at play in "Scarlet," in which a woman's worth is measured by how well she can hold the attention of men: "She is a very intimidating woman and she is afraid that if she does not step up to the challenge with this attractive man that she is very fond of, then she will be looked at differently."The body—the specifically gendered body—holds power here, even if it is a fleeting power.

85 Further, the male gaze is strong in the stories written by men, and it is generally a gaze attuned to women's *bodies*. In "The Little Dream Girl," the athletic narrator practices alone—or so she thinks:

86 She grabs the ball and shoots again, and makes it. As the janitor at the other end of the courts weeps up the popcorn and candy bar wrappers, he watches Ashley drain shot after shot as she practices late into the evening. Ashley will never quit, and she is still determined to win that scholarship for the state school. The next day, she is invited to attend a few liberal arts colleges and the State University. Eventually, she picks her school and works incredibly hard to make the starting team by her sophomore year and plays in the NCAA tournament her junior year. All went well for the little dream girl from Edgewood, Nebraska.

87 Even in this story, one which seemingly ends with an empowered woman stretching the bounds of gender norms, we encounter a male eyeing a woman's body in motion. What is he thinking? It is impossible to tell, but his presence highlights a reality: our bodies, particularly women's bodies, are under scrutiny—perhaps especially in this case, in which the young woman being constructed in the narrative is also being constructed as both a feminist and somebody stepping slightly outside her assigned gender role. She, and her gender transgressions, must be watched carefully.

Critiques and conclusions

88 What does such an approach to writing about gender teach us and our students? What can we learn—personally, politically, and pedagogically—from experimenting with Califia-Rice's call to compose narratives of virtual gender swapping? In "On Becoming a Woman: Pedagogies of the Self," Romano remarks on some of the potential goals of feminist compositionist practice. She suggests that what may be "crucial to the production of equitable discourse is the possibility that when many women are present and differ in their self-representations, then 'women' as a category—represented variously—can be taken back from its reductive forms and rebuilt as multiple" (462). Part of the goal of my paired fiction exercises was certainly to expand students' sense of the multiple ways that women—and men—exist as gendered beings in the world. But we also experienced, in writing and analyzing those narratives, a sense of the gendered *body* and how gender finds itself written on—and read from—the bodies we inhabit and through which we both derive and articulate a sense of self. Those bodies, though, are never simply personal; they are profoundly politicized bodies, called to a gendered scrutiny, sculpting, and legibility that determine which bodies are male and female, powerful and weak.

89   Interestingly enough, transgender and transsexual theorists such as Prosser have argued forcefully that it is in the examination of *narrations* of gender that we come to a fuller and richer understanding of its "composition"—both personally and politically, in mind and on body. Prosser argues, for instance, that "transsexual and transgendered narratives alike produce not the revelation of the fictionality of gender categories but the sobering realization of their ongoing foundational power" (11). We might be tempted to think of gender as a set of roles, many stereotypical, that can be critiqued and cast off, like so many changes of clothing. But Prosser maintains, as my students' narratives reveal, that gender inscribes itself at the level of the flesh. This is particularly true when considering narratives of gender transition: "Transsexuality reveals the extent to which embodiment forms an essential base to subjectivity; but it also reveals that embodiment is as much about feeling one inhabits material flesh as the flesh itself" (7). For Prosser, examining such narratives is the key to opening up a more expansive and thorough discussion of gender; as he maintains, "To talk of the strange and unpredictable contours of body image, and to reinsert into theory the experience of embodiment, we might begin our work through [..] autobiographical narratives" (96).

90   As a pedagogue invested in the expansive possibilities of feminist compositionist practices, I must ask myself what potential for actual critical agency lies in a closer attention to the body and its composition in gender narrations. On one hand, I believe that my students may have encountered powerfully in the paired fiction exercise how gender functions in our society to condition certain expectations and norms for how women and men are to behave—at least stereotypically. In this way, the exercise is in line with Will Banks's recent call for working with students on creating "embodied writing," or writing that takes into consideration the specific needs, desires, and beingness of particular bodies and of particular experiences of the body. As Banks suggests, such writing "offers us and our students spaces to think through all those multiple and shifting signifiers at work on us so that we come up with sharper understandings of ourselves and those around us" (38).

91   At the same time, though, the narrative "performances" of my students are suggestive of the double bind of gender—a double bind neatly evoked by transsexuality, which itself evokes tropes both of boundary crossing and the power of boundaries to (re)inscribe norms. For Stryker, transsexuality

92   [...] is simultaneously an elaborately articulated medico-juridical discourse imposed on particular forms of deviant subjectivity, and a radical practice that promises to explode dominant constructions of self and society.(594)

93   In a new historical survey and analysis, *How Sex Changed: A History of Transsexuality in the United States*, Joanne Meyerowitz argues in a similar vein—that transsexuality in particular is a simultaneous reification, on one hand, of gender norms and expectations, and, on the other hand, a mobilization of gender:

94   Transsexuals, some argue, reinscribe the conservative stereotypes of male and female and masculine and feminine. They take the signifiers of sex and the prescriptions of gender too seriously. They are "utterly invested" in the boundaries between female and male. Or they represent individual autonomy run amok in the late modern age. [...] some theorists identify transsexuals as emblems of liberatory potential. (11, 12)

95   Did my students experience that liberatory potential? Our discussions postexercise were revealing, thoughtful, and even critical. We could spot stereotypes "in action," noting

how we craft stories for ourselves—and others—in which the most limiting and even sexist of gender norms are deployed again and again, for both "traditional" sexes and genders.

96   But does such recognition in a classroom exercise translate into increased sociopolitical agency? I am less sure about that, as indeed are many feminist compositionists. Donna LeCourt, in her essay "Writing (without) the Body: Gender and Power in Networked Discussion Groups," describes her experiences with using electronic discussion venues to help women students foster and experiment with multiple voices and modes of expression, thus potentially "subvert[ing] and/or resist[ing] the power relationships that silence them in other realms" (171). LeCourt hopes that "[m]aking students metacognitive of their discursive positions and how those already constructed embody different relations of power would create a context in which the forms of textual resistance so productive in the electronic space could become consciously employed, and perhaps more importantly, equally possible in the classroom space" (173). The emphasis in LeCourt's position has to be placed on "perhaps" and "could," with metacognition *potentially* translating from a pedagogical venue to a more "real-world" one. Indeed, I believe my students and I used the paired fiction exercise to think metacognitively about gender in some very critical ways; but did the fiction writing lead to resistances to gender norms outside the space of the exercise, or outside the classroom? I can't be certain, particularly since those norms, as Stryker and Meyerowitz suggest, are so persistent and so powerful.

97   I am not sure that our narratives of gender swapping and transition were necessarily helping liberate participants from gender norms, even though I believe they offered us opportunities to explore useful insights. If anything, they revealed the extent to which gender is much more than a set of roles and rhetorical tropes; there is a rhetoric of the body that needs careful consideration as well. As one of the students wrote in one of the stories, "[Y]ou only survive if you can fit into a society." And a significant way in which we fit in—or do *not* fit in—has to do with how our bodies are perceived as complying with or deviating from sets of highly gendered norms. In *Transgender Warriors*, Feinberg argues pointedly that gender is more than just a process of naming, a performance of roles: "When I say I am a gender outlaw in modern society, it's not rhetoric. I have been dragged out of bars by police who claimed I broke the law when I dressed myself that evening. I've heard the rap of a cop's club on the stall door when I've used a public women's toilet. And then there's the question of my identity papers" (61).

98   Ultimately, I maintain that working with students on the narration and construction of gender is perhaps better served by metaphors and tropes that capture some of the lived and embodied complexity of gender. Performativity has been useful as a trope. Transgenderism and transsexuality may be even better. Indeed, to what extent do *many* of us steadily "transit," even unknowingly, from the bodies we are born with to the culturally idealized gendered bodies images of which surround us in the media? At the very least, the paired fiction exercise has taught me that it is crucial when considering *discourses* of gender with students to recognize the material realities constructed by, maintained by, and perhaps even at times enabling of those discourses. And, pedagogically, considering with students gender *beyond* its rhetorical dimensions is not to leave rhetoric behind, but to think about rhetoric in a more materially grounded way. Wendy Hesford argues that "[i]t is particularly important that the pedagogical process enables students to explore the self as a discursive and cultural construct in courses that rely on autobiographical experiences" (60). While I agree, I also believe that such autobiographical experiences might involve a bit of play, such as the creative play of paired fiction writing, that might remind our students (and us) of the additional dimensions of the self "as a discursive and cultural construct"—namely the embodied

and material self that is also written, composed, and narrated. Trans theorists can help us undertake this work.

Appendix: Students' paired fiction narratives
"Unsafe"/m to f

99 In this place you can see that is very big, crowed, full of lights, and people. This place is place is huge it is full of tall buildings, cars it is crowed everywhere you go. There are some very dark street where nobody walks by, restaurants that nobody is willing to eat in because there nasty smells, but there are places out there that are beautiful with nice flowers around, big gardens and nice smells.

100 I, Sarah, am terrified of large cities. They are big and smelly, but I have to live in one because I am going to school at Berkley University. The changes that I have had to make are huge for me and they are hard to deal with every day. My goal every day is to survive to the next day. I have lived in a little town my whole entire life and I loved it there. Everyone knew everyone and in the city nobody knows who you are. I feel so lost and lonely. The only way I can cope living in this city is by talking to my friends back at home. They tell me not to worry and that my beautiful looks can get me anywhere I want. I have been heref or almost 2 months and I don't know anybody, I have get rob two times in my apartment and I don't have anybody to help me. My loneliness is indescribable and I don't even like this city I am just trying to be successful with my life but my every day is come alone, there are day that I don't even speak a word out of my mouth because I don't have anybody to talk with. I am trying to get a job in a restaurant serving tables but the people that lives in this neighborhood is very scary and those are the ones I will be serving even that I don't want to work there I have to need the money because I got all stolen the last time they broke in my apartment.

101 I now have a home security system in my apartment. Now if anyone tries to break in, then the police will be notified immediately. My landlord put metal bars on my windows so that no one could break in from the outside and I personally put in a hidden video camera for anyone that does get in. I now feel secure at home but I think that I will always feel unsafe in my home.

"Mr. Football"/ f to m

102 The sun's warm rays beat down on my skin. Sitting here sipping a tropical coconut drink in the sand. The ocean waves crash into the beach repetitiously creating a relaxing, peaceful ambience. All you can see for miles is the blue sky meeting the horizon of the blue sparkling waters. There is no one else for miles on this beach. There is no noise aside from the ocean waves beating against the shore and the seagulls that soar above.

103 Then a tall, muscular man walks on to the beach. He is the hottest man you will ever see. He has brown hair and brown eyes. He's very tan and he has blond streaks in his hair from the sun. He's a college football player at the University of Florida so he is always outside. Also, he's very athletic in many different sports. He has a great 8-pack and well-defined muscles. He's around 6'4" and weighs around 210 (pure muscle). This mysterious boy has perfect straight and white teeth and when he smiles he has the biggest dimples. Mr. Football loves the beach and spends all day out here laying around and playing in the water.

104 Now Mr. Football loves to come to the beach to think and straighten out all his thoughts. As he walks down the beach in his normal fashion he sees a blob laying up ahead, intrigued he moves closer. He becomes very interested in this and begins to poke at it. The second he touches it he feels the electric current of a jellyfish flow through his hand. In this shocked state he begins to move backwards and then falls over something behind him, breaking his ankle. In those few seconds his football career is over for the year.

105 Now Mr. Football will have to stay away from partying and playing sports for the summer because he needs to heal his foot. If he doesn't play football he won't be able to afford school. His scholarship pays for all of his school needs. So, Mr. Football will have to lay around for the rest of the summer and heal up!

"Scarlet"/m to f

106 Setting: An 80s pop dance club in Soho. Everyone is beautiful and wild hair and funky outfits are seen under the lights. The theme of this popular haven is black and white cubism. The waitresses wear white and black spandex and the drinks are never colored. The building is very dimly lit, and usually packed with pretty people in bright colors, to exhibit their individualism and self-gratification which was popular in the 80s. Many young people and one 75-year-old man flock to the dance floor, bars, and few VIP rooms to live it up. In the back, there are "drug rooms" where many people experiment with white and black cocaine powder. The room usually smells of expensive perfume, cigarette smoke, and alcohol. The walls are 2 to 3 stories high, and a large projector screen shows silent movies from old science fiction B movies. The doorway has a receptionist desk and coat area filled with black and white plants, and an aquarium with black, white, and transparent fish. The only art or décor of the building is found in the comfy furniture in wild shapes and the interesting dance floor design of cubist black and white shapes.

107 Main Character: her name is Scarlet Weathers or that is what people know her as, she is a very mysterious woman. When she walks into the bar everyone stops and looks to her. All the guys begin to swarm her. She wears a bright red sequin dress, unlike many of the others in the club who wear black and white and insanely bright colors like yellow. She seems rich, like no other woman in the club. No one really knows her age because she is very mysterious. She always has a lit cigarette, but rarely puts it to her mouth. She is always the center of attention when she walks into a room.

108 Problem: A figure enters the club and approaches Scarlet. The figure is a large man looking to be about 29 years of age. He looks attractive, and wears a business suit. He seems to be the male version of Scarlet, just a little older and mature. As he sits next to Scarlet on the black stool at the white bar, he lights her cigarette with a suave smile and begins talking to her about normal single and looking type things. They talk, and laugh, while certain eyes peer over to what seems to be an important gossip topic. Soon they disappear together into the back next to the "drug rooms." The man, named Timothy, asks Scarlet: "Would you like some crack? I don't mean this cheap stuff the club offers, but what I brought in. It's much more expensive and I won't take any other buzz than this. Care to join me?" Scarlet looks at Timothy and wonders what this kind of cocaine is, as she has never done drugs before.

109 Solution: Scarlet has this "hard-ass" attitude that she wants to maintain. She is a very intimidating woman and she is afraid that if she does not step up to the challenge with this attractive man that she is very fond of, then she will be looked at differently. Scarlet goes along with plan and begins to snort a few lines of the coke. As minutes pass she begins to feel the effects of the coke and cannot focus on what she is doing. She begins to admit things that she has done in her past, such as help with murder plots. She feels the guy grab her hands and place handcuffs on them and escorts her out the backdoor. Timothy turned out to be a crooked cop whose brother was killed by someone that Scarlet was associated with. Scarlet was then taken to prison and this is where the story starts, of her plot to kill Timothy's brother.

"Amanda"/m to f

110 The setting is a dreary and dank street corner that the smells of city pollution is wretched and you cant wait to get on the bus and get the hell out of there. Its so hot out that you think that you might melt onto the sidewalk and break into small pieces that mix in with all

the cigarette buds and squished pieces of gum you're standing there sweating your balls off when the lady sitting on the bench that has an insurance advertisement on it with graffiti and everything says to you that you should stand behind the half bent over utility pole if you want to stay cool and out of the sun. I don't think that will help much considering that I can see the cityscape in the horizon through all of the insidious haze that plagues the city and the street corner that you are standing at. While wasting your time you look across the street and see a bunch of kids that obviously have never heard of air-conditioning playing with the water coming out of a fire hydrant and chasing each other around in the street almost getting hit by cars and then you see all the drug deals going down the corner and you begin to be concerned with your safety. Man this place is like a scene from hell and no matter how bad you think it is it only gets worse when it starts to rain and the water brings down all the pollution for the wretched rooftops that line the street.

111   This is the first time that Amanda has been outside the quiet setting of her hometown. Amanda was brought up in a nice and quiet suburban area with no crime and where everyone knew everyone else. This area was one of her least favorite places in the town where she was now in college. She just didn't fit in. She wore the wrong clothes, talked differently, and was even a different race. Amanda was in the middle of a Ghetto wearing the worst possible thing, Abercrombie and Finch. There was no chance of her fitting in. Surrounded in this area of filth and slime the only job that she could find was a job at a local convenience store. She had only been working there for about two weeks and she had already been robbed twice. This added to the fear that she had of this place and the loathing that she had to get away from there. She knew this was the only place that gave the degree that she wanted and she was determined to remain there. She would get her degree, yet right now she was just worried about survival.

112   Amanda had a decision to make, whether to stay in this hell hole for 4 years and get her degree or whether to take the short term gain and go home to her parents and tell them that she no longer had any interest in getting a college degree. Her parents were never real keen on her going to college in the first place because they just didn't see the need, so if she went home in shame, where she could also rejoin her boyfriend, her parents would do the equivalent of an "I told you so" speech. She would live the rest of her life wondering what might have been if she would just have stuck out the ghetto for a few years. As she was working at the convenience store during the afternoon and putting up with all the shit she got from the local neighborhood kids, "do you want to feel my joe joe" she had a profound realization ... she didn't have to do either.

113   Amanda came to one realization during her time in the ghetto; you only survive if you can fit into a society. Amanda met many people in that small convenience store, but only one seemed to be decently civil with her, a man name Johnny. Johnny was not your normal guy and she seemed to like him. There was only one problem, Johnny was a drug dealer. Johnny and Amanda began to talk and after a few weeks things began to change. The neighborhood kids left Amanda alone, the store was not getting robbed at all, and everyone seemed to have taking a liking to Amanda. Amanda was slowly drug down into the filth and slime of the world that she lived in. Johnny had taken what used to be a little innocent angel and turned her into a victim of the ghetto. Amanda did not give up her dream of getting her degree; she just found another way to pay for it. Amanda became a large time drug dealer in the ghetto; her and Johnny did get married, although it was not for the best. Johnny didn't have too many friends in the ghetto. One night about a month after their first child had been born a black 1960s model Lincoln rolled by their house and there was a clatter of bullets hitting the pavement. After that silence. Now Amanda did not get lucky enough to escape that hellhole, but Johnny and their child had. Both had been killed in the incident. Of course Amanda could not report this to the police and she was forced to live the rest of her life in sadness, even though her life only lasted a few more days.

"The Little Dream Girl"/ m to f

114 Setting: A high school cafeteria/gym. Puke green and orange colored walls and hardwood basketball floors. Smells like meat loaf, pizza, and the end of a full contact basketball game. It is very old, complete with black scuffmarks on the floors and very dusty. Very run down, and not well maintained.

115 Ashley Days sits in the middle of the bleachers. She stairs at the basketball hoop, still in her uniform, and a basketball in her hands. Ashley is the star forward of Edgewood high's girls' basketball team. She is a senior at the school and she hopes to someday win a scholarship to play in college. Since her family doesn't have too much money, and she has 3 brothers and a baby sister, she needs this scholarship to further her goal of becoming an English professor and free lance writer. She enjoys writing fiction, mostly impromptu fiction, as it is a great strength to her just like basketball is. She spends her days practicing basketball, reading, writing, and just being a normal high school teen. She is 6 feet tall, with curly blonde hair to her shoulders. She has a boyfriend, but she doesn't think it will carry on through high school. He is more or less the high school sweetheart prom date. Now, she has just lost the big game to the cross-town rival with a missed three point shot at the buzzer. And she heard that a college scout had been in attendance that night in her little school.

116 Conflict: Ashley was very upset because of her poor performance on the court, she gets into the game when she plays and sometimes can be taken as a trouble maker on the court when she back talks the refs when they call her for a foul. She saw her hopes of getting the scholarship fade as well as her hopes of becoming a English Professor/Freelance writer. She prays that she will hear from the basketball scout that was at her last game, or she will not be able to reach her goal of going to college.

117 Wrap up: She is very depressed about her future beyond high school, and contemplates her other options. She likes her boyfriend John, and his father owns the grocery shop in town. She could get married and be supported when John takes over the family business. Yet, she wouldn't be completely happy. Because after she wrote a paper about feminism, she sees herself as wanting an impressive career. After many thoughts, and many prayers, she gets up, steps to the free throw line, and takes a shot. Miss. She grabs the ball and shoots again, and makes it. As the janitor at the other end of the court sweeps up the popcorn and candy bar wrappers, he watches Ashley drain shot after shot as she practices late into the evening. Ashley will never quit, and she is still determined to win that scholarship for the state school. The next day, she is invited to attend a few liberal arts colleges and the State University. Eventually, she picks her school and works incredibly hard to make the starting team by her sophomore year and plays in the NCAA tournament her junior year. All went well for the little dream girl from Edgewood, Nebraska.

"Turnabout"/F to M

118 A setting is an apartment. It is small yet cozy. There is no particular smell to the apartment. The furniture is not expensive; it's just what you would expect from a typical college student. I'm a struggling student who works two jobs with 40 hours a week of hard labor. Not to mention I'm a computer science engineer, I spend most of the day at school pulling my hair out to understand why I'm actually in this major to begin with. As I come home from classes I go straight to Bally total fitness to manage, part time. It's an easy job, and it allows me to get in shape while being paid. Not too bad for someone as busy as me. My jobs alternate each day between Bally's and working at the children's hospital. Yeah, sounds kind of weird that I'm a computer science nerd, health freak who cares about his looks, and works at the children's hospital.

119 I'm dating a girl who is just annoying the hell out of me. At one time the two of us were like best friends and I would tell her everything. But now I don't even feel like talking to her anymore. I don't have that much available time anymore and she's always complaining that I don't spend any time with her. Well if I actually had free time I think I would be able to. What is even worse is that I work with her best friend. One night after work I took her home and next thing you know I was still there the next morning. I don't know what to do now. I can't face my girlfriend and I'm scared she's going to find out what I did. I don't want to break her heart but I don't care much for her anymore either. I've just been avoiding her for as long as possible. When I got home from work today I got a voicemail from her saying that we have to talk. Now I'm kind of scared because I don't know if she knows what I did and I don't know what to expect.

120 How can this be happening? I've got such a hectic life already. I can't afford to make some life-changing decision that conflicts with my schedule. I'm up all night thinking about what to do with this situation and what to say to her when "we talk". I figure that if I care for this girl she deserves to know what happened. But on the other hand I don't have any interest for her anymore, so it wouldn't hurt to not say anything. But if she does know what happened between her best friend, and me then she'll be the one to break up with me. And then I'll end up going through a state of depression for no reason at all. And I don't need that in my life, not right now.

121 I decide that I'm going to tell her what happened and tell her that "we" aren't working anymore. I know she's going to assume that I'm breaking up with her to be with her best friend, and I hate when girls do that. They just flip out over something that doesn't even exist. And this isn't fair to me because I'm putting myself in a bad situation. So I decide to call her up and discuss what we need to talk about. I told her everything about what happened between her best friend and me, and I also included that we're just not working well together anymore. She, of course, got pissed and yelled, bitched and screamed on the phone. Then she told me that that's not what she wanted to talk about. She also had something to tell me... she slept with my best friend as well.

Notes

[1] For a fuller discussion of feminism and the teaching of writing, see the wonderful collection, *Feminism and Composition: A Critical Sourcebook*, edited by Gesa E. Kirsch et al., which anthologizes "classic," early feminist approaches to composition as well as more recent trends in thinking about gender in the writing classroom.

[2] I experimented earlier in my career with such pedagogies, particularly in pseudonymous online chat, in which participating students pretended to "wake up" in a world in which homosexuality was the norm and heterosexuality the stigmatized sexuality. An examination of this kind of role playing and alternative narration exercise can be found in my article "Out of the Closet and into the Network: Sexual Orientation and the Computerized Classroom," published in 1997 in *Computers and Composition*.

[3] For a fuller discussion of why it is "tricky" but nonetheless useful to consider such terms as trans, transgender, and even transsexuality more broadly, see my introduction to *Bisexuality and Transgenderism: InterSEXionsof the Others*.

[4] *Hir* is a gender-neutral, third-person singular pronoun (from Wikipedia, http:// en.wikipedia.org/wiki/Hir).

[5] For a good discussion of the more "contentious" aspects of the debate between Butler and some feminist thinkers, see Butler's essay, "Against Proper Objects," and Rosi Braidotti's

interview with Butler, "Feminism by Any Other Name," both included in the collection *Feminism Meets Queer Theory*.

[6] Butler self-corrects in her book following *Gender Trouble, Bodies That Matter*, maintaining that her formulation of performativity in *Gender Trouble* does *not* mean that gender can be taken on and off like a suit of clothes. More recently, in Kate More's interview with Butler, "Never Mind the Bollocks: Judith Butler on Transsexuality," Butler offers a new articulation:

> There's a kind of forward moving effort to reconceive and redefine what counts as real. So for me the performative theory of gender was not about putting on a masquerade that hides a reality, or that is derived from a higher reality, but it's actually about a certain way of inhabiting norms that alters the norms and alters our sense of what is real and what is liveable. [...] I think I'm interested in disrupting the symbolic in order to rearticulate it in more expansive ways. (297)

[7] Kate Bornstein's *My Gender Workbook* has a section entitled "Back into the Classroom: Three Gender Performance Workshops" (225-42) that may be just as useful as Califia-Rice's questions for inspiring classroom activities to explore the performance and construction of gender narrations.

[8] For more on Hochman's paired fiction writing exercise, see his "Transactional Dynamics of Paired Fiction Writing."

[9] Many other feminist compositionists have promoted the use of autobiography or personal narratives as pedagogical tools for understanding the relationship between power and gender, as well as other sociocultural markers and signifiers. Wendy Hesford, in *Framing Identities: Autobiography and the Politics of Pedagogy*, argues forcefully for writing pedagogies that use autobiography and personal narrative in creative and critical ways. She says, "Autobiographical acts [...] do not reflect unmediated subjectivities; rather, they are acts of self-representation that are ideologically encoded with historical memories and principles of identity and truth. [...] I am less interested in autobiography as a chronological record of a life already lived or as the retrieval of an essential essence or truth [...] than I am with examining autobiographical acts as social signifying practices shaped by and enacted within particular institutional contexts and their histories" (xxiii). Put another way, Hesford is interested in pedagogical uses of autobiography that are not excavations of an essentialist notion of self unearthed through an expressivist exercise, but rather a social-epistemic approach to narrations of self that understands the construction, articulation, and representation of subjectivity as always already existing within and inflected by a sociopolitical and historically bounded matrix. As a consequence, she argues "for the primacy of students' autobiographical texts in a feminist multicultural writing curriculum," and "urge[s] writing teachers to recognize the identity negotiations and interplay of social discourses articulated through the processes of writing and reading autobiography" (56).

[10] In this essay, I have chosen six stories, included in the appendix, to discuss. Of the ten stories produced, all of which are intriguing and insightful, these six stories generated the most in-class discussion. Students have given me permission to quote from and discuss their work.

Credit

Alexander, Jonathan. "Transgender Rhetorics: (Re)Composing Narratives of the Gendered Body." *College Composition and Communication* 57.1. Copyright © 2005 by the National Council of Teachers of English. Reprinted by permission.

Tlilli Tlapalli: The Path of the Red and Black Ink

GLORIA ANZALDÚA

1
> "Out of poverty, poetry; out of suffering, song."
> —Mexican saying

2 When I was seven, eight, nine, fifteen, sixteen years old, I would read in bed with a flashlight under the covers, hiding my self-imposed insomnia from my mother. I preferred the world of the imagination to the death of sleep. My sister, Hilda, who slept in the same bed with me, would threaten to tell my mother unless I told her a story.

3 I was familiar with *cuentos* – my grandmother told stories like the one about her getting on top of the roof while down below rabid coyotes were ravaging the place and wanting to get at her. My father told stories about a phantom giant dog that appeared out of nowhere and sped along the side of the pickup no matter how fast he was driving.

4 Nudge a Mexican and she or he will break out with a story. So, huddling under the covers, I made up stories for my sister night after night. After a while she wanted two stories per night. I learned to give her installments, building up the suspense with convoluted complications until the story climaxed several nights later. It must have been then that I decided to put stories on paper. It must have been then that working with images and writing became connected to night.

Invoking Art

5 In the ethno-poetics and performance of the shaman, my people, the Indians, did not split the artistic from the functional, the sacred from the secular, art from everyday life. The religious, social and aesthetic purposes of art were all intertwined. Before the Conquest, poets gathered to play music, dance, sing and read poetry in open-air places around the *Xochicuahuitl, el Árbol Florido,* Tree-in-Flower. (The *Coaxihuitl* or morning glory is called the snake plant and its seeds, known as *oloiuhqui,* are hallucinogenic.) The ability of story (prose and poetry) to transform the storyteller and the listener into something or someone else is shamanistic. The writer, as shape-changer, is a *nahual*, a shaman.

6 In looking at this book that I'm almost finished writing, I see a mosaic pattern (Aztec-like) emerging, a weaving pattern, thin here, thick there. I see a preoccupation with the deep structure, the underlying structure, with the gesso underpainting that is red earth, black earth. I can see the deep structure, the scaffolding. If I can get the bone structure right, then putting flesh on it proceeds without too many hitches. The problem is that the bones often do not exist prior to the flesh, but are shaped after a vague and broad shadow of its form is discerned or uncovered during beginning, middle and final stages of the writing. Numerous overlays of paint, rough surfaces, smooth surfaces make me realize I am preoccupied with texture as well. Too, I see the barely contained color threatening to spill over the boundaries of the object it represents and into other "objects" and over the borders of the frame. I see a hybridization of metaphor, different species of ideas popping up here, popping up there, full of variations and seeming contradictions, though I believe in an ordered, structured universe where all phenomena are interrelated and imbued with spirit. This almost finished product seems an assemblage, a montage, a beaded work with several leitmotifs and with a central core, now appearing, now disappearing in a crazy dance. The whole thing has had a mind of its own, escaping me and insisting on putting together the pieces of its own puzzle with minimal direction from my will. It is a rebellious, willful entity, a precocious girl-child forced to grow up too quickly, rough, unyielding, with pieces of feather sticking out here and there, fur, twigs, clay. My child, but not for much longer. This female being is angry, sad, joyful, is *Coatlicue*, dove, horse, serpent, cactus. Though it is a flawed thing – a clumsy, complex, groping blind thing – for me it is alive, infused with spirit. I talk to it; it talks to me.

7   I make my offerings of incense and cracked corn, light my candle. In my head I sometimes will say a prayer – an affirmation and a voicing of intent. Then I run water, wash the dishes or my underthings, take a bath, or mop the kitchen floor. This "induction" period sometimes takes a few minutes, sometimes hours. But always I go against resistance. Something in me does not want to do this writing. Yet once I'm immersed in it, I can go fifteen to seventeen hours in one sitting and I don't want to leave it.

8   My "stories" are acts encapsulated in time, "enacted" every time they are spoken aloud or read silently. I like to think of them as performances and not as inert and "dead" objects (as the aesthetics of Western culture think of art works). Instead, the work has an identity; it is a "who" or a "what" and contains the presences of persons, that is, incarnations of gods or ancestors or natural and cosmic powers. The work manifests the same needs as a person, it needs to be "fed," *la tengo que bañar y vestir*.

9   When invoked in rite, the object/event is "present"; that is, enacted, "it is both a physical thing and the power that infuses it. It is metaphysical in that it "spins its energies between gods and humans" and its task is to move the gods. This type of work dedicates itself to managing the universe and its energies. I'm not sure what it is when it is at rest (not in performance). It may or may not be a "work" then. A mask may only have the power of presence during a ritual dance and the rest of the time it may merely be a "thing." Some works exist forever invoked, always in performance. I'm thinking of totem poles, cave paintings. Invoked art is communal and speaks of everyday life. It is dedicated to the validation of humans; that is, it makes people hopeful, happy, secure, and it can have negative effects as well, which propel one towards a search for validation.

10   The aesthetic of virtuosity, art typical of Western European cultures, attempts to manage the energies of its own internal system such as conflicts, harmonies, resolutions and balances. It bears the presences of qualities and internal meanings. It is dedicated to the validation of itself. Its task is to move humans by means of achieving mastery in content, technique, feeling. Western art is always whole and always "in power." It is individual (not communal). It is "psychological" in that it spins its energies between itself and
its witness.

11   Western cultures behave differently toward works of art than do tribal cultures. The "sacrifices" Western cultures make are in housing their art works in the best structures designed by the best architects; and in servicing them with insurance, guards to protect them, conservators to maintain them, specialists to mount and display them, and the educated and upper classes to "view" them. Tribal cultures keep art works in honored and sacred places in the home and elsewhere. They attend them by making sacrifices of blood (goat or chicken), libations of wine. They bathe, feed, and clothe them. The works are treated not just as objects, but also as persons. The "witness" is a participant in the enactment of the work in a ritual, and not a member of the privileged classes.

12   Ethnocentrism is the tyranny of Western aesthetics. An Indian mask in an American museum is transposed into an alien aesthetic system where what is missing is the presence of power invoked through performance ritual. It has become a conquered thing, a dead "thing" separated from nature and, therefore, its power.

13   Modern western painters have "borrowed," copied, or other-wise extrapolated the art of tribal cultures and called it cubism, surrealism, symbolism. The music, the beat of the drum, the Blacks' jive talk. All taken over. Whites, along with a good number of our own people, have cut themselves off from their spiritual roots, and they take our spiritual art objects in an unconscious attempt to get them back. If they're going to do it, I'd like them to be aware of what they are doing and to go about doing it the right way. Let's all stop importing Greek myths and the Western Cartesian split point of view and root ourselves in the mythological soil and soul of this continent. White America has only attended to the body of the earth in order to exploit it, never to succor it or to be nurtured in it. Instead of surreptitiously ripping off the vital energy of people of color and putting it to commercial use, whites could allow themselves to share and exchange and learn from us in a respectful way. By taking up *curanderismo,* Santeria, shamanism, Taoism, Zen and otherwise delving into the spiritual life ceremonies of multi-colored people, Anglos would perhaps lose the white sterility they have in their kitchens, bathrooms, hospitals, mortuaries and missile bases. Though in the conscious mind, black and dark may be associated with death, evil and destruction, in the subconscious mind and in our dreams, white is associated with disease, death and hopelessness. Let us hope that the left hand, that of darkness, of femaleness, of "primitiveness," can divert the indifferent, right-handed, "rational" suicidal drive that, unchecked, could blow us into acid rain in a fraction of a millisecond.

Ni cuicani: I, the Singer

14 For the ancient Aztecs, *tlilli, tlapalli, la tinta negra y roja de sus códices* (the black and red ink painted on codices) were the colors symbolizing *escritura y sabiduría* (writing and wisdom). They believed that through metaphor and symbol, by means of poetry and truth, communication with the Divine could be attained, and *topan* (that which is above – the gods and spirit world) could be bridged with *mictlán* (that which is below – the underworld and the region of the dead).

> Poet: she pours water from the mouth of the pump, lowers the handle then lifts it, lowers, lifts. Her hands begin to feel the pull from the entrails, the live animal resisting. A sigh rises of from the depths, the handle becomes a wild thing in her hands, the cold sweet water gushes out, splashing her face, the shock of nightlight filling the bucket.

15 An image is a bridge between evoked emotions and conscious knowledge; words are the cables that hold up the bridge. Images are more direct, more immediate than words, and closer to the unconscious. Picture language precedes thinking in words; the metaphorical mind precedes analytical consciousness.

The Shamanic State

16 When I create stories in my head, that is, allow the voices and scenes to be projected in the inner screen of my mind, I "trance." I used to think I was going crazy or that I was having hallucinations. But now I realized it is my job, my calling, to traffic in images. Some of these film-like narratives I write down; most are lost, forgotten. When I don't write the images down for several days or weeks or months, I get physically ill. Because writing invokes images from my unconscious, and because some of the images are residues of trauma which I then have to reconstruct, I sometimes get sick when I *do* write. I can't stomach it, become nauseous, or burn with fever, worsen. But, in reconstructing the traumas behind the images, I make "sense" of them, and once they have "meaning" they are changed, transformed. It is then that writing heals me, brings me great joy.

17 To facilitate the "movies" with soundtracks, I need to be alone, or in a sensory-deprived state. I plug up my ears with wax, put on my black cloth eye-shades, lie horizontal and unmoving, in a state between sleeping and waking, mind and body locked into my fantasy. I am held prisoner by it. My body is experiencing events. In the beginning it is like being in a movie theater, as pure spectator. Gradually I become so engrossed with the activities, the conversations, that I become a participant in the drama. I have to struggle to "disengage" or escape from my "animated story," I have to get some sleep so I can write tomorrow. Yet I am gripped by a story which won't let me go. Outside the frame, I am film director, screenwriter, camera operator. Inside the frame, I am the actors – male and female – I am desert sand, mountain, I am dog, mosquito. I can sustain a four-to-six hour "movie." Once I am up, I can sustain several "shorts" of anywhere between five and thirty minutes. Usually these "narratives" are the offspring of stories acted out in my head during periods of sensory deprivation.

18 My "awakened dreams" are about shifts. Thought shifts, reality shifts, gender shifts: one person metamorphoses into another in a world where people fly through the air, heal from mortal wounds. I am playing with my Self, I am playing with the world's soul, I am the dialogue between my Self and *el espíritu del mundo*. I change myself, I change the world.

19 Sometimes I put the imagination to a more rare use. I choose words, images, and body sensations and animate them to impress them on my consciousness, thereby making changes in my belief system and reprogramming my consciousness. This involves looking my inner demons in the face, then deciding which I want in my psyche. Those I don't want, I starve; I feed them no words, no images, no feelings. I spend no time with them, share not my home with them. Neglected, they leave. This is harder to do than to merely generate "stories." I can only sustain this activity for a few minutes.

20 I write the myths in me, the myths I am, the myths I want to become. The word, the image and the feeling have a palpable energy a kind of power. *Con imágenes domo mi miedo, cruzo los abismos que tengo por dentro. Con palabras me hago piedra, pájaro, puente de serpientes arrastrando a ras del suelo todo lo que soy, todo lo que algún día seré.*

> *Los que están mirando (leyendo),*
> *los que cuentan (o refieren lo que leen).*
> *Los que vuelven ruidosamente las hojas de los códices.*
> *Los que tienen en su poder*
> *la tinta negra y roja (la sabiduría)*
> *y lo pintado,*
> *ellos nos llevan, nos guían,*
> *nos dicen el camino.*

Writing Is A Sensuous Act

21 *Tallo mi cuerpo como sí estuviera lavando un trapo. Toco las saltadas venas de mis manos, mis chichis adormecidas como pájaras al anochecer. Estoy encorvada sobre la cama. Las imágenes aletean alrededor de mi cama como murciélagos, la sábana como que tuviese alas. El ruido de los trenes subterráneos en mi sentido como conchas. Parece que las parendes del cuarto se me arriman cada vez más cerquita.*

22 Picking out images from my soul's eye, fishing for the right words to recreate the images. Words are blades of grass pushing past the obstacles, sprouting on the page; the spirit of the words moving in the body is a concrete as flesh and as palpable; the hunger to create is as substantial as fingers and hand.

23 I look at my fingers, see plumes growing there. From the fingers, my feathers, black and red ink drips across the page. *Escribo con la tinta de mi sangre.* I write in red. Ink. Intimately knowing the smooth touch of paper, its speechlessness before I spill myself on the insides of trees. Daily, I battle the silence and the red. Daily, I take my throat in my hands and squeeze until the cries pour out, my larynx and soul sore from the constant struggle.

Something To Do With the Dark

[24]
> *Quien canta, sus males espanta,*
> *—un dicho*

[25] The toad comes out of its hiding place inside the lobes of my brain. It's going to happen again. The ghost of the toad that betrayed me – I hold it in my hand. The toad is sipping the strength from my veins, it is sucking my pale heart. I am a dried serpent skin, wind scuttling me across the hard ground, pieces of me scattered over the countryside. And there in the dark I meet the crippled spider crawling in the gutter, the day-old newspaper fluttering in the dirty rain water.

[26]
> Musa bruja,venga. Cúbrese con una sábana y espante mis demonios que a rempujones y a cachetadas me roban la pluma me rompen el sueño. Musa, ¡misericordia!

[27]
> Óigame, musa bruja, ¿Por qué buye uste' en mi cara? Su grito me desarrolla de mi caracola, me sacude el alma. Vieja, quítese de aquí con sus alas de navaja. Ya no me despedaze mi cara. Vaya con sus pinche uñas que me desgarran de los ojos basta los talones. Váyese a la tiznada. Que no me coman, le digo, Que no me coman sus nueve dedos caníbales.

[28]
> Hija negra de la noche, carnala, ¿Por qué me sacas las tripas, por qué cardas mis entrañas? Este bilvanando palabras con tripas me está matando. Jija de la noche ¡vete a la chingada!

[29] Writing produces anxiety. Looking inside myself and my experience, looking at my conflicts, engenders anxiety in me. Being a writer feels very much like being a Chicana, or being queer – a lot of squirming, coming up against all sorts of walls. Or its opposite: nothing defined or definite, a boundless, floating state of limbo where I kick my heels, brood, percolate, hibernate and wait for something to happen.

[30] Living in a state of psychic unrest, in a Borderland, is what makes poets write and artists create. It is like a cactus needle embedded in the flesh. It worries itself deeper and deeper, and I keep aggravating it by poking at it. When it begins to fester I have to do something to put an end to the aggravation and to figure out why I have it. I get deep down into the place where it's rooted in my skin and pluck away at it, playing it like a musical instrument – the fingers pressing, making the pain worse before it can get better. Then out it comes. No more discomfort, no more ambivalence. Until another needle pierces the skin. That's what writing is for me, an endless cycle of making it worse, making it better, but always making meaning out of the experience, whatever it may be.

[31]
> My flowers shall not cease to live;
> my songs shall never end:
> I, a singer, intone them;
> they become scattered, they are spread about.
> *—Cantares mexicanos*

[32] To write, to be a writer, I have to trust and believe in myself as a speaker, as a voice for the images. I have to believe that I can communicate with images and words and that I can do it well. A lack of belief in my creative self is a lack of belief in my total self and vice versa – I cannot separate my writing from any part of my life. It is all one.

[33] When I write it feels like I'm carving bone. It feels like I'm creating my own face, my own heart – a Nahuatl concept. My soul makes itself through the creative act. It is constantly remaking and giving birth to itself through my body. It is this learning to live with *la Coatlicue* that transforms living in the Borderlands from a nightmare into a numinous experience. It is always a path/state to something else.

In *Xóchilt* in *Cuícatl*

[34] She writes while other people, sleep. Something is trying to come out. She fights the

words, pushes them down, down, a woman with morning sickness in the middle of the night. How much easier it would be to carry a baby for nine months and then expel it permanently. These continuous multiple pregnancies are going to kill her. She is the battlefield for the pitched fight between the inner image and the words trying to recreate it. *La musa bruja* has no manners. Doesn't she know, nights are for sleeping?

35   She is getting too close to the mouth of the abyss. She is teetering on the edge, trying to balance while she makes up her mind whether to jump in or to find a safer way down. That's why she makes herself sick – to postpone having to jump blindfolded into the abyss of her own being and there in the depths confront her face, the face underneath the mask.

36   To be a mouth – the cost is to high – her whole life enslaved to that devouring mouth. *Todo pasaba por esa boca, el viento, el fuego, los mares y la Tierra.* Her body, a crossroads, a fragile bridge, cannot support the tons of cargo passing through it. She wants to install "stop" and "go" signal lights, instigate a curfew, police Poetry. But something wants to come out.

37   Blocks (*Coatlicue* states) are related to my cultural identity. The painful periods of confusion that I suffer from are symptomatic of a larger creative process: cultural shifts. The stress of living with cultural ambiguity both compels me to write and blocks me. It isn't until I'm almost at the end of the blocked state that I remember and recognize it for what it is. As soon as this happens, the piercing light of awareness melts and the block and I accept the deep and the darkness and I hear one of my voices saying, "I am tired of fighting. I surrender. I give up, let go, let the walls fall. On this night of the hearing of faults, *Tlazolteotl, diosa de la cara negra,* let fall the cockroaches that live in my hair, the rats that nestle in my skull. Gouge out my lame eyes, rout my demon from its nocturnal cave. Set torch to the tiger that stalks me. Loosen the dead faces gnawing my cheekbones. I am tired of resisting. I surrender. I give up, let go, let the walls fall."

38   And in descending to the depths I realize that down is up, and I rise up from and into the deep. And once again I recognize that the internal tension of oppositions can propel (if it doesn't tear apart) the *mestiza* writer out of the *metate* where she is being ground with corn and water, eject her out as *nahual,* an agent of transformation, able to modify and shape primordial energy and therefore able to change herself and others into turkey, coyote, tree, or human.

39   I sit here before my computer, *Amiguita,* my altar on top of the monitor with the *Virgen de Coatlalopeuh* candle and copal incense burning. My companion, a wooden serpent staff with feathers, is to my right while I ponder the ways metaphor and symbol concretize the spirit and etherealize the body. The Writing is my whole life, it is my obsession. This vampire which is my talent does not suffer other suitors. Daily I court it, offer my neck to its teeth. This is the sacrifice that the act of creation requires, a blood sacrifice. For only through the body, through the pulling of flesh, can the human soul be transformed. And for images, words, stories to have this transformative power, they must arise from the human body – flesh and bone – and from the Earth's body – stone, sky, liquid, soil. This work, these images, piercing tongue or ear lobes with cactus needle, are my offerings, are my Aztecan blood sacrifices.

Credit _____

Andrea A. Lunsford

Toward A Mestiza Rhetoric
ANDREA A. LUNSFORD

1   I will have my voice: Indian, Spanish, white. I will have my serpent's tongue—my
woman's voice, my sexual voice, my poet's voice. I will overcome the tradition of silence.

—Gloria Anzaldúa, Borderlands/La Frontera

2   Gloria Anzaldúa has not had an easy time of having what she calls her "own voice." Born
in 1942 and raised in the border country of south Texas (in Jesus Maria of the Valley),
Anzaldúa learned early that she was different, an "alien from another planet" who didn't
quite fit with the norms and expectations of her family and community, didn't "act like a
nice little Chicanita is supposed to act" ("La Prieta," 199, 201). Describing some of her
early experiences in "La Prieta," Anzaldúa rejects ongoing efforts to label her differences in
various ways—as lesbian, as feminist, as marxist, as mystic, as "other:" "Ambivalent? Not
so. Only your labels split me," she says (205).

3   In this early essay, Anzaldúa announces the multiplicity of her "self" and her "voice."
She is a "wind-swayed bridge, a crossroads inhabited by whirlwinds"; she is "Shiva, a
many-armed and legged body with one foot on brown soil, one on white, one in straight
society, one in the gay world, the man's world, the woman's, one limb in the literary world,
another in the working class, the socialist, and the occult worlds. A sort of spider woman
hanging by one thin strand of web" (204). And indeed, much of Anzaldúa's work has been
devoted to making a space where such multiplicity could be enacted, This Bridge Called
My Back, edited with Cherie Moraga, grew out of an experience at a 1979 women's retreat
during which Anzaldúa was made (once again) to feel she was being labeled—tokenized
as a "Third World woman" and as an outsider, an exoticized other to the white feminists
there. Characteristically, Anzaldúa turned that experience into a means of affirming her
commitment to women of color by providing a forum in which their multiple voices—and
her own—could be heard. In 1987 came her groundbreaking Borderlands /La Frontera, the
book in which she has most thoroughly rendered and theorized the borderland space that
is home to her multiple identities and voices. And then in 1990—after years of waiting for
someone "to compile a book that would continue where This Bridge Called My Back left
off"—Anzaldúa edited the luxuriant and sprawling collection Making Face, Making Soul/
Haciendo Caras. (She has also given voice to two bilingual children's picture/story books,
including: Prietita Has a Friend/ Prietita tiene un amigo and Friends from the Other Side/
Amigos del otro lado).

4   Taken together, Anzaldúa's work (including a number of essays not cited here) stands
testimony to her personal triumph over the "tradition of silence" and to her ability to
imagine, enact, and inhabit spaces that go beyond dichotomies of all kinds: beyond male /
female; beyond reason/ emotion, beyond gay /straight; beyond other/white; beyond mythic/
real; beyond mind/body; beyond spirit/matter; beyond orality/literacy; beyond I/you. In
every case, Anzaldúa rejects either/or in favor of both/and then some, of an identity that is
always in process. As she says in "To(o) Queer the Writer," identity can never be reduced
to a "bunch of little cubbyholes. [...] Identity flows between, over, aspects of a person.
Identity is a river, a process" (252-53). This process, which Anzaldúa represents both
as occurring on the borderland, the in-between, and in the act of making faces / souls
can enable transformations that, while often brutally painful, can allow for nonbinary
identity, for new states of mestiza consciousness, and for multiple writing strategies (what
AnaLouise Keating calls "mestizaje écriture" and what I am calling a "mestiza rhetoric").

5   In these moments, it is possible to take in the labels of society and to transform
them, to find all others in one's self; one's self in all others. Learning to live such
transformations calls for a "new mestiza" who has "a tolerance for contradictions, a

tolerance for ambiguity," who "learns to be an Indian in Mexican culture, to be Mexican from an Anglo point of view. She learns to juggle cultures. [. . .] Not only does she sustain contradictions, she turns the ambivalence into something else" *(Borderlands* 79). In turn, living in and rendering such contradictions and transformations calls for a new kind of writing style. In Anzaldúa's case, this means a rich mixture of genres — she shifts from poetry to reportorial prose to autobiographical stream of consciousness to incantatory mythic chants to sketches and graphs, and back again — weaving images and words from her multiple selves and from many others into a kind of tapestry or patchwork quilt of language. It also means an insistence that visual images and words belong together in texts of all kinds as well as a rich mix of languages — some English, some Spanish, some Tex/Mex, some Nahuatl — and registers. In "How to Tame a Wild Tongue," she denounces "linguistic terrorism," saying "I am my language. Until I can take pride in my language, I cannot take pride in myself. Until I can except as legitimate Chicano Texas Spanish, Tex-Mex, and all other languages I speak, I cannot accept the legitimacy of myself. Until I am free to write bilingually and to switch codes without having to translate, [. . .] *(Borderlands 59)*. In the interview that follows, Anzaldúa comments on all of these issues. She also has much to say about her prior experiences with and current relationship to writing and to a form of collaboration, aspects of her work that will be of special interest to rhetoric and composition students.

6   As we might expect, Anzaldúa's relationship to language and to writing is extremely complex. If books, as she says in the preface to *Borderlands /La Frontera* "saved [her] sanity" and taught her "first how to survive and then how to soar," she often figures the act of writing as daring and dangerous *(Bridge* 171) or as painful, as a terrifying ride in the "nightsky" *(Borderlands* 140-41), as like "carving bone" (73), as giving birth, an endless cycle of "making it worse, making it better, but always making meaning out of the experience" (73), as a "blood sacrifice" (75). Writing is for Anzaldúa thus inextricably related to the process of making (or writing) faces /souls as well as a primary means of enabling the kinds of ongoing transformations necessary of inhabiting the borderlands. *"There is no separation between life and writing,"* she says in "Speaking in Tongues: A Letter to Third World Women Writers," so *"Why aren't you riding, writing,* writing?" (emphasis hers). And most important, she cautions, "It's not on paper that you create but in your innards, in your gut and out of living tissue—*organic* writing, I call it" *(Bridge* 172.).

7   Given her commitment to multiplicity and inclusivity, Anzaldúa is naturally drawn to forms of collaboration—with artists in her children's books, with co-editors and with collectives in other works, even—as she says in the following interview—with the architect and designers who have helped to expand her home. Anzaldúa represents herself as in constant conversation, a dialogue between her many selves, her multiple audiences/readers, and the texts that emerge in the process (with their own intertexts and interfaces) that hum along on her computer screen. "That's what writers do, we carry on a constant dialogue between language and hands and images, one or another of our identities trying desperately to get in a word, an image, a sound," she says in a passage in *Making Face* that is highly reminiscent of Bakhtinian dialogism (xxiv). In fact, Anzaldúa's discussions of the crucial role audiences / others play in her own writing provide a fine example of what Bakhtin means by "answerability," which Anzaldúa refers to as "responsibility," literally the ability to respond, to answer, to join in a conversation that is always ongoing. As she says in this interview, "I do the composing, but it's taken from little mosaics of other people's lives, other people's perceptions." These mosaics are her own collaborative response-abilities (for a further explanation of this aspect of Anzaldúa's work, see Susan Bickford's "In the Presence of Others") and reveal the degree to which she is aware of the politics of address, of her need to answer or respond in ways that

will create a readership at the same time that it teaches how to "read" her respondings (Making *Face* xviii).

8 During this interview, Anzaldúa remarks that she has been shocked to "find composition people picking me up" (she was interviewed at a CCCC meeting in 1992 by Donna Perry). Given that composition has long been equated with the hegemony of "standard" English and with gatekeeping, Anzaldúa's surprise is—well, not surprising. As this interview reveals, however, she has experienced in her own schooling both the limiting and the liberatory impulses in composition, the latter in the company of longtime writing teacher, theorist, and critic Jim Sledd. Close attention to this doubled experience with composition and a close reading of this interview suggests to me that, among her many selves, Anzaldúa includes a writing theorist as well as an accomplished rhetor and a prolific writer. She is also a teacher. When I asked her whether she thought mestiza consciousness could be taught, she said yes, though with great difficulty and pain. In *Making Face,* she speaks directly of her own teaching goals: "I wanted a book which would teach ourselves and whites to read in nonwhite narrative traditions" (xviii); moreover, she wants to teach others to acquire voices without becoming *periquitas* (parrots) and to use theory to "change people and the way they perceive the world" (xxv). "We need *teorias,*" she says, "that will enable us to interpret what happens in the world, that will explain how and why we relate to certain people in specific ways, that will reflect what goes on between inner, outer, and peripheral 'I's within a person and between the personal 'I's and the collective 'we' of our ethnic communities. *Necesitamos teorias* that [. . .] cross borders, that blur boundaries—new kinds of theories with new theorizing methods" (xxv). Here and elsewhere Gloria Anzaldúa calls for a new rhetoric, a mestiza rhetoric, that she is clearly in the process of helping to make.

CRLOCRLOLOCR

9 **Q.** What are some of your very early memories of writing? I'm using writing very broadly here to include drawing, marking, any kind of language use that seems like writing.

10 **A.** Sí, the whole activity of writing and the conditions that surround it as distinct from writing on a piece of paper started early on orally with me: it started as a defense against my sister. When we were growing up, we had to work after school. We had chores, we had fieldwork, we had housework. And then it was time for bed, and I didn't get to do my reading. So I would read under the covers with a flashlight in bed with my sister. And my brothers were in the same room, but my sister and I shared the same bed. And she was ready to tell my mom. To keep her entertained, I would tell her a story. I would make up a story—just something that had happened during the day, and I would make it all kind of like an adventure or a quest of the happenings of these little girls, my sister and myself, and, you know, I kind of embroidered it. And so she would settle down and go back to sleep and wouldn't tell my mom the next day. And then the following night she would want the same thing. Every night I learned to tell a little story. So I was writing stories very early.

11 **Q.** Your own version of *A Thousand and One Nights?*

12 **A.** And then this is what happened: she wanted two. So I got into doing serials. I would tell a part of the story and then break it off and say, "You know, if you don't tell, you'll get the rest of it tomorrow." *It* was like I turned the tables on her. So for me, writing has always been about narrative, about story; and it still is. Theory is a kind of narrative. Science—you know, physics —that's a narrative, that's a hit on reality. Anthropology has its narrative. And some are master narratives, and some are outsider narratives. There's that whole struggle in my writing between the dominant culture's traditional, conventional narratives about reality and about literature and about science and about life and about politics; and my other counternarratives as a *mestiza* growing up in this country, as an internal exile, as an inner exile, as a postcolonial person, because the Mexican race in the United States is a colonized people. My ancestors were living life on the border. The band was part of the state of Tamaulipas, Mexico, and then the U.S. bought it, bought half of Mexico, and so the Anzaldúas were split in half. The Anzaldúas with an accent, which is my family, were north of the border. The Anzaldúas without an accent stayed on the other side of the border, and as the decades went by we lost connection with each other. And so the Anzaldúas and the Anzaldúas, originally from the same land, the state of Tamaulipas in the nation of Mexico, all of a sudden became strangers in our own land, foreigners in our own land. We were a colonized people who were not allowed to speak our language, whose ways of life were not valued in this country. Public education tried to erase all of that. So here I am now, a kind of international citizen whose life and privileges are not equal to the rights and privileges of ordinary, Anglo, White, Euro-American people. My narratives always take into account these other ethnicities, these other races, these other cultures, these other histories. There's always that kind of struggle.

13   **Q.** I know that art and drawing are central to much of your work, and I think of drawing as a kind of writing too. As a child, did you draw a lot?

14   **A.** Yes. I wanted to be an artist. I wasn't sure whether I wanted to be a visual artist or a writer, or something else, but I started out as an artist, and in fact the teaching that I did in high school as a student teacher was in literature and in art. But I never could get a job teaching art in the public schools. I got one teaching composition, teaching English, teaching literature, but not art. But I have a degree in art. I had two areas of focus in my M.A., "majors" I guess was the word, and one was art education and the other was literature.

15   **Q.** If you define writing broadly enough to include drawing, then you certainly began writing very, very early in your life.

16   **A.** Yes. I started drawing very early on, and besides telling my sister these stories, I started keeping a journal because my sister, my whole family is ... I don't know how to explain it. We would talk a lot and fight a lot and quarrel a lot.

17   **Q.** You were a very verbal family?

18   **A.** Very verbal. In some ways like your average family in the U.S., abusive verbally, or not aware of the vulnerabilities a child might have. So I was always gotten after for being too curious, for reading. I was being selfish for studying and reading, rather than doing housework. I was selfish because I wasn't helping the family by reading and writing. So anyway I had all of these emotions. I wanted to fight back and yell, and sometimes I did. But I would watch my sister have temper tantrums, and she would have temper tantrums so severe that she would pee in her pants.

19   **Q.** She is younger than you, right?

20   **A.** A year and three months. And she would eat dirt. She would get so upset, you know, and I didn't want to be with her. I started shutting down emotions, but I had to find a release for all these feelings. I was feeling alienated from my family and I was fighting against society—you know, your typical preadolescent and adolescent angst. So I started keeping a journal. I attribute my writing to my grandmothers who used to tell stories. I copied them until I started telling my own, but I think it was my sister who forced me to find an outlet to communicate these feelings of hurt and confusion. So I started keeping journals.

21   **Q.** Did you keep them throughout school?

22   **A.** Yes. I have all of them lined up on top of my closet, but I think the earlier ones are still back home, so I'm going to try to hunt those up. I always keep journals and I do both my little sketches and some texts. The pamphlet I gave you [which includes several drawings] came from a workshop in Pantla that I did at the Villa Montalbo, a writer's residency right here in Saratoga. These people saw an essay that I had done, *"Nepantla,"* about the in-between state that is so important in connecting a lot of issues—the border, the borderland, *nepantla*. It was an essay I had done for a catalog, on border art as being the place that a lot of Chicanas do our work from—you know, the site of cultural production. These people wrote up a grant and got some money, and so five of us (I got to pick some of the other artists) worked for five weeks on a project together and had an exhibit at the San Jose Latino Arts Center. My presentation was both textual and visual. I had the visual image and I had the text and they exhibited them together on the wall.

23 So, yes, if you define writing as any kind of scribble, any kind of trying to mark on the world, then you have the oral, the dance, the choreography, the performance art, the architects—I had a feminist architect help me design this addition to my study. It's all marking. And some of us want to take those marks that are already getting inscribed in the world and redo them, either by erasing them or by pulling them apart, which involves deconstructive criticism. Pulling them apart is looking at how they are composed and what the relationship is between the frame and the rest of the world. In this country it's White. The dominant culture has the frame of reference. This is its territory, so any mark we make on it has to be made in relationship to the fact that they occupy the space. You can take any field of disciplinary study, like anthropology: that frame is also Euro-American, it's Western. Composition theory, that's very Euro-American. Thus any of us trying to create change have to struggle with this vast territory that's very, very powerful when you try to impinge on it to try to make changes. It's kind of like a fish in the Pacific Ocean, with the analogy that the Pacific Ocean is the dominant field and the fish is this postcolonial, this feminist, or this queer, or whoever is trying to make changes. I think that before you can make any changes in composition studies, philosophy, or whatever it is, you have to have a certain awareness of the territory; you have to be familiar with it and you have to be able to maneuver in it before you can say, "Here's an alternative model for this particular field, for its norms, for its rules and regulations, for its laws." And especially in composition these rules are very strict: creating a thesis sentence, having some kind of argument, having kind of a logical step-by-step progression, using certain methods, like contrast, like deductive versus inductive thinking. I mean all the way back to Aristotle and Cicero with his seven parts of a composition.

24 So for anyone like me to make any changes or additions to the model takes a tremendous amount of energy, because you're going against the Pacific Ocean and you're this little fish and you have to weigh the odds of succeeding with the goal that you have in mind. Say my goal is a liberatory goal: it's to create possibilities for people, to look at things in a different way so that they can act in their daily lives in a different way. It's like a freeing up, an emancipation. It's a feminist goal. But then I have to weigh things. Okay, if I write in this style and I code-switch too much and I go into Spanglish too much and I do an associative kind of logical progression in a composition, am I going to lose those people that I want to affect, to change? Am I going to lose the respect of my peers—who are other writers and other artists and other academicians—when I change too much, when I change not only the style, but also the rhetoric, the way that this is done? Then I have to look at the students, the young students in high school and in elementary school who are going to be my future readers, if my writing survives that long. And I look at the young college students, especially those reading *Borderlands:* how much of it is a turnoff for them because it's too hard to access? I have to juggle and balance, make it a little hard for them so that they can stop and think, "You know, this is a text, this is not the same as life, this is a representation of life." Because too often when people read something, they take that to be the reality instead of the representation. I don't want to

turn those students off. So how much do you push and how much do you accommodate and be in complicity with the dominant norm of whatever field it happens to be?

25   **Q.** So if you are a fish in this vast ocean, which is the Anglo-European framework, you can't just reject the water outright but rather try to change it?

26   **A.** Yes. Let me show you a little drawing, so you can see what I am saying:

No's I of ras – A DRAWING NEEDS TO BE ADDED OR JPG! -Hillary

27   I want to speak of the *nosotras* concept. It used to be that there was a them and an us. We were over here, we were the "other" with other lives, and the *"nos"* was the subject, the White man. And there was a very clear distinction. But as the decades have gone by, we, the colonized, the Chicano, the Blacks, the Natives in this country, have been reared in this frame of reference, in this field. So all of our education, all of our ideas come from this frame of reference. We are complicitous for being in such close proximity and in such intimacy with the other. Now I think that us and them are interchangeable. Now there is no such thing as an other. The other is in you, the other is in me. This White culture has been internalized in my head. I have a White man in here, I have a White woman in here. And they have me in their heads, even if it is just a guilty little nudge sometimes. So, when I try to articulate ideas, I try to do it from that place of occupying both territories: the territory of my past and my ethnic community, my home community, the Chicano Spanish, the Spanglish; and the territory of the formal education, the philosophical educational ideas, and the political ideas that I have internalized just by being alive. Both of these traditions are inherent in me. I cannot disown the White tradition, the Euro-American tradition, any more than I can the Mexican, the Latino, or the native, because they are all in me. And I think that people from different fields are still making these dichotomies—I think.

28   **Q.** Would you describe yourself as being in one or more fields?

29   **A.** Composition, feminism, postcolonialism ... I didn't even know I belonged into this postcolonial thing until Patricia Cloud said in a bookflap that I am a feminist, postcolonial critic. And then there is me the artist, me the teacher, and all the multicultural stuff. It's hard to keep up with the reading, so I don't even try anymore. For preparation for this interview, one of your questions was "Who has influenced you as a postcolonial critic?" and I couldn't think of anyone. All of the reading that I've done has been in terms of particular articles for a class. When Homi Bhabha was here, I did some reading and I went to his lecture, which I couldn't understand. When Spivak was here it was the same thing. I took a class with Donna Haraway in feminist theory, and when I had to read "Can the Subaltern Speak?" it took me weeks to decipher one sentence. Well, not weeks, but you know what I'm saying. And then I read a couple of JanMohamed's essays too. Of course, way back I read a little bit of Frantz Fanon's *The Wretched of the Earth,* and Paulo Freire's *The Pedagogy of the Oppressed,* but just little snippets. And then for your interview I got a copy of this postcolonial studies reader. But you know, I didn't have time to really study a lot, so I made little notes about the things that I wanted to think about and maybe respond to in writing.

30   **Q.** One of the reasons Lahoucine Ouzgane[1] and I wanted particularly to talk to you about postcolonial studies is that we are interested in why there hasn't been more confluence between postcolonial studies and composition studies. One reason is no doubt the historical association of the English language with colonialism. We think that another of the reasons may well be that postcolonial studies has very quickly theorized itself into very high abstract language that is inaccessible. I think Homi Bhabha is a very good example of the kind of scholar who is speaking on a level of abstraction that just seems completely foreign to a student in a first-year writing class, who may come from southern Texas and be a speaker of Spanish as a first language. Yet it seems a shame that these fields don't talk more to one another. In our perspective, you're a person who does talk to both fields, and in ways that are accessible. My first-year students read parts of *Borderlands,* for example, and they are more threatened than they are puzzled. They are threatened because they think they can't imagine you. Many of my students are from small farming communities in Ohio. Most of them are Anglo, and they say things like, "She sounds so mad. Is she mad? And who is she mad at?" So that's one of the reasons we wanted to talk with you, and to see if in doing so we could find some means of getting both composition and postcolonial studies to think about their own discourses, and the ways in which some of those discourses are very exclusionary- they shut people out.

31   **A.** I think that you came at the right time, because the first half of one of the book projects that's currently on my back burner is about composition and postcolonial issues of identity. Most of the questions that you've asked are there, plus others. I have about four different chapters of notes and rough drafts for this book in my computer that have to do with the writing process, that have to do with rhetoric, that have to do with composition. Not just that, but taking it over into how one composes one's life, how one creates an addition to one's house, how one makes sense of all the kinds of coincidental and random things that happen in one's life, how one gives it meaning. So it's my composition theme, *compustura*. In fact, that's the title of one of the chapters: "Compustura." Compustura used to mean for me being a seamstress; I would sew for other people. Compustura means seaming together fragments to make a garment which you wear, which represents you, your identity and reality in the world. So that's why when you and Lahoucine called me, I thought, yes, there's finally somebody out there who's making the connection.

32   **Q.** You have already talked about the risks you take and about the stylistic borders you cross. Are there any things about writing that are particularly hard for you? Or easy?

33   **A.** Yes, there are. I think one problem is for me to get into a piece of writing, whether it is theory, or a story, or a poem, or a children's book, or a journal entry. I am always rethinking and responding to something that I value, or rethinking somebody else's values. If the value is competition, then I start thinking about how when you compete, there is a certain amount of violence, a certain amount of struggle. Okay, behind that violence and that struggle I experience some kind of emotion: fear, hesitancy, sadness, depression because of the state of the world, whatever. In order to backtrack to the theoretical concepts, I have to start with the feeling. So I dig into the feeling and usually the feeling will have a visual side while I'm pulling it apart. One of the visuals that I use is Coyochauqui, the Aztec moon goddess who was the first sacrificial victim. Her brother threw her down the temple stairs and when she landed at the bottom she was dismembered. The act of writing for me is this kind of dismembering of everything that I am feeling, taking it apart to examine it and then reconstituting it or recomposing it in a new way. So that means I really have to get into the feeling— the anger, the anguish, the sadness, the frustration. I have to get into this heightened state, which I access sometimes by being very, very quiet and doing some deep breathing, or by some little tiny meditation, or by burning some incense, or whatever gets me in there. Sometimes I walk along the beach. So I access this state, I get all psyched up, and then I do the writing. I work four, five, six hours; and then I have to come off that. It is like a withdrawal, I have to leave that anger, leave that sadness, leave that compassion, whatever it is that I am feeling; I have to come off that heightened, aware state. If I want to do some honest writing, I have to get into that state, if you want to do a mediocre job, you do a kind of disembodied writing which has nothing to do with your feelings or with yourself or with what you care about. You care, maybe, only intellectually about putting out this essay so that your peers can respect you. So that is one problem of writing for me: engaging in an emotional way, and then disengaging. So disengage you have to take another walk, wash the dishes, go to the garden, talk on the telephone, just because it is too much. Your body cannot take it. So that is one problem.

34   Some of the other things that come up for me—and I wrote them down, because I knew you were going to ask me this—one other problem is that you want to avoid that stage. You practice avoidance, you procrastinate. It takes you a while to go to the computer. You circle around the stuff over and over. You do not want to get to the dissertation, to the master's thesis, to that paper that is due for this quarter, because you are going to be struggling with these things. That is the problem of avoidance, of not doing the work. Every day I have to recommit myself with the writing. It is like making a date with myself, having an appointment to do this writing. And some days I don't feel like going to meet that appointment. It's too hard on my body, especially since I have diabetes; it takes out too much.

35   **Q.** Do you try to write at a regular time? Every day?

36   **A.** Not in terms of clock time, but in terms of my routine, because my internal clock changes. I get up later and go to bed earlier and sometimes I write at night and sometimes I write during the day; but yes, I have a certain routine. I get up and I inject myself with insulin and I have my food. Generally after that I have some activity like this interview. Or maybe two hours of filing and returning people's calls and letters—the stuff that I don't like to do. And then a walk, and then I dive into four, five, or six hours of this appointment with myself. Sometimes I can only do two or three hours, and other times I can do it around the clock. After writing, I take a break for lunch or the second meal, whatever it is, and then I do some reading: serious theoretical stuff for maybe an hour or two, and then some escapist reading. I love mysteries, horror.

37   **Q.** Do you compose at the word processor?

38   **A.** Yes, I do, at my desk, and sometimes I take my little laptop to the coffee house or to the beach, or just outside.

39   **Q.** Do the words seem to come out as well from the ends of your fingers typing as they did when you were scripting?

40   **A.** Yes, except that when I was at an artist's retreat for four weeks just last month, my computer broke down and I had to resort to handwriting. What started happening was that I started writing poems. I had gone there to revise *24 Stories,* which is this book I'm working on. I had taken nineteen of the stories in hard copy, so I was able to revise on paper, but the rest of the time I was doing poems and I was doing composition theory. I ended up doing a lot of stuff on composition theory. I also did work on a large book that I have in progress—the creative writing manual that I told you about. I did writing exercises for that book: some meditation, some hints and elements of writing, some fictive techniques. I didn't plan on doing any of that. I just wanted to do the stories, but not having a computer switched me over.

41   So anyway, those are two problems: the problem of engaging and disengaged, and the problem of avoidance. Then there is the problem of voice. How am I going to write the forward for the encyclopedia I agreed to do? What voice, tone, am I going to take? How much can I get away with the Spanish? How much can I get away with the Spanglish? This is a pretty formal reference book. Another example is the bilingual series of children's books. How much can I get through the censors in the state of Texas in any particular children's book? The state of Texas has more stringent censorship rules than the other states, and most publishers can only do one book for all of the states. So the publishers tend to be conservative, because they want to get these books into the schools. How much can I get away with pushing at the norms, at the conventions? That's another problem, and sometimes it's my biggest problem: if I can't find a voice, a style, a point of view, then nothing can get written. All you have are those notes, but you don't have a voice to speak the style. The style is the relationship between me, Gloria, the author; you, the person reading it, my audience, the world, and the text. So there are three of us. Or are there more than three of us?

42   **Q**. A lot more, probably. At least four, maybe, when you bring the text in?

43   **A**. Well, in the author there is the outside author, there is the author who is the writer, and there is the narrative-voice author; and then in the reader there are all these different readers. And then the text changes according to the reader, because I think that the reader creates the text.

44   So I'm grappling with this voice and how much I can push in order to make people think a little more differently, or to give them an emotional or intellectual experience when they can go and say, "Oh, so that's the Pacific Ocean?" Not quite that blatantly. Another example is Toni Morrison's *The Bluest Eye*. You never look at another Black child without what you took from that text. It has changed your way of looking at Black children. The problem of voice is the third problem.

45   I think another more external problem is one of censorship. With the very conservative path that this country has taken in terms of the arts, these times are hard. I know artists who can't exhibit nude photographs of their children because that's like an obscenity. When you apply for the NEA or any of these grants, you're limited. That's external censorship from the right, of morality and family values. Then there is the external censorship from my family. "Gloria, don't write about that; that's a secret." You're not supposed to devalue the Chicano culture. I was being disloyal to my mother and my culture because I was writing about poverty and abuse and gender oppression. So there's a kind of weightiness on you *not* to write, not to do your art in as honest a way as possible. You're supposed to make nice, like you were talking about being Southern girls.

46   I write a lot about sexuality in my stories. And—I don't know if you read "Immaculate, Inviolate" in *Borderlands*—but when I sent my brother the book, and he read it, he had a fit. He was going to show it to my uncle, and my uncle was going to sue me, because that was his mother I was talking about, my grandmother. I talked about how my grandfather lifted her skirt to do his thing, and how he had three other *mujeres con familia*. He would spend three days and three nights with my grandmother, and two days and two nights with the next mistress, and two days with the next one. The children from all the families played together, and my grandmother was ashamed of that and felt so humiliated. I'm not supposed to write about that. I'm constantly asked by my family to choose my loyalty. When I choose who I'm going to be loyal to, myself or them, I'm supposed to choose them. I don't, and I never have, and that's why I'm accused of betraying my culture, and that's why I'm a bad girl: selfish, disobedient, ungrateful.

47   **Q**. And also why you are a writer.

48   **A**. To take the problem of censorship one step further, there is also internal censorship. I've internalized my mom's voice, the neoconservative right voice, the morality voice. I'm always fighting those voices.

49   **Q**. I was just going to ask you about that again. The visual that you showed me earlier had "us" and "them," and you said very beautifully that both of these—the "them" and the "us"—are now in you. You're very aware of that mixture of voices inside yourself. I think that many teachers of composition would like to be able to find ways to help students recognize their own multiple voices, especially the Anglo students who don't see themselves as having any race, any ethnicity, and often they don't even think they have any range of sexuality. They're just "man" or "woman," that's it. How do we help those students really hear those other voices? How do we help them get Gloria's voice in them? They have the *nos* so much in their head that they don't have any other voices. One of the reasons work like yours is so important to the future of composition studies is that it gives concrete evidence of many voices in a text, many voices speaking out of who you are, many voices that you allow to speak. Many, on the other hand, are not only monolingual in the strict sense of English being the only language, but deeply, internally monolingual as well. And composition studies really hasn't done much of anything in the past to help them out of that.

50   A. I think that the only recourse is a kind of vicarious move of immersing themselves in the texts of people who are different, because the fastest way for them to recognize that they have diversity, that they have these values, that they have these experiences and beliefs, is to jerk them out into another country where they don't speak the language, they don't know the food. It's like taking a fish out of water. The fish doesn't know that it lives in the element of water until it jerks onto the beach and can't breathe. You can't do that to every student. But sometimes a traumatic experience can do that, it can open up a window. What education and the schools can give is this vicarious experience via the text, via reading *The Bluest Eye,* or *Borderlands.*

51   In terms of composition, I think teachers need to look at alternate models. What I want to do with the chapters of the textbook that I've been talking to you about is to offer other ways of considering how to write a story, a poem, or a paper. And again, that alternate way is colored by the Western frame of everything. What I'm trying to present to you is another way of ordering, another way of composing, another rhetoric; but it is only partly new. Most of it is cast in the Western tradition, because that's all that I was immersed in. The symbol is to see the university as this walled city, and somebody brings the Trojan Horse, the Trojan *Burra,* into the city gates. At night the belly of the burra opens, and out comes the "other" trying to make changes from inside. And I have a visual for that. . . . There's your Trojan Burra. It's kind of hard, because the university wall or city is very seductive, you know? There's something very seductive about fitting in, and being part of this one culture, and forgetting differences, and going with the way of the norm. Western theory is very seductive, and pretty soon instead of subverting and challenging and making marks on the wall, you get taken in.

52   Q. Certainly some in composition studies have thought that that's what the university was for, that's what the composition teacher was for: to help the students become assimilated into the university, rather than to help them challenge the reality of the university.

53   A. Yes. This is also what traditional therapy tries to do. It tries to assimilate you to life, to reality, to living.

54   Q. So here, in the night, out of the burra, come the challengers?

55   A. Yes, these different ways of writing: the inappropriate ways, the bad girls not making nice. It's really hard because you are one of only a few.

56   Q. One of the things I like best about teaching composition is that sometimes I can make a place, as a teacher, for students to do dangerous and experimental kinds of writing. But then they have to go and pass the tests and pass the history essays and do the inside-the-lines kind of writing.

57   A. This is what I was talking about earlier: that in order to make it in this society you have to be able to know the discipline, if it's teaching, if it's composition, if it's carpentry. Whatever field it is, you have to know your way around. You have to know how to wire the house before you can start being an innovative electrician.

58   The question is, how can you change the norm if the tide is so tremendous against change? But you can do something. You are in the field of composition, right? And somehow you respect my ideas and my writing. Otherwise, you wouldn't be here. So for me to be effective in making whatever little changes I can, I have to get this respect, this acceptance, this endorsement from my peers. All of these academics who teach my writings are endorsing me, and they make it possible for me to reach a wider audience.

Whatever little changes I can make in people's thoughts, it is because they first allowed me through the gate. If you absolutely hated my stuff and everybody else hated my stuff, no matter how innovative it was, nobody would ever see it because it wouldn't get through the peer gate. I couldn't do any of this without you.

59   **Q.** Well, you could do it, and you have done it; but reaching the very, very largest audience in the United States certainly does take that.

60   **A.** Which is my next step. One of my goals is to have a larger audience, which is what I'm trying to accomplish with this book of fiction. Fiction is a genre that more than just people from the academy can accept. I mean, community people do read my books—the children's book especially goes into the community, and *Borderlands*—but it's still beyond the scale of most people. My family doesn't do any serious reading. They will look at my stuff —my sister will read a little bit of it, and my brother—but they don't do serious reading. They don't sit down on a daily basis like you and I do and read stuff on composition and theory.

61   **Q.** But they might read a book of stories.

62   **A.** Yes, and what I'm trying to convey to you about composition and postcoloniality I am trying to do thorough story. You can theorize through fiction and poetry; it's just harder. It's an unconscious kind of process. The reader will read this and wonder about it. Instead of coming in through the head with the intellectual concept, you come in through the back door with the feeling, the emotion, the experience. But if you start reflecting on that experience, you can come back to the theory.

63   **Q.** I wonder if that's partly why the boundaries between fiction and nonfiction seem to be so permeable right now. It's hard sometimes to say what is a short story and what is an essay.

64   **A.** The way that one composes a piece of creative nonfiction and the way one composes fiction are very similar. In composing nonfiction, you're very selective and you take little fragments here and there and you piece them together in a new way. So right off the bat you're not being true to the nonfiction. It's fiction already, just in manipulating it.

65   **Q.** And then the representation itself—you said earlier that the representation is not the same as the experience; it's the representation.

66   **A.** The borders are permeable, and I like the fact that at this turn of the century these borders are transparent and crossable. And when we get past the millennium, the fin *de siécle,* some of these things will settle down into another kind of reality. At every turn of the century everything is up for grabs: the categories are disrupted, the borders are crossable. Then you get to another plateau where things become more fixed in cement, but not really. Then you wait for the next period of insurgency, when everything is up for grabs again. I think it goes like that in cycles. So this is why I'm so hopeful and so glad that I'm alive right now, because I can partake of this confusion. But still, back to your students, what's going to help them?

67   **Q.** Well, the book you're working on may help them, but I often find students so anxious to be able to work within the framework and to be part of the system, and so fearful of what will happen if they're not part of the system (and often with very good reason!), that they resist taking risks and they resist trying to get in touch with things that might hurt.

68   **A.** Yes, we come back to the same thing: fear of being different. You don't want to stick out, you don't want to be different—especially at their age. You and I have already passed midlife. We can have a sense of identity and of self that is not so much based on other people's reactions anymore. But theirs is very much a relational type of identity, so that if this group of people disapproves of them and finds their difference to be problematic, they won't be able to function. They won't be able to get their degree, they won't get the grant, they won't get the job. So how do you teach them to take risks? How do you teach them to stand up and say, "I'm different and this is who I am, and your way is maybe a good way, but it's not the only way." How do you get them to do that? And I think that writing and post-colonial studies are trying to do that in terms of getting people to think about how they are in the world.

69   Writing is very liberating and emancipatory; it frees you up. In the process of writing, you're reflecting on all of the things that make you different, that make you the same, that make you a freak. You're constantly grappling with identity issues. Postcoloniality looks at this power system discipline—whether it's a government, whether it's anthropology, or composition—and it asks, "Who has the voice? Who says these are the rules? Who makes the law?" And if you're not part of making the laws and the rules and the theories, what part do you play? How is that other system placed in your mind? You get into the neocolonization of people's minds. You get into the erasure of certain histories, the erasure of ideas, the erasure of voices, the erasure of languages, the erasure of books. A lot of the Mayan and Aztec codices were burned, and a whole system of knowledge wiped out. Postcoloniality comes and asks these questions. What reality does this disciplinary field, or this government, or this system try to crush? What reality is it trying to erase? What reality is it trying to suppress? Writing is about freeing yourself up, about giving yourself the means to be active, to take agency, to make changes. So I see both writing and postcoloniality as emancipatory projects, about how to get from here to there.

70   **Q.** May I ask a question about English? One of the first things that brought me to your work was your mixture of languages. As a teacher of writing who believes that writing and literacy can be liberatory, it was very frightening and disorienting and hurtful when I began to realize the degree to which writing and language could be just the opposite: the ways in which they could enslave, keep down, exclude, hurt, silence. To have to face my own doubleness within the discipline of writing was hard for me, because I wanted to embrace the goals of liberation, and I didn't want to face the fact that teaching any kind of a system involves constraints and hurts, or the degree to which English is hegemonic and silencing, the way in which English tends to drown out. I also think about the way in which English, throughout its whole history as a language, has been like a sponge, sucking up words from Norse, or German, or French, or I think now of Spanish, from which English is absorbing enormous amounts. I don't know how I feel about that. I don't know whether I think that it's good that the language is alive and growing, or whether I think that English is exerting its power once more and trying to surround Spanish, let's say and take it in. Those are very confusing issues to me. I'm also very I'm also very much aware that students quite often fear other languages in the same way they fear other people that they perceive as different. So how are you feeling about the state of English today? How do you feel about the English-only legislation which passed in the Congress last summer?

71   **A.** Well I think that English is the dominant symbology system. Language is a representational system, a symbology system. But what happens with the language, this particular symbolic system, is that it displaces the reality, the experience, so that you take the language to be the reality. So say you had Hindi, or Spanish, or Hopi, or whatever the language happens to be. That language attempts to create reality; not just shape it but create it; not just mold it but create it and displace it. I think all languages do that. Then you take a country like the United States, where via the industrial age and the electronic age and the age of the Internet, the dispersal of English is faster and more widespread than any other language thus far. It's going to become the planetary language if we're not careful. Other countries are going to become—I don't want to say "Americanized," because I don't want to use the word "America" to represent the United States—but it's

going to have this kind of United Statesian-culture-swallowing-up-the-rest-of-the-world kind of mouth. As for me, I like English and I majored in English at that I wasn't allowed Spanish. I never took any Spanish courses other than a Spanish class in high school. I took some French and some Italian—which didn't do me any good because I can't remember any of it now. The way I grew up with my family was code switching. When I am my most emotive self, my home self, stuff will come out in Spanish. When I'm in my head, stuff comes out in English. When I'm dealing with theory, it's all in English, because I didn't take any classes in which theory was taught in Spanish. So the body and the feeling parts of me come out in Spanish, and the intellectual, reasoning parts of me come out in English.

72 **Q.** Do you dream in Spanish?

73 **A.** I dream in both Spanish and English. What's happening more and more with English is that I get the ideas in Spanish and I get them in visuals. Like one of the ideas that I'm working with is *conocimiento,* the Spanish word for knowledge, for ways of knowing. Those ideas come to me in Spanish and in visuals. So when I think "conocimiento," I see a little serpent for counter-knowledge. This is how it comes to me that this knowledge, this "counter-knowledge," is not acceptable, that it's the knowledge of the serpent of the garden of Eden. It's not acceptable to eat the fruit of knowledge; it makes you too aware, too self-reflective. So how do you take this *conocimiento* and have the student speculate on it, when all the student knows and is immersed in is the kind of knowledge that crosses this one out? For a student to do this, there has to be some kind of opening, some kind of fissure, crack, gate, *rajadura*—a crack between the world is what I call it—the hole, the interfaces.

74 **Q.** Before we began taping, you remembered that people generally assume that you have read a lot of theory, since your books enact so many of the concepts poststructural theory has espoused. You must have read Foucalt, you must have read Derrida, you must have read Irigaray or Cixous. You said that you hadn't read them before you wrote *Borderlands,* but that the ideas—they're "out there."

75 **A.** Yes, the ideas are out there because we are all people who are in more or less the same territory. We occupy the world of the academy and of the late twentieth century. We've read some of the same books, we've seen some of the same movies, we have similar ideas about relationships, whether we're French or born in the United States or raised here. In reflecting on what we know and on our experiences, we come up with these paradigms, concepts of what it is that life is about, about how interactions and power struggles work. Those theorists give it different terms than I do; a lot of my terms are in Spanish, like *conocimiento.* A lot of the concepts that I have about composition and postcoloniality are attempts to connect pre-Columbian histories and values and systems with the postcolonial twentieth century. A lot of times I will start with a cultural figure from the precolonial: *Coatlicue or la Llorona.* Then I look at the experience in 1997 that Chicanos and Chicanas are going through, and I try to see a connection to what was going on then. I want to show a continuity, to show a progression. I try to give a term, to find a language for my ideas and my concepts that comes from the indigenous part of me rather than from the European part of me, so I come up with *Coatlicue,* and *la facultad,* and *la frontera,* and *Nepantla*—concepts that mean: "Here's a little nugget of a system of knowledge that is different from the Euro-American. This is my hit on it, but it's also a *mestizo /mestiza* cognitive kind of perception, so therefore this ideology or this little nugget of knowledge is both indigenous and Western. It's a hybridity, a mixture, because I live in this liminal state in between worlds, in between realities, in between systems of knowledge, in between symbology systems." This liminal, borderland, terrain or passageway, this interface, is what I call *Nepantla.* All of the concepts that I have about composition, all of the concepts that I have about postcoloniality, come under this umbrella heading of *Nepantla*. which means *el lugar en medio,* the space in between, the middle ground. I first saw that word in Rosario Castellano's writings. When they dug up the streets of Mexico City to build the subway system, they found the *Templo Mayor*. In it they found the statue of *Coatlicue*, and they found all these artifacts, and they found murals on the walls, and one of the murals was *Nepantla*. There are also all these words that begin with *Nepantla* and end in other endings in *Nahuatt*. One of them is "between two oceans:" that's the *Nepantla*. Whenever two things meet there's the *Nepantla*, so they have tons and tons of words with the root word *Nepantla*. *Borderlands* falls into that category, but *Borderlands* is just one project of this overall umbrella project that is my life's work, my life's writing. *Borderlands* is just one hit on it. And this new book that I'm working on now, on composition and on the process of writing, and on identity, and on knowledge, and on the construction of all of these things, is like a sequel to *Borderlands*. All of my books are parts of this project.

76   **Q.** And the book of short stories that you're working on, too?

77   **A.** Yes, and the process for my composing all these projects is very much Coyochauqui, the moon goddess that got dismembered. In composing, you take things apart and everything is fragmented, and then you struggle to put things together.

78   **Q.** Is there any sense of weaving in what comes after the tearing apart, from the language? I also think of weaving as a metaphor for what happens at some points in writing.

79   **A.** Yes, there is—a kind of weaving, a rearranging. Anyway, I'm enumerating the different stages of my writing process. And what's funny is that I started out just talking about writing, and then I branched off into other art forms: into musical composition, dances that get choreographed, film, video—all of these arts have elements in common. Even architecture and building construction have something in common with composition, even though in the construction of a building you have to have all the details first—where the electrical outlets have to be, where the windows are, what the dimensions are. Then you're allowed to be creative; you can manipulate things, you can move the light switch a little bit. But with writing, you can approach it from an outline, from something that's already framed for you; or you can start composing with a loosely held-together frame; or you can jump into it and start anywhere. You can start in the end and go to the beginning, or you can start in the middle and go both directions, toward the beginning and the end. The frames for all of these art forms vary a little bit, but a lot of the process of the composition is very similar.

80   Okay, so once I found that out, I started looking at how I create aspects of my identity. Identity is very much a fictive construction: you compose it of what's out there, what the culture gives you, and what you resist in the culture. This identity also has this kind of projection of your self into a future identity. You can say here's the image of Gloria, or here's the image of Andrea that I want to project in the next seven years, the kind of person that I'd like to be in the future; and then you start building that Andrea. You can start building that Andrea by saying, "I'm going to make more time for myself, I'm going to value solitude, I'm going to get rid of the clutter, I'm going to find out what my own goals are and what my agenda is, and go with that instead of what my mother, or my family, or the academy, or my husband wants, and these are the projects that I'm going to concentrate on." You reshape yourself. But first you get that self-image in your head, and then you project that out into the world. When you look at it ten years later, you won't recognize yourself. When you go back home to your mom and to your brothers and sisters, you'll be an entirely different person, and they won't see how you came from there to here. So you keep creating your identity this way.

81   Then I took all of this knowledge a step further, to reality. I realized that if I can compose this text, and if I can compose my identity, then I can also compose reality

out there. It all has to do with the angle of looking at things. Say all your life you've perceived Andrea as being this one kind of person, you've perceived an essay to be this one kind of composition, you've perceived the planet earth and the United States to be this kind of country and this kind of reality. Then you find out that you don't have to write the essay this way, that you don't have to be the Andrea that you've been all your life, and that if you see that shed, and that sky and that sea and all that happens in it from this other angle, then you will see something else. You can recreate reality. But you're going to need some help, because it's all done in relationship with other people. When we are born we are taught by our culture that that is up, and this is down, and that's a piece of wood, and that's a no-no. To change the tree, the up and down, and the no-no, you have to get the rest of your peers to see things in this same way—that that's *not* a tree, and that's *not* a no-no. You know what I'm saying. It's all of us that created this physics, this quantum mechanics; now we all have to recreate something different. A scientist will be the first to give us an idea of this other universe, of this other atom; the writer will be the first to give us an idea of this other emotional experience, this other perception, this other angle. It has to be one of the members of the tribe to start making that aperture, that little hole, that crack. It has to be one of the members of the community to say, "Yeah, this is a different way of looking at reality." Then everybody else will say, "Yeah, why didn't I think of that? That's true." All of a sudden you'll have a congress, a consensual basis for this reality that you're observing. And once you have this consensual view of reality, along comes Anzaldúa, who says, "No, that's just the reality that your particular people—who are Indo-European, or Western, or Inuit, or whatever—that's just your gift. Here's a different way of looking at reality."

82 **Q.** When you were talking about your architect, it made me think about what you later said about the importance of other people and always having other people around you. When I think of the feminist architect that you worked with for the addition to your house, that person brought a lot to the project but you were important to the project, too, and then the electricians and the plumbers. Was it a deeply collaborative project?

83 **A.** Yes. They consulted with me, but they knew that I didn't have the know-how. They said, "What kind of space do you want to live in?" and I said "Tall, a lot of opening, a lot of window space." And then they said, "Well, how tall?" Then there is the city code. You have to have a certain amount or free territory in your lot; you can only build so many square feet. I was limited to that, so I said, "I'll go up." Then there are the neighbors. I had to get permission, because some of these windows overlook them. There's a public hearing if you build a two-story, because you're impinging on somebody else's space. So anyway, all of those people and the architect had their visions of what they wanted the space to be like, and I had mine, and I wanted them to co-create it with me. I didn't want it to just be me. There's always negotiating. The corner windows are two or three hundred dollars more expensive than the regular windows, and I said, "I can't afford that." But the architect was invested in having these corner windows—which had been my idea in the first place—so I said, "Well, this is your project, too, so we'll go with that." I wanted only one door, because I felt that French doors were not as secure, but then I talked to the carpenter, who said, "No, this glass is very durable." It's all very collaborative.

84 **Q.** I was just looking at your children's book: obviously you collaborated with the artist on that project, too.

85 **A.** Well, it wasn't quite a straight collaboration, because I did the text first and then I gave it to the artist. But now I am doing a project for a middle-school girl readership, and there I will be working with the artist. But I also think that there is no such thing as a single author. I write my texts, but I borrow the ideas and images from other people. Sometimes I forget that I've borrowed them. I might read some phrase from a poem or fiction, and I like the way it describes the cold. Years and years go by, and I do something similar with my description, but I've forgotten that I've gotten it somewhere else. Then I show my text in draft form to a lot of people for feedback: that's another level of co-creating with somebody. Then my readers do the same thing. They put all of their experience into the text and they change *Borderlands* into many different texts. It's different for every reader. It's not mine anymore.

Q. Does that feel okay to you? You don't feel possessive about your writing as your "property?"

A. No, I don't; I've always felt that way about writing. I do the composing, but it's taken from little mosaics of other people's lives, other people's perceptions. I take all of these pieces and rearrange them. When I'm writing I always have the company of the reader. Sometimes I'm writing with my friends in mind, and sometimes I'm writing for people like you who teach writing. In writing, I'm just talking with you without your being here. This is where style comes in. Style is my relationship with you, how I decide what register of language to use, how much Spanglish, how much vernacular. It's all done in the company of others, while in solitude—which is a contradiction.

Q. Are there some stylists that have been really important to you?

A. Well, I know that thematically, Julio Cortazar has influenced me. He was an Argentinean writer living in France who wrote *Hopscotch,* and *End of the Game and Other Stories,* and he wrote a lot about these in-between places of reality impinging on each other. In terms of my feminist ideas, my gender liberation ideas, *Jane Eyre* influenced me. I read it thirteen times when I was growing up. I really like how this little girl is so assertive. I like her being able to support herself differently from gender roles that were assigned to women. In terms of style, I recently read a mystery by Ruth Rendell, *No Night Is Too Long.* She writes popular stuff under the name Barbara Vine. She can really get into the rhythm of the lines, the words, the voice. I read Cormac McCarthy's *All the Pretty Horses.* I didn't finish the book, but I thought it had a style very similar to mine.

Q. You mentioned Toni Morrison. Have you read a lot of her work?

A. Yes, in the past I did. I think *Song of Solomon* was the last book of hers that I read. I stopped reading her a few years ago; I don't know why. I have her books, and I'm going to pick them up again.

Q. Have you read Borges?

A. Yes. I have his entire collected works.

Q. I was thinking about the story "The Aleph" and that certain spot where, if you lie down and you put your eye there, you can see everything.

A. Yes, when I talk about borders with my students, I use a visual of the aleph.

Q. Didn't Borges write in both Spanish and English as you do?

A. I think he wrote mainly in Spanish, but was heavily influenced by English writers. He read Poe and Hawthorne and people like that.

Q. I picked up a book the other day called the *History of Reading,* written by Alberto Manguel, who lived in Argentina for a time and who read to Borges for several years. And he would go there at night and Borges would say, "shall we have Kipling tonight, or shall we have Poe?" and he would read.

A. Style is a very difficult concept. Often I go to visuals to clarify my concepts, as I've said. For example, I think what's going on now at the turn of the century is exemplified by the *remolino,* the whirlwind, the vortex. North of the equator, the movement is clockwise, so all of our knowledge on this side moves clockwise. South of the equator, the movement is counterclock-wise. The rivers flow the other way here. As a mestiza, I'm living on the equator. Some of my culture, the indigenous and the Mexican culture, pulls me counterclockwise. This comes with its own perception of being. And over here, in North America, all of the knowledge that I learned in school, all of the ways that I've learned to look at life, is pulling me the other way. I'm pulled in two different ways. I think that postcoloniality is situated right here. If you consider the counterclockwise to be the colonized cultures and the clockwise to be the colonizer cultures, then there is this tension and you're trying to accommodate both of these cultures and still be comfortable. But it's a struggle to find this peace, this settlement. You have to change the clockwise movement to be counterclockwise once in a while, and sometimes you have to change this counterclockwise movement to move like the North. It's a state that's very unsettling. It's also the state you are in when you are trying to compose. Moving clockwise is everything that has been written: the literature, the norm, the genre laws. As a writer, you are trying to add to those genre laws, to that knowledge, to that literature, to that art. You have to go along with it in some ways, but to create some changes you have to go counterclockwise. This is the struggle for a writer like me: how much can you get away with without losing the whole thing? All of these metaphors come around and around: to style, to composition itself, to identity, to the creation of knowledge, and to the creation of experience.

101   **Q.** When I look at your writing, I think yours is a mixture of styles. Have you seen other people that mix things up the way you do?

103   **A.** Well other Chicanas were mixing Spanglish in poetry, but not in theory, not in academic writing. And I think of style as trying to recover a childhood place where you code-switch. If I am fictionalizing a certain experience, I go back to the reality of the experience in my memory, and it takes place in both languages. So I get into that style. But I think that what I was trying to do by code-switching was to inject some of my history and some of my identity into this text that White people were going to read or Black people were going to read or Native American people were going to read. I was trying to make them stop and think. Code-switching jerks readers out of their world and makes each think, "Oh, this is my world, this is another world, this is her world where she does this, where it's possible to say words in Spanish." It's like taking the counterclockwise and injecting it into the clockwise. I think that's why I started that. And now a lot of Chicanas are doing it.

104   **Q.** Think of the same thing about injecting, but injecting the discourse of lesbianism or alternative sexuality of any kind into traditional hetero-sexuality. It does the same thing. It insists that we go this way and it helps readers to inhabit other ways of being, other ways of knowing. Isn't that very important too?

105   **A.** And you know we live in the *remolino,* the vortex, the whirlwind; and in this time everything is very much confused: values, ideology, identity. The student is caught in her own little vortex. What I would like to do is what Carlos Castaneda was told to do by Don Juan the shaman: to stop the world. The world is this reality and the world is also the description we have of it in our heads. How do you stop that and say, "No, this other world exists, this other possibility, this other reality." You have to stop this world a little bit to get the other one in. So I would like to stop the *remolino* for just a second, the second that it takes the reader to say, "I didn't know that Chicano Spanish was the bastard language. And if Chicano Spanish is a bastard language, what registers of English are also bastards and not allowed into the academy?" Then they start looking at British English, Australian English, Canadian English, United States English. Then at all of the dialects and all of the registers: academic, formal, slang. And then maybe the reader will say, "I don't know, I'm a redneck and this is my language, and maybe I should write about this language for this particular class. Just for that little second it stops them. Does this make sense to you? Or maybe I'm being too presumptuous and I don't really do that. Anyway, I think that writing has that faculty, but it has to be honest writing and it has to be writing the struggle.

106   **Q**. When bell hooks says that language is a place of struggle, I think that's what she means: you're struggling to get language out of the clock-wise just for the second and into the counterclockwise, and it's a terrible struggle. It goes on your whole life—if I understand her correctly. Did you have any teachers that. . .

107   **A**. ... pointed me in this direction?

108   **Q**. Or that nurtured you in your writing and in your reading and thinking?

109   **A**. I had a favorite teacher when I was in elementary, who influenced the way I look at history and the teacher-student dynamic and at power, domination, and subordination. He would have students teach the class. I was a shy little Chicanita, but I was known as "the brain" because I had the best grades. So he would have me do stuff. I liked to help the other kids. I was his pet: I would grade the papers, and I ended up making up the tests. He would leave me in the classroom. He'd go outside for twenty minutes, and I would be like the little teacher. I learned a lot about power and about teaching.

110   Then when I was in high school, they put me in the accelerated section. There were plus one, two, three, four sections and regular one, two, three, four sections. Chicanos were put in the one, two, three, four sections, and the Whites were all in the plus, except me and Danny—we were put in the plus. There were also some Whites who were in the one, two, three, four. I was put in the "accelerated" level with Danny, but I had no interaction with the White kids because they looked down on me. I was with the White kids for English, Math, Science—for everything except Health, PE, and Homeroom, which I had with Chicanos. One of the teachers that I had was really into building vocabulary. I remember opening dictionaries and encyclopedias and reading whole chunks. I loved to look at the meanings of words. The whole time I was very studious and very withdrawn from other people, very shy. That particular teacher said that I had a facility with words, but that I needed to be trained. But then she would ignore me and pay attention to the White kids. So it was like a put-down rather than praise. Then I had a teacher in college who felt one of the pieces I wrote should be published.

111   Then I went to grad school after I got my B.A., and I had a teacher named James Sledd at the University of Texas. He was the first person ever to encourage me to talk about cultural stuff. I wrote an essay for him called "Growing up Chicana," which was the basis for the *Prieta* in *This Bridge Called My Back*. It was also the basis for a manuscript that I did on my memories, which I then took parts of and made into *Borderlands*. And now I have taken part of it and made it into this book of stories, and other segments of it are going into *La Llorona: Theorizing Identity, Knowledge, Composition*. All of that has its roots in the very first essay that I wrote for James Sledd. He encouraged me to talk about cultural things, and I used some Mexican words and some terms in Spanish. I had written some stories way back when I was working on my B.A., and some when I was working on my M.A.. They all code-switched, but when I wrote for James Sledd we were doing something different. We were trying to write formally: what we would call now theorizing; what was called then criticism. His encouragement was very important to me, and he was also very important to me as a role model. He was very much a maverick against the university; he was very much at odds, an outsider. From him I learned that an outsider is not just somebody of a different skin; it could be somebody who's White, who's usually an insider but who crosses back and forth between outsider and insider. So he was my model to think about insider/outsider, and then I had my whole life to think about *Nosotras*, us and them.

112   **Q**. Did you mention an undergraduate teacher who said that something you had written could be published?

113   **A**. Yes. This was at Texas Women's College in Denton. But I couldn't afford to go to Denton. So then I had to get out for two years and work. I saved money for two years, and then I went to Pan American. I published the essay from my first year in a little Pan

American quarterly. Few of the teachers encouraged me. When I was working on my M.A., I would constantly be marked down on my papers for being too subjective, for not following the rhetoric of Aristotle and Cicero. You know, the model that people value, with the logical development of ideas. I would constantly get marked down. Across the board, all of the professors—in Comp. Lit., in English Lit., in all of the classes that I took for my M.A., and later on while working for a Ph.D. in Austin—all of the professors marked me down. Even the ones I took here at UC-Santa Cruz, teachers who were using my book as a textbook —when I turned in my papers, they would subtly want me to write the status-quo way, even though they would use my book as a model for how to do things differently.

114 So it was a great shock to me several years ago, when the CCCC conference invited me to speak. The very same discipline, the very same teachers who had marked me down and had said that I was writing incorrectly, all of a sudden invited me to speak. Then I started getting requests for reprints in composition readers. That was such a shock to me. Finding that composition people were reading me was a bigger shock than finding that anthropologists were reading me or that women's studies people were reading me. Just a few days ago I was sent a book, a textbook for students. One of the sections is on place, and they took a little segment of chapter seven, *"La Conciencia de la Mestiza,"* where I talk about the valley and returning to the valley. The students are supposed to take that little piece of writing, and write a letter saying what I wrote, assuming my place, and signing the letter "Gloria Anzaldúa." I'll show you the book if you don't believe it. I don't know how the students are supposed to do this.

115 **Q.** English in colleges and in universities has traditionally been a gatekeeper, functioning to keep the gate closed. Only in the last twenty-five years or so have people in English, and mostly people in composition, said, "We don't want to do that anymore. If we are going to be gatekeepers, we want to be opening the gate." That is a very, very big change.

116 **A.** It was a big shock for me to find composition people picking me up, and only a slightly smaller shock to find Spanish and Portuguese modern language people putting my stuff in their readers. Because we Chicanas were not part of Latino writing. They just included Mexican, South American, and Central American writers, not Chicanas. They put Sandra Cisneros in there, they put me in there. I am now a Latina writer. Can you believe that?

117 **Q.** We have talked about some of these issues of unity, rationality, organization, and coherence; and of how we can make a space for intuition, emotion, and the body in writing and in the construction of knowledge — what Kenneth Burke calls the paralogical, to go along with the logical, and the logical has had a strangle hold on the teaching of writing. You have to start with A and you must end with Z. You can't start with Q.

118 **A.** I use "paralogical" in the forward to the encyclopedia in talking about spirituality and reality. When I use these terms, sometimes I think I made them up. I know "paranormal," so I think "paralogical."

119 **Q.** Before our time is over, would you talk at least a little bit about activism and working for change? Because in your writing, it's very clear that you see writing and activism as related. I think that it's less dear how we engage others in doing that kind of activism.

120 **A.** Well, I think that a lot of the activism for writers and for artists stems from trying to heal the wounds. You've been oppressed as a woman, or oppressed as a queer, or oppressed racially as a colonized person, and you want to deal with that oppression, with those wounds. Why did this happen to you? Why is it so hard? Who are these people that are oppressing you, and why do they have a license to oppress you? For me it started as a child. Children don't have any recourse. They can be abused by their parents. They don't have any rights. Society doesn't protect them. In my case, I was such a freak, such a strange little thing, that I felt all of the ill winds that were blowing. I really felt them. I had a very low threshold of pain. The differences that I felt between me and other people were so excruciating. I felt like such a freak. I was trying to make meaning of my existence and my pain, and that in turn led me to writing. In writing I'm trying to write about these moments where I took things into my own hands and I said, "This is not the way things are supposed to be. Girl children are not supposed to be treated this way. Women are not supposed to be battered; they're not supposed to be second-class citizens. Chicanas shouldn't be treated in this way in society." I started grappling with those issues, and writing became a way of activism, a way of trying to make changes. But it wasn't enough just to sit and write and work on my computer. I had to connect the real-life, bodily experiences of people who were suffering because of some kind of oppression, or some kind of wound in their real lives, with what I was writing. It wasn't a disembodied kind of writing. And because I am a writer, voice—acquiring a voice, covering a voice, picking up a voice, creating a voice—was important. And then you run into this whole experience of unearthing, of discovering, of rediscovering, of recreating voices that have been silenced, voices that have been repressed, voices that have been made a secret. And not just for me, but for other Chicanas. Look at all these women who have certain realities that are similar to mine, but they don't really see them. But when they read a text by Toni Morrison or when they read *Borderlands,* they say, "Oh, that went on in my life, but I didn't have the words to articulate it. You articulated it for me, but it's really my experience." They see themselves in the text. Reading these other voices gives them permission to go out and acquire their own voices, to write in this way, to become an activist by using Spanglish, or by code-switching. And then they go out and they read the book to their little girls, or their neighbor's kids, or to their girlfriend, or to their boyfriend.

121   **Q.** It's like links in a chain or a circle that keeps expanding?

122   **A.** Yes. As with my children's book *La Llorona,* it's really very much a cultural story. All that these Chicanitos read is White stuff, and then along comes *La Llorona* and they say, "Yeah, my grandmother used to tell me stories like that." And it feels really good for them to be in a book. There's this little kid—six, seven, eight, nine, ten—who never sees himself represented, so unearthing and nurturing that voice is part of the activism work. That's why I try to do so many anthologies. That's why I promote women, especially women of color and lesbians of all colors, and why I'm on editorial boards for magazines: because I want to get their voices out there. I believe that says something about activism. Because in the process of creating the composition, the work of art, the painting, the film, you're creating the culture. You're rewriting the culture, which is very much an activist kind of thing. So that writers have something in common with all of these people doing grass-roots organizing and acting in the community: it's all about rewriting culture. You don't want a culture that batters women and children. By the year 2005, fifty percent of the group that is going to be labeled "poverty stricken"—fifty percent of it—are going to be women and children. That's a whole new thing, women out of jobs, homeless children. It's a reality that we need to speak of. Twenty years ago, incest was not part of consensual reality. It was the writers who wrote about it, feminists who talked about it, who made films about it, and who did art about incest and child abuse, who changed reality. Before that, it was just a given. You beat your wife, that's part of it. Having abusive sex with your wife is not rape. Consensual reality has been redefined by these people rewriting a culture. Now it's part of culture that when you batter someone, you're supposed to be responsible. It's not something you can get away with unless you're a psychopath.

123   **Q.** What you just said makes me think of one of the things that's important about your work for postcolonial studies. Your work goes beyond the deconstructive—which has been a large part of the very important work that postcolonial studies has done—to show what colonialism has done and been. But the kind of work that you're talking about creates a new reality. It goes beyond the deconstructing and the showing of old oppressions and hurts.

124   **A.** When you get into reading and writing the "other," into assuming some kind of authority for the "other"—whether you are the "other" or you are the subject—there's a community involved. And I think what you are saying is that postcolonial theorists sometimes forget what's going on here in the community, in the world that we inhabit.

125   **Q.** And so do teachers of writing, I hasten to add.

126   **A.** Yes. There's a responsibility that comes with invoking cultural and critical authority, and I think you could call that responsibility being open to activism and being responsible for your actions. No?

127   **Q.** I want to ask one other thing. Suppose you and I had a little child here, and we wanted to watch her grow up and be a writer. What would be your wildest dream for that little child in becoming a writer? What would you most hope for?

128   **A.** Well, I think what I would most hope for is probably not something that is possible. I would hope for her to have a peaceful community in all the different worlds, in all the different cultures, in all the different realities. I would hope for her to be a true mestiza, and I don't think it's possible right now because the powers that decide the laws of man are very much monolithical. It's not an equal kind of thing.

129   **Q.** Do you have any hopes that the situation might change in the future?

130   **A.** Yes, I do. I think we're drifting toward that. The distinction between the people with power and the people without power will get eased, so that the people without any agency now take on a little agency, and the people that were all-powerful now become a little powerless. There will be this kind of hybridity of equal parts, instead of a graft and a major tree. And I would like her to be able to explore the world and not to fear that she's going to be attacked, not to suffer being wounded. To live is to be in pain. To live is to struggle. Life hurts, but we can mitigate that hurt a little bit by having a society where the little girl child can pursue her interests and her dreams without being too much constrained by gender roles or racial law or the different epistemologies that say, "This is the way reality is." I don't know if that's ever going to happen. But I hope so. Sometimes I think so.

Credit _____

Lunsford, Andrea A. "Toward a Mestiza Rhetoric: Gloria Anzaldúa on Composition and Postcoloniality" by Andrea A. Lunsford from *Crossing Borderlands: Composition and Postcolonial Studies*, edited by Andrea A. Lunsford and Lahoucine Ouzgane, copyright © 2004. Reprinted by permission of the University of Pittsburgh Press.

VIEWPOINT
The Laugh of the Medusa
HELENE CIXOUS

Translated by Keith Cohen and Paula Cohen

1   I shall speak about women's writing: about *what it will do*. Woman must write herself: must write about women and bring women to writing, from which they have been driven away as violently as from their bodies-for the same reasons, by the same law, with the same fatal goal. Woman must put herself into the text-as into the world and into history-by her own movement.

2   The future must no longer be determined by the past. I do not deny that the effects of the past are still with us. But I refuse to strengthen them by repeating them, to confer upon them an irremovability the equivalent of destiny, to confuse the biological and the cultural. Anticipation is imperative.

3   Since these reflections are taking shape in an area just on the point of being discovered, they necessarily bear the mark of our time – a time during which the new breaks away from the old, and, more precisely, the (feminine) new from the old (*la nouvelle de l'ancien*). Thus, as there are no grounds for establishing a discourse, but rather an arid millennial ground to break, what I say has at least two sides and two aims: to break up, to destroy; and to foresee the unforeseeable, to project.

4   I write this as a woman, toward women. When I say "woman," I'm speaking of woman in her inevitable struggle against conventional man; and of a universal woman subject who must bring women to their senses and to their meaning in history. But first it must be said that in spite of the enormity of the repression that has kept them in the "dark" – that dark which people have been trying to make them accept as their attribute – there is, at this time, no general woman, no one typical woman. What they have in *common* I will say. But what strikes me is the infinite richness of their individual constitutions: you can't talk about a female sexuality, uniform, homogeneous, classifiable into codes – any more than you can talk about one unconscious resembling another. Women's imaginary is inexhaustible, like music, painting, writing: their stream of phantasms is incredible.

5   I have been amazed more than once by a description a woman gave me of a world all her own which she had been secretly haunting since early childhood. A world of searching, the elaboration of a knowledge, on the basis of a systematic experimentation with the bodily functions, a passionate and precise interrogation of her erotogeneity. This practice, extraordinarily rich and inventive, in particular as concerns masturbation, is prolonged or accompanied by a production of forms, a veritable aesthetic activity, each stage of rapture inscribing a resonant vision, a composition, something beautiful. Beauty will no longer be forbidden.

6   I wished that that woman would write and proclaim this unique empire so that other women, other unacknowledged sovereigns, might exclaim: I, too, overflow; my desires have invented new desires, my body knows unheard-of songs. Time and again I, too, have felt so full of luminous torrents that I could burst-burst with forms much more beautiful than those which are put up in frames and sold for a stinking fortune. And I, too, said nothing, showed nothing; I didn't open my mouth, I didn't repaint my half of the world. I was ashamed. I was afraid, and I swallowed my shame and my fear. I said to myself: You are mad! What's the meaning of these waves, these floods, these outbursts? Where is the ebullient, infinite woman who, immersed as she was in her naiveté, kept in the dark about herself, led into self-disdain by the great arm of parental-conjugal phallocentrism, hasn't been ashamed of her strength? Who, surprised and horrified by the fantastic tumult of her drives (for she was made to believe that a well-adjusted normal woman has a ... divine composure), hasn't accused herself of being a monster? Who, feeling a funny desire stirring inside her (to sing, to write, to dare to speak, in short, to bring out something new), hasn't thought she was sick? Well, her shameful sickness is that she resists death, that she makes trouble.

7 And why don't you write? Write! Writing is for you, you are for you; your body is yours, take it. I know why you haven't written. (And why I didn't write before the age of twenty-seven.) Because writing is at once too high, too great for you, it's reserved for the great-that is, for "great men"; and it's "silly." Besides, you've written a little, but in secret. And it wasn't good, because it was in secret, and because you punished yourself for writing, because you didn't go all the way; or because you wrote, irresistibly, as when we would masturbate in secret, not to go further, but to attenuate the tension a bit, just enough to take the edge off. And then as soon as we come, we go and make ourselves feel guilty-so as to be forgiven; or to forget, to bury it until the next time.

8 Write, let no one hold you back, let nothing stop you: not man; not the imbecilic capitalist machinery, in which publishing houses are the crafty, obsequious relayers of imperatives handed down by an economy that works against us and off our backs; and not *yourself*. Smug-faced readers, managing editors, and big bosses don't like the true texts of women-female-sexed texts. That kind scares them.

9 I write woman: woman must write woman. And man, man. So only an oblique consideration will be found here of man; it's up to him to say where his masculinity and femininity are at: this will concern us once men have opened their eyes and seen themselves clearly.[1]

10 Now women return from afar, from always: from "without," from the heath where witches are kept alive; from below, from beyond "culture"; from their childhood which men have been trying desperately to make them forget, condemning it to "eternal rest." The little girls and their "ill-mannered" bodies immured, well-preserved, intact unto themselves, in the mirror. Frigidified. But are they ever seething underneath! What an effort it takes – there's no end to it – for the sex cops to bar their threatening return. Such a display of forces on both sides that the strug-gle has for centuries been immobilized in the trembling equilibrium of a deadlock.

11 Here they are, returning, arriving over and again, because the unconscious is impregnable. They have wandered around in circles, confined to the narrow room in which they've been given a deadly brainwashing. You can incarcerate them, slow them down, get away with the old Apartheid routine, but for a time only. As soon as they begin to speak, at the same time as they're taught their name, they can be taught that their territory is black: because you are Africa, you are black. Your continent is dark. Dark is dangerous. You can't see anything in the dark, you're afraid. Don't move, you might fall. Most of all, don't go into the forest. And so we have internalized this horror of the dark.

12 Men have committed the greatest crime against women. Insidiously, violently, they have led them to hate women, to be their own enemies, to mobilize their immense strength against themselves, to be the executants of their virile needs. They have made for women an antinarcissism! A narcissism which loves itself only to be loved for what women haven't got! They have constructed the infamous logic of antilove.

13 We the precocious, we the repressed of culture, our lovely mouths gagged with pollen, our wind knocked out of us, we the labyrinths, the ladders, the trampled spaces, the bevies – we are black and we are beautiful.

14 We're stormy, and that which is ours breaks loose from us without our fearing any debilitation. Our glances, our smiles, are spent; laughs exude from all our mouths; our blood flows and we extend ourselves without ever reaching an end; we never hold back our thoughts, our signs, our writing; and we're not afraid of lacking.

15 What happiness for us who are omitted, brushed aside at the scene of inheritances; we inspire ourselves and we expire without running out of breath, we are everywhere!

16   From now on, who, if we say so, can say no to us? We've come back from always.

17   It is time to liberate the New Woman from the Old by coming to know her – by loving her for getting by, for getting beyond the Old without delay, by going out ahead of what the New Woman will be, as an arrow quits the bow with a movement that gathers and separates the vibrations musically, in order to be more than herself.

18   I say that we must, for, with a few rare exceptions, there has not yet been any writing that inscribes femininity; exceptions so rare, in fact, that, after plowing through literature across languages, cultures, and ages,[2] one can only be startled at this vain scouting mission. It is well known that the number of women writers (while having increased very slightly from the nineteenth century on) has always been ridiculously small. This is a useless and deceptive fact unless from their species of female writers we do not first deduct the immense majority whose workmanship is in no way different from male writing, and which either obscures women or reproduces the classic representations of women (as sensitive-intuitive-dreamy, etc.)[3]

19   Let me insert here a parenthetical remark. I mean it when I speak of male writing. I maintain unequivocally that there is such a thing as marked writing; that, until now, far more extensively and repressively than is ever suspected or admitted, writing has been run by a libidinal and cultural-hence political, typically masculine-economy; that this is a locus where the repression of women has been perpetuated, over and over, more or less consciously, and in a manner that's frightening since it's often hidden or adorned with the mystifying charms of fiction; that this locus has grossly exaggerated all the signs of sexual opposition (and not sexual difference), where woman has never her turn to speak – this being all the more serious and unpardonable in that writing is precisely *the very possibility of change*, the space that can serve as a springboard for subversive thought, the precursory movement of a transformation of social and cultural structures.

20   Nearly the entire history of writing is confounded with the history of reason, of which it is at once the effect, the support, and one of the privileged alibis. It has been one with the phallocentric tradition. It is indeed that same self-admiring, self-stimulating, self-congratulatory phallocentrism.

21   With some exceptions, for there have been failures – and if it weren't for them, I wouldn't be writing (I-woman, escapee) – in that enormous machine that has been operating and turning out its "truth" for centuries. There have been poets who would go to any lengths to slip something by at odds with tradition-men capable of loving love and hence capable of loving others and of wanting them, of imagining the woman who would hold out against oppression and constitute herself as a superb, equal, hence "impossible" subject, untenable in a real social framework. Such a woman the poet could desire only by breaking the codes that negate her. Her appearance would necessarily bring on, if not revolution – for the bastion was supposed to be immutable – at least harrowing explosions. At times it is in the fissure caused by an earthquake, through that radical mutation of things brought on by a material upheaval when every structure is for a moment thrown off balance and an ephemeral wildness sweeps order away, that the poet slips something by, for a brief span, of woman. Thus did Kleist expend himself in his yearning for the existence of sister-lovers, maternal daughters, mother-sisters, who never hung their heads in shame. Once the palace of magistrates is restored, it's time to pay: immediate bloody death to the uncontrollable elements.

22   But only the poets-not the novelists, allies of representationalism. Because poetry involves gaining strength through the unconscious and because the unconscious, that other limitless country, is the place where the repressed manage to survive: women, or as Hoffmann would say, fairies.

23 She must write herself, because this is the invention of a *new insurgent* writing which, when the moment of her liberation has come, will allow her to carry out the indispensable ruptures and transformations in her history, first at two levels that cannot be separated.

24 a) Individually. By writing herself, woman will return to the body which has been more than confiscated from her, which has been turned into the uncanny stranger on display – the ailing or dead figure, which so often turns out to be the nasty companion, the cause and location of inhibitions. Censor the body and you censor breath and speech at the same time.

25 Write yourself. Your body must be heard. Only then will the immense resources of the unconscious spring forth. Our naphtha will spread, throughout the world, without dollars – black or gold – nonassessed values that will change the rules of the old game.

26 To write. An act which will not only "realize" the decensored relation of woman to her sexuality, to her womanly being, giving her access to her native strength; it will give her back her goods, her pleasures, her organs, her immense bodily territories which have been kept under seal; it will tear her away from the superegoized structure in which she has always occupied the place reserved for the guilty (guilty of everything, guilty at every turn: for having desires, for not having any; for being frigid, for being "too hot"; for not being both at once; for being too motherly and not enough; for having children and for not having any; for nursing and for not nursing ...) – tear her away by means of this research, this job of analysis and illumination, this emancipation of the marvelous text of herself that she must urgently learn to speak. A woman without a body, dumb, blind, can't possibly be a good fighter. She is reduced to being the servant of the militant male, his shadow. We must kill the false woman who is preventing the live one from breathing. Inscribe the breath of the whole woman.

27 b) An act that will also be marked by woman's *seizing* the occasion to *speak*, hence her shattering entry into history, which has always been based *on her suppression*. To write and thus to forge for herself the antilogos weapon. To become at will the taker and initiator, for her own right, in every symbolic system, in every political process.

28 It is time for women to start scoring their feats in written and oral language.

29 Every woman has known the torment of getting up to speak. Her heart racing, at times entirely lost for words, ground and language slipping away – that's how daring a feat, how great a transgression it is for a woman to speak – even just open her mouth – in public. A double distress, for even if she transgresses, her words fall almost always upon the deaf male ear, which hears in language only that which speaks in the masculine.

30 It is by writing, from and toward women, and by taking up the challenge of speech which has been governed by the phallus, that women will confirm women in a place other than that which is reserved in and by the symbolic, that is, in a place other than silence. Women should break out of the snare of silence. They shouldn't be conned into accepting a domain which is the margin or the harem.

31 Listen to a woman speak at a public gathering (if she hasn't painfully lost her wind). She doesn't "speak," she throws her trembling body forward; she lets go of herself, she flies; all of her passes into her voice, and it's with her body that she vitally supports the "logic" of her speech. Her flesh speaks true. She lays herself bare. In fact, she physically materializes what she's thinking; she signifies it with her body. In a certain way she inscribes what she's saying, because she doesn't deny her drives the intractable and impassioned part they have in speaking. Her speech, even when "theoretical" or political, is never simple or linear or "objectified," generalized: she draws her story into history.

32 There is not that scission, that division made by the common man between the logic of oral speech and the logic of the text, bound as he is by his antiquated relation – servile, calculating – to mastery. From which proceeds the niggardly lip service which engages only the tiniest part of the body, plus the mask.

33 In women's speech, as in their writing, that element which never stops resonating, which, once we've been permeated by it, profoundly and imperceptibly touched by it, retains the power of moving us – that element is the song: first music from the first voice of love which is alive in every woman. Why this privileged relationship with the voice? Because no woman stockpiles as many defenses for countering the drives as does a man. You don't build walls around yourself, you don't forego pleasure as "wisely" as he. Even if phallic mystification has generally contaminated good relationships, a woman is never far from "mother" (I mean outside her role functions: the "mother" as nonname and as source of goods). There is always within her at least a little of that good mother's milk. She writes in white ink.

34 *Woman for women.* – There always remains in woman that force which produces/is produced by the other – in particular, the other woman. *In* her, matrix, cradler; herself giver as her mother and child; she is her own sister-daughter. You might object, "What about she who is the hysterical offspring of a bad mother?" Everything will be changed once woman gives woman to the other woman. There is hidden and always ready in woman the source; the locus for the other. The mother, too, is a metaphor. It is necessary and sufficient that the best of herself be given to woman by another woman for her to be able to love herself and return in love the body that was "born" to her. Touch me, caress me, you the living no-name, give me myself as myself. The relation to the "mother," in terms of intense pleasure and violence, is curtailed no more than the relation to childhood (the child that she was, that she is, that she makes, remakes, undoes, there at the point where, the same, she others herself). Text: my body – shot through with streams of song; I don't mean the overbearing, clutchy "mother" but, rather, what touches you, the equivoice that affects you, fills your breast with an urge to come to language and launches your force; the rhythm that laughs you; the intimate recipient who makes all metaphors possible and desirable; body (body? bodies?), no more describable than god, the soul, or the Other; that part of you that leaves a space between yourself and urges you to inscribe in language your woman's style. In women there is always more or less of the mother who makes everything all right, who nourishes, and who stands up against separation; a force that will not be cut off but will knock the wind out of the codes. We will rethink womankind beginning with every form and every period of her body. The Americans remind us, "We are all Lesbians"; that is, don't denigrate woman, don't make of her what men have made of you.

35 Because the "economy" of her drives is prodigious, she cannot fail, in seizing the occasion to speak, to transform directly and indirectly all systems of exchange based on masculine thrift. Her libido will produce far more radical effects of political and social change than some might like to think.

36 Because she arrives, vibrant, over and again, we are at the beginning of a new history, or rather of a process of becoming in which several histories intersect with one another. As subject for history, woman always occurs simultaneously in several places. Woman un-thinks[4] the unifying, regulating history that homogenizes and channels forces, herding contradictions into a single battlefield. In woman, personal history blends together with the history of all women, as well as national and world history. As a militant, she is an integral part of all liberations. She must be farsighted, not limited to a blow-by-blow interaction. She foresees that her liberation will do more than modify power relations or toss the ball over to the other camp; she will bring about a mutation in human relations, in thought, in all praxis: hers is not simply a class struggle, which she carries forward into a much vaster movement. Not that in order to be a woman-in-struggle(s) you have to leave the class struggle or repudiate it; but you have to split it open, spread it out, push it forward, fill it with the fundamental struggle so as to prevent the class struggle, or any other struggle for the liberation of a class or people, from operating as a form of repression, pretext for postponing the inevitable, the staggering alteration in power relations and in the production of individualities. This alteration is already upon us – in the United States, for example, where millions of night crawlers are in the process of undermining the family and disintegrating the whole of American sociality.

37   The new history is coming; it's not a dream, though it does extend beyond men's imagination, and for good reason. It's going to deprive them of their conceptual orthopedics, beginning with the destruction of their enticement machine.

38   It is impossible to *define* a feminine practice of writing, and this is an impossibility that will remain, for this practice can never be theorized, enclosed, coded – which doesn't mean that it doesn't exist. But it will always surpass the discourse that regulates the phallocentric system; it does and will take place in areas other than those subordinated to philosophico-theoretical domination. It will be conceived of only by subjects who are breakers of automatisms, by peripheral figures that no authority can ever subjugate.

39   Hence the necessity to affirm the flourishes of this writing, to give form to its movement, its near and distant byways. Bear in mind to begin with (1) that sexual opposition, which has always worked for man's profit to the point of reducing writing, too, to his laws, is only a historico-cultural limit. There is, there will be more and more rapidly pervasive now, a fiction that produces irreducible effects of femininity. (2) That it is through ignorance that most readers, critics, and writers of both sexes hesitate to admit or deny outright the possibility or the pertinence of a distinction between feminine and masculine writing. It will usually be said, thus disposing of sexual difference: either that all writing, to the extent that it materializes, is feminine; or, inversely – but it comes to the same thing – that the act of writing is equivalent to masculine masturbation (and so the woman who writes cuts herself out a paper penis); or that writing is bisexual, hence neuter, which again does away with differentiation. To admit that writing is precisely working (in) the in-between, inspecting the process of the same and of the other without which nothing can live, undoing the work of death – to admit this is first to want the two, as well as both, the ensemble of the one and the other, not fixed in sequences of struggle and expulsion or some other form of death but infinitely dynamized by an incessant process of exchange from one subject to another. A process of different subjects knowing one another and beginning one another anew only from the living boundaries of the other: a multiple and inexhaustible course with millions of encounters and transformations of the same into the other and into the in-between, from which woman takes her forms (and man, in his turn; but that's his other history).

40   In saying "bisexual, hence neuter," I am referring to the classic conception of bisexuality, which, squashed under the emblem of castration fear and along with the fantasy of a "total" being (though composed of two halves), would do away with the difference experienced as an operation incurring loss, as the mark of dreaded sectility.

41   To this self-effacing, merger-type bisexuality, which would conjure away castration (the writer who puts up his sign: "bisexual written here, come and see," when the odds are good that it's neither one nor the other), I oppose the other bisexuality on which every subject not enclosed in the false theater of phallocentric representationalism has founded his/her erotic universe. Bisexuality: that is, each one's location in self (repérage en soi) of the presence-variously manifest and insistent according to each person, male or female – of both sexes, nonexclusion either of the difference or of one sex, and, from this "self-permission," multiplication of the effects of the inscription of desire, over all parts of my body and the other body.

42   Now it happens that at present, for historico-cultural reasons, it is women who are opening up to and benefiting from this vatic bisexuality which doesn't annul differences but stirs them up, pursues them, increases their number. In a certain way, "woman is bisexual"; man – it's a secret to no one – being poised to keep glorious phallic monosexuality in view. By virtue of affirming the primacy of the phallus and of bringing it into play, phallocratic ideology has claimed more than one victim. As a woman, I've been clouded over by the great shadow of the scepter and been told: idolize it, that which you cannot brandish. But at the same time, man has been handed that grotesque and scarcely enviable destiny (just imagine) of being reduced to a single idol with clay balls. And consumed, as Freud and his followers note, by a fear of being a woman! For, if psychoanalysis was constituted from woman, to repress femininity (and not so successful a repression at that – men have made it clear), its account of masculine sexuality is now hardly refutable; as with all the "human" sciences, it reproduces the masculine view, of which it is one of the effects.

43   Here we encounter the inevitable man-with-rock, standing erect in his old Freudian realm, in the way that, to take the figure back to the point where linguistics is conceptualizing it "anew," Lacan preserves it in the sanctuary of the phallos (ø) "sheltered" from *castration's lack*! Their "symbolic" exists, it holds power – we, the sowers of disorder, know it only too well. But we are in no way obliged to deposit our lives in their banks of lack, to consider the constitution of the subject in terms of a drama manglingly restaged, to reinstate again and again the religion of the father. Because we don't want that. We don't fawn around the supreme hole. We have no womanly reason to pledge allegiance to the negative. The feminine (as the poets suspected) affirms: ". . . And yes," says Molly, carrying Ulysses off beyond any book and toward the new writing; "I said yes, I will Yes."

44   *The Dark Continent is neither dark nor unexplorable.* – It is still unexplored only because we've been made to believe that it was too dark to be explorable. And because they want to make us believe that what interests us is the white continent, with its monuments to Lack. And we believed. They riveted us between two horrifying myths: between the Medusa and the abyss. That would be enough to set half the world laughing, except that it's still going on. For the phallologocentric sublation[5] is with us, and it's militant, regenerating the old patterns, anchored in the dogma of castration. They haven't changed a thing: they've theorized their desire for reality! Let the priests tremble, we're going to show them our sexts!

45   Too bad for them if they fall apart upon discovering that women aren't men, or that the mother doesn't have one. But isn't this fear convenient for them? Wouldn't the worst be, isn't the worst, in truth, that women aren't castrated, that they have only to stop listening to the Sirens (for the Sirens were men) for history to change its meaning? You only have to look at the Medusa straight on to see her. And she's not deadly. She's beautiful and she's laughing. Men say that there are two unrepresentable things: death and the feminine sex. That's because they need femininity to be associated with death; it's the jitters that gives them a hard-on! for themselves! They need to be afraid of us. Look at the trembling Perseuses moving back-ward toward us, clad in apotropes. What lovely backs! Not another minute to lose. Let's get out of here.

46   Let's hurry: the continent is not impenetrably dark. I've been there often. I was overjoyed one day to run into Jean Genet. It was in Pompes *funébres*.[6] He had come there led by his Jean. There are some men (all too few) who aren't afraid of femininity.

47   Almost everything is yet to be written by women about femininity: about their sexuality, that is, its infinite and mobile complexity, about their eroticization, sudden turn-ons of a certain miniscule-immense area of their bodies; not about destiny, but about the adventure of such and such a drive, about trips, crossings, trudges, abrupt and gradual awakenings, discoveries of a zone at one time timorous and soon to be forthright. A woman's body, with its thousand and one thresholds of ardor – once, by smashing yokes and censors, she lets it articulate the profusion of meanings that run through it in every direction – will make the old single-grooved mother tongue reverberate with more than one language.

48   We've been turned away from our bodies, shamefully taught to ignore them, to strike them with that stupid sexual modesty; we've been made victims of the old fool's game: each one will love the other sex. I'll give you your body and you'll give me mine. But who are the men who give women the body that women blindly yield to them? Why so few? Because so few women have as yet won back their body. Women must write through their bodies, they must invent the impregnable language that will wreck partitions, classes, and rhetorics, regulations and codes, they must submerge, cut through, get beyond the ultimate reserve-discourse, including the one that laughs at the very idea of pronouncing the word "silence," the one that, aiming for the impossible, stops short before the word "impossible" and writes it as "the end."

49   Such is the strength of women that, sweeping away syntax, breaking that famous thread (just a tiny little thread, they say) which acts for men as a surrogate umbilical cord, assuring them – otherwise they couldn't come – that the old lady is always right behind them, watching them make phallus, women will go right up to the impossible.

50   When the "repressed" of their culture and their society returns, it's an explosive, utterly destructive, staggering return, with a force never yet unleashed and equal to the most forbidding of suppressions. For when the Phallic period comes to an end, women will have been either annihilated or borne up to the highest and most violent incandescence. Muffled throughout their history, they have lived in dreams, in bodies (though muted), in silences, in aphonic revolts.

51   And with such force in their fragility; a fragility, a vulnerability, equal to their incomparable intensity. Fortunately, they haven't sublimated; they've saved their skin, their energy. They haven't worked at liquidating the impasse of lives without futures. They have furiously inhabited these sumptuous bodies: admirable hysterics who made Freud succumb to many voluptuous moments impossible to confess, bombarding his Mosaic statue with their carnal and passionate body words, haunting him with their inaudible and thundering denunciations, dazzling, more than naked underneath the seven veils of modesty. Those who, with a single word of the body, have inscribed the vertiginous immensity of a history which is sprung like an arrow from the whole history of men and from biblico-capitalist society, are the women, the supplicants of yesterday, who come as forebears of the new women, after whom no intersubjective relation will ever be the same. You, Dora, you the indomitable, the poetic body, you are the true "mistress" of the Signifier. Before long your efficacity will be seen at work when your speech is no longer suppressed, its point turned in against your breast, but written out over against the other.

52   *In body.* – More so than men who are coaxed toward social success, toward sublimation, women are body. More body, hence more writing. For a long time it has been in body that women have responded to persecution, to the familial-conjugal enterprise of domestication, to the repeated attempts at castrating them. Those who have turned their tongues 10,000 times seven times before not speaking are either dead from it or more familiar with their tongues and their mouths than any-one else. Now, I-woman am going to blow up the Law: an explosion henceforth possible and ineluctable; let it be done, right now, in language.

53   Let us not be trapped by an analysis still encumbered with the old automatisms. It's not to be feared that language conceals an invincible adversary, because it's the language of men and their grammar. We mustn't leave them a single place that's any more theirs alone than we are.

54   If woman has always functioned "within" the discourse of man, a signifier that has always referred back to the opposite signifier which annihilates its specific energy and diminishes or stifles its very different sounds, it is time for her to dislocate this "within," to explode it, turn it around, and seize it; to make it hers, containing it, taking it in her own mouth, biting that tongue with her very own teeth to invent for herself a language to get inside of. And you'll see with what ease she will spring forth from that "within "– the "within" where once she so drowsily crouched – to overflow at the lips she will cover the foam.

55   Nor is the point to appropriate their instruments, their concepts, their places, or to begrudge them their position of mastery. Just because there's a risk of identification doesn't mean that we'll succumb. Let's leave it to the worriers, to masculine anxiety and its obsession with how to dominate the way things work – knowing "how it works" in order to "make it work." For us the point is not to take possession in order to internalize or manipulate, but rather to dash through and to "fly."[7]

56   Flying is woman's gesture – flying in language and making it fly. We have all learned the art of flying and its numerous techniques; for centuries we've been able to possess anything only by flying; we've lived in flight, stealing away, finding, when desired, narrow passageways, hidden crossovers. It's no accident that voler has a double meaning, that it plays on each of them and thus throws off the agents of sense. It's no accident: women take after birds and robbers just as robbers take after women and birds. They (*illes*)[8] go by, fly the coop, take pleasure in jumbling the order of space, in disorienting it, in changing around the furniture, dislocating things and values, breaking them all up, emptying structures, and turning propriety upside down.

57   What woman hasn't flown/stolen? Who hasn't felt, dreamt, performed the gesture that jams sociality? Who hasn't crumbled, held up to ridicule, the bar of separation? Who hasn't inscribed with her body the differential, punctured the system of couples and opposition? Who, by some act of transgression, hasn't overthrown successiveness, connection, the wall of circumfusion?

58   A feminine text cannot fail to be more than subversive. It is volcanic; as it is written it brings about an upheaval of the old property crust, carrier of masculine investments; there's no other way. There's no room for her if she's not a he. If she's a her-she, it's in order to smash everything, to shatter the framework of institutions, to blow up the law, to break up the "truth" with laughter.

59   For once she blazes *her* trail in the symbolic, she cannot fail to make of it the chaosmos of the "personal" – in her pronouns, her nouns, and her clique of referents. And for good reason. There will have been the long history of gynocide. This is known by the colonized peoples of yesterday, the workers, the nations, the species off whose backs the history of men has made its gold; those who have known the ignominy of persecution derive from it an obstinate future desire for grandeur; those who are locked up know better than their jailers the taste of free air. Thanks to their history, women today know (how to do and want) what men will be able to conceive of only much later. I say woman overturns the "personal," for if, by means of laws, lies, blackmail, and marriage, her right to herself has been extorted at the same time as her name, she has been able, through the very movement of mortal alienation, to see more closely the inanity of "propriety," the reductive stinginess of the masculine-conjugal subjective economy, which she doubly resists. On the one hand she has constituted herself necessarily as that "person" capable of losing a part of herself without losing her integrity. But secretly, silently, deep down inside, she grows and multiplies, for, on the other hand, she knows far more about living and about the relation between the economy of the drives and the management of the ego than any man. Unlike man, who holds so dearly to his title and his titles, his pouches of value, his cap, crown, and everything connected with his head, woman couldn't care less about the fear of decapitation (or castration), adventuring, without the masculine temerity, into anonymity, which she can merge with without annihilating herself: because she's a giver.

60   I shall have a great deal to say about the whole deceptive problematic of the gift. Woman is obviously not that woman Nietzsche dreamed of who gives only in order to.[9]

Who could ever think of the gift as a gift-that-takes? Who else but man, precisely the one who would like to take everything?.

61   If there is a "propriety of woman," it is paradoxically her capacity to depropriate unselfishly: body without end, without appendage, without principal "parts." If she is a whole, it's a whole composed of parts that are wholes, not simple partial objects but a moving, limitlessly changing ensemble, a cosmos tirelessly traversed by Eros, an immense astral space not organized around any one sun that's any more of a star than the others.

62   This doesn't mean that she's an undifferentiated magma, but that she doesn't lord it over her body or her desire. Though masculine sexuality gravitates around the penis, engendering that centralized body (in political anatomy) under the dictatorship of its parts, woman does not bring about the same regionalization which serves the couple head/genitals and which is inscribed only within boundaries. Her libido is cosmic, just as her unconscious is worldwide. Her writing can only keep going, without ever inscribing or discerning contours, daring to make these vertiginous crossings of the other(s) ephemeral and passionate sojourns in him, her, them, whom she inhabits long enough to look at from the point closest to their unconscious from the moment they awaken, to love them at the point closest to their drives; and then further, impregnated through and through with these brief, identificatory embraces, she goes and passes into infinity. She alone dares and wishes to know from within, where she, the outcast, has never ceased to hear the resonance of fore-language. She lets the other language speak – the language of 1,000 tongues which knows neither en-closure nor death. To life she refuses nothing. Her language does not contain, it carries; it does not hold back, it makes possible. When id is ambiguously uttered – the wonder of being several – she doesn't defend herself against these unknown women whom she's surprised at becoming, but derives pleasure from this gift of alterability. I am spacious, singing flesh, on which is grafted no one knows which I, more or less human, but alive because of transformation.

63   Write! and your self-seeking text will know itself better than flesh and blood, rising, insurrectionary dough kneading itself, with sonorous, perfumed ingredients, a lively combination of flying colors, leaves, and rivers plunging into the sea we feed. "Ah, there's her sea," he will say as he holds out to me a basin full of water from the little phallic mother from whom he's inseparable. But look, our seas are what we make of them, full of fish or not, opaque or transparent, red or black, high or smooth, narrow or bankless; and we are ourselves sea, sand, coral, seaweed, beaches, tides, swimmers, children, waves .... More or less wavily sea, earth, sky – what matter would rebuff us? We know how to speak them all.

64   Heterogeneous, yes. For her joyous benefit she is erogenous; she is the erotogeneity of the heterogeneous: airborne swimmer, in flight, she does not cling to herself; she is dispersible, prodigious, stunning, desirous and capable of others, of the other woman that she will be, of the other woman she isn't, of him, of you.

65   Woman be unafraid of any other place, of any same, or any other. My eyes, my tongue, my ears, my nose, my skin, my mouth, my body-for-(the)-other – not that I long for it in order to fill up a hole, to provide against some defect of mine, or because, as fate would have it, I'm spurred on by feminine "jealousy"; not because I've been dragged into the whole chain of substitutions that brings that which is substituted back to its ultimate object. That sort of thing you would expect to come straight out of "Tom Thumb," out of the *Penisneid* whispered to us by old grandmother ogresses, servants to their father-sons. If they believe, in order to muster up some self-importance, if they really need to believe that we're dying of desire, that we are this hole fringed with desire for their penis – that's their immemorial business. Undeniably (we verify it at our own expense – but also to our amusement), it's their business to let us know they're getting a hard-on, so that we'll

assure them (we the maternal mistresses of their little pocket signifier) that they still can, that it's still there – that men structure themselves only by being fitted with a feather. In the child it's not the penis that the woman desires, it's not that famous bit of skin around which every man gravitates. Pregnancy cannot be traced back, except within the historical limits of the ancients, to some form of fate, to those mechanical substitutions brought about by the unconscious of some eternal "jealous woman"; not to penis envies; and not to narcissism or to some sort of homosexuality linked to the ever-present mother! Begetting a child doesn't mean that the woman or the man must fall ineluctably into patterns or must recharge the circuit of reproduction. If there's a risk there's not an inevitable trap: may women be spared the pressure, under the guise of consciousness-raising, of a supplement of interdictions. Either you want a kid or you don't – *that's your business*. Let nobody threaten you; in satisfying your desire, let not the fear of becoming the accomplice to a sociality succeed the old-time fear of being "taken." And man, are you still going to bank on everyone's blindness and passivity, afraid lest the child make a father and, consequently, that in having a kid the woman land herself more than one bad deal by engendering all at once child-mother-father-family? No; it's up to you to break the old circuits. It will be up to man and woman to render obsolete the former relationship and all its consequences, to consider the launching of a brand-new subject, alive, with defamilialization. Let us demater-paternalize rather than deny woman, in an effort to avoid the co-optation of procreation, a thrilling era of the body. Let us defetishize. Let's get away from the dialectic which has it that the only good father is a dead one, or that the child is the death of his parents. The child is the other, but the other without violence, bypassing loss, struggle. We're fed up with the reuniting of bonds forever to be severed, with the litany of castration that's handed down and genealogized. We won't advance backward anymore; we're not going to repress something so simple as the desire for life. Oral drive, anal drive, vocal drive – all these drives are our strengths, and among them is the gestation drive – just like the desire to write: a desire to live self from within, a desire for the swollen belly, for language, for blood. We are not going to refuse, if it should happen to strike our fancy, the unsurpassed pleasures of pregnancy which have actually been always exaggerated or conjured away – or cursed – in the classic texts. For if there's one thing that's been repressed here's just the place to find it: in the taboo of the pregnant woman. This says a lot about the power she seems invested with at the time, because it has always been suspected, that, when pregnant, the woman not only doubles her market value, but – what's more important – takes on intrinsic value as a woman in her own eyes and, undeniably, acquires body and sex.

66   There are thousands of ways of living one's pregnancy; to have or not to have with that still invisible other a relationship of another intensity. And if you don't have that particular yearning, it doesn't mean that you're in any way lacking. Each body distributes in its own special way, without model or norm, the nonfinite and changing totality of its desires. Decide for yourself on your position in the arena of contradictions, where pleasure and reality embrace. Bring the other to life. Women know how to live detachment; giving birth is neither losing nor increasing. It's adding to life an other. Am I dreaming? Am I mis-recognizing? You, the defenders of "theory," the sacrosanct yes-men of Concept, enthroners of the phallus (but not of the penis):

67   Once more you'll say that all this smacks of "idealism," or what's worse, you'll splutter that I'm a "mystic."

68   And what about the libido? Haven't I read the "Signification of the Phallus"? And what about separation, what about that bit of self for which, to be born, you undergo an ablation – an ablation, so they say, to be forever commemorated by your desire?

69   Besides, isn't it evident that the penis gets around in my texts, that I give it a place and appeal? Of course I do. I want all. I want all of me with all of him. Why should I deprive

myself of a part of us? I want all of us. Woman of course has a desire for a "loving desire" and not a jealous one. But not because she is gelded; not because she's deprived and needs to be filled out, like some wounded person who wants to console herself or seek vengeance: I don't want a penis to decorate my body with. But I do desire the other for the other, whole and entire, male or female; because living means wanting everything that is, everything that lives, and wanting it alive. Castration? Let others toy with it. What's a desire originating from a lack? A pretty meager desire.

70   The woman who still allows herself to be threatened by the big dick, who's still impressed by the commotion of the phallic stance, who still leads a loyal master to the beat of the drum: that's the woman of yesterday. They still exist, easy and numerous victims of the oldest of farces: either they're cast in the original silent version in which, as titanesses lying under the mountains they make with their quivering, they never see erected that theoretic monument to the golden phallus looming, in the old manner, over their bodies. Or, coming today out of their infans period and into the second, "enlightened" version of their virtuous debasement, they see themselves suddenly assaulted by the builders of the analytic empire and, as soon as they've begun to formulate the new desire, naked, nameless, so happy at making an appearance, they're taken in their bath by the new old men, and then, whoops! Luring them with flashy signifiers, the demon of interpretation – oblique, decked out in modernity – sells them the same old handcuffs, baubles, and chains. Which castration do you prefer? Whose degrading do you like better, the father's or the mother's? Oh, what pwetty eyes, you pwetty little girl. Here, buy my glasses and you'll see the Truth-Me-Myself tell you everything you should know. Put them on your nose and take a fetishist's look (you are me, the other analyst – that's what I'm telling you) at your body and the body of the other. You see? No? Wait, you'll have everything explained to you, and you'll know at last which sort of neurosis you're related to. Hold still, we're going to do your portrait, so that you can begin looking like it right away.

71   Yes, the naives to the first and second degree are still legion. If the New Women, arriving now, dare to create outside the theoretical, they're called in by the cops of the signifier, fingerprinted, remonstrated, and brought into the line of order that they are supposed to know; assigned by force of trickery to a precise place in the chain that's always formed for the benefit of a privileged signifier. We are pieced back to the string which leads back, if not to the Name-of-the-Father, then, for a new twist, to the place of the phallic-mother.

72   Beware, my friend, of the signifier that would take you back to the authority of a signified! Beware of diagnoses that would reduce your generative powers. "Common" nouns are also proper nouns that disparage your singularity by classifying it into species. Break out of the circles; don't remain within the psychoanalytic closure. Take a look around, then cut through!

73   And if we are legion, it's because the war of liberation has only made as yet a tiny breakthrough. But women are thronging to it. I've seen them, those who will be neither dupe nor domestic, those who will not fear the risk of being a woman; will not fear any risk, any desire, any space still unexplored in themselves, among themselves and others or anywhere else. They do not fetishize, they do not deny, they do not hate. They observe, they approach, they try to see the other woman, the child, the lover – not to strengthen their own narcissism or verify the solidity or weakness of the master, but to make love better, to invent

74   *Other love.* – In the beginning are our differences. The new love dares for the other, wants the other, makes dizzying, precipitous flights between knowledge and invention. The woman arriving over and over again does not stand still; she's everywhere, she exchanges, she is the desire-that-gives. (Not enclosed in the paradox of the gift that takes nor under the illusion of unitary fusion. We're past that.) She comes in, comes-in-between herself me and you, between the other me where one is always infinitely more than one and more than me, without the fear of ever reaching a limit; she thrills in our becoming. And we'll keep on becoming! She cuts through defensive loves, motherages, and devourations: beyond selfish narcissism, in the moving, open, transitional space, she runs her risks. Beyond the struggle-to-the-death that's been re-moved to the bed, beyond the love-battle that claims to represent ex-change, she scorns at an Eros dynamic that would be fed by hatred. Hatred: a heritage, again, a remainder, a duping subservience to the phallus. To love, to watch-think-seek the other in the other, to despecularize, to unhoard. Does this seem difficult? It's not impossible, and this is what nourishes life – a love that has no commerce with the apprehensive desire that provides against the lack and stultifies the strange; a love that rejoices in the exchange that multiplies. Wherever history still unfolds as the history of death, she does not tread. Opposition, hierarchizing exchange, the struggle for mastery which can end only in at least one death (one master – one slave, or two nonmasters ≠ two dead) – all that comes from a period in time governed by phallocentric values. The fact that this period extends into the present doesn't prevent woman from starting the history of life somewhere else. Elsewhere, she gives. She doesn't "know" what she's giving, she doesn't measure it; she gives, though, neither a counterfeit impression nor something she hasn't got. She gives more, with no assurance that she'll get back even some unexpected profit from what she puts out. She gives that there may be life, thought, transformation. This is an "economy" that can no longer be put in economic terms. Wherever she loves, all the old concepts of management are left behind. At the end of a more or less conscious computation, she finds not her sum but her differences. I am for you what you want me to be at the moment you look at me in a way you've never seen me before: at every instant. When I write, it's everything that we don't know we can be that is written out of me, without exclusions, without stipulation, and everything we will be calls us to the unflagging, intoxicating, unappeasable search for love. In one another we will never be lacking.

Notes

[1] Men still have everything to say about their sexuality, and everything to write. For what they have said so far, for the most part, stems from the opposition activity/passivity, from the power relation between a fantasized obligatory virility meant to invade, to col-onize, and the consequential phantasm of woman as a "dark continent" to penetrate and to "pacify." (We know what "pacify" means in terms of scotomizing the other and mis-recognizing the self.) Conquering her, they've made haste to depart from her borders, to get out of sight, out of body. The way man has of getting out of himself and into her whom he takes not for the other but for his own, deprives him, he knows, of his own bodily territory. One can understand how man, confusing himself with his penis and rushing in for the attack, might feel resentment and fear of being "taken" by the woman, of being lost in her, absorbed, or alone.

[2] I am speaking here only of the place "reserved" for women by the Western world.

[3] Which works, then, might be called feminine? I'll just point out some examples: one would have to give them full readings to bring out what is pervasively feminine in their significance. Which I shall do elsewhere. In France (have you noted our infinite poverty in this field?-the Anglo-Saxon countries have shown resources of distinctly greater conse-quence), leafing through what's come out of the twentieth century – and it's not much – the only inscriptions of femininity that I have seen were by Colette, Marguerite Duras, ... and Jean Genet.

[4] "De-pense," a neologism formed on the verb penser, hence "unthinks," but also "spends" (from depenser) (translator's note).

[5] Standard English term for the Hegelian Aufhebung, the French la releve.

[6] Jean Genet, Pompesfunebres (Paris, 1948), p. 185.

[7] Also, "to steal." Both meanings of the verb voler are played on, as the text itself explains in the following paragraph (translator's note).

[8] Illes is a fusion of the masculine pronoun ils, which refers back to birds and robbers, with the feminine pronoun elles, which refers to women (translator's note).

[9] Reread Derrida's text, "Le Style de la femme," in Nietzsche aujourd'hui (Paris: Union Generale d'Editions, Coll. 10/18), where the philosopher can be seen operating an Aufhebung of all philosophy in its systematic reducing of woman to the place of seduction: she appears as the one who is taken for; the bait in person, all veils unfurled, the one who doesn't give but who gives only in order to (take).

Credit _____

Cixous, Helene. "The Laugh of the Medusa," translated by Keith Cohen and Paula Cohen, from *Signs*, Vol. 1, No. 4. Copyright © 1976. Reproduced with permission of University of Chicago Press - Journals in the format Textbook via Copyright Clearance Center.

Autism and Rhetoric
PAUL HEILKER AND MELANIE YERGEAU

1
> **Paul Heilker** is associate professor of English at Virginia Tech, where he teaches courses in rhetoric, writing, and composition pedagogy and serves as co-director of the doctoral program in rhetoric and writing. He is author of The Essay: Theory and Pedagogy for an Active Form (NCTE, 1996) and coeditor of Keywords in Composition Studies (Heinmann, 1996). His work has appeared I such journals as College Composition and Communication, Rhetoric Review, Composition Studies, and Writing on the Edge.
>
> **Melanie Yergeau** is a PhD candidate in rhetoric, composition, and literacy at The Ohio State University. A recipient of the 2009 Karios Best Webtext Award and the 2008 Karios-Bedford/ St. Marin's Graduate Student Award for Service, she researches how disability studies and digital technologies complicate our understandings of writing and communication. Active in the neurodiversity movement, she serves on the Board of Directors of the Autistic Self-Advocacy Network (ASAN) and directs its Central Ohio chapter.

2
Public awareness and public discourse about autism are approaching critical mass. April 2, 2008, was the first World Autism Awareness Day, which was voted into existence by the United Nations General Assembly. CNN marked the occasion by launching one of its "worldwide investigations," devoting the entire days programming to discussions of autism. Three recent documentary films, *Autism Every Day, Autism: The Musical,* and *Her Name Is Sabine,* all attempt to broaden the public's understanding of the condition. A 2009 feature film, *Adam,* depicts the awkward love story of an autistic man and his nonautistic neighbor. In 2010, HBO produced a biopic on autistic author Temple Grandin, portrayed by Claire Danes, *Parenthood,* a new, high-profile drama on the NBC television network, features a story line about a family with an autistic child. Generation Rescue has purchased significant ad space annually for the past several years in the *USA Today,* imploring lawmakers to "green our vaccines," and a multi-year Autism Speaks television vision campaign compares autism incidence with statistics on lightning strikes, car crashes, and the likelihood of becoming a professional athlete (AutismSpeaksVids; Autism Speaks, "Learn the Signs – Ad Council Campaign"). In the past two years, corporations such as Barnes & Noble, Toys "R" Us, Lindt chocolates, and Starbucks have publicly promoted the fight against autism – with $1 paper puzzle pieces sold in the checkout lane, with pithy coffee-cup quotes and book promotions, and with chocolate rabbits in special gold wrappers. And in May 2010, NASCAR hosted its first Autism Speaks 400 stock car race.

3
We could go on, but what, we wonder, despite this amazing increase in public discourse about autism, can we really communicate about it? The new welter of voices exhorting the public to become more aware and increase our understanding of autism really has very little to offer. In its own advertising in April 2008, CNN noted that autism "remains one of the greatest mysteries of medicine […] Although autism will be diagnosed in more than 25,000 U.S. children this year, scientists and doctors still know very little about the neurological disorder." And a contemporaneous article on autism published in *Newsweek* is titled simply, "Mysteries and Complications" (Kalb).

4
Here, then, is the first way that autism is rhetorical: we are being swamped by a massive increase in fundamentally uncertain yet persuasive discourse. Let us recall Aristotle's ancient distinction between the necessary and the contingent: the proper domain of rhetoric, he wrote, is not the realm of the necessarily true, certain, of stable, but rather the realm of the contingent, possible, and probably (1357a par. 4). We do not yet know what causes autism. In addition, there is considerable argument about what, exactly, autism is, how we should think about it, and how we should respond to it. Is it a disease? A disability? A diversity issue? All these things, and more? How meaningful – and to whom – is the concept of autism spectrum disorders (ASD) (and all that such a rainbow metaphor entails)? How meaningful – and to whom – are the distinctions among autism, high-

functioning autism, Asperger syndrome, and pervasive development disorder-not otherwise specified (PDD-NOS). And how meaningful – and to whom – are the distinctions between people on the autism spectrum and those who are often presented as their polar (and more desirable) opposites, the neurologically typical?

5   Whatever else it may be, autism is a profoundly rhetorical phenomenon. And we are – parents, educators, caregivers, policymakers, the public, and autistic people themselves – would be significantly empowered to understand and respond to it as such. In the continuing absence of stable scientific or medical knowledge about autism, we need to shine a bright and insistent light on how brazenly rhetorical any utterance, especially any highly visible utterance, about autism really is – and, equally important, on how rhetorical any silence about neurotypicality really is. There is an enormous amount of work to be done on this front for anyone interested in rhetoric, public discourse, or medical rhetoric. Every text about autism in the ever-increasing barrage of public discourse on the subject – every news story, every memoir, every popular magazine article, every website, every journal article (including this one), every television broadcast, every blog entry – every public text on autism is begging for a rhetorical analysis.

6   We understand that to professionals in our field, the idea that all texts are rhetorical is now self-evident. What we want to suggest here, however, does not strike us so: we contend that human neurology itself, autistic or other, is likewise a profoundly rhetorical phenomenon. We contend that autism itself is a rhetoric, a way of being in the world through language, a rhetoric we may not have encountered or recognized frequently in the past nor value highly in academic contexts, but a rhetoric nonetheless. If autism is a rhetoric, then we are beholden to respond to it with cultural sensitivity, ethical care, and pedagogical complexity. And if autism is a rhetoric and autistics are minority rhetors, English faculty already possess all the tools and experience they will need to do exactly that.

Autism is a Rhetoric

7   Let us proceed, then, with some definitions. Though the definitions of *rhetoric* are legion, what most have in common is their focus on language use in the social realm. Most definitions of rhetoric focus on the role of communication in social interaction. Kenneth Burke, for instance, writes that the "basic function of rhetoric [is] the use of words by human agents to form attitudes or to induce actions in other human agents" (41). Similarly, Marc Fumaroli says, "Rhetoric appears as the connective tissue peculiar to civil society and to its proper finalities" (253-54). And Gerard A. Hauser maintains simply that "[r]hetoric is communication that attempts to coordinate social action" (2). Though the definitions of *autism* are also legion, what they, too, have in common is a focus on language use in the social realm, a focus on communication in social interaction. Indeed, two of the three primary descriptors of autistic behavior, two of the three traditionally cited, fundamental ways that autism presents itself in the world, per the medical establishment, have to do with communication in the social realm. The National Institute of Health defines autism as "a spectrum that encompasses a wide range of behavior" but whose "common features include impaired social interactions, impaired verbal and nonverbal communication, and restricted and repetitive patterns of behavior" ("Autism" par. 3). Likewise, the Centers for Disease Control and Prevention (CDC) says, "Autism spectrum disorders (ASDs) are a group of developmental disabilities defined by significant impairments in social interaction and communication and the presence of unusual behaviors and interests" (par. 1).

8   Given the definitional confluence of autism and rhetoric in communication and social interaction, it is simple to assert that autism is a rhetorical phenomenon. But we want to go further. According to Jim Corder, "Each [of us] is a rhetorical creation. Out of an inventive world (a past, a set of capacities, a way of thinking) [...we are] always creating structures of meaning and generating a style, a way of being in the world" (152). Following Corder, then, who defines rhetoric here as a way of being in the world through language, through invention, structure, and style, we contend that autism itself is a rhetoric, that autism is a way of being in the world through language, through invention, structure, and style. According to Corder, "Every utterance belongs to, exists in, issues from, and reveals a rhetorical universe. Every utterance comes from somewhere (its inventive origin), emerges as a structure, and manifests itself as a style" (141). But sometimes it doesn't. Sometimes, Corder says, an utterance gets blocked in invention and cannot move into structure or style. According to Corder, sometimes we block into a portion of our invention that is so private, so secret, so truly original with ourselves that it will give rise only to private forms of structure and style, ones that will not sustain communication with others. Sometimes, he maintains, such blockages in invention occur when a person "refuses conflicts by refusing to come out into structure and style." And sometimes the blockage occurs in structure, Corder contends, when we simply stall in a structure or keep returning to it, "unable to move backward to explore or to use an inventive world and also unable to move forward and realize [ourselves] through a unique style" (142).

9   *Paul Heilker speaks: When I understand autism as a rhetoric, as a way of being in the world through language, I thus have a very different sense of the silences I often inhabit in the presence of my autistic son. A rhetorical perspective on autism allows me to see how sometimes Eli may be blocked into a portion of his invention so private, so secret, so truly original with him, that it will give rise only to private forms of structure and style that will not sustain communication with others. Eli occasionally speaks to himself even when others are present, quietly, but urgently, above a whisper but at a volume clearly directed to no one but himself. When I ask what he is doing, he says simply, "I'm talking to myself." A rhetorical perspective on autism likewise lets me understand there are times when Eli refuses conflicts by refusing to come out into structure and style. I now have a rhetorical explanation for why, when he was in seventh grade, Eli literally pulled his head inside his shirt for an entire class period because he did not want to make an oral presentation. When he gets angry and frustrated as he tries to articulate something, when he stops and says aloud, "Unnhhh, how do I SAY this?" – I now know that something in his invention is not getting out into structure and style, that it has stalled there, that he is working through a rhetorical process. When he returns to his obsessive topics of interest, as people on the spectrum tend to do, talking about America's Funniest Videos, homestarrunner. com, SpongeBob SquarePants, for instance, understanding autism as a rhetoric lets me see that he is returning to his favorite inventive universes, that he wants to share topoi in those universes which he continues to find valuable over long stretches of time, that bear repeated usage. When he recites long strings of stock discourse – reciting the entire script of the movie Toy Story, as he did once on a long vacation car ride – I understand that he is choosing to repeat – to inhabit for a short time, in a world that is endlessly in flux – a very familiar and comforting rhetorical structure.*

10   *Melanie Yergeau speaks: Understanding autism as a rhetoric brings a certain level of legitimacy to what I might consider my commonplaces – repetitive hand movements, rocking, literal interpretation, brazen honestly, long silences, long monologues, variations in voice modulation – each its own reaction, or a potentially autistic argument, to a discrete set of circumstances. For instance, I grew up understanding autism (that is, my way of being in the world through language, through invention, structure, and style) as distinctly "less than," as a journal entry I wrote shortly after dropping out of high school suggests:*

11   *I've always been quiet. For as long as I can remember, adults have been telling me to speak louder and more often. After being told this, I usually speak inaudibly and less frequently. I've never really been a people person either. Don't get me wrong, I like people; I just don't like being around them. They make me nervous and I never know what to say. I'm sort of hyper and fidgety and do weird things with my hands, and always*

263

have twenty things going through my mind at once. [...] I imagine about everyone's life but my own, probably because I always tend to screw up mine with the way I act. I have a hard time smiling at people. That's just pitiful. It is like an intoxicating disease, spreading from my voice all the way to my nervous system. It rusts up my joints and leaves me with overemphasized, robotic movements.

12 *Coming to autism rhetorically recasts items such as "difficulty smiling" – from pitiful disease symptom into autistic discourse convention, from a neurological screwup into an autistic confluence of structure and style. So too has understanding neurotypicality as a rhetoric legitimized my autistic ways of communicating: such an understanding involves calling attention to normalized discourse patterns frequently portrayed as desirable and ideal, involves calling attention to ways of being that are not the ways of being.*

13 Sometimes, Corder says, the difficulty arises not because an utterance gets stuck somewhere along the line from invention to structure to style, but rather from "[i]nstances of traffic colliding as [an utterance] tries to cross from one rhetorical universe into another, [which results] in frequent interruption in the flow of ideas, in *apparent* illogicality, in the occurrence of strange words and coinages" (143; emphasis added). Sometimes, he notes, "different portions of invention try to move simultaneously into structure and style" and two or more inventive sets try "to be known through one sequence of structure and style" (144).

14 **Paul speaks:** *Understanding autism as a rhetoric helps me understand Eli's longstanding habit of radically shifting the topic of conversation without warning and without transition, without signaling the shift. When he was in grade school, one of his teachers said that talking with Eli was like listening to an old eight-track tape player, that he shifted topics the way an eight-track shifted songs at the touch of a button. To use a different technological analogy, Eli changes topics so radically and rapidly and easily that he sometimes seems to be listening to multiple channels of some invisible radio simultaneously, moving instantaneously from one channel to another. From Corder's rhetorical perspective, though, what may otherwise appear as interruption, illogicality, and strangeness may instead be more usefully understood as differing portions of Eli's invention trying to move simultaneously, or close to simultaneously, into structure and style, that multiple inventive sets are trying to work through the same sequence of structure and style.*

15 *Such a rhetorical perspective also offers an explanation for two of Eli's "autistic" behaviors that no other discourse about autism has provided. The first of these is his overweening interest in puns. A pun is an instance of a word inhabiting two distinctly different rhetorical worlds at the same time. Indeed, the farther apart these worlds are conceptually or culturally, the better the pun, typically. Eli's intense interest in puns, indeed, his delight in finding utterances that pile up a long series of individual puns to create an even larger collective pun (such as jokes ending with punch lines like "Only Hugh can prevent florist friars," "Chess nuts boasting in an open foyer," "He was a super-callused, fragile mystic hexed by halitosis," and so on) is a function of his desire to have multiplex and disparate inventive universes work through singular sets of structure and style. The second of these is Eli's remarkable ability to find points of intersection between divergent data sets. He will regularly point out connections between texts, for instance, that I think probably no one else has detected, such as "Did you notice that 'The Blue Monkey' is a diamond in* Looney Tunes Back in Action *and a night club in* Inspector Gadget 2*?" His familiarity and ease with having multiple inventive worlds move simultaneously through singular structures and styles seem to help Eli to see connections between disparate events or items, connections that other people typically cannot or do not see.*

Listening and Silence

16 We could and should continue this kind of analysis, using other rhetorical concepts as lenses through which to view and understand autism. We might ask, for instance, which kind of rhetoric – judicial, epideictic, or deliberative – do autistics tend to employ, and what might that mean? Or what are the characteristic troops in autistics' discourse, and what might that signify?

17 The kind of work we are suggesting involves what Krista Ratcliffe calls *rhetorical listening,* a practice that urges us to fundamentally alter how we hear and respond to the discourses of others. Defined generally as a trope for interpretive invention, she says, rhetorical listening signifies a stance of openness that a person may choose to assume in relation to any person, text, or culture. Defined more particularly as a "code of cross-cultural contact," Ratcliffe writes, "*rhetorical listening* signifies a stance of openness that a person may choose to assume in cross-cultural exchanges" (1). The goal of rhetorical listening, she contends, is "to generate more productive discourses, whether they be in academic journals or over the dinner table" (46). Ratcliffe challenges us to consider just how open our stances really are in relation to autistics and their rhetorics, their ways of being in the world through language.

18 Let us consider, for instance, *echolalia,* a characteristic kind of language use among autistics, in which they repeat stock words and phrases verbatim that they have heard other speakers use. Typically, this behavior is seen as an impairment, a deficiency that needs to be alleviated. But if we listen rhetorically, this repeated use of stock material starts sounding more like a traditional and valued kind of invention. In the middle ages and early Renaissance, students were trained to keep what were known as "commonplace" books, large journals in which they meticulously copied down, verbatim, words, phrases, sentences, and even entire dialogues and passages from other speakers that they thought noteworthy. And they were likewise trained to deploy this stock material regularly as they composed. From a disease model perspective, an autistic's preferred echolalic reverting to stockpiles of quotations from films, television programs, websites, and books, rather than generating "original" formulations, is seen as a pervasive developmental delay. When we choose to listen rhetorically, though, when we purposefully adopt a stance of cross-cultural openness toward autistic discourse, we can begin to see that we engage in similar, though not identical, echolalia in academic settings, when doing research and citing sources. As Ratcliffe suggests, such a stance offers the possibility of generating a more productive discourse, a way to value autistic rhetoric and build upon it, rather than try to eradicate it.

19 Similarly, rhetorical listening allows us to generate a more productive discourse about autism and the rhetorical triangle. Ratcliffe contends that rhetorical listening "does not presume a naïve, relativistic empathy, such as 'I'm OK, you're OK' but rather an ethical responsibility to argue for what we deem fair and just while questioning that which we deem fair and just" (25). Empathy – a loaded worded in autism discourse, a characteristic that autistics are said to lack – presumes that one can be so in tune with another person as to actually understand that person's emotional state, to even perhaps vicariously experience it. But empathy involves a certain level of erasure, and as Dennis Lynch writes, "whatever empathy's expressed aims may be, asking people to empathize usually locates the obstacles to empathy – to listening and being heard – solely in the minds and habits of individual participants, and so obscures or ignores the political and economic and bodily dimensions of social struggles" (5-6). So too, Lynch notes, does empathy necessitate "bodily displacement" (10). Thus, when psychologists and rhetoricians alike suggest that autistics cannot imagine or acknowledge the mental states of others, that autistics cannot emotionally or rhetorically reciprocate, that autistics cannot gauge the needs and expectations of an audience, these scholars stand, as neurotypicals, presuming to know what they cannot possibly know, to have experienced what they cannot possibly have experiences. In a flagrantly arrogant construction, such scholars suggest that autistics cannot write or read in a rhetorically effective manner because they are empathetically challenged, because they lack empathy for neurotypical readers; yet, neurotypicals can read and write about autism and autistics because *their* empathy is so fully realized: they understand autistics better than autistics understand themselves. By and large, our various disciplinary assumptions about empathy are normalized constructs, and rhetorical listening can help us complicate out understanding of empathy and theory of mind ad rhetorical concepts: the supposed ability to read minds, to invoke audiences, in the words of Lisa Ede and Andrea Lunsford, and to imagine how those audiences will feel, react, connect, identify. In listening rhetorically, that is, in "consciously standing under discourses that surround us and others while consciously acknowledging all our particular – and very fluid – standpoints" (Ratcliffe 28), we can recognize autistic ways of knowing and empathizing as differences rather than neurological deficits, differences which can usefully complicate a host of normative and unchallenged assumptions in the field.

20   Indeed, adopting a rhetorical perspective on autism and rhetorically listening to autistics could radically revise what we think we know about autism, could fundamentally challenge some of our most foundational assumptions about autism and autistics. In *Unspoken,* or instance, Cheryl Glenn suggests we should come to understand "silence *as a rhetoric,* as a constellation of symbolic strategies that (like spoken language) serves many functions" (xi). Silence, she notes, "has long been considered a lamentable essence of femininity, a trope for oppression, passivity, emptiness, stupidity, or obedience" (2). Whereas, "speaking or speaking out continues to signal power, liberation, culture, or civilization itself," Glenn writes, "[t]hat seeming obverse, silence, signals nothingness" (3). And nowhere is this more true than in the discourse surrounding autism, where an autistic's silence is construed as both a heartbreaking tragedy and the cancellation of personhood. In a 2005 *USA Today* article, for instance, Thomas Insel, director of the National Institute of Mental Health, described autism as "a tremendously disabling brain disease, which really robs a child and a family of the personhood of this child" (qtd. in Jayson par. 5).

21   But a rhetorical perspective offers us new, different, and more useful ways of thinking about at least some autistics' silences. As Glenn notes, "[S]ilence takes many forms and serves many functions, particularly as those functions vary from culture to culture" (15). Moreover, she asserts that "all human silences are a form of communication; listeners and observers will attach various and individualized meaning(s) to the silence, regardless of the silent person's intent." Glenn then begins to list the many things silence might mean, including agreement, disagreement, boredom, indecision, uncertainty over someone else's meaning, impoliteness, over politeness, anger, communion, thoughtfulness, a lack of information, a lack of urgency, fearfulness, empathy, or a lack of attention (16).

22   Rhetorical theory maintains that we speak in order to address some exigence, some social situation which compels us to speak, about which we cannot remain silent. There is some gap, some break, some disruption, some failure, some need that is not being addressed, not being met, and about which the speaker cannot remain silent (see Bitzer, for example). All of our chatter, in other words, is an indication of how very needy we are, a manifestation of our desperation to use language in an ultimately impotent attempt to bridge our biological separateness, as Burke notes (21).

23   ***Paul speaks:*** *Thinking again of my son, a rhetorical perspective on autism makes me wonder, how many different silences does Eli have? And what do these various silences signify? What are their rhetorical functions? What are they intended to communicate? And to what audiences? My experiences with Eli suggests that a rhetorical perspective on some autistic silences, at least, offers a very different way of understanding and valuing this characteristic of his rhetoric. Eli is highly verbal, witty, fully mainstreamed in school, and a sociable guy. We talk a lot. But one of his characteristic ways of being in the world through language is to embody and enact extended silences. We have a fifteen-minute drive to school in the morning, and there are often extended silences in the car, silences I feel compelled to fill up but he does not. While I can't stand the silence, he is comfortable*

in it. He does not feel the exigence, the gap, the break, the disruption, the failure, the need in the social fabric. He is not compelled to speak, therefore he does not speak. In other words, rather than being some kind of deficit or delay or withdrawal, rather than signifying his entrapment, frustration, depression, or loneliness, his silence signifies his contentment, his satisfaction, his fully realized development, and his fully successful rhetoric. His silence during our car rides is a manifestation of his fully successful integration into the world – he has no compelling gaps, needs, or failures that must be addressed. He is not silent because he is withdrawn; he is silent because his integration in the social world is unproblematic, because he has no exigence. As Glenn suggests, sometimes, even for autistics' "Words are unnecessary because no tensions need to be resolved with conversation or words" (17).

24 The range of abilities and disabilities, of gifts and deficits of those on the autistic spectrum is enormous, of course, but we do think that adopting a rhetorical perspective on autism allows us, indeed, requires us, to critically reexamine and reevaluate our assumptions about autistic silences, perhaps even the silences of nonverbal autistics.

Embracing Difference

25 Emerging from the social upheavals of the 1960s, college composition teachers of the day were forced to wrestle with difficult questions about diversity, language, and identity. As the Conference on College Composition and Communication (CCCC) put it, "What should the schools do about the language habits of students who come from a wide variety of social, economic, and cultural backgrounds? [...] Should the schools try to uphold language variety, or to modify it, or to eradicate it?" ("Students' Right" 709). These concerns spurred the field of composition to publish "Students' Right to Their Own Language" in 1972, a resolution adopted by the National Council of Teachers of English as an official position statement in 1974 and reaffirmed in 2003:

26 We affirm the students' right to their own patterns and varieties of language – the dialects of their nurture of whatever dialects in which they find their own identity and style [...] The claim that any one dialect is unacceptable amounts to an attempt of one social group to exert its dominance over another [...] A nation proud of its diverse heritage and its cultural and racial variety will preserve its heritage of dialects. (710-11)

27 *Melanie speaks: I first noticed the banner on my way home from a campus colloquium on disability and narrative. I have just delivered a paper of my own, a paper in which I outed myself as an Asperger's autistic – only to be greeted by a giant, hand-painted image of a baby-blue jigsaw puzzle piece three houses down the road. The image on the banner was somewhat masked by a fold in the fabric, but I recognized it instantly as a local version of the iconic logo for Autism Speaks. Puzzle pieces hold a special place in my heart. That is, I hate them. They symbolize so much of what is wrong with popular autism discourse – representing autistic people as puzzling, mysterious, less-than-human entities who are "short a few cognitive pieces," who are utterly self-contained, disconnected, and need to "fit in." Tacked to the upper story of the sorority house, the puzzling banner provided details for a campus cookout fundraiser, all proceeds to be donated to Autism Speaks, which had recently formed a student chapter at my university.*

28 *To be perfectly clear: when it comes to Autism Speaks, I'm biased. I'm autistic and I don't feel that they speak for me. And I the president of my university chaired their Walk for Autism in 2008, and when he said that "it [autism] should not exist," I wrote him a letter. And when I came across an Autism Speaks U flyer boasting "Got questions? We've got answers!" – I wrote the faculty advisor a letter. And when the president of my university responded with what seemed like a polite yet automated response, I felt frustrated. And when the Autism Speaks advisor insisted that she "empathized with my position" and implied that I, on the basis of my diagnosis, could not empathize with hers – I wrote to the president of the Autistic Self-Advocacy Network (ASAN) and began forming, with* another autistic graduate student, an alternative autism group at my university. And when the campus newspaper, in a one-month period, released a series of autism-related articles that featured student quotes such as "The rate of diagnosis has increased. [...] It's such an alarming thing" and "I think it is in our best interest, especially for those of us who carry a burden for ASD individuals, to make an effort to help in any way we can" – I felt the burn. Alarming and burdensome, indeed.

29 In my estimation, the missing piece from the so-called autism puzzle seems quite obvious – autistic people. And I say this not in some metaphorical, autism-has-trapped-our-souls vein. Popular autism discourse has infiltrated my campus, above and beyond the walls of the psychology and allied health departments, and I worry. I worry about the transparency of this discourse. I worry about how (un)knowingly and (un)critically my students and my colleagues and my professors have digested it. Nonautistic autism discourse seems to have attached to the linings of many an intestinal wall.

30 But what I perhaps fear most is the construction of the autist as an inherently arhetorical being. Certainly, diagnostic criteria describe autistics as lacking in social and emotional reciprocity, as ultra-individualistic and perhaps noncommunicative – what we in the rhetoric and composition fold might denote as egocentricity or lack of audience awareness (see Furecic). The autist, as medically constructed, is self-focused, a two-pointed rhetorical triangle floating outside the context bubble. And yet such a stance on autism and audience awareness is itself autism audience unaware. As Tyler Cowen suggests,

31 The more likely truth is that autistics and nonautistics do not always understand each other very well. It's odd that the people who make this charge so often, in the very act of doing so, fail to show much empathy for autistics or to recognize their rich emotional lives. Even when the cognitive capabilities of autistics are recognized – most commonly in the cases of savants – it is too often accompanied by a clichéd and inaccurate picture of a cold, robotic, or less than human personality. (par. 19)

32 I would here posit that in the same manner that neurotypicals find autistics mysterious, so too do autistics find neurotypicals mysterious. Predicting the expectations of a mysterious audience is indeed a difficult task, a difficulty that would seem understandable – and yet when audience issues occur on the part of the autist, the result is considered pathological.

33 In my role as a spectrumite student, I'm much more likely to be pathologized than I am in my role as a teacher. My behaviors as a student – lack of eye contact, fixation on narrow topics, odd manner of speaking – are explained by the documentation sitting in the university's disability services office. And, with the exception of large lecture courses, I've yet to have a professor who hasn't commented on the way I speak, variously describing me as quiet, as socially inept, as unable to produce spontaneous speech. When I succeed in the realm of speech, I become the subject of a triumphant mini-narrative, one in which success is defined as "overcoming" my autistic tendencies. And herein lies the catch (and frustration) – by virtue of achieving this normalized concept of success, I'm categorized as a "high-functioning" autistic. And the labeling doesn't end there. When I describe myself as autistic, I frequently feel compelled to denote myself as mild or high functioning – and not because I like the labels. If I don't make some reference to the mildness factor, colleagues at conferences and coffee shops often fumble, "But you don't look autistic." Or they suggest that I must be high functioning even for a high-functioning person, because I "cope" so well. High functioning has come to denote my "ability" to play neurotypical, to pass.

34 Although teachers of English have generally become more tolerant and acceptable of language diversity based on race, gender, class, and ethnicity, for instance, there will soon be a rapid increase in the number of students coming to college whose identity is formed by and reflects a very different culture, one with its own preferred forms of socialization and language use, its own diverse rhetoric. Understanding autism as a rhetoric puts us on familiar footing, however, lets us call upon our considerable though occasionally vexed experiences of dealing with difference, of responding to issues of diversity, language, and identity in our classrooms. We have substantial collective wisdom we can draw upon to help this newer minority population try to learn, as other minority populations have tried to learn, to both appropriate the language of wider communication and to maintain the language of their home cultures and identities. Still, it remains to be seen, as increasing numbers of autistics begin writing and speaking in the archly constructed discursive spaces on higher education, the extent to which they, too, might be allowed to exercise their right to their own language.

35   Conceiving of autism as a rhetoric, as a way of being in the world through language, allows us to reconstrue what we have historically seen as language deficits as, instead, language *differences*. Students on the autism spectrum, like all students, have their own culturally and individually distinctive topoi, tropes, dialects, and so on, and their rhetorics thus constitute both cultural and individual representations of their selfhood. If we can come to see our autistic students through the lens of rhetoric more than through a stock and overdetermined lens of autism, we might come to better appreciate what they do have to offer instead of fixating on what they do not. Indeed, if we give them the opportunity, we might get a chance to learn how they see themselves. We purposefully conclude here without imparting prescriptive advice, if only because no prescription can help an instructor authentically respond to a student, regardless of neurology. We have no illusions about the challenges English faculty will face as increasing numbers of autistic students come to college, and we are vividly aware of how intractable some autistics' uses of language can be. But if we in the academy can learn another from popular autism discourse, it's this: there are people speaking about autistics, and then there are autistics speaking. Misinformation and unethical representations of autism and autistics abound – in the media and even on our college campuses – and we might do best to unlearn everything we think we have learned about autistics, who, as a group, are about as amorphous and diverse as neurotypicals.

36   Finally, if we accept the idea of autism as a rhetoric, then we have to acknowledge the possibility of what Corder calls "a biorhetoric, the rhetoric imperative one serves" (161). Understanding the verbal and nonverbal manifestations of autism as a rhetorical imperative does much to dissolve the idea of otherness, to give credence to the idea of a single, inclusive, broad spectrum representing all of human neurology. And as the sense of otherness diminishes, we fellow rhetors, we—as parents, educators, caregivers, policymakers, the public, and people on the autism spectrum themselves—will come to understand our common dilemma and our common hope. As Corder concludes, "There is no normality: we search for inventive-structural-stylistic-contextual sets that will give, amid some pain, some peace of understanding or fruitful work or whatever one can find to live with" (168).

Credit _____

Heilker, Paul and Melanie Yergeau. "Autism and Rhetoric." *College English* 73.5. Copyright © 2011 by the National Council of Teachers of English. Reprinted by permission.